D1453114

THE CULTURE OF POWER

*The Lin Biao Incident in the
Cultural Revolution*

JIN QIU

The Culture of Power

The Lin Biao Incident in the Cultural Revolution

STANFORD UNIVERSITY PRESS

STANFORD, CALIFORNIA

Stanford University Press
Stanford, California
© 1999 by the Board of Trustees of the
Leland Stanford Junior University

Printed in the United States of America

CIP data appear at the end of the book

To my parents,
   my brother and sisters,
   and all those who
   suffered unduly

Contents

6 pages of photos follow p. 106

■ Foreword

Elizabeth J. Perry

The best works of social science, if we reflect on their origins, can usually be traced to some deeply felt engagement on the part of the author. But if outstanding scholarship is rarely disinterested, seldom can an author claim as interesting a perspective on the subject matter as Jin Qiu in her study of the Lin Biao affair. The daughter of one of the (alleged) principals in the mysterious incident, the author writes with a personal commitment—derived from an insider's position—that is virtually unique among Western analysts of contemporary Chinese politics.

The core argument of Jin Qiu's book, which highlights the significance of family pressures on elite decision making in China, assumes added credibility by virtue of the author's own experiences as a member of an elite Chinese family. But this account is not simply—or even primarily—a personal narrative. It is, rather, the outcome of meticulous research conducted in a wealth of firsthand sources, including published and unpublished memoirs, party and government documents, and interviews with numerous participants. Jin Qiu's own background permits access to a variety of otherwise unavailable materials. Importantly, however, she complements this insider status with an outsider's standards of evidence and explanation. Dr. Jin's conclusions are shaped by insights from Western social science, drawn especially from the field of political psychology. Holding a U.S. doctoral degree, she combines personal engagement and insider information with advanced training in Western methodology and theory. The result is not only a new interpretation of the Lin Biao affair, but a fresh approach to elite-level Chinese politics in general.

For those accustomed to thinking of elite decision making as the product of highly rational individual calculations, Dr. Jin's account will come as something of a shock. Here we encounter few well-considered choices based on clearheaded calculations of the connection between means and ends.

Instead, we find that physical and mental illness, irrational fears and jealousies, family feuds, spur-of-the-moment interactions, and drug-induced confusion characterized elite behavior during the Cultural Revolution. Even some of Mao Zedong's most famous ideological contributions are linked to the psychological insecurities of an aging charismatic personality.

Sensibly, Jin Qiu does not present her book as an analysis of the Cultural Revolution as a whole. As she notes, that decade-long movement was far too complex to be captured by a study of the machinations surrounding the Lin Biao incident. Even as a reinterpretation of one bizarre event within the Cultural Revolution, her account raises a number of nagging unanswered questions. Why, for example, did Lin Biao's son reveal his conspiratorial designs to his sister—toward whom he felt such intense rivalry, if not outright enmity? Why did Lin Biao's faithful bodyguard desert the vice-chairman during his hour of greatest need? And why, in the end, did the renegade plane crash over Mongolia?

Although the author does not supply definitive explanations for all of the uncertainties connected to this puzzling event, she does suggest that the answers lie in an appreciation of the contingencies of human interaction. Jin Qiu's contention that, narrowly construed, the Lin Biao affair was "accidental" fits well with recent approaches which recognize the unpredictability of Chinese revolutionary history in general. In place of a once-dominant structural determinism that stressed the historical inevitability of the revolution, scholars have come to emphasize the decisive role of individual initiatives and accidental occurrences.

It may well be the case that the "extra-institutional" factors—of personality, family dynamics, and the like—to which Jin Qiu directs our attention are especially salient determinants of elite decision making during periods of exceptional turmoil such as the Cultural Revolution. Yet one would be hard-pressed to identify many turmoil-free moments of "tranquility" or "normalcy" in contemporary Chinese history. Furthermore, as Jin Qiu points out, the lack of a clear demarcation between leaders and institutions continues to characterize the Chinese political system to this day, rendering it highly susceptible to extra-institutional influences.

In many respects, the Lin Biao incident—extraordinary though it was—lays bare the contradictions of Chinese communism, in which boundaries between the personal and the political are highly permeable. Jin Qiu's revealing portrait of one catalytical event thus offers an instructive lesson about the larger revolutionary drama in which it is embedded. Her fascinating analysis of this turning point in contemporary Chinese history forcefully reminds us of the power of volatile emotions, individual inclinations, family tensions, and unintended consequences in setting the course of revolutionary change.

■ Preface

This study of the Lin Biao incident is in a sense the result of personal struggle and a determination to set the historical record straight. My father, General Wu Faxian, commander-in-chief of the Chinese air force under Marshal Lin Biao, was convicted of assisting Lin Biao in an alleged attempted coup d'état—something I never believed my father had done. I therefore decided to find out what had really happened to Lin Biao on the night of September 12–13, 1971, a night that changed my life forever. For almost ten years, our family heard not a word from my father, who had been secretly arrested two weeks after the fateful night. Then, in 1980 my father was sentenced to seventeen years in prison after being subjected to a "special trial" along with Lin's other major "accomplices." The families of those purged also suffered the consequences. My mother and brother, for example, were kept under house arrest for seven years before they were sent to do forced labor on prison farms for another three years, where they were subjected to all kinds of humiliation. They were guilty simply because they were related to my father. My two younger sisters, only eleven and thirteen years old in 1971, had to struggle to survive on their own, since our parents had disappeared overnight.

What happened to my family, however, was hardly unique during the crazy decade of the Chinese Cultural Revolution (1966–76). I have deep compassion for many people who fell victim to the purges that followed the Lin Biao incident. During those purges, Mao not only removed thousands of senior and junior officials from office; he also had them imprisoned or detained under house arrest. These people, together with their families, experienced personal traumas as great as my family's, if not greater.

My interest in researching the Lin Biao incident became keener after I arrived in the United States to study in 1989, when I realized that I was probably the only person, among the tens of thousands of victims of Mao's purges after the incident, who had both the opportunity and the linguistic competence to conduct research in the West. My purpose is to make known to the public the other side of the story, from the viewpoint of the victims of Mao's purges after the Lin Biao incident.

Thus, personal motivation and determination were the major forces that carried me through the difficulties in conducting my research. Fortunately, I have not been alone in my struggle first to survive in the United States, then to transform life stories into an academic work. Many people helped me with their warm hearts and much-needed encouragement, and I would like to take this opportunity to express my genuine gratitude to each of them, including those I am unable to name here.

I am profoundly indebted to my dissertation adviser, Stephen Uhalley, Jr., whose generous help made it possible for me to conduct my research in the United States. With his unflagging encouragement and support, I made the transition from being a daughter who wanted to get her family's story out to being a scholar who sought to understand personal experiences in a larger context. Academically, I am also indebted to other professors at the University of Hawaii, especially the members of my dissertation committee, Harry Lamley, Roger Ames, John Stephan, and Sharon Minichiello. I enjoyed working with them and am grateful for their warm support and constructive suggestions. I wish especially to thank Idus Newby, then chair of the History Department, who edited my dissertation.

Several institutions have generously supported my research. The History Department at the University of Hawaii offered me essential financial support. The Center for Cultural and Technical Exchange between East and West (the East-West Center) in Honolulu provided a four-year fellowship, during which I completed all requirements for the Ph.D., and also supported my field trips to the libraries at Harvard University, Columbia University, Stanford University, the University of California, Berkeley, and the Library of Congress. The Center for Chinese Studies at the University of Hawaii supported my research in Hong Kong and the People's Republic of China in 1993. I am especially grateful to the Center for Chinese Studies, a component of the Institute of East Asian Studies at the University of California, Berkeley, which awarded me a postdoctoral fellowship for the academic year 1995–96 to revise my dissertation for publication. I would like to thank the center's director, Wen-hsin Yeh, who went to considerable trouble to make sure my manuscript found a publisher. It is a pleasure to express my gratitude to these people and institutions.

I am also grateful to Frederic E. Wakeman, Jr., Hong Yung Lee, and Lowell Dittmer at the University of California, Berkeley; Parris Chang at Pennsylvania State University; Elizabeth Perry and Roderick McFarquhar at Harvard University; Michael Ying-mao Kau at Brown University; and

Thomas Robinson at Georgetown University, who provided me with many illuminating insights and constructive suggestions at different stages of my research. I also want to express my deep appreciation to Muriel Bell, executive editor of Stanford University Press, whose support and editing made a better piece of my work. I am also truly grateful to Nathan MacBrien and Janet Mowery at Stanford University Press for their excellent work in the editing and production of the book.

Various libraries and their staffs generously supported and assisted my research. I am especially indebted to Annie K. Chang, Jeff Kapellas, and Alison Altstatt at the Library of the Center for Chinese Studies, University of California, Berkeley; Nancy Hearst at the library of the John King Fairbank Center for East Asian Research, Harvard University; Julia W. Tung of the East Asian Collection at the Hoover Institution, Stanford University; Wang Ji at the East Asian Collection of the Library of Congress; and Jean Hung of the Universities Service Center at the Chinese University of Hong Kong.

I deeply appreciate the help given me by my interviewees and by Chinese scholars, who shared their information and experiences with me even though in doing so they ran the risk of harassment by the Chinese government. I am especially grateful to Lin Doudou, Lin Biao's daughter, and Zhang Qinglin, her husband, who generously shared with me their memories of the Lin Biao incident. I greatly admire the courage and honesty of my interviewees and regret that I cannot mention all of their names here.

I wish to express deep appreciation to my friends Allan and Patricia Sparks for their efforts to make my trip to the United States possible, and also to Carol and Frank Jung and Patricia and Clyde Huston for unflagging encouragement and support.

I am grateful to my friends and colleagues in the History Department of the University of Hawaii; I profited greatly from our exchanges of opinions. I wish especially to thank Peter Martin Worthing, who spent a tremendous amount of time discussing and editing my work. Ken Robinson, Paul Lococo, Kim Jin-kyung, Kevin Daily, Sylvia Sun, and John Kieschnick also helped me at various stages of my research.

Finally, I would like to thank my parents and my brother and sisters, whose love and confidence in me have been an inexhaustible source of support. Without their personal sacrifice and unconditional support over these years, I would never have be able to complete this research. After years of suffering, my parents are living a relatively quiet life in retirement. I sincerely hope that this book will only add happiness to their lives.

J.Q.

THE CULTURE OF POWER

*The Lin Biao Incident in the
Cultural Revolution*

1

Introduction

In the months before his death in 1976, the longtime leader of the People's Republic of China, Mao Zedong, was prone to look back over his life sorting out his accomplishments and failures. "I did two things in my life," he told his designated successor, Hua Guofeng, on one nostalgic occasion. "The first was to fight against Jiang Jieshi [Chiang Kai-shek] for several decades and drive him to a few islands and send the Japanese back home after the eight-year war against Japan." The second accomplishment Mao pointed to was the Cultural Revolution of 1966–76. Not surprisingly, Mao was confident of the success as well as the significance of the first of his accomplishments, but he seemed uncertain how history would judge the second. "Only a few people agree with me [and] quite a few people oppose me," he told Hua in an uncharacteristic moment of self-doubt. "Neither of these [two accomplishments] was finally [i.e., fully] accomplished and [the resulting problems] will be passed to the next generation."[1] Mao was thus evidently concerned about his legacy, even in areas that he considered his most important accomplishments. Would his be a legacy of peace, he wondered, or of "a foul wind and a rain of blood." "Only heaven knows what you are going to do," Mao said with a sigh to Hua.[2]

The sigh seemed to confess Mao's disappointment with the outcome of the Cultural Revolution, a dramatic social upheaval to which he devoted all of his thought and energy during the last ten years of his life. When he started the Cultural Revolution, he had wanted to ensure a path of continuous revolution for at least the next several generations. He never expected the revolution to be the crowning disgrace of his life. Ten years later, at the end of his life, he regretfully admitted that time was running out on his effort to bequeath to his successor a China that was everything he intended it to be. He was not even sure whether China could maintain peace and integration after he was gone. It was finally clear even to Mao that the Cultural Revolution had failed to achieve what he had intended.

Mao's concern over the Cultural Revolution has been verified by events since his death. In 1981, five years after Mao died, the Sixth Plenum of the Eleventh Congress of the Chinese Communist Party (CCP) acknowledged that the Cultural Revolution was "responsible for the most severe setback and the heaviest losses suffered by the party, the state, and the people since the founding of the People's Republic."[3] Thereafter, neither the government nor the people who lived through the Cultural Revolution had anything positive to say about it. Mao's adventurous pursuit of a utopian dream became one of the Chinese people's worst nightmares. The governments of Mao's successors have shown understandable caution in criticizing the Cultural Revolution, but they have reversed nearly everything it stood for.[4]

I wish to emphasize that this is not a study of the Cultural Revolution as such. Indeed, the Cultural Revolution, which lasted from 1966 to 1976, was a multidimensional phenomenon that no single volume can cover comprehensively.[5] From a macrohistorical viewpoint, the Cultural Revolution was in fact many revolutions related in form but with considerable diversity in content and process. The Cultural Revolution intended by party leaders, particularly Mao, was quite different from the cultural revolutions that actually occurred. Moreover, the Cultural Revolution in Guangdong differed from that in Sichuan, which in turn differed from those in Yunnan, Xinjiang, and elsewhere. Each province and even each city had its own revolution. Obtaining archival materials from across China and conveying the complexity of the Cultural Revolution itself are daunting challenges to any researcher seeking to write its comprehensive history. Nevertheless, the Cultural Revolution does provide organizing themes for scholars looking into individual facets of Chinese politics and society in the last decade of the Mao era.

In a broad sense, the Cultural Revolution exemplifies the series of public and political crises China endured in the twentieth century. Politically, the Cultural Revolution was the result of conflict between a charismatic leader and a bureaucratic government in the process of institutionalizing itself. It was a systematic effort to rejuvenate a rigid administrative system that provided civil servants with no career alternatives and no means of exiting with dignity. Socially, it was an expression of accumulated frustrations with bureaucracy itself, as Mao himself understood. Culturally, it was a clash between traditional Confucian values and the Communist revolutionary spirit. And economically, it was an experiment aimed at creating a "socialist economy" based on egalitarian peasant principles, and as such was a rejection of capitalist, market-oriented economies.[6]

This study examines certain extra-institutional factors that fueled Chinese politics during the Cultural Revolution. By extra-institutional factors I mean such elusive details as personality, individual experience, and social relationships, including family ties, personal connections (*guanxi*), and individual loyalties as these function in the political sphere. I use the term "extra-institutional" in particular to emphasize a distinction between two political phenomena—those that characterize or constitute political *systems*, and those that inform or pervade the *context* in which those systems function and generate meaning.

Western studies of recent Chinese politics have always focused on institutional factors, including organizations, ideology, and formal policy-making apparatuses.[7] Studies of the political elite have addressed less formal group processes, including the functioning of sociopolitical factions, opinion and interest groups, informal groups, and situational groups.[8] Such studies contribute notably to our understanding of the nature of the Chinese Communist system, especially those that grasp the dynamics of Chinese politics. The best of them provide good accounts of the interaction between collective behavior and group decision-making. They also put Chinese politics in the broad framework of international politics and thereby provide bases for informed comparative study.

As more information became available after the Cultural Revolution, it became apparent that the gap between theory and reality in Communist politics in China was always quite large. Scholars now find themselves overwhelmed by newly available details in primary sources, including information about the private lives of political leaders.[9] They have access to oral accounts by leading participants in important political events. The resulting wealth of new information has made it necessary to modify previous interpretations. It has also made it easier to research specific topics and to add contextual factors to studies of recent political institutions and elites. The latest studies published in China are thus rich in detail but often lack perspectives informed by Western social science.

This book extends the study of recent Chinese politics to familial and personal levels of inquiry. I believe that new microinformation at these levels can shed light on the macroperspectives already well established in Western works on recent Chinese politics. As a historian, I am interested in whether events can be interpreted differently through an examination of personal and even seemingly tangential data. More particularly, I hope to establish a persuasive framework with which to credibly reconstruct the series of events that led to the Lin Biao incident. I may not be able to prove my case definitively and I will undoubtedly bring a share of my own biases to the topic, but complex historical events always admit of a variety of interpretations among well-meaning and open-minded historians. I hope to illustrate that Lin Biao's death is understandable only if one takes into consideration extra-institutional factors that explain not just the incident but also a good deal else in modern Chinese politics. Moreover, I intend to illustrate how extra-institutional factors interact with institutional factors in the political life of the People's Republic. Such a study should help explain to what extent traditional Chinese culture and values influence individual and group behavior in the political arena.[10]

Of all the major events in the Cultural Revolution, the Lin Biao incident remains the most mysterious. Many scholars suggest that the day of the incident, September 13, 1971, was also the day of the greatest crisis in Mao's China. On that day, Lin Biao, then sole vice-chairman of the Chinese Communist Party, officially designated as the closest comrade-in-arms of and heir apparent to Mao Zedong, was supposedly defecting to the Soviet Union when the aircraft in which he was fleeing crashed in the People's Republic of Mongolia. Everyone on the plane was killed, including Lin and his wife and son.

More than a quarter-century later, the incident remains an unsolved mystery. At the time, Chinese officials issued strongly worded accusations of an aborted coup d'état and a plot to assassinate Mao, both allegedly masterminded by Lin Biao. These accusations framed the official verdict on the event, which was "confirmed" a decade later at a show trial in 1980–81. Nonetheless, the accusers never established a convincing link between Lin and the crimes attributed to him.[11] Three key questions concerning the incident remain unanswered: Why would Lin, the brilliant architect of major victories in the Chinese civil war and a man who had always been doggedly loyal to Mao, suddenly attempt an ill-conceived coup? Why, when the alleged coup effort failed, would he have attempted to escape the country by fleeing to the Soviet Union? Finally, why—and most important, how—did his plane crash?

The Lin Biao incident shocked everyone in China, and then in the rest of the world. As every Chinese knew, Lin had come to the forefront of national politics five years earlier, when he was elevated from minister of defense to sole vice-chairman of the Communist Party. Lin's position as Mao's heir apparent was reconfirmed in the party constitution of 1969, when the party honored Lin as Mao's "closest comrade-in-arms" and "successor." Thereafter Lin accompanied Mao on every public occasion, always clutching a copy of the "little red book" of Mao's quotations.[12]

What is even more incongruous is that only two days before Lin's plane crashed the Xinhua News Agency reported that a book of photographs that included several of Mao and Lin together would be published shortly as part of the celebration of the 50th anniversary of the CCP. "This will make people feel encouraged," stated the Xinhua report, "that Comrade Lin Biao is a bright example for the whole party, the whole army, and the whole country to learn from."[13] In addition, the cover of the September issues of *Hongqi* (*Red Flag*) carried for the third time in 1971 a color photograph of Mao and Lin together.[14] Even after the Lin Biao incident but before it was made public, Lin's name continued to appear in newspapers in Beijing and other cities, though less frequently than it had before. In remote areas, Lin's name still appeared in local media until the end of 1971.[15]

Lin's sudden death triggered the biggest political crisis in Mao's party since 1949. How could Mao make his people believe that their "beloved vice-chairman," who had helped whip the country into the frenzied cult of Mao's personality, had turned overnight into a would-be assassin of Mao himself and a traitor to the country? Mao needed time to determine how best to cushion the shock to his people and to the world and had to act with caution. Instead of releasing an announcement of Lin's death, the Party Central Committee issued, between late September 1971 and March 1972, a set of documents exposing Lin's "crimes" and disseminated the documents incrementally to officials and other Chinese according to their rank and position in the political hierarchy. During the Cultural Revolution, the party grouped the Chinese into different social categories according to their political backgrounds and attitudes. While rank and position within the party separated party officials, party members in general had more political privilege than nonparty members. Certain Chinese were specified as politically unreliable because of their "class origins" and their political attitudes. Even the overseas Chinese and foreigners were identified as either "friends" or "enemies" of China. This politicization of Chinese society during the Cultural Revolution still exerts a strong influence over Chinese society today.

For more than a week, Mao restricted the news of the incident to Politburo members, and it was two additional weeks before he circulated the first document on the incident among high-ranking party officials in the provinces.[16] According to a circular of September 28, only members of local Party Standing Committees, military officers ranking above division commander, and provincial officials could have access to CCP documents concerning the incident.[17] The circular also made it mandatory that no one should take notes or make copies or even talk about these documents.

Finally, two months after the incident, the government made its first announcement to ordinary Chinese that Lin had died.[18]

When the party finally decided to circulate documents at the grass-roots level, it stamped all of them "strictly confidential" and allowed only the party organizations at the county or equivalent level to have custody of them. The party instructed leaders to "borrow" the documents from party organizations and read them aloud to everyone authorized to hear them. A circular from the Party Central Committee instructed, "Landlords, rich peasants, counter-revolutionaries, bad elements, rightists, and capitalists, as well as those who have serious historical problems and who are under investigation, cannot listen to the readings of the documents. Nor are any foreigners to hear them." The circular also directed that party members be the first to hear the documents, followed by workers, peasants, and soldiers, and only then other Chinese. The circular ended by announcing that the party would issue a supplementary directive describing how the documents should later be read to "patriotic overseas Chinese, foreign experts, and foreigners with Chinese citizenship."[19]

The following is one man's recollection of how he learned about the Lin Biao incident:

> Marshal Lin Biao died in September 1971, but we ordinary Chinese first heard about the incident in July 1972, ten months later. I was then a high school student in a country town in Hunan province. At first, we knew only that something frightening and immensely important had happened. The Communist Party members among the students and teachers were called away from classes and shut up for a week of meetings in the County Revolutionary Committee compound. Armed guards stood before the meeting hall, and, despite the summer heat, the windows were heavily curtained, muffling the megaphone inside. Then a Party member was permitted to visit his sick wife and the incredible news leaked: our revered First Vice-Chairman Lin Biao had conspired to kill our beloved Chairman Mao and had died in a plane crash in Mongolia while he, his wife, his son, and a handful of coconspirators were trying to escape to the Soviet Union in a Trident jet. This we could hardly accept, but there must have been some truth in it since our informant immediately lost his Party membership and was thrown into jail for a year and a half for breach of discipline.
>
> We got more information soon enough. After the Party members had been briefed, it was our turn for a week of meetings. We listened to readings from official documents in the mornings, were made to discuss and criticize Lin and his policies in the afternoons. What we heard confused us more than any of the shifts in the political wind that had us spinning about dizzily since the start of the Cultural Revolution in 1966.[20]

Meanwhile, the party carefully withheld information concerning the Lin Biao incident from the outside world. The Central Committee warned that anyone who "leaked" information to inappropriate or unauthorized persons would be severely punished. Chinese embassies around the world received instructions to remain silent if queried about Lin Biao. On November 30, 1971, and again in March 1972, the central government issued documents reiterating the need to maintain secrecy from the outside world.[21] Thus, Lin's whereabouts remained a puzzle outside China. Despite widespread speculation in those months about what had happened to Lin, the Chinese government never officially announced his death. Even when Mao himself finally confirmed Lin's death in talks with Ceylon's prime minister Sirimavo Bandaranaike and French foreign minister Maurice Schumann in the summer of 1972, his remarks shed little light on how Lin had died.[22]

With all mysterious happenings at the highest levels of government, speculation feeds on the absence of reliable information. Unofficial explanations of Lin's death, however, were even less convincing than the official one. The best known of the unofficial explanations appeared in a book by Yao Ming-le (a pseudonym), which seven well-known publishers outside China issued simultaneously in 1983.[23] Yao claimed that Lin died not in a plane crash in Mongolia but on his way home from Mao's villa in Beijing, where Mao had invited him for a "last supper." Few students of the subject have taken this version seriously, chiefly because the sources, to which Yao claimed to have exclusive access, were never made available to others.[24]

Despite much speculation, the official explanation of the Lin Biao incident has remained the most widely accepted interpretation. When the initial shock of Lin's death had passed, many Chinese, as well as most scholars in and outside of China, came to accept the official explanation, even though few found the evidence for it convincing. According to this explanation, Lin authorized plans for a coup d'état and the assassination of Mao and died fleeing to the Soviet Union after both plans had failed.[25]

The dearth of reliable sources of alternative explanations and the secretive nature of Chinese politics are the simplest explanations for the widespread but grudging acquiescence in the official account. The historiography of Chinese politics since 1949 is largely a creature of the official control of primary sources. The availability of such sources, as the political scientist Michel Oksenberg has noted, determines not only what subjects scholars can research but what they can say about their subjects as well.[26] In the years before and during the Cultural Revolution, because primary sources on Chinese politics were limited in number and had also been officially screened, scholars had to scrutinize every available item of information using a method that came to be called "Pekingology" (after "Kremlinology," developed by students of Soviet politics), which encouraged the closest possible reading of texts. Without complete background information, however, they sometimes misinterpreted what they read.[27]

This situation still prevails for students of politically sensitive topics like the Lin Biao incident. Accounts of the incident rely heavily on official and semiofficial sources, which include the documents issued by the government in 1971–72 announcing the "crimes" of the "Lin Biao and Chen Boda anti-party clique"; the official publications of the 1980–81 trials of the "Lin Biao and Jiang Qing counter-revolutionary cliques"; and the literature produced by party historians and journalists.[28] In the early 1970s, Western scholars obtained through secret channels copies of the 1971–72 documents just mentioned, including what was supposedly Lin's plan for a coup, a document entitled "An Outline of Project 571."[29] The difficulty of obtaining these confidential documents itself enhanced their apparent authenticity and thus the authenticity of the information they contained and convinced many scholars that charges against Lin Biao must be true.[30] Otherwise, some scholars wondered, why would the Chinese government invest so much effort in fabricating so bizarre a story about Lin Biao, a story that made no one, not even Mao himself, look good? And why would the Chinese government go to such lengths to keep fabricated documents confidential?

As reasonable as these questions seem, careful examination of the evidence supporting the official accusations against Lin suggests that many of the documents were written after the incident to justify the official explanation and the subsequent purge of Lin's followers; but the explanations they offer are largely unconvincing. First, they contain noticeable inconsistencies about Lin's "crimes." The most serious charge, the alleged coup attempt, was missing entirely from the first group of CCP documents issued immediately after the incident. In the first six documents concerning the incident, including Zhongfa nos. 57, 60, 61, 62, 64, and 65, the government described Lin as "a traitor to the country," "an attempted assassin of Mao," and "a conspirator who planned to establish a separate government in Guangzhou [Canton]."[31] It was not until November 14, 1971, that the Central Committee issued another circular, Zhongfa no. 74, announcing the "discovery" of the "Outline of Project 571." The "Outline," the government charged, was the plan for Lin's coup attempt, and after it failed, Lin and his family fled the country in haste. However, the total omission of this "chief crime" of the Lins in early documents and the two-month interval between the incident in September and the "discovery" of Lin's plan indicate that the government at the least failed to establish convincingly a cause-and-effect connection between Lin's "escape" from the country and the alleged attempted coup. In other words, the government did not know anything about Lin's "attempted coup" until two months after the incident.

There were other significant discrepancies between the denunciations of 1971–72 and the publications during and after the trials ten years later. At the trials, the government dropped one of the early charges against Lin—that he had plotted to establish a separatist government in Guangzhou. It also repudiated the original charges that Lin's generals were involved in the plots to assassinate Mao and stage the coup, even though Lin and his wife were found guilty of these offenses.[32] The differences in the two sets of documents were responses to political developments in the decade between 1971–72 and 1980–81. The earlier documents were compiled by the Central Investigation Group for Special Cases (*zhongyang zhuanan zu*, or *zhuanan zu*, Special Case Group) headed by Zhou Enlai, Jiang Qing (Madame Mao), and Wang Dongxing, the director of the General Office of the Party Central Committee.[33] By the time of the trials in 1980–81, most of the key people in that group had either died or lost their political importance, and the people who oversaw the trials belonged to what Hong Yung Lee has called "the group of the purged" during the Cultural Revolution.[34] The differences between the two groups were reflected in the accounts of the incident in the two sets of documents: Jiang Qing and her associates, who were in charge of the purge of Lin and his group in 1971, were themselves on trial with Lin as his "colleagues" in 1981! It explains why in the early 1980s Deng Xiaoping's government believed it was necessary to change some of the early charges against Lin Biao and his group for the sake of current politics.

Even the key evidence, Lin's alleged coup plan, does not support the official allegations.[35] Even if we assume that the document is authentic, the "Outline of Project 571" is ostensibly the rough draft of a plan authorities found in a notebook left on a table in a house at the air force academy, where Lin's son, Lin Liguo, an air force officer, and his colleagues often gathered. Whoever found it there supposedly sent it to Zhou Enlai on October 9, 1971, four weeks after the Lin Biao incident.[36]

It was not until November 1971, two months after the incident, that Mao decided to use the notebook as evidence of Lin Biao's plot. Mao's physician, Li Zhisui, reports in his memoir that Mao had long suspected that Lin Biao "wanted him dead and was even afraid that Lin might try to poison him." Nevertheless, Dr. Li reported, Mao never believed that "Lin Biao might be plotting to assassinate him and seize power himself."[37] One of my interviewees, whose father was in charge of the Central Investigation Group for Special Cases organized for the Lin Biao incident, also confirmed that when his father presented the newly discovered "Outline of Project 571" to Mao and Zhou Enlai, Mao did not believe at all that it was Lin's plan. However, despite Zhou's hesitation, Mao decided to publicize it as such in order to further incriminate Lin's group.[38]

Furthermore, the notebook copy of the alleged plan reads more like a political proclamation than a plan for a coup. Only two of its nine parts discuss the use of force. The parts concerning politics are far more interesting than those concerned with military aspects of a coup. Many of the document's criticisms of Mao and the Cultural Revolution appear to anticipate those made after Mao's death. In fact the "Outline" contains one of the earliest criticisms of the Cultural Revolution.[39]

Whoever drafted the plan had limited knowledge of military tactics and organization. For example, the "basic strengths" of the conspirators were said to be in the Fourth and Fifth Air Force Armies, the Ninth, Eighteenth, and Thirty-fourth Air Force Divisions, the Twenty-first Tank Regiment, and, strangely, the Civil Aeronautics Administration. Thus, the estimate of the author of the plot was that no more than half a dozen military units would support the coup. It is difficult to imagine that Lin, who had commanded a million troops and had intricate knowledge of the requirements of every military situation, would accept such an estimate of forces as sufficient to carry out a coup. It is equally doubtful that Lin would have relied so heavily on the air force to ensure success. Even the author of the "Outline" noted that "at present the preparation of our strength is still not adequate."[40] Given Lin's military record, one might reasonably have expected him to do a much better job of planning a military action against Mao. Further, the language in the "Outline" is not what Lin would have used. Judging from their dogged loyalty to Mao over three decades of struggle against their common enemies, it is difficult to imagine that Lin or anyone else in the generation of old revolutionaries would refer to Mao as "B-52."

According to Chinese officials, the author of this "Outline" was Yu Xinye, who was a secretary in the General Office of the Party Committee of the air force. The only connection between Lin Biao and Yu Xinye that could be established was that Yu was a colleague of Lin Biao's son, Lin Liguo. The only link that the Chinese officials established between Lin Biao and the coup plan was the "confession" of another colleague of Lin Liguo's, Li Weixin, the lone survivor among those who boarded a helicopter trying to escape from Beijing after Lin's plane took off from Beidaihe on September 13, 1971. Li Weixin "confessed" that Yu Xinye told him on September 11,

1971, that Liguo had brought the plan with him and left it with "Shou zhang" (Lin Biao) and the "director" (Lin Biao's wife, Ye Qun) at Beidaihe.[41] His statement, however, could hardly be considered sound evidence connecting Lin Biao and Ye Qun with the alleged plot, especially given the conditions under which Li had "confessed"; the Central Investigation Group for Special Cases is known to have coerced people to make false confessions. Moreover, the oddest thing about the plan is that no one, including Li Weixin, ever admitted seeing a written plan for a coup before the Lin Biao incident, not even Lin's "coconspirators" identified in any of the documents the party circulated in 1971–72 or in the trial records of 1980–81. Li only claimed that he had *heard* Yu Xinye mention such a plan, but said he himself had never seen it.

In sum, what makes the incident a mystery are the notable differences between Lin's life as a brilliant military planner and Mao loyalist and the descriptions of his bizarre death while fleeing to a foreign country, the party's slow and awkward response to the incident and to Lin's death, and the implausibility of the official explanations. How could or did Mao's "best student" turn overnight into a traitor? Why did it take so long for the government to inform its own cadres and the Chinese people of Lin's death? And why was the government so reluctant to release the information about Lin's death to the outside world? If the charges against him were true, Lin was unique among the old revolutionaries who achieved high rank, whether before or during the Cultural Revolution: he was the only high official ever charged with attempting to assassinate Mao, with attempting to escape from the country in a way that implied an arrangement with the Soviet Union, or with plotting a coup against the revolutionary government and thus presumably against the revolution itself.[42]

To me, the problem in assessing the Lin Biao incident is less one of fact than of interpretation. By the tenets of Western political theory, the official version of the incident is plausible, perhaps even convincing. The factional nature of Chinese politics, which Western theory emphasizes, is sufficient to explain the incident. According to this theory, Mao and Lin were on a collision course after the Second Plenum of the Ninth Party Congress of 1970, whether because Lin's army had become a force competing with Mao's party or because Mao and Lin disagreed on major matters of foreign policy.[43] Many scholars believe Lin was unhappy with Mao's rapprochement with the United States, though there is little solid evidence to sustain that belief.[44] With so many bases for conflict between Lin and Mao, this line of reasoning continues, it would not have been unreasonable for Lin to resort to extreme measures had he concluded that his hold on power was slipping away in his struggle against Mao. Such reasoning is plausible, however, only if Lin, Mao's designated heir, was so eager for power that he could not wait for the elderly Mao, who was 78 years old in 1971 and thirteen years Lin's senior, to die or retire. In fact, it was crucial to the case against Lin that the government create an image of Lin as a power-hungry, impatient, and even desperate man. So far, this tactic has largely succeeded. In conducting my research, I found that my fellow Chinese were comfortable only with the image of Lin Biao created by official propaganda. However, if we question this assumption of an ambitious Lin Biao, we open a Pandora's box of possibilities about Lin's fall, and even about the incident itself. Some scholars have already pursued this line of investigation. In their 1996 study of Lin Biao, Frederick Teiwes and Warren Sun present a revisionist view of Lin Biao's role in the Cultural Revolution that challenges the generally accepted image of Lin Biao.[45]

Dissatisfied with official explanations and possessing inside information about some of the people involved, I decided to look into the Lin Biao incident. I have read extensively in the available primary and secondary materials on the subject and have interviewed people directly and indirectly involved in the events leading up to the incident and in the incident itself, including my father, Wu Faxian, an air force general under Lin Biao. After the Lin Biao incident, the party accused my father of being one of Lin's chief coconspirators and sentenced him to seventeen years in prison. My belief in my father's innocence encouraged me to question the official version of the incident, and in doing so I came to believe a quite different version. Even the official evidence, I found, can be made to support conclusions quite different from the official ones. This is especially so if one considers the evidence in an extra-institutional context. For example, I have become convinced that without the involvement of Lin's wife and son in politics, Lin would never have agreed to board the plane by which he ostensibly sought to "escape" from China, and he and his family members would not have died a dishonorable death in the Mongolian desert.

Like Lin's unexpected fall, the Cultural Revolution itself was an aberrant episode in the history of the People's Republic, one that brought all the problems and contradictions in both party and society to the surface. In an important sense, the Cultural Revolution was Mao's way of resolving a crisis of his own—his personal, late-in-life rejection of an institutional apparatus he himself had created and over which he found himself presiding. It was Mao who initiated and sustained the Cultural Revolution, and the revolution in turn bore the marks of his persona. This is the consensus of Chinese scholars today. Even the party itself, which has tried hard to preserve Mao's reputation as a political and social leader, has conceded that the events and consequences of the Cultural Revolution "have proved that Comrade Mao Zedong's principal theses for initiating this revolution conformed neither to Marxism-Leninism nor to Chinese reality. They represent an entirely erroneous appraisal of the prevailing class relations and political situation in the party and state."[46]

Among the things that account for this extraordinary assessment are the extra-institutional factors that were so important during the Cultural Revolution. For several years during the revolution, China was literally in chaos. Social rules and political norms broke down. Because of the disruptions in the functioning of political institutions, temporary organizations emerged to keep the country functioning. Among these at the national level were the Central Cultural Revolution Small Group (CCRSG, *zhongyang wenge xiaozu*) and the Working Group of the Central Military Committee (*junwei banshi zu*), and at the provisional and local levels an assortment of ad hoc committees. For a while, the CCRSG, headed by Madame Mao, Jiang Qing, functioned as a stand-in for the Politburo and the central government. Because of the ad hoc nature of these institutions and the personal ties that held them together, individuals gained power by taking advantage of personal relationships rather than working through normal bureaucratic processes.

In this environment, the political involvement of family members of important individuals increased notably, and families began to experience the consequences of political ups and downs. Mao's wife, Jiang Qing, and Lin Biao's wife, Ye Qun, both previously obscure women, became actively involved in politics once the Cultural Revolution commenced. They took advantage of the eminence of their husbands to achieve positions of power for themselves. Jiang Qing helped Mao further his revolutionary agenda, only to become a scapegoat when the revolution backfired. In contrast, Ye Qun's activities contributed notably to the ill fortune of her husband and culminated in the plane crash in Mongolia. Ye Qun manipulated important aspects of Lin's public career during the Cultural Revolution, and the Lin Biao incident suggests how the involvement of family members in a political crisis can limit a person's professional decisions.

In this study, I believe that I present a balanced and factual account of Lin Biao and the incident that bears his name. I hope to shine new light on the events that led to the incident and to show the need for further study of Chinese politics under Mao. This introductory chapter lays out the problem; in Chapters 2 and 3, I discuss and analyze Mao's personal role in the Cultural Revolution and the pattern of the political purges during his rule. Chapter 4 presents a description of Lin Biao and his activities during the Cultural Revolution that is completely at odds with the one presented in official sources. During the Cultural Revolution, Lin was in fact a sickly and passive figure who bore little resemblance to the pathologically ambitious and forceful individual described in official accounts. Chapter 5 discusses the rupture between Mao and Lin at Lushan in August 1970 and reinterprets events between that time and the Lin Biao incident. It illustrates a pattern of behavior among Mao's associates that influenced their relationship with Mao himself and through that relationship Mao's understanding of the Lin Biao incident. Chapter 6 discusses the role of the elite families in Chinese politics and the manifestations of that role in the incident; Chapter 7 reconstructs the Lin Biao incident of September 12–13, 1971, based on a close reading of relevant literature and interviews with many key witnesses and participants. The final chapter presents my conclusions concerning Lin and the incident that bears his name.

2

Mao Zedong and Theories of the Cultural Revolution

The Lin Biao incident can be defined in two ways. In the narrow sense, the incident was what happened to Lin Biao and his family on the night of September 12–13, 1971. In a broader sense, the incident was the result of the events that developed between the Second Plenum of the Ninth Party Central Committee in August 1970, when the rupture between Mao and Lin began, and September 1, 1971. To understand Lin's unexpected fall, we should first examine Chinese politics during, and even before, the Cultural Revolution, an event that brought to the surface the fundamental problems and contradictions within both the Chinese Communist Party (CCP) and Chinese society. Lin's name, like Mao's, was closely associated with the Cultural Revolution. Mao's personal sponsorship allowed Lin to climb the political ladder after the revolution started. Lin rose from minister of defense to sole vice-chairman of the CCP in 1966 and was named Mao's designated successor in 1969. Only two years later, his sudden death can be seen as a metaphor for the total failure of the Cultural Revolution.[1] Today, however, he and Madame Mao are officially singled out as responsible for Mao's second revolution, while most others who supposedly opposed Mao during the Cultural Revolution have been rehabilitated.

Although studies of the period have already covered many of the facts about the Cultural Revolution and revealed various possible origins of the event, one important question remains to be answered: why did Mao want a second revolution in 1966 that would paralyze the institutions established by the first revolution two decades earlier? In this chapter, I focus on the impact of Mao's personal views and political style on the decision-making processes of party and government institutions. By reconstructing some major events before and during the Cultural Revolution, I establish the connection between Mao's thinking and party theories, Mao's patterns of behavior, and his relationship with his chief lieutenants. By doing so, I want to provide plausible answers to an even more puzzling question: why Mao, with a few aides, was able to turn the whole country upside down for several years. Extra-institutional factors, such as personal ideas, behaviors, and personalities are at least as important as the institutional factors that functioned in the Chinese political system under Mao.

In a real sense, the Cultural Revolution was Mao's personal assault on the political institutions he and his comrades had created and institutionalized beginning in 1949. Those institutions, he came to see, were filled with "revisionists." From theory to practice, Mao closely supervised each step of the new revolution. His own ideas became the party's only guiding principles, and every policy had to have his endorsement. The Cultural Revolution became Mao's personal revolution, beginning with his ambition to reorganize the state and party institutions and ending with his death and the arrest of his wife, Jiang Qing.

A leader must have followers, of course.[2] During the Cultural Revolution, Mao's comrades practiced a cult of personality so extreme that they elevated Mao to the position of a demigod. The masses seemed to worship him blindly. This, as well as a political culture and tradition that tolerated authoritarian rulers, endowed Mao with enormous power over the country and the people, and he in turn mobilized the masses to carry out his revolution. Whatever he said was "ultimate truth," and whoever expressed doubt about any of it was subject to severe punishment, including death. During the Cultural Revolution, thousands of people accused of the crime of "disrespecting Mao" became counter-revolutionaries. For example, a person who accidentally stepped on Mao's picture or wrapped something with a piece of newspaper that contained Mao's words or a picture of him could end up in prison or even be executed. Mao used such rules to get rid of his political opponents and to experiment with his utopian fantasies.

Chinese scholars today tend to blame party theories developed in the mid-1960s for the occurrence of the Cultural Revolution, especially Mao's theory of "continuing revolution under the dictatorship of the proletariat" (*jixu geming*), which provided major justification for the necessity of the Cultural Revolution. It dominated Chinese politics in the decade 1966–76. Some believe that the Cultural Revolution probably would not have happened had the party not accepted this misguided theory. Mao's strong belief in the theory, according to official party historians, caused him to misjudge the situation and to turn against many of his colleagues. They say, however, that only the "political careerists" such as Lin Biao and Madame Mao should be blamed for the misfortunes that resulted from the Cultural Revolution, because they took advantage of Mao's "mistakes" to advance their personal interests and to engage in "criminal activities" against Mao's victims.

Some Chinese scholars have questioned ascribing the theory of continuing revolution to Mao, saying that Mao himself never wrote anything referring to it and that the concept never appeared in Mao's published works.[3] They conveniently forget that during the Cultural Revolution party propaganda hailed the theory as Mao's most innovative contribution to Marxist-Leninist theory. Evidence shows that Mao closely supervised the development of this theory and allowed it to bear his name when it was published. Wang Li, one of Mao's assistants in drafting Cultural Revolution documents, attested that Mao himself came up with the concept in a conversation with Wang on February 12, 1967. Although nearly all the central documents during the Cultural Revolution were drafted by Chen Boda, Zhang Chunqiao, Yao Wenyuan, Wang Li, and others, they worked under Mao's close supervision. In many cases Mao personally edited drafts several times before they were published.[4]

Several months after the Cultural Revolution started, Mao felt the need to justify the revolution theoretically. In February 1967, Wang Li told Chen Boda that Mao had given him the task of doing just that. Wang Li carefully studied Mao's speeches on the subject of the Cultural Revolution and incorporated the major points he found there in an editorial in the October issue of *Hongqi* (*Red Flag*) in honor of the twentieth anniversary of the publication of Mao's essay "On the Correct Handling of Contradictions Among the People."[5] It was in this editorial that Wang Li first discussed the concept of continuing revolution. More explicit discussion of the theory appeared later in an editorial published simultaneously on November 6, 1967, in *Renmin ribao* (*People's Daily*), *Hongqi*, and *Jiefangjun bao* (*People's Liberation Army Daily*), entitled "March Along the Socialist Path Established by the October Revolution." Before publishing the editorial, Chen Boda and Yao Wenyuan sent a draft of it to Mao for his approval. "We revised this editorial again," Chen and Yao said in their letter to Mao. "We added new materials for the chairman's six new ideas and also quotations from Lenin. . . . All of us sincerely hope that the chairman will take a look at the draft and revise it."[6] After editing the revised draft, Mao approved it for publication. The editorial explained "continuing revolution" as follows:

1. Socialist society is a long historical period, during which struggles between classes and between the socialist and capitalist roads will continue for a long time. The danger of a restoration of capitalism also persists during this historical stage.

2. Class struggle under the dictatorship of the proletariat is, in essence, related to the question of power. In other words, the capitalists will attempt to overthrow the proletariat. The proletariat has to achieve an overall dictatorship over the bourgeoisie in the superstructural and cultural areas.

3. The struggle between the two classes and the two roads will definitely be reflected within the party. A handful of capitalist roaders in positions of authority will be the major targets of the revolution continuing under the dictatorship of the proletariat.

4. The way to continue revolution under the dictatorship of the proletariat is to mobilize the masses to stage a cultural revolution.[7]

This editorial became one of the most important documents of the Cultural Revolution. It clarified not only the purposes of the Cultural Revolution but also its methodology, its use of force, and its targets. Based on an assumption of the continuing existence of classes and thus of class struggle in socialist society, the theory revealed the basis for conflict within the revolutionary party: the still-existing bourgeois class would use its representatives in the revolutionary party to try to regain the power it had lost. The solution to this problem, as Mao saw it, was to stage a continuing revolution from the bottom.

Many studies of the theory of continuing revolution focus on its philosophical and political implications. Most criticisms of the theory center on whether the theory conformed to Marxist-Leninist principle or whether it was based on domestic and international realities. The problem, however, is not *what* the theory suggests, but *why* and *how* Mao came to believe that relations within a socialist society and within the revolutionary party were fundamentally antagonistic. When the theory first surfaced, there is little evidence that Mao really believed that his long-term comrades had become "class enemies." He knew that neither Liu Shaoqi nor Deng Xiaoping, who were cited as the heads of a capitalist faction within the party, had openly challenged him or objected to his major ideas once they became party policies, and they probably would never do so. What Deng Xiaoping did after he returned to power upon Mao's death has proved this. When Deng finally had the chance to get even with Mao, he chose not to become "China's Khrushchev." Largely through his efforts, Mao remains a "great leader" today. According to Wang Li, Mao initially just wanted to "teach a lesson" to Liu and Deng because he believed they could no longer be trusted to follow all of his orders, especially after he died. Nevertheless, Mao mentioned several times after their fall that Liu and Deng should remain members of the Party Central Committee owing to their earlier contributions to the original revolution of 1949.[8]

On what basis then did Mao believe that a "bourgeois class" had already formed within the CCP, and how was he able to persuade the whole party and whole country to go along with him? To answer these questions, we should trace the development of Mao's understanding of conflict in socialist society based on his own experience as a leader after 1949, especially after the economic failures of 1958–59. It is also necessary to consider Mao's characteristics as a charismatic leader. As Lowell Dittmer points out, three elements are necessary to "continue" a revolution: a charismatic leader, an illegitimate authority structure, and sustained mobilization of mass support.[9] In light of Dittmer's formulation, Mao's role in the Cultural Revolution is best explained by his being a charismatic leader whose charisma was a legacy of his sacrifices and leadership in the wars before 1949, by the CCP's still questionable legitimacy for ruling China, and by Mao's personal senility and paranoia. The last two of these conditions required regular reassertion of the legitimacy of the revolution and its progeny.

Mandate of the People: Creation of a Charismatic Leader

The People's Republic of China was established by a group of revolutionaries who fought continuously for 30 years before they finally succeeded in taking power. This struggle created a party of 4.5 million members, an army of more than 4 million men, and a military elite, including Mao himself. The establishment of the revolutionary state in 1949 legitimized the rule of the Communist Party in the light of Chinese political tradition.[10] In Weberian terms, the legitimacy of the new state rested on charismatic as well as traditional factors.[11]

Mao's charisma derived from the charm and forcefulness of his personality as well as his personal contribution to the revolutionary cause. In comparison with most of the poorly educated revolutionaries, Mao was considered a sage for his knowledge, imagination, and intuitive resources.[12] Mao impressed educated people with his intelligence as well as his guile in surviving the long harsh struggle. By 1949, Mao had achieved the status of unchallenged and unchallengeable leader of the CCP and the genuine respect of his comrades. When Lin Biao insisted that Mao was a genius, he was not the only one to do so. Liu Shaoqi had exalted Mao as early as the Seventh Party Congress in 1945. At an enlarged meeting of the Central Military Committee on August 17, 1959 (a meeting of the regular members plus others specially invited to attend), Liu repeated his exaltation and criticized Peng Dehuai for opposing the idea of "the cult of personality":

I always actively advocate the idea of "the cult of personality," although the concept itself may not be totally appropriate. . . . What I mean by this is that I will actively enhance the prestige of Chairman Mao. I have held this opinion for a long time and I pronounced [the greatness of] Chairman Mao even before the Seventh Party Congress. . . . I am doing it now, and I will also advocate "the cult of personality" of Comrade Lin Biao and Comrade [Deng] Xiaoping. . . . It is absolutely wrong for someone [like Peng Dehuai] to oppose "the cult of personality" of Mao with the excuse that in the Soviet Union "the cult of personality" of Stalin was destroyed. [To oppose Mao's personality cult] is a destructive action against the proletarian cause.[13]

Liu Shaoqi's speech elucidated an already widely accepted view within the party—that Mao personified the party. To many of his colleagues, Mao deserved this status because of his leadership during the brutal struggle before 1949. In those trying times he had established himself as a capable leader who made sound assessments of situations and outsmarted his enemies with superior strategies and tactics. Whether it was the result of luck, talent, or something else, winning the war established Mao as a charismatic leader in the eyes of his colleagues and the Chinese people alike. Most of his colleagues openly supported Liu's statement on the cult of personality. One of them expressed his respect for Mao this way: "[We should] believe Mao with a blind faith and follow Mao unconditionally."[14] This crystallization of party power in Mao's person institutionalized Mao's authority—and created a charismatic leader who eventually elevated himself above the party and ultimately nearly destroyed it.

Chinese political tradition provided its own justifications for recognizing and accepting a charismatic leader. The concept of the "mandate of heaven" had traditionally been used to sustain the legitimacy of dynastic rulers. Mao and his comrades conveniently transformed it into the modern concept of the "mandate of the people," which they repeatedly used to legitimize CCP rule. Mao himself once wrote on this subject: "What is the 'mandate of heaven?' It is nothing but the 'mandate of the people.' Is our power granted by heaven? Our power is granted by the people, and above all, by the working class as well as the poor and lower-middle-class peasants."[15] A *Hongqi* editorial of 1968 elaborated on Mao's ideas:

Who grants power to us? It is granted by the working class, by the poor and lower-middle-class peasants, and by the broad laboring class that constitutes 90 percent of our population. We represent the proletariat and the broad masses. The people support us because we crushed the enemy of the people. One fundamental principle for the Communist Party is to rely directly on the broad revolutionary masses.[16]

Chinese political tradition not only facilitated the acceptance of a charismatic leader like Mao; it also exerted a strong influence on Mao's own mentality as leader. Mao saw himself as the savior of the Chinese people entrusted with the noble task of rescuing them from "an abyss of misery." A man who views himself this way is unlikely to see himself as an ordinary human being.[17] Mao enjoyed this fantasy with increasing enthusiasm. His bodyguards witnessed a change in his attitude as early as 1947, when for the first time he received a hail of *wansui* (long live . . .) from a crowd of poor peasants as he passed by. Mao was so touched by the salutation that he accepted it with tears in his eyes. He and his colleagues took this as a sign of the legitimacy of their struggle to rule China in the future.[18]

After 1949, Mao was much more at ease with adulation from the people. In 1952 his appearance at Wuhan attracted more than 10,000 people, who cheered and saluted him uncritically. The spontaneous outpouring of enthusiasm caused his bodyguards great anxiety as they tried to protect him from the crowd. Showing no sympathy for the guards' plight, Mao said jokingly, "I almost could not leave Huanghe Lou" (Building of Yellow Crane). On another occasion he deliberately ignored warnings not to attract attention from people on the street while dining in a second-floor restaurant in Tianjin in 1958. He showed himself in the windows and was immediately "discovered" by a woman on the street below. When the woman cried out, "Long live Chairman Mao!" people rushed from all directions to the restaurant. Rejecting pleas for caution from his guards, Mao went to the window six times, waving and shouting to the crowd. After four hours of this, Mao was able to leave the restaurant only with the assistance of extra guards sent over from the Tianjin garrison.[19]

In the past, said one of his bodyguards, Mao would have been angry when anyone shouted *wansui* while he was among the people, because the ensuing chanting and celebration kept him from speaking. During the incident at Tianjin, however, Mao thoroughly enjoyed the attention he attracted. Benjamin Schwartz, who studied Mao through careful readings of Mao's speeches between 1957 and 1958, concludes that by the fall of 1958 Mao was fully comfortable with the idea that he was the spiritual leader of the Chinese people.[20]

The experience of being worshiped had a transforming effect on Mao, reinforcing his sense of himself as the savior of the Chinese people. In a sense, the Cultural Revolution was a consummation of this personal fantasy. A revolutionary song expressed the idea precisely: "The east is red, there rises the sun, there emerges in China Mao Zedong, who brings people happiness and is the great savior of the people." During the Cultural

Revolution, the song was performed upon Mao's arrival whenever he appeared in public, and it gained such popularity that some suggested it be made the national anthem. The effect of this on Mao was understandable. He must have believed that he was the greatest when he stood atop the Tiananmen (the Gate of Heavenly Peace) facing thousands of cheering Chinese. From August to November 1966, Mao regularly appeared on the Tiananmen or at Tiananmen Square in a convertible car to receive the worship of the visiting Red Guards with ever-increasing enthusiasm. On several such occasions, Mao told his comrades with pride and confidence that the masses had really mobilized behind him. The resulting demonstrations of support confirmed Mao's conviction that his power had been legitimized and confirmed by the "mandate of the people."

Challenge the Earth

Before 1949 the legitimacy of the CCP rested on its war record. After 1949, however, the CCP confronted a less heroic experience: the task of building state institutions, developing a national economy, and solving intractable social problems. One major problem for the CCP war veterans was their lack of administrative and economic expertise. Hong Yung Lee has concluded that the factors that helped the CCP achieve power in 1949 thereafter restricted its capacity for state-building and economic development. Comparing China's experience in co-opting technical experts into the bureaucracy with that of Eastern European countries, Lee notes that the Chinese experience, which lasted more than 30 years, was of much longer duration than that in Eastern Europe. The prolonged transition of the leadership from revolutionary cadres to professionals, Lee suggests, was responsible for a number of economic and bureaucratic disasters, including the Great Leap Forward.[21]

To Mao, however, the major problem was not transforming his elite cadres into professional administrators for the purposes of state-building and economic development, but maintaining CCP legitimacy by showing the people that the party was equipped to bring them dignity and wealth. Although he did not completely ignore technical training for his cadres, Mao was confident, at least until 1959, of the CCP's ability to build in China first a socialist and then a communist society, where the Chinese would live happily thereafter.

Mao's confidence was boosted by the performance of the national economy from 1949 to 1952 and by the unexpectedly rapid transformation of the nation's economic structure from 1949 to 1956.[22] In 1952 grain output was 308.8 billion jin, an increase of 42.8 percent over 1949. The value of the gross industrial output in 1952 reached 34.33 billion yuan, 144.9 percent above the level of 1949.[23] According to party publications, the socialist transformation of agriculture, handicrafts, and industries was completed in 1956. The peasants had been placed in agricultural cooperatives, private enterprises had organized into handicraft cooperatives, and capitalist industries and commercial enterprises were transformed into joint state-private enterprises. In comparison with the Soviet Union and Eastern European countries, where these transformations had generated widespread resistance, the process in China had gone relatively smoothly, with less resistance and bloodshed. According to a party resolution of 1981, 1957 was the best year in economic terms since the founding of the PRC.[24]

These economic successes temporarily overshadowed the problem of an underqualified workforce but by no means made it disappear. Administrators continued to employ techniques developed during the war, such as issuing arbitrary orders and counting on the power of the human will in organizing economic work. Li Yinqiao, one of Mao's chief bodyguards, told Mao in 1955 that the party cadres in his hometown had forced peasants to join cooperatives. Party cadres went to the village and called everybody together, Li reported. Then they announced, "Those who would follow Jiang Jieshi [Chiang Kai-shek, the leader of Guomindang, the Chinese Nationalist Party] go to that side and work on your own; those who would follow Chairman Mao, stay on this side and join the cooperatives." Of course, no one dared reject the cooperatives. Mao admitted, after hearing of this practice, that the cadres were too simple-minded, but he never saw this as a serious problem. Mao simply wrote a letter to the provincial leader, asking him to criticize the party cadres who did this.[25]

Such problems did not loom only at the lower levels of administration. Most members of the Party Central Committee, including Mao himself, believed that economic development could be sparked by a revolutionary spirit among the masses. During the Great Leap Forward in 1958, the party attempted to accelerate economic progress, and the party newspaper *Renmin ribao* took the lead in spreading unrealistic expectations for the economy. In an editorial on August 3, 1958, *Renmin ribao* praised such absurd slogans as "The bolder you are, the more the land will produce" and "The amount the land produces depends on your courage, so forget about 'restrictionists.'"[26] False reports of grain output appeared in newspapers; one claimed, for instance, that the wheat harvest had reached 5,000 kilograms per mu, with a record annual output of 15,000 kilograms per mu.[27] Provincial leaders outdid one another in falsifying their grain production reports. So widespread and thoroughgoing were these exaggerations that even some scientists provided "scientific proof" that absurdly high production levels were possible. A well-known physician, for example, published an article in *Zhongguo qingnian* (*Chinese Youth*) "proving" that it was possible to produce twenty times the old average of 1,000 kilos per mu by using just 30 percent of the available annual solar energy. Mao, who came from a peasant family, hardly believed these exaggerations, but he refused to discourage the masses, being a firm believer in the human will. In Shanghai in 1959, responding to a question from Li Rui, one of his former secretaries, about how he could have believed the falsified grain reports, Mao simply blamed scientists for providing misleading information. "You also joined in the bragging without being on firm ground," Mao said jokingly to one scientist. "But your view is correct as a way of thinking."[28]

Another well-known example of a misguided policy was the "mass campaign to boost iron and steel production." Bo Yibo, who was in charge of state industry at the time, described twenty years later how the policy was formulated:

> Between June and July 1958, Mao said to me, "Now we know how to do it in terms of agriculture. The method is to 'let grain take the lead in producing other agricultural products.' . . . The problem concerning agricultural policy has been solved, but what about industry?" [I knew that] Mao meant to ask me to come up with a slogan to illustrate the idea of surpassing Great Britain, which was the largest producer of steel and iron at 22 million tons a year. *Without much thinking,* I replied, "Then, we can say, 'Let steel take the lead in other industries.'" "Good," Mao replied, "Let's do it."[29]

Thus was a national policy made. Soon thereafter, the Politburo issued a communiqué entitled "The Enlarged Politburo Conference Calls on the Whole Party and Whole People to Strive to Produce 10.7 Million Tons of Steel." Accomplishing this goal would mean doubling the 1957 production of 5.35 million tons. Since production through August 1958 was a mere 4 million tons, it was clearly impossible to achieve the goal of 10.7 million by the end of the year. Mao and many others, however, professed to believe it could be done. Why? According to Wang Heshou, minister of metallurgy at the time, they counted on a mass movement to do the job.

To reach the quota, party leaders at all levels organized campaigns to boost iron and steel production. The Party Central Committee called four telephone conferences to pressure local cadres to fulfill their quota. The

Central Secretariat organized a telephone conference on September 24, demanding a "campaign by big regiments" to boost daily production of steel to 60,000 tons. The Party Central Committee accompanied such demands with threats to punish cadres who fell short of their quota. The army also mobilized to increase iron and steel production. By the end of 1958 more than 600,000 small "backyard" blast furnaces were operating across the country. The number of people mobilized to work the mines and furnaces jumped from 240,000 in August to 50 million by September and eventually reached 90 million. Iron and steel production spread everywhere—to the fields, the schools, the streets, the courtyard of the Ministry of Foreign Affairs, even to State Vice-Chairman Madame Song Qingling's backyard.[30] Many veteran communists came to see the effort as a new war to "challenge the earth." The Great Leap Forward rested on the idea that by mobilizing the masses to boost production China would make the "leap" to become a true communist society in a few years.

This wishful thinking had disastrous consequences. It appeared at first that iron and steel production did increase through the nationwide efforts. The state announced on December 19 that the goal of 10.7 million tons of steel had been met twelve days ahead of schedule. Only 72 percent of the total, however, was of standard quality.[31] The campaign wasted large amounts of material, labor, and money; damaged equipment through overuse; and produced a great deal of steel of such low quality that it was useless. Furthermore, the huge demand for wood to fuel inefficient backyard furnaces destroyed the natural environment over an extensive area.

The damage done to agriculture and other industries was even greater. The movement exhausted so much rural labor (38.2 million peasants stopped farming to produce steel) that crops went unharvested. Damage to other industries was no less significant. The excessive consumption of power and raw materials interrupted normal operations of many factories in light industry. The imbalance between industry and transportation was also exacerbated.[32]

By early 1959 the disruptive consequences of this mass movement were apparent to most party leaders. The misguided policies and irrational behavior combined with a series of severe natural disasters in a three-year period to reduce grain output dramatically. According to economist Wen Tiejun, the first economic crisis was fully evident from 1958 through 1960. In those three years, the state deficit increased from 5.6 percent to 14.3 percent. The total deficit over three years amounted to 20 billion yuan.[33] The accompanying table illustrates population changes between 1957 and 1961.

*Population Before and After Mao's Great
Leap Forward (1958), 1957–1961*

Year	Crude death rate (percent)	Natural increase rate (percent)	Population change
1957	10.80%	23.23%	18,250,000
1958	11.98	17.24	13,410,000
1959	14.59	10.19	12,130,000
1960	25.43	−4.57	−10,000,000
1961	14.24	−3.78	−3,480,000

SOURCE: Yao Xinwu and Yin Hua, *Zhongguo changyong renkou shujuji*, p. 9.

In reality, the situation was even worse than the figures indicate. By January 1959 the food supply for residents of Beijing had been reduced to one cabbage per household per day. The problem was worse in the countryside, especially in poor provinces like Henan and Gansu. Although grain output decreased after 1958, the amount of grain that peasants had to hand over to the state increased, rising from 24.6 percent of the total in 1957 to 39.6 percent in 1959, and to 35.7 percent in 1960. Many peasants suffered from malnutrition, and in the worst-hit areas thousands died of starvation. No official figures are available for how many people died in the "three hard years"—estimates range from 10 to 30 million. In Gansu province alone, perhaps 1.3 million people died, a figure equal to one-tenth of the total population.[34]

How could this happen? Lack of technical expertise among revolutionary cadres, misguided policies, and deep-seated social and political problems all contributed to the disaster, but the greatest responsibility lay with Mao and his colleagues. Mao was behind all the policies, many of which reflected his personal beliefs, even his own personality. To emphasize Mao's personal role is not to deny that profound social, political, institutional, and cultural problems were also at work.[35] Rather, the above discussion illustrates one of the special problems that plagued the PRC until Mao's death—the conflict between a charismatic leader and the process of institutionalization. Political institutions during the Great Leap Forward placed few restrictions on the power of Mao, who was in reality the leader of a group of war veterans who believed that the strategies that brought them to power would be equally effective in building the national economy. Although decision-making processes were more complicated than those described here, in the first decades of the People's Republic, CCP leaders tended to make economic policy on the basis of their estimates of the capabilities of human will rather than careful calculations of economic realities. This does not mean that the party completely ignored economic factors in making policy. From time to time, Mao himself listened to the advice of experts and economic specialists. However, the Great Leap Forward itself was more a result of Mao's ignorance of professional opinions. Mao and his colleagues carried their wartime experiences into their efforts at state-building and economic development. Thus they relied almost exclusively on courage and persistence to build their socialist society. "I simply do not believe that it will be more difficult to develop industry and agriculture than to fight a war," Mao said at the Nanning Meeting of January 20, 1958.[36] On another occasion, Mao said it would be necessary for the party to wage a new war—a war against nature—to develop the economy.[37]

This was not just a matter of rhetoric. Mao and his comrades constantly drew nostalgic comparisons between their war experiences and their effort to build the national economy. Mao himself once put it this way:

> In the past, millions of us steeled [ourselves] through class struggle into communist fighters supported by the masses. [We] practiced the supply system, led a communist life—this was a Marxist style of work as opposed to a bourgeois style of work. In my view, the rural work style and guerrilla practices are, after all, better. In twenty-two years of war we were victorious. Why is it that building communism doesn't work? Why do [we] have to use a wage system? This is a concession to the bourgeoisie; [we are] allowing the rural work style and guerrilla practices to be used to belittle us [and] the result is the development of individualism.[38]

Like Mao, many other war veterans showed absolute faith in this style of war communism. Liu Shaoqi also shared the enthusiasm for war methods. During the Great Leap Forward, while a vice-chairman of the PRC, Liu fantasized about building a successful socialist economy by waging several campaigns at once, much as the CCP had done in the late 1940s in defeating the Nationalists. Liu advocated an "experiment in communism" in Xushui county in Hebei province, where everybody would have an equal share of life's necessities.[39]

Before 1960, Mao made no effort to familiarize himself with economic theories. He had little trust in "bookish" knowledge, and preferred to rely on his own experience and intuition. "I never read any books on commanding a war," he told a group of foreign guests in March 1965. "We should read fewer books. Reading too many books is no good."[40] He mocked agricultural "experts" who could not tell one crop from another. He repeatedly made analogies between himself and emperors who, with little or no education, ruled China successfully. Only after serious problems developed in the economy in 1959 did Mao organize a group to study political economy. According to party historian Shi Zhongquan, this was the first and only time in his life that Mao undertook a study of economics.[41]

Mao trusted intellectuals even less than he trusted book learning. After the anti-communist uprising in Hungary in 1956, Mao estimated that 80–90 percent of Chinese intellectuals—about 5 million people—still belonged to the bourgeois class. Thus it was not rich peasants, landlords, or compradors who threatened proletarian power; it was bourgeois intellectuals.[42] In March 1958, after the "anti-rightist movement," which was aimed at purging independent-thinking intellectuals, Mao proposed a theory of "two exploiting classes," one of which included intellectuals.[43] His bias against intellectuals not only meant that he disregarded expert opinion in economic development, but also eventually led to a broad purge of intellectuals during the Cultural Revolution, when a popular belief was "the more books you read, the more reactionary you become."

"Do Not Lose the Heart of the People"

The misguided policies of the Great Leap Forward soon had their full impact on the economy, and in late 1958 the party made its first efforts to adjust its economic policies. From November 1958 to April 1959, the Politburo held a series of meetings at Zhengzhou, Wuchang, and Shanghai. There, Mao criticized "leftist" ideas, including the tendency to blur the distinction between socialism and communism as illustrated by missteps in the movement to set up people's communes in 1958. Some rural cadres believed that they could deprive peasants of their labor as well as their products without paying compensation, on the assumption that in a people's commune, everything belonged to the people.[44] Mao tried to educate the cadres on the difference between ownership in a people's commune, which was a "collective ownership" in nature, and "socialist ownership by the people." He meant that at the present stage of socialism, products should still be distributed according to one's labor instead of to everyone equally. He also rejected proposals to abolish commodity production and exchange.[45] The Sixth Plenum of the Eighth Party Central Committee held in Wuhan in November and December 1958 adopted a resolution emphasizing that the people's communes must continue to distribute products according to the amount of work a person performed. The resolution also cautioned that communism would not soon be established in China.

Although Mao acknowledged problems with the people's communes, he would tolerate no criticism of the decision to establish communes in the first place. He endeavored to convince the people and his comrades that the problems in the communes were minor, involving work methods and the proper understanding of Marxist theories. There was nothing wrong with the "three red flags"—that is, the party's general line, the Great Leap Forward, and the people's communes. Mao was especially sensitive about criticism of the communes, which he took as personal criticism. The communes represented an experiment in his long-cherished utopian dream of peasant egalitarianism. Having been a peasant himself, Mao believed nothing was more exciting than the prospect of setting up places where peasants could eat without having to pay for doing so. According to Li Rui, Mao had outlined his dream for a new society for China as early as 1919: a plot of ideal land with "new-style villages" consisting of "new-style families," "new-style schools," and other new-style staff.[46] This may reflect the influence on young Mao of Kang Youwei's *Da tong shu* (*The Book of Universal Commonwealth*) and European utopian socialist ideas, but Mao never gave up his desire to establish an ideal society in China. During the Cultural Revolution, he made a clearer statement of his vision in his famous "May 7 Directive." In this directive, Mao laid out a blueprint for China as a self-sufficient society where soldiers would simultaneously defend the country and work in industry and agriculture; workers and peasants would be able to assist each other while also performing their major tasks, and so forth.[47]

Throughout his life, Mao had a keen concern for the peasants. Few leaders in Chinese history had paid as much attention to the peasants as Mao did. He once said that the happiest moment in his life was not when the CCP took power in China, but when he learned that most peasants had been organized into agricultural cooperatives.[48] Once, before the Great Leap Forward, according to Li Yinqiao, Mao was in tears when he saw a piece of cornbread, dark in color and bitter in taste, brought back by a bodyguard from his home village. He could not sleep that night, murmuring repeatedly, "We are in a socialist society and we have to find a way [to provide better food for peasants]."[49] His concern over the peasants partly explains why Mao supported and vehemently defended the Great Leap Forward and the people's communes.

However, Mao became cautious when things turned sour. He was willing to adjust his policies and accepted some of the blame after hearing the peasants' complaints while traveling the countryside in mid-1958. Although worried about losing "people's hearts" if he ignored their complaints, he would not allow anyone to question the legitimacy of his rule or the "correctness" of his policy of the "three red flags." This finally led to his conflict with Minister of Defense Peng Dehuai at the Lushan Conference of 1959, which destroyed all of his previous efforts to adjust economic policy within the party.

The enlarged Politburo meeting and the Eighth Plenum of the Eighth Central Committee were held in July and August 1959 at Lushan. These meetings were among the most important meetings in CCP history. In a sense, the Lushan Conference of 1959 marked a turning point in the relationship between Mao and his close comrades. Peng Dehuai's indirect criticism of Mao indicated that some of his comrades began to lose faith in him as an infallible leader.

The subsequent fall of Peng Dehuai, who was the defense minister and vice-chairman of the Central Military Committee, and other leaders became the first of Mao's worst purges of his longtime comrades after 1949.[50] In the long run, the victory of Mao over Peng and others resulted in the continuation of fatally flawed economic policies, cost millions of lives in the next few years, and also set an example for dealing with inner-party struggle—men were purged because they voiced opinions different from Mao's. Above all, the conference reinforced Mao's power over the party and ensured that few people would ever again dare to tell Mao a truth he did not want to hear. In this sense, the events of Lushan set a precedent for Mao's later purges in the Cultural Revolution, including those of Liu, Deng, Chen Yi, Tan Zhenlin, and above all Lin Biao. It became clear at the 1959 Lushan Conference that anyone who disagreed even slightly with Mao would be considered a counter-revolutionary. This unwritten law was later practiced to an extreme during the Cultural Revolution and epitomized by the ill fortune of Lin Biao at another Lushan Conference more than a decade later.

The enlarged Politburo meeting began calmly enough. Many participants took the occasion as an opportunity to vacation at Lushan, a famous mountain resort in Jiangxi province. The purpose of the meeting was "a further summing up of past experiences" and correcting "leftist errors that had come to the leadership's notice." Mao's initial speeches were positive discussions of past party work. Believing that most problems had been solved by previous efforts, Mao set the tone by characterizing the current situation as one of "great achievements, numerous problems, and a bright future."[51] Not everyone shared this view, however, especially Mao's evaluation of the "three red flags." Halfway through the scheduled sessions, the party was divided over how to evaluate mistakes made in the recent past. Some wanted to view the situation positively, while others emphasized the immediate economic problems facing the country. Peng Dehuai was the most outspoken in the latter group. The following are excerpts from Peng's remarks during group discussions:

Morning, July 3
The rate of increase in production in the commune of Mao's hometown was actually not that great. As far as I know, production increased by only 16 percent. I asked Comrade Zhou Xiaozhou,[52] who told me that the commune's production increased by only 14 percent, even with much help and funding from the state. The chairman has been to that commune. I asked the chairman, "What do you think?" He told me that he had not discussed this matter when he was there. I think he did.

Morning, July 4
[We should] learn a lesson, not just complain or find fault. Everybody bears some responsibility, including Comrade Mao Zedong, who decided on 10.7 [million tons of steel]. How can he not share some responsibility? He criticized himself at the Shanghai Conference, admitting that he had been somewhat hotheaded.[53] I also bear some responsibility. At the least, I did not oppose [the ideas] at the time. What is great about the chairman is that he can figure out problems in time and make a quick adjustment.

Morning, July 7
The people's communes, I believe, were established too early . . . without any prior experimentation. It would be better if we had experimented for a year before they were set up.

Morning, July 8
Mao has such great prestige within the party and among the Chinese people that he has no match in the whole world. However, this prestige should not be misused. It caused many problems when the chairman's opinions were communicated loosely.

Morning, July 10
After liberation, a series of victories made many people hotheaded. Therefore, reports that were positive and advantageous were sent to Mao. After a great victory, it's easy to overlook and reject opposite opinions.[54]

What Peng said must have received some general support. Other people, including Li Rui, Zhou Xiaozhou, and Zhang Wentian, shared Peng's opinions, and all of them were later purged along with Peng Dehuai. After the group discussions, Peng felt obliged to let the chairman know his opinions directly, since Mao did not participate in group discussions and there was little time left before the conference was to end on July 15. On the night of July 14, Peng wrote a letter to Mao and sent it to him the next day. Nobody expected that letter to end Peng's political career and turn him into an "anti-party element."

Read today, Peng's letter seems to be only a request that the party draw lessons from past experience, not a challenge to Mao as party leader.[55] Peng took pains to avoid any misunderstandings between Mao and himself. Unlike the speeches quoted above, the letter directed no personal criticism at Mao. The first part focused on achievements under Mao's leadership, but in the second part Peng listed "petty-bourgeois fanaticism" as one of the causes of current problems. Huang Kecheng, secretary of the Central Secretariat and another victim of the Lushan Conference, immediately recognized Peng's mistake when Peng later showed him the letter, but the letter had already been sent. "It is not very well written," commented Huang, "because there is 'sting' in it"—"sting" meaning wording that might offend Mao.[56]

Huang was right. Peng's letter indeed offended Mao. Mao said to Wang Renzhong the day after he got Peng's letter that he would not make any immediate comments on the phrase "petty-bourgeois fanaticism."[57] In CCP history, the expression "petty bourgeois" was used to refer to those who did not belong to the proletariat. Intellectuals, for example, were considered petty bourgeois. Mao was from a rich peasant family and went to school before he joined the revolution. He was thus especially sensitive to criticism directed at the "petty bourgeoisie."

Mao did not control his anger long. "Can you allow me to speak for a little while since you have said so much? I took sleeping pills three times [last night], but I still could not sleep."[58] With these words, Mao launched his counterattack on July 23, eight days after receiving Peng's letter.[59] Then his words fell into the hall like bombshells:

> Now some wind is blowing both inside and outside the party. [The rightists said] nothing good about us and [expected] we would fall. . . . All the rightists' opinions have been repeated [at the meeting]. . . . Some of those [who made criticisms] are rightists and wavering elements themselves. They cannot hold an overall view and are angry [about what happened]. [Some of them] will change after some work, but some of them [will not] because they also had problems in the past and were criticized before. . . . This time, [those] at the meeting ganged up with [those] outside the meeting. It's a pity that we cannot invite them [rightists] all, because Lushan is too small. Just invite them all, the likes of Luo Longji and Chen Mingshu, but the hall is indeed too small![60]
>
> . . . Then, I will go to the countryside and lead the peasants to overthrow the government. If your People's Liberation Army will not follow me, I will go looking for the Red Army. I will organize another PLA. I think the PLA will follow me. . . .
>
> I will not say anything more today because I have to go to bed. You can continue the meeting if you want to, but I have to go. Do I speak for too long? It is not for two hours yet. The meeting adjourns![61]

According to Li Rui, who has provided the most detailed account of the Lushan Conference, most people present were shocked by the tone of Mao's speech. At least seven times Mao mentioned the phrase "petty-bourgeois fanaticism." After the speech, Peng tried to explain to Mao that the letter he wrote was nothing but an expression of his own opinions to the chairman. He did not think it right for Mao to distribute the letter at the conference. Peng asked Mao to return the letter, but it was too late. The chairman had made up his mind not to let him off.

At first, it was not easy for Mao to settle his personal score with Peng. Despite the personal problems he had with some of his colleagues, Peng enjoyed a high reputation in the party. For several days after Mao's speech, criticism of Peng and others did not reach the level Mao had expected. While criticizing Peng, many participants also made self-criticisms, admitting that they had not taken the letter as a serious problem before the chairman's speech. Some of them even tried to help Peng by emphasizing repeatedly that Peng did not mean anything malicious by the letter.

On July 26, word from the chairman reached the meeting. According to Li Rui's notebooks, Mao's directive said this: "Do not point just to the letter, but to the person as well. Draw clear distinctions [between party lines] and elucidate the problems. No ambiguity."[62] Most people realized by now that Mao considered the problem between Peng and himself to be much more severe than a difference of opinion over party policy. The chairman wanted more than criticism of Peng's letter: he wanted criticism of Peng himself. On the same day, Peng, on the advice of several comrades, reluctantly made his first self-criticism. Peng noted later in his diary that he was depressed and uneasy about making a self-criticism against his will and admitting things he did not mean. "I felt as bad as if ten thousand swords had stabbed my heart," he wrote.[63]

Nevertheless, Mao would not let the matter drop. With keen political sensitivity sharpened by the harsh experiences of war, he saw much more in the situation than a difference of opinion regarding the Great Leap Forward and the people's communes. Peng's letter provided Mao with an opportunity to mute dissenting voices inside as well as outside the party. He would let people know that to deny the "three red flags" was to deny the correctness of his leadership, and denial of his leadership within the party would not be tolerated.

While Peng Dehuai was making involuntary self-criticisms, Mao was elevating the struggle to a higher level of principle. Soon thereafter, Tian Jiaying told Li Rui that a document concerning an "anti-party clique" was being drafted and that Zhou Xiaozhou was listed as a member.[64] Tian wanted Li to pass the word to Zhou to choose his words more cautiously in the future.

On July 29, Mao decided to call the Eighth Plenum of the Eighth Central Committee to meet on August 2 and continue discussing the problem of "rightist tendencies" in the party. Before the plenum, Peng received severe criticism at two enlarged Politburo meetings on July 31 and August 1. Mao took the lead, focusing on Peng's past problems. Liu Shaoqi, Zhou Enlai, Zhu De, and Lin Biao participated in the meeting, and Peng Dehuai, Peng Zhen, He Long, Huang Kecheng, Zhou Xiaozhou, and Li Rui audited the meeting. Li Rui kept a record of it, producing thereby what turned out to be a very important historical document. Li Rui was so pained by the criticism of Peng that he could hardly keep his hand steady when he wrote. No one present stood up in Peng's defense.[65]

The plenum identified Peng Dehuai, Huang Kecheng, Zhang Wentian, and Zhou Xiaozhou as the chief members of an anti-party clique. The Party Central Committee took several actions, among them "A Decision Concerning the Mistakes of the Anti-Party Clique Headed by Comrade Peng Dehuai" and "A Decision Concerning the Removal of Comrade Huang Kecheng from His Position as Secretary of the Central Secretariat."[66] On August 16, Mao wrote an important document entitled "Jiguanqiang he pojipao de laili ji qita" ("The Origins of the Machine Gun, Mortar, and Other Weapons"), in which he presented the dispute at Lushan as "a continuation of a life-and-death struggle between the two contradictory classes, the proletariat and the bourgeois, during the process of socialist revolution in the past ten years." The struggle would continue, Mao said, until the final extinction of classes, as long as 50 more years.[67]

This unexpected turn of Peng Dehuai's political career illustrated one recurring problem in the relationship between Mao and his chief lieutenants. Because of nationwide economic and social problems, Mao became increasingly insecure and sensitive about the "correctness" of his leadership. As a revolutionary leader, Mao's power was largely based on personal loyalty and trust between himself and his followers. There were no institutional constraints to stabilize the relation between the leader and the led. Mao relied on loyalty and respect from his followers, who in turn depended on Mao's trust to advance in their careers. If this patron-client tie were broken, either Mao's leadership or someone else's career would be in jeopardy. This was the cause of many inner-party conflicts under Mao. Mao had little choice but to condemn opinions that differed from his own in order to maintain power over his comrades and the country.

However, Mao could not use personal reasons to justify the elimination of a high official. One way to accomplish his goal while maintaining public support was to "raise the issue to a higher level" (*shang gang shang xian*). In the case of Peng Dehuai, what began as a difference of opinion became a class struggle. In this sense, what happened at the Lushan Conference in 1959 anticipated Mao's many other purges later in the Cultural Revolution, including that of Lin Biao and his generals at and after the Lushan Conference in 1970.

Events after the 1959 Lushan Conference, however, soon posed a greater threat to Mao's leadership. Despite Mao's victory at Lushan and in the subsequent anti-rightist struggle, the economy continued to deteriorate, and famine spread across the countryside. Even those who firmly supported Mao in his struggle against Peng began to question Mao's handling of it. On January 11, 1962, a working conference of the Central Committee, also known as the Conference of Seven Thousand People (*qiqian-ren dahui*), met in Beijing. In his speech at the conference, Liu Shaoqi reported nationwide problems much more frankly than anyone had before, though he included exaggerated compliments for past achievements to mitigate the bad news. What was most alarming to Mao in the report was that Liu described the problems as due "30 percent to natural disaster, but 70 percent to human factors." This assessment contradicted Mao's and in fact was consonant with Peng's early notion on the problems of party leadership. Many scholars have since maintained that it was Liu's report at the Conference of Seven Thousand People that first provoked Mao's distrust of Liu.[68] Whether this was true or not, Mao never forgot this event. Later, at the Eleventh Plenum of the Eighth Party Central Committee in 1966, Mao referred to "the problem of 1962" in his big-character poster announcing his split with Liu.[69] Jiang Qing gave a clearer indication of Mao's resentment of Liu's report when she said later that "the Cultural Revolution finally enabled [us] to give vent to the anger nursed since the Conference of Seven Thousand People."[70]

To his dismay, Mao finally had to relinquish personal direction of economic activities, which he had taken over in 1956 after his severe criticism of Chen Yun (a vice-premier in charge of economic policies), Zhou Enlai, and others for their opposition to Mao's ideas for a rapid acceleration of economic development. After the Conference of Seven Thousand People, Liu Shaoqi presided over an enlarged meeting of the Standing Committee that discussed the national budget and economy. When the meeting was over, Liu Shaoqi, Zhou Enlai, and Deng Xiaoping went together to Wuhan to report to Mao, asking for his endorsement of their decisions to restore the Small Group on Central Finance and Economy, which Mao had abolished in 1956, and to appoint Chen Yun to head it. The requests were actually pleas to Mao to yield responsibility for directing the economy to Chen Yun. Mao saw the requests as a personal humiliation, a sign that he was no longer an "infallible" and unchallengeable leader in his colleagues' eyes. This was probably what Jiang Qing meant when she referred to Mao's "nursed anger."

Although it was difficult for Mao to acknowledge failure, he was forced to do so this time. As the head of the party and the state, Mao could not deny responsibility for the economic disasters since 1956. Nor could he ignore the fact that millions of people were starving to death, having seen with his own eyes how starved his own daughter was when she came home from boarding school. Whether Mao ever regretted what he had done is unknown, but he did refuse to have meat with his meals for at least seven months beginning in the summer of 1960.[71]

Mao had already retired from the front line of leadership after voluntarily stepping down from the position of state chairman in 1959. Now he was forced to accept further compromise by agreeing to the group's requests. But he did not surrender easily. As Peng Dehuai had said privately to a friend during the Lushan Conference, "The first emperor who established a new dynasty was usually great but, at the same time, terrible." To Mao's disappointment, he could not easily find fault with his successors' economic leadership. The state economy began recovering through the efforts of Chen Yun and others in 1962. There was a 25 million jin increase in grain output in 1962, a 6.2 percent improvement over 1961.[72] The average worker's salary also increased by 6 percent. In fact, the national economy reached an all-time high in 1966, when the Cultural Revolution began.[73] Economic achievements proved the effectiveness of the collective leadership of Liu Shaoqi, Deng Xiaoping, Zhou Enlai, and Chen Yun. But what did this mean to Mao? Could China continue to develop under a collective leadership without Mao's authority? Answers came soon.

Continuing the Revolution Under the Dictatorship of the Proletariat

Mao had long been the major theorist of the CCP, though what came to be known as Mao Zedong Thought included the collective efforts of many others. While other leaders in the early 1960s concentrated on reviving the national economy, Mao spent his time contemplating how to compensate for his loss by making a breakthrough in the field of Marxist social theory. In August 1962 at the working conference of the Central Committee at Beidaihe, he began maneuvering to refocus party work from the economy to politics by reemphasizing the theory of class struggle. The original agenda called for the conference to focus on agricultural and commercial policies. However, on the first day of the conference Mao raised the question of class struggle and contradictions in socialist society. "If the proletariat overlooks its responsibility for leadership," Mao warned, "capitalist restoration is quite possible." Mao thereby changed the agenda for the conference, the remainder of which was devoted almost entirely to discussions of class struggle.[74] At the following Tenth Plenum of the Eighth Party Central Committee, Mao continued: "Never forget class struggle," Mao warned the party. "From now on, we should talk about it year by year, month by month, and day by day. We will talk about it at every meeting, every party conference, and whenever [we] hold a meeting until we have a clearer Marxist-Leninist line on this."[75] Mao's arbitrary directive severely impeded the regular work of the party.

The party simply had no way to constrain its mighty but capricious leader. Liu Shaoqi and others repeatedly deferred to Mao on important issues. The constant concession to Mao's arbitrary decisions not only disrupted economic planning but also led to the tragic purges of many leaders during the Cultural Revolution. Ironically, Liu himself probably did not realize until it was too late that in supporting Mao's theory of class struggle he put his political career and even his life in jeopardy. When he joined Mao in talking about class struggle and the threat of "bourgeois restoration" in China, he never imagined that Mao would one day accuse him of being the leader of resurgent capitalism.

The communiqué of the Tenth Plenum of the Eighth Party Central Committee reflected, once again, Mao's victory over the party, which accepted his idea of class struggle without reservation. It took Mao only seven months—from the Conference of Seven Thousand People in January 1962 to the Beidaihe Conference in August—to reassert his control of the party and redirect its attention from economic problems to the theory of class struggle. The August communiqué, which Mao edited himself, declared that class struggle would continue through the entire transitional period from socialism to communism. It would inevitably influence the party itself and could become the source of revisionism within the party.[76] The message was clear: because of the danger of revisionism, the party would treat any difference of opinion within its ranks as a difference between Marxism and revisionism.

Mao needed only one more thing to justify his theory of continuing revolution—an illegitimate authority structure to target in the next phase. The conflict between the CCP and the Communist Party of the Soviet Union since the late 1950s made finding that target easy. Mao had felt personally threatened by Khrushchev's denunciation of Stalin not long after Stalin's death. Mao watched with dismay as a respected Communist leader was turned into an "enemy of the people" overnight. Witnessing the Soviet example, Mao realized that his own comrades could do him more harm than his enemies outside the party because the comrades would be in position to disguise their purposes, as in the case of Khrushchev, who had appeared loyal to Stalin before Stalin died. To Mao, "capitalist restoration" in the Soviet Union began with the denunciation of Stalin. Thus he made what seemed to him a logical connection between protecting his personal reputation and that of the party.

Mao was energized by the challenge posed by the new enemy—revisionists within the party. He decided to launch a nationwide struggle against revisionism to protect the country from "capitalist restoration." In February 1963, the working conference of the Party Central Committee in Beijing decided to launch two campaigns, one of "five antis" (*wu fan*) in the cities and another in support of "four cleans" (*si qing*) in the countryside.[77] Mao traveled extensively after the conference to organize forces for these campaigns but found little enthusiasm among provincial leaders. He complained in May 1963 that only two officials in eleven provinces, Liu Zihou, first secretary of the Party Committee in Hebei province, and Wang Yanchun, secretary of the Party Committee of Hunan province, mentioned the Socialist Education Movement.[78] Mao believed the problems of revisionism were not confined to party cadres at the lowest level.

The Socialist Education Movement was something of a prelude to the Cultural Revolution. It was Mao's first campaign against revisionists within the party. Its most significant consequence was the clash between Mao and Liu Shaoqi over differing conceptions of the movement itself. Liu held that the movement should address problems at the lower levels of the party structure, whereas Mao wanted to use the movement to purge "the capitalist roaders within the party."[79] This disagreement deepened Mao's personal animosity toward Liu. If in 1962 Mao had hesitated to turn against Liu Shaoqi, who had been one of his most loyal followers for 30 years, he now began to consider seriously the possibility of doing just that.[80] Mao was irritated that Liu was unimpressed by Mao's claim that there were capitalists in the party. Although Liu did not challenge the claim directly and even agreed that there were some cadres within the party taking a "capitalist road," he suggested that it could be an exaggeration to consider them a faction. Liu was worried that the wholesale pursuit of capitalist roaders would make too many party cadres vulnerable, especially on the provincial level.

Liu's anxiety was well founded. As early as the Lushan Conference of 1959, Mao was detecting "machine guns" within the party. He then clarified in the document of 23 items that the problem of capitalist roaders should be a focus of the Socialist Education Movement, an indication that he had decided to cleanse the party from within. Mao professed to be especially pessimistic about the situation in 1963–64. "One third of the power in the country is no longer in our hands, but in the hands of our enemies," Mao told a Central Committee working conference on June 8, 1964.[81] Mao assessed the situation as follows:

> Class enemies of all descriptions [*niu gui she shen*] will be at large everywhere, but our cadres still totally ignore them. Many of us, not knowing the distinction between enemies and friends, will cooperate with the enemy or be corrupted by the enemy. . . . Many workers, peasants and intellectuals will also be turned to their side through their weakness in the face of various [enemy] tricks. If things go on like this, it won't be long, a few years to ten years at the least and several decades at the most, [before reactionaries] inevitably succeed in their nationwide counter-revolutionary restoration. The Marxist party will be turned into a revisionist party and a fascist party, and the whole country will change color. Please think about this, comrades. What a dangerous situation this will be![82]

Mao was convinced that although the problems he saw emerged at the bottom their roots were at the top. In January 1965 he therefore began to prepare his comrades for a split in the Central Committee. "What are you going to do if revisionism appears in the Central Committee?" Mao asked responsible cadres in the provinces.[83] Mao's warnings on this point became more frequent and serious until he finally announced in the same year his discovery that "a Khrushchev is right beside us." Thus, Mao believed he was fully justified in starting his second revolution, or rather in continuing the first one.

In conclusion, the theory of "continuing the revolution under the dictatorship of the proletariat" summed up Mao's vision and practice after 1949. In many ways, it reflected Mao's own experience and personality. Mao and his comrades were nostalgic about their wartime experience and tried to keep the revolutionary spirit alive for the work of developing the economy. They were extremely eager to achieve economic success in order to maintain their legitimacy as rulers of China. Driven by their communist ideology, Mao and his comrades wanted to prove that their system was superior to the capitalists'. They launched one "great leap forward" after another in economic areas, hoping to show that China could achieve much faster economic growth than the bourgeois societies had achieved in the previous hundred years. Unfortunately, the economy did not develop as Mao and his comrades wanted. On the contrary, arbitrary decisions and blind belief in wartime experience ended in a nationwide economic crisis. The result was a dramatic decrease in population by 10–30 million people in the early 1960s.[84]

Despite economic setbacks, Mao refused to admit the problems in his leadership and ignored the fact that his party cadres lacked the preparation and qualifications to lead economic development. He took all criticism personally, as a challenge to his leadership or to the ruling party's legitimacy. In 1957 the party launched a large-scale anti-rightist movement against the challenge to party leadership from outside. More than 100,000 people, most of them intellectuals, were labeled "rightist" and persecuted. In 1959, Mao turned against his own comrades who criticized the party's economic policies. This led to the purge of Peng Dehuai and other high officials, and the consequent "anti-rightist-deviation" movement claimed 365,000 victims within the party itself.[85]

When Mao finally had to accept partial blame for the disastrous economic policies pursued from 1958 through 1961, he was upset as well as resentful. As a charismatic leader, he simply did not believe that anything was beyond his ability. In his reply to a question about Mao's most striking characteristic, Li Yinqiao replied, "his courage in facing challenges," citing the following. One day at Beidaihe, Mao was suddenly in a mood to go swimming despite the extremely rough waters. Stubbornly ignoring all cautions from his staff, he rushed into the roaring sea, shouting to his bodyguards behind him, "Come on, I don't think it is any worse than the seven brigades of Liu Kan."[86] One big wave knocked all of them down on the beach. Seeing his guards in a frenzy, Mao laughed and yelled to the sea, "Good, I finally found my match. I will see who is the winner!" He also got angry with his bodyguards. "If you lose your courage to follow me, you may leave. I will organize other forces to fight," he yelled. For a second and third time he rushed into the water surrounded by his guards, only to be thrown back by the mountainous waves. When he finally had to give up, he was still muttering about going back into the water.[87]

Mao's personal preferences and beliefs reflected his defiant character. As one Chinese scholar puts it, Mao most dreaded a pedestrian life without challenges. He loved hot peppers and liked his food very hot. To him, all good revolutionaries should be able to stand hot food. He kept experimenting with new ideas and simply would not abandon his personal dream of creating a new society. He could not face the loss of his authority and became furious when his ideas were challenged. He knew he was not infallible, but he did not need someone else to point this out to him. A combination of his early utopian dream and what degenerated into senile paranoia inspired him to engage in one struggle after another. He never wanted the revolution to stop because a continuing revolution would ensure his indispensability as a revolutionary leader.

This drive may have added to Mao's personal charm, but it was a disaster for the party and for the country. Just several months after he retired from economic leadership he came back brandishing the sword of class struggle. With this, he knocked down most of his colleagues and revitalized the myth of the invincible leader. Thus began the most disastrous period in the history of the People's Republic.

3

Chinese Gerontocracy and
the Cultural Revolution

In their studies of Mao Zedong, Chinese party historians have drawn a clear distinction between the "great Mao" of his prime and the "erroneous Mao" of his later years. They describe both the Great Leap Forward and the Cultural Revolution as mistakes made by an aging leader. They also compare Mao to Stalin in his later years and suggest thereby that mighty leaders who rule too long engender political instability. Few of these scholars, however, have tried to elucidate what it was exactly that differentiated the "great Mao" from the "erroneous Mao." Even among the more extensive and diverse studies of Mao by Western scholars, only a few offer analyses of Mao's physical and psychological problems in his later years.[1]

Any inquiry into the probable physical and psychological effects of aging on Mao leads one to the concept of gerontocracy, government by the elderly, and to gerontology, the study of the effects of aging on human behavior. It is not my purpose here to make a systematic study of the elderly Mao exclusively from a gerontocratic or gerontological perspective. It is, rather, to draw connections between the Cultural Revolution and Mao's personal circumstances, including the fact that he was 73 years old in 1966 when the Cultural Revolution began. One of the most important features of national politics during the Cultural Revolution was Mao's continuing purge of high officials. More or less suddenly, Mao turned against almost all his longtime party comrades. This behavior suggests that Mao suffered from what psychologists call senile paranoia. That diagnosis does not answer all questions about the Cultural Revolution, but it does add insight and information to discussions of the origin and course of the Cultural Revolution.

According to general theories of social gerontology, the physical and psychological changes many people undergo in later adulthood can affect their ability to function efficiently. Most such changes affect persons of advanced age, particularly those over 75.[2]

If aging is a difficult experience for most people, the prospect of dying is especially painful for powerful political leaders without heirs to perpetuate their legacy. In a discussion of "the politics of rejuvenation," Angus McIntyre identifies the behavior patterns of such political leaders. Prominent among the patterns is reliance on the ego-defense mechanism of denying death by fantasizing about immortality or indispensability. Another prominent pattern is the manic defense of idealization—conjuring up a renovated image of their youthful political selves as an antidote to their envy of younger peers.[3] Many of McIntyre's insights are especially pertinent to the elderly Mao. Indeed, several of Mao's biographers have already established a connection between Mao's inner struggle against old age and his role in the Cultural Revolution. Robert J. Lifton has suggested that Mao sought to deny his imminent death by seeking immortality through the Cultural Revolution.[4]

Giving Life Meaning Through the Cultural Revolution

Among the characteristic concerns of later adulthood identified by psychologists is an ongoing internalized struggle to accept one's life as lived and to develop an acceptable approach to death. Erik Erikson described this as the conflict between integrity and despair in later adulthood.[5] In searching for the meaning of one's life, an individual is "inevitably vulnerable to some degree about the limitations of his accomplishments." In order to overcome the fear of death, aged adults may exaggerate their own importance by associating their existence with something grandiose. Such an aging adult may also try to develop a sense of effectiveness and vitality to "lessen the threat of death as a blow to narcissism."[6]

In Mao's case, the personal psychology of an elderly individual had implications far beyond the man himself. Mao's psychological adjustment to aging was not that of a person coming to terms with himself and his family and immediate circumstances, but that of a man exaggerating the relationship between himself as a powerful charismatic leader and the people, the country, and the causes he had led. The idea of "continuing revolution" discussed in the preceding chapter could also be interpreted as Mao's remedy for his own psychological dilemmas as an old man. It provided a logical link between the meaning of his own life and China's political future. As Lucian Pye put it, psychologically, Mao confused the meaning of the 1949 revolution with the meaning of his own life. The aged Mao was thus unable to "distinguish between the moment in history when he was the appropriate revolutionary leader and the need for a different role for future revolutionary spirits in China."[7] The older he grew, the more deeply Mao became obsessed with the revolution that gave meaning to his life. It was too painful for him to accept that, having led the revolution of 1949, he was incapable of leading the economic transformation the country needed after the revolution. One result of his effort to prove otherwise was the Great Leap Forward.

Psychologically, Mao was unprepared to deal with failure in later adulthood. After the failure of his bold experiment to accelerate economic development by force of human will, he reasserted his leadership of the revolution by developing the theory of continuing revolution. This theory, Mao hoped, would guarantee the future of Communist China, thus affirming the immortality of his generation and its revolutionary accomplishments. Mao saw these issues as measures in a personal war to save China from "revisionists" and "capitalist restoration." The fantasy both validated for himself, and he hoped for the country as well, his own indispensability and immortality, and satisfied his nostalgia for revolutionary experience. The theory of continuing revolution provided Mao with a perfect vehicle for immortality by connecting his life with China's future.

Cognitive Impairment and the Decision to Undertake a Cultural Revolution

Examining Mao's decision to launch the Cultural Revolution from a cognitive point of view offers a different psychological perspective. This point of view suggests that motivational as well other forces may have affected Mao's decision. According to Yaacov Vertzberger, motivational biases "arise from emotions, personal motives and needs, and have ego-defensive functions," whereas biases that lack such motivation are the "products of complexity of the environment, the inherent limitations on cognitive capabilities, and the strategies used to overcome them."[8]

In the case of Mao, the influence of both types of bias was obvious in many of his decisions before and during the Cultural Revolution. The connection between Mao's theory of the Cultural Revolution and his pursuit of personal immortality has already been noted. The chairman became increasingly stubborn in forcing his own ideas on the party, and his stubbornness, which increased as he aged, was largely a result of motivational biases in Mao's outlook. Aging, according to Vertzberger, tends to produce rigidity and overconfidence in the individual and a preference for either/or choices.[9]

However, other elements may also have contributed to Mao's miscalculations. Mao's well-articulated worries about China's future sounded valid to many of his comrades. There indeed existed worldwide hostility toward Mao's China during the first two decades of the republic. The Soviet Union, which Mao had considered a "big brother" under Stalin, became an enemy under Khrushchev. In China itself, corruption and bureaucratization within the party and the government worsened in the early 1960s. Until the eve of the Cultural Revolution, few of Mao's colleagues questioned the need for reform, or even for a full-scale cultural revolution. Indeed, it was Liu Shaoqi who chaired the enlarged Politburo meeting in May 1966 at which the party decided to stage the Cultural Revolution. What eventually cost Mao the support of most of his colleagues during that revolution was not his belief in the need for the Cultural Revolution but the way he conducted it—by mobilizing the Red Guards and the masses to destroy virtually all state and party institutions. Many of Mao's comrades accepted Mao's theory readily. Even in the 1990s, Chinese government and party officials still repeat Mao's concern of "peaceful evolution" (*heping yanbian*) to capitalism, which, by Mao's definition, is happening everywhere in China today.

When Mao blended his need for immortality with his perceptions of problems in the party and the government, his own cognitive biases seemed to disappear for him and were less visible to his comrades. According to Vertzberger, once motivational biases become part of the internal cognitive process, a leader may become even more certain that his decisions are correct and "consequently ignore or even distort the interpretation of information indicating the need for major policy change." This process may be more pronounced in an elderly leader; even if he realizes his motivational biases, he is less likely than a younger person to attempt to correct them because of the psychological discomfort such a correction may arouse.[10] This was precisely the case with Mao during the Cultural Revolution. Oblivious to anything like the cognitive considerations mentioned above, he believed his decisions were fully justified and based on a sound understanding of reality. By the time of the 1971 Lin Biao incident, Mao was at least intermittently aware of his errors in the Cultural Revolution, but the elderly Mao was psychologically no longer capable of correcting his mistakes. He was thus preoccupied for the rest of his life with defending the Cultural Revolution, his last "contribution" to China and the one that would guarantee his immortality, and he continued to victimize his comrades who expressed reservations about the Cultural Revolution.

Fear of Death and the Rejuvenation of Society

In discussing the different types of aging of leaders, McIntyre refers to reparative and destructive narcissistic leadership. The former type is characterized by a leader's protection of "his grandiose self by idealizing his supporters" and the latter by a leader's protection of "his grandiose self by devaluing his opponents." Sometimes the two types may coexist in the same leader.[11]

Applying McIntyre's concepts, we find in the elderly Mao's behavior during the Cultural Revolution a standard case of shifting between reparative and destructive leadership. From its beginning the Cultural Revolution was characterized by the mobilization of youth to rebel against older authority figures and by extensive purges of senior party officials. Scholars have proposed several hypotheses to link these two phenomena. Some have suggested that Mao mobilized the Red Guards in order to overthrow his political opponents.[12] Others have proposed a reverse cause-and-effect relationship—that is, that the downfall of large numbers of senior officials was the logical result of Mao's outrageous efforts to rejuvenate society by unleashing a new revolutionary spirit.[13] Following McIntyre's classification, we may infer a third hypothesis: Mao's shifting between the reparative and destructive forms of leadership suggests a parallel instead of causal relationship between the two phenomena. When Mao idealized Chinese youth, his distrust of colleagues of his generation went deeper. The two attitudes paralleled each other. The Cultural Revolution began with Mao's dual intentions to "rejuvenate and revitalize the entire society" on the one hand, and to clear the party of capitalist roaders on the other.[14]

There is an obvious link between the narcissistic Mao and his mobilization of the Red Guards to launch the revolution. Like many other aged leaders, Mao responded to his own old age by identifying with the younger generation. Knowing that the death of his own revolutionary generation was inevitable, Mao may have been able to reduce his psychological pain by witnessing the revolutionary spirit flourishing in the young. In Robert Lifton's words, Mao unconsciously transformed his dread of the "historical death" of the revolution into an exaggerated image of the revolutionary spirit of Chinese youth.[15] Lowell Dittmer has posited a three-stage change in Mao's attitude toward youth with his advancing age. Mao's skeptical attitude toward youth in the 1930s turned into ambivalence in the mid-1950s, which in the mid-1960s gave way to an exaggerated belief in the ability of youth to perpetuate the revolution and thus Mao's own immortality.[16] "This generation of our young people will build our poor country into a great socialist power with their own hands," Mao wrote to college students in 1965. "Chinese youth with strong resolution and high aspiration will wholly devote themselves to fulfilling this great historical mission."[17]

Mao also nostalgically identified youth with his own rebellious self. When he was young, he often had serious conflicts with his teachers. He switched from one school to another, failing to find a niche in any of them. Mao never forgot the humiliation he felt as an assistant in the library at Peking University. "My office was so low that people avoided me," he recalled.[18] This personal experience explains in part Mao's acute distrust of intellectuals in general for the rest of his life. He respected knowledge, but he resented the condescending air he associated with the intellectuals who had embarrassed him. Once he encouraged a niece to rebel against school rules by refusing to return to school on time: "Tell them [school authorities] 'I will listen to Mao because I am his relative. I will rebel because I listen to him.'"[19] On another occasion, Mao spoke to a nephew of his bias against professors: "Reform of education is in essence a reform of teachers," Mao said. "Teachers usually have only so much to offer and are no good without their lecture notes."[20] It is no wonder that as soon as the Cultural Revolution began schoolteachers became the victims of rebellious students.

Mao took increasing pleasure in educating young people in his later years. He told American journalist Edgar Snow that he wanted to be remembered only as a teacher when the two of them discussed the four popular titles he had received during the Cultural Revolution.[21] The youth were his hope. Identifying himself with them not only assuaged the pain of facing an impending death but also gave him renewed vitality and energy. At the same time, Mao always worried about the genuineness of young people's commitment to the revolution. In a talk with his nephew, Mao expressed his deep concern over the softness of the younger generation:

> You think only about yourself and your own problems. Your father remained faithful and unyielding before his enemies, because he was serving the majority of the people. You probably would have surrendered and begged for your life if you had been him. Many of our family members were killed by the Guomindang and U.S. imperialists. You were brought up on eggs and candy and have never known hardship. I will be quite content if you remain a *zhongjianpai* [middle-of-the-roader]. How can you be a leftist if you have never suffered?[22]

Mao concluded that what the young people needed was the disciplining experience of a "great revolutionary storm." When Mao learned that students were organizing themselves in high schools, he immediately supported the idea and later made use of them as Red Guards. On August 1, 1966, Mao wrote a personal letter to the Red Guards:

> Allow me to express my warm support for you. At the same time, I sincerely support the big-character poster, which spelled out the reasons to rebel, put up by the Red Flag Fighting Group from the secondary school attached to Peking University, as well as the revolutionary speech by Comrade Peng Xiaomeng, who represented the Red Flag Fighting Group at the June 25 meeting of all the faculty and students at Peking University.[23]

As the leader of the country, Mao surely knew that it was imprudent to support anything rebellious students might do. But he was determined to do so, despite differences of opinion on the subject within the central government. Mao's letter was not written just to support the students, but to challenge his party colleagues. He had the letter printed and distributed during the Eleventh Plenum of the Eighth Party Central Committee (August 1–12, 1966). In doing so, Mao forced the Central Committee to go along with him, thereby confirming the legitimacy of the Red Guard organizations.

On August 18, 1966, the Red Guards held their first rally at Tiananmen. Concerns about whether the young people were ready to continue the revolution had previously dampened Mao's personal pleasure in receiving mass adulation. Mao told Wang Li and others in mid-August 1966 that one reason revisionism had succeeded in the Soviet Union was that only a limited number of people had had the chance to see Lenin in person. He would therefore see that Chinese youth had numerous chances to see their revolutionary leader—the more the better.[24] Before deciding to receive the Red Guards publicly and on a large scale, Mao had been much impressed by the emotions his appearance had aroused at a Red Guard office on an earlier occasion. He was convinced that direct contact between leader and young people was crucial to implanting in them the revolutionary spirit. In his excitement at the Tiananmen rally, he even changed one student's name from Song Binbin (meaning "refined and courteous") to Song Yaowu (meaning "wants to be armed") when she gave him a Red Guard armband.

This was the beginning of what was later known as "establishing contacts" (*dachuanlian*). On September 5, the Central Committee and the State Council issued a directive to facilitate establishing contacts. The directive asked various government agencies to provide free transportation, board, and lodging for Red Guards. The central government would absorb the cost. From August to November 1966, more than 13 million Red Guards came to Beijing to attend eight rallies and to see Mao.[25] Mao was impressed and excited by their vitality. But the move to establish contacts soon produced nationwide disarray, as tens of thousands of students flocked to Beijing and other cities and swarmed into famous historical places, such as Shaoshan, Mao's hometown, and Jinggangshan, where Mao's revolution had started. The army helped with the resulting logistical problems by offering the students shelter, transportation, and food. From time to time, the air force had to drop food and clothing from planes and helicopters to people stuck in Shaoshan and other mountainous areas.[26] In late October the central government expressed its desire to end this chaotic movement, but Mao still reveled in the excitement and suggested the establishment of permanent stations nationwide to receive Red Guards. He dropped the suggestion only after Zhou Enlai and others pointed out its impracticality.

It was not long before out-of-control Red Guards began to engage in disruptive activities and to turn against one another instead of following Mao's directives to grasp power from "capitalist roaders." Mao admitted at the Central Working Meeting in October that he was at fault for publicizing the poster at Peking University, for his unqualified support of the Red Guards, and for promoting "establishing contacts."[27] In January 1967, only six months after condemning Liu Shaoqi and Deng Xiaoping for sending government work teams to schools to maintain order, Mao himself dispatched soldiers and workers to the schools to contain the rampaging students.[28] The next year, on July 28, 1968, in a meeting with student leaders, Mao was in tears when he said to Kuai Dafu, one of the best-known Red Guard leaders, "You have let me down, and what is more, you have disappointed the workers, peasants, and soldiers in China."[29] Finally disillusioned with the Red Guards, Mao exiled millions of them to the countryside after 1968.

A Bourgeois Headquarters in the Party
and Mao's Destructive Defense

During the Cultural Revolution, Mao oscillated between two defense mechanisms: idealizing Chinese youth and destroying his enemies. Mao's suspicion of his comrades increased to the point of paranoia, especially after Khrushchev denounced Stalin. Mao was increasingly concerned about identifying potential enemies and disarming them before they struck at him. In a speech at the Twelfth Plenum of the Eighth Party Central Committee in October 1968, he explained: "In the past, we fought from the north to the south. That kind of war was easy to fight because the enemies were clear to us. The Great Proletarian Cultural Revolution is much more difficult than that type of war."[30] The problem, he continued, was the confusion of antagonistic contradictions (enemies) with non-antagonistic contradictions (comrades who make mistakes). There was something of a quixotic fantasy in such statements. Even if he could not identify his enemies, Mao was ready to confront them, and his inability to identify them increased his certainty that enemies were everywhere.

Although not all of Mao's worries were unjustified, he certainly exaggerated the problem of internal enemies. In order to gain "an illusory security," Mao resorted to increasingly aggressive actions against his comrades.[31] It is not an overstatement to say that most purges of high officials after 1949 were at least partly the consequence of Mao's paranoia.

In the case of Peng Dehuai, the letter Peng wrote Mao at Lushan was by no means the sole reason for Peng's fall. His ouster was largely the result of Mao's distrust of Peng. Peng was not the only person who complained to Mao about the Great Leap Forward and the people's communes. Li Yunzhong, deputy director of the Bureau of Infrastructure of the State Planning Commission, had written a similar letter to Mao.[32] Liu Shaoqi explained later, in 1962, that nothing had been really wrong with Peng's letter. The problem was the "clique" Peng had formed within the party.[33]

Mao and Peng did not trust each other for specific historical reasons. Mao reviewed his feuds with others in a speech at the Seventh Plenum of the Eighth Central Party Committee in April 1959, right before the Lushan Conference. As he named those who had opposed him in the past, he interjected, "Peng hates me with an all-consuming passion."[34] Mao's problem with Peng went back at least to the Yanan period. In 1945, at a meeting called the East-China Forum, Mao and his party comrades had criticized Peng for his direction of the controversial Hundred Regiments Campaign and for his "tendency to seek independence from the Party Central Committee." Although Peng made a self-criticism at the meeting, he never admitted his alleged errors.[35] In an emotional moment at Lushan in 1959, Peng shouted at Mao, "You screwed me for 40 days at Yanan. Why can't you allow me to screw you for twenty days?"[36] Peng's vulgar language shocked people, and later Peng angrily refused Mao's suggestion that they talk things over.[37] Understandably, such an outburst made it more difficult for Mao to forgive Peng, and Mao later repeated Peng's words at three high-level meetings. In 1962, at the Tenth Plenum of the Eighth Party Central Committee, for example, Mao said, "The first Lushan Conference was meant to discuss our work. But Peng Dehuai came out [with vulgar language]. This 'screw' by Peng messed up everything and interrupted our work."[38]

Mao also had a personal score to settle with Peng. In his letter to Mao, Peng had quoted a Chinese proverb that says anyone who creates something new runs the risk of having no descendants, meaning that the individual risks punishment from heaven. In criticizing Peng's letter on July 23, 1959, an emotional Mao responded to Peng: "Should the person who made a start lose his descendants? Should I have no descendants? One of my sons was killed and another has a mental problem. Should I have no descendants because of this?"[39] Everyone at the meeting was touched when they saw tears in Mao's eyes, for they knew that Mao's eldest son, Mao Anying, was killed during the Korean War while serving under Peng Dehuai's command. Mao never publicly blamed Peng for the death of his son, but Peng should have known better than to provoke Mao with the idea of having no descendants. Mao's reference to his son's death in his criticism of Peng won his audience over. The death of his son had been one of the heaviest emotional blows in Mao's life. According to Mao's daughter-in-law, Liu Songlin, Mao was in such enormous pain when he broke the news of Mao Anying's death to her that his hands turned icy cold.[40] Some Chinese scholars believe that if his son had outlived Mao the chairman would not have felt so keenly about the problem of succession.

Psychologically, Mao was no longer able to detach personal feelings or "motivational bias" from political decision-making. He fell into a cognitive vicious circle—his personal feelings and suspicions led to motivational biases toward people like Peng, which in turn worsened his paranoia and thus his unfounded perception that the party was full of conspirators against him. For example, on the day he delivered his "counterattack" speech at Lushan, Peng told one of his bodyguards that Peng Dehuai's original name was Peng Dehua (*dehua* means "to obtain China"). "It means that Peng harbored ambitions to control China," Mao claimed.[41] Mao's suspicions of Peng were intensified by Peng's trip to the Soviet Union and several Eastern European countries in April 1959. Mao heard that in one of their talks Khrushchev had acknowledged Peng as an "international hero," which aroused Mao's suspicion of cooperation between Peng and Khrushchev.[42] There is some evidence that Peng and Khrushchev exchanged opinions during Peng's earlier visit to the Soviet Union. According to Clare Hollingworth, Khrushchev had private conversations with Peng, during which Khrushchev criticized the Great Leap Forward and the formation of people's communes. Khrushchev allegedly urged Peng to write to Mao from Tirana, itemizing the points Khrushchev had raised. Hollingworth's version, however, still awaits corroboration.[43]

Nevertheless, Mao charged Peng with collaborating with Khrushchev. At the enlarged Politburo meeting on August 1, 1959, Mao exclaimed, "You, Peng Dehuai, always want to reform the party and the world in accordance with your ideas. For some reason, however, you never got the chance. This time, you got advice from *abroad*.... You picked up the other's scent about the Great Leap Forward and the people's communes."[44]

A chance event during the Lushan Conference deepened Mao's suspicion of Peng's "organized conspiracy." After Mao's speech of July 23, Li Rui felt depressed and went to see Zhou Xiaozhou. Zhou suggested that the two of them go together to talk to Huang Kecheng. At first, Huang refused, fearing that people (or Mao) might misinterpret their get-together as a group activity, which had repeatedly caused trouble in the party. Huang later changed his mind when Zhou insisted on coming to see him.[45] What made things worse was that during their ensuing talk, Peng, who was staying just a few doors down from Huang, also came over. According to Peng, he came to discuss a telegram for the Tibet Military Region.[46] None of the men stayed long, but their brief meeting proved to be a fatal mistake. When word of their meeting reached Mao, he took it as evidence that Peng Dehuai, Huang Kecheng, Zhang Wentian, Zhou Xiaozhou, and Li Rui had formed a "clique" against him. Within the CCP, an accusation of organized anti-party activity was the worst thing that could happen in one's political career. There was no way for the accused to defend themselves. Even the fact that all but Zhang were from Hunan was held against them. They were indicted as a "Hunan clique" first, and then as a "military club."

Peng never admitted the charges. In his fury, he shouted at the enlarged meeting of the Central Military Committee held after the Lushan Conference, "You can expel me from the party and have me shot! If any of you are members of the 'military club,' step forward to admit it yourselves."[47] Nobody believed the meeting of Peng Dehuai, Huang Kecheng, Zhou Xiaozhou, and Li Rui on the evening of July 23 had been an innocent get-together. Liu Shaoqi, for example, said several years later, "The reason we staged the struggle against the anti-party clique headed by Comrade Peng Dehuai at Lushan is that for a long time Comrade Peng Dehuai formed a faction within the party. He even joined the anti-party clique of Gao Gang and Rao Shushi."[48] Li Rui probably would not have been labeled a member of this counter-revolutionary clique had he not happened to go to Huang's that night. Years later, Li Rui still regretted that he had done so. While imprisoned after Lushan, Li composed a poem entitled "On the Evening of July 23" to express his regret over going to Huang's quarters.[49]

What happened at Lushan was not unique, though some purges of high party officials were political and accidental, and others were histori-cal and personal; some were necessary, but others were contingent. A four-step pattern characterized inner-party struggles in Mao's era. A struggle always began with Mao's distrust of a particular person. The chairman then would begin to "work on public opinion" against him by spreading complaints among cadres at various levels. Then came the stage of criticism and self-criticism, during which Mao mobilized forces to criticize the person and in turn compelled him to make a self-criticism. Once the individual admitted to a mistake, the party pronounced a ver-dict of guilty. Invoking his charismatic power, Mao then transferred his personal dislike and distrust into a fully "justified" party condemnation of the person's outrageous crimes, such as having formed an anti-party clique in an attempt to split the party.

The fate of those who thus fell from Mao's favor was largely deter-mined by their relationship with Mao and with other leaders. Those who had historical and personal feuds with Mao usually fared less well. In many cases, the criticism mounted until the victim was politically, if not physically, destroyed. Mao was ruthless in these inner-party struggles be-cause he gradually lost the ability to distinguish between personal feud and party conflict. Mao told his bodyguards many times that he fought only to protect the party, not for personal reasons.[50] He also insisted that he would never compromise on questions of "principle."[51] Once Mao identified someone as a rival, he seldom gave him a chance to fight back. If the victim were lucky enough to survive, he might be rehabilitated by Mao or Mao's successor, as Deng Xiaoping was. The less lucky might be rehabilitated posthumously after Mao's death, as were Liu Shaoqi and Peng Dehuai. Those with no luck at all continued to serve, also posthu-mously, as scapegoats to be invoked during Mao's subsequent purges of others; this was the fate of Chen Boda and Lin Biao.

Nearly all Mao's purges in the post-1949 period conformed to this pat-tern, including those of Huang Kecheng, Liu Shaoqi, Deng Xiaoping, Peng Zhen, Luo Ruiqing, Lu Dingyi, Yang Shangkun, Chen Yi, Tan Zhenlin, and Lin Biao. Space limitations preclude in-depth discussions of each of these cases here. The purge of Liu Shaoqi, however, illustrates an important as-pect of the problem of Mao's successors and how personal, emotional, and historical factors interacted at Mao's court. In a sense, Liu's fall in the Cul-tural Revolution was inevitable because he had started to lose Mao's trust as early as 1962. The final split between Mao and Liu during the Cultural Revolution, however, was probably more a result of Liu's position as Mao's successor than the consequence of factional politics or differences over policy.

Charismatic Mao and the Problem of Succession

Throughout his life, Mao's personality displayed extreme contradictions and ambivalences. His intelligence enabled him to make sound and rational judgments, but his capriciousness and ego often caused him deep psychological distress afterward. The resulting ambiguities showed themselves in every aspect of his life. For example, he detested the cult of personality, opposed the naming of cities and streets after leaders, including himself, and forbade his colleagues to celebrate his birthday.[52] He told Edgar Snow in 1970 that he had disliked being worshiped in the Cultural Revolution;[53] but he had obviously enjoyed receiving the Red Guards' adulation on Tiananmen. He once confessed to his bodyguards that it would not do for them to treat him as a leader, but that it also would not do if they did *not* treat him as a leader.[54] On another occasion, Mao admitted to Mei Bai, a member of his staff, that he regretted having mentioned Hai Rui at the Seventh Plenum of the Eighth Party Central Committee.[55] "I felt regret after I mentioned Hai Rui," Mao told Mei, "I will not be able to stand it if a Hai Rui really emerges."[56] Mao's prediction proved correct. At Lushan, he reacted strongly to Peng Dehuai's outspoken criticism of his leadership. His resentment of Peng's frankness continued into the Cultural Revolution. Mao sponsored the publication of articles criticizing literary works about Hai Rui, for he believed that the works drew implicit comparisons between Hai Rui's dismissal from office and Peng Dehuai's fall at Lushan. Yet Mao's best self-evaluation came in a letter to his wife, Jiang Qing, in 1966. According to Lucian Pye, "Mao himself identified the character of his inner ambivalence as a clash between self-confidence and self-doubt, between solid strength and impish trickiness." Mao described himself as a combination of "self-assured" tiger and "spontaneous and affect-free" monkey.[57]

The ambiguity in Mao's character manifested itself most clearly on the issue of succession. Mao began to prepare for his own retirement as early as 1958, when he was 64 years old. That year he told Gao Zhi, one of his former secretaries, that he did not want to be the state chairman anymore. The reason, Mao explained, was that he wanted to forgo routine work, such as receiving credentials from foreign ambassadors, so he could concentrate on more significant things.[58] In 1961 in a conversation with Lord Montgomery, Mao mentioned for the first time that Liu Shaoqi would be his successor.[59]

When Mao proposed his own retirement, however, he expected the masses to object. He also expected a call to shoulder leadership once again "whenever the nation is urgently in need" of his service and "if the party decides to recall him."[60] To Mao's dismay, however, his colleagues seemed ready to accept his retirement.[61] He likely felt more and more like a "shelved father" whom no one cared to consult. He may not have wanted to continue in the position of state chairman, but he could not tolerate his colleagues' willingness to cease treating him as state chairman.

Because of his deep fear of being left out of the national leadership, Mao was especially sensitive about having access to information. In 1961 he became furious upon discovering that his colleagues at a Central Working Meeting had drafted key changes in a plan concerning the reorganization of the people's communes without consulting him.[62] Mao finally found a chance to vent his accumulated anger at a Central Working Meeting in December 1964. Before the conference, Deng Xiaoping had suggested to Mao that because of his health, Mao need not attend this routine meeting. Mao was annoyed by the suggestion, and the next day he appeared at the meeting with the state and the party constitutions in hand. "I am still a party member and a citizen," he told the meeting. "One of you [Deng Xiaoping] forbade me to attend the meeting, and another [Liu Shaoqi] did not allow me to speak!"[63] The episode was a turning point in relations between Mao and Liu. Although he made a self-criticism later, Liu never regained Mao's confidence.

Mao was 72 in 1965. Although physically still in good shape, he began to prepare himself and China for an era without him.[64] In Chinese tradition, 73 and 84 are fateful numbers for the elderly. In popular belief, it is unusual for a person to live beyond the age of 73, but if one does, one will likely live until 84. Mao was obviously aware of this notion when he quoted the following Chinese saying to Lord Montgomery in 1961, "73 and 84, you will go to the king of hell even if he does not invite you." He told Montgomery that he had only one more "five-year" plan for himself, since he was 68 at the time.[65] In 1964 he told Edgar Snow that he was "getting ready to see God very soon."[66] Mao even fantasized about five different ways he might die: from a gunshot; in a plane or train crash; by drowning; or from disease.[67]

The search for a reliable successor assumed great importance for Mao in the mid-1960s since he believed he had little time left. In June 1966, Mao revealed his anxiety to Ho Chi Minh, leader of the Democratic Republic of Vietnam, "Both of us are over 70 now and we will be invited to join Marx sooner or later. Who will be the successor? We don't know whether he will be E. Bernstein, K. Kautsky, or Khrushchev. We should get ready while we still have time."[68] As part of his preparations, Mao accelerated the process of looking for a successor. Mao wanted to make sure that his successor would carry on what he had begun. But could he trust Liu?

Since 1962 it had appeared more and more clear to Mao that he could not. Mao could not forget Liu's suggestion that Mao was personally responsible for the disastrous Great Leap Forward or Liu's disagreement with him about the ultimate goal of the "four cleans" in 1964. Accordingly, even before the Cultural Revolution, Mao had already began to "work on public opinion" against Liu. In November 1964, shortly after the meeting on the "four cleans," Mao publicly condemned Liu in the following terms:

> I am chairman, and you are the first vice-chairman. A storm may arise from a clear sky [i.e., Mao may die a sudden death]. Once I die, you probably will still be unable to fit into my position. So, I will give you my title right now. You become chairman, and you become Qinshihuang [the first emperor of the Qin dynasty]. I have my weak points. I have no reason to scold the mother now. It will not work anymore. You are tough, so you took the lead in scolding the mother.[69]

In January 1965, Mao criticized Liu several times at Central Working Meetings. On January 13 he first asked provincial leaders what they would do if revisionism appeared within the central government and then revealed to them his concerns about China's future. On January 14, Mao rejected a document about the Socialist Education Movement drafted by a group under Liu's direction.[70] He again raised the question of revisionism in the Central Committee at the Central Working Meeting of September–October 1965. "What will you do if revisionism appears within the Central Committee?" he asked. "It is very likely and is most dangerous."[71] The following March, Mao bade Kang Sheng and others to get ready to "attack the Central Committee." The same instruction appeared again in a CCP document in mid-May.[72] As one Chinese scholar put it, a "Chinese Khrushchev" had become Mao's worst nightmare.[73] He had to find him, no matter what the cost.

A chance event increased Mao's alarm over the possibility of a conspiracy in the central government. After Khrushchev was ousted in 1964, Zhou Enlai and He Long headed a delegation to attend the celebration of the 47th anniversary of the October Revolution in Moscow. On November 7, Marshal Rodion Malinovsky, the Soviet defense minister, told He Long, "Now we have gotten rid of Khrushchev. You should follow our example and get rid of Mao, too." He immediately reported the conversation to Zhou, who lodged a protest with Brezhnev, who in turn later apologized to the Chinese delegation.[74] No one will ever know exactly how much this upset Mao, but he surely responded. In the next couple of years, preventing a coup became Mao's major concern. In December 1965, he asked several local military leaders, including the commander of the Nanjing Military Region, Xu Shiyou, what they would do if there were a coup in Beijing.[75] Lin Biao's speech at an enlarged Politburo meeting on May 18, 1966, reflected Mao's anxieties:

> In recent months, Chairman Mao has paid particular attention to the adoption of many measures toward preventing a counterrevolutionary coup d'état. After the Lo Jui-ch'ing problem, he talked about it. Now that the P'eng Chen problem has been exposed, he has again summoned several persons and talked about it, dispatched personnel and had them stationed in the radio broadcasting stations, the armed forces, and the public security systems in order to prevent a counterrevolutionary coup d'état and the occupation of our crucial points. This is the "article" Chairman Mao has been writing in recent months. This is the "article" he has not quite finished and printed, and because of this, Chairman Mao has not slept well for many days. It is a very profound and serious problem. This is the endeavor of Chairman Mao that we ought to learn from.[76]

While more evidence is needed to establish a link between Mao's fear of a coup and the fall of Luo Ruiqing, the PLA chief of staff, in December 1965, such a fear definitely played a role in the fall of Peng Zhen, the mayor of Beijing, and He Long in 1966. On February 3, 1967, Mao told Albanian guests how nervous he had been the previous May. He had thought about the possibility of sabotage while he reorganized the Beijing municipal government. "We transferred two divisions of garrison troops [to Beijing]," Mao told his guests. "[That is why] you can now wander around Beijing and so can we."[77]

By May 1965, Mao felt he was losing power and was surrounded by conspirators. Some of his colleagues, he felt certain, were forming "independent kingdoms" to expel him from the leadership, while others were preparing a coup d'état. He criticized Deng Xiaoping and Li Fuchun, a premier, for their "independent kingdoms" in the Central Secretariat and the State Planning Commission. He then leveled the same charge at Peng Zhen and charged Peng with plotting a coup. Luo Ruiqing lost his position as chief of staff of the PLA in December 1965, and several months later He Long faced charges for his alleged role in the "February Mutiny plot," based entirely on evidence provided by Red Guard big-character posters.[78] Mao also removed Yang Shangkun from his position as director of the General Office of the Party Central Committee for allegedly bugging Mao and secretly recording Mao's private conversations. In retrospect, it is clear that there were no valid charges against any of these victims of the Cultural Revolution. That all had held key positions and were rehabilitated after Mao's death in 1976 suggests that all were victims of Mao's paranoid fear of a coup against him.

Mao did charge Peng Zhen and others with an attempted coup, but many were condemned simply because Mao no longer trusted them. The purges of Liu Shaoqi and Deng Xiaoping, however, were more complicated, for several reasons. First, as state chairman, Liu held a higher position than anyone previously purged. Second, Liu's case had the widest national impact, owing to the mass criticism sessions introduced during the stage of criticism and self-criticism. The device of mass criticism broke the usual pattern for dealing with inner-party cleavages and ultimately cost Liu Shaoqi and many other high officials their lives during the Cultural Revolution. Finally, the increasing absurdity of the criticism of Liu suggests that he was actually the victim of a dynamic mass movement that got out of control.[79]

In this sense, Liu Shaoqi was a victim not only of Mao's mistrust but also of the mass movement. At the beginning of the Cultural Revolution, Mao probably did not want to destroy Liu Shaoqi physically.[80] The explosive dynamic of the Cultural Revolution simply exceeded anything Mao had had in mind when he launched it. According to Wang Li, Mao had a three-year plan for the Cultural Revolution, during which a great number of veteran cadres would be criticized and ousted as "capitalist roaders." Mao wanted, however, only to teach the cadres a lesson, after which he would rehabilitate most of them and return them to office properly chastised. He told Wang Li in July 1967 that he would keep Liu and Deng in the Central Committee. Even Peng Zhen, who was accused of being a traitor, should, Mao said, be allowed to remain a party member and be assigned some work after the Culture Revolution because of his early contribution to the Chinese revolution.[81]

What happened later went far beyond Mao's expectations. First, the Red Guards, whom Mao mobilized to carry out the Cultural Revolution, disappointed him. Second, many of the leading cadres engaged in an outburst of criticism of the Cultural Revolution, which was later known as the February Adverse Current. Mao became more and more agitated by the reluctance of his colleagues to cooperate with his ideas on the Cultural Revolution. This reluctance threatened to leave the Cultural Revolution and thus Mao's work itself unfinished. "I cannot die, and I should hold on for a while," Mao told a provincial leader. Mao believed that China still needed a leader like himself, someone to represent the interests of the masses now that the relationships between the cadres and the masses and the party and the masses were deteriorating.[82]

In many localities the Cultural Revolution resulted in total chaos. Mass organizations divided into factions and fought among themselves.[83] Efforts by the central government to promote unity among the masses (*dalianhe*) and to grasp power (*duoquan*) from capitalist roaders did little to stabilize the situation nationwide. Mao felt the need for radical methods to guarantee the success of the Cultural Revolution. In March 1967 he decided to encourage mass criticism (*dapipan*) of Liu Shaoqi to divert attention from struggles between Red Guard factions. In May, *Hongqi* published an article by Qi Benyu, a member of the Central Cultural Revolution Small Group (CCRSG), openly accusing Liu of being a "representative of imperialism, feudalism, and a reactionary bourgeois class," "a false revolutionary," and a "Chinese Khrushchev."[84]

Labeling Liu Shaoqi the number one enemy served a dual purpose: it answered Mao's psychological need to find a "Chinese Khrushchev," and it provided a common target for mass criticism, one that gave "polemical focus to a movement that threatened to get out of hand."[85] Liu himself commented after he read Qi's article that "the inner-party struggle has never been conducted in such an absurd way." He wrote several letters to Mao and the Central Committee refuting the accusations against him, but of course Mao turned a deaf ear to his appeals. To carry the Cultural Revolution to a successful end, Mao was determined to break all party regulations and expose inner-party cleavages to the masses. Editorials in central newspapers under Mao's control and pronouncements from the CCRSG usurped the authority of resolutions and decisions of the Central Committee. Instead of receiving nonviolent criticism and conducting self-criticism within the party, subjects being criticized found themselves in prisons or quasi prisons known as "study groups" (*xuexi ban*). Among those jailed after December 1966 were 30 or so veteran cadres in Shifangyuan, a western suburb of Beijing, including Lu Dingyi, Huang Kecheng, Tan Zheng, Peng Dehuai, Peng Zhen, Luo Ruiqing, He Long, Wan Li, Li Jingquan, Liu Ren, and Chen Zaidao.[86] Mao's decision to subject them to mass criticism left them in the hands of the Special Case Groups and reduced their chances for survival. Liu Shaoqi died of exposure on November 12, 1969; He Long died on June 19, 1968; and Peng Dehuai on November 19, 1974. All three died while in the charge of the Special Case Groups.

Mao's attitude toward Deng Xiaoping, however, was noticeably different. On July 14, 1967, Mao told Wang Li in Wuhan that he himself did not want to link Liu and Deng as allies. He said, "[I just want to] oust them for one year, or two years at most. Others [the masses] want to expose them, so we have to go along with the idea. . . . If Lin Biao cannot function effectively anymore because of his poor health, I will restore Deng to the leading position."[87] Personally, Mao never completely lost trust in Deng. Mao told Wang Li as early as 1963 that the three people he trusted most were Luo Ronghuan, Deng Xiaoping, and Chen Yun. Mao believed that he could expect their lifelong cooperation, especially that of Luo and Deng.[88] Chen Boda also recalled that when he used the phrase "Liu-Deng line" in his draft of a political report to the Ninth Party Congress, Mao instructed him to delete it: "Comrade Deng Xiaoping commanded many wars, so he is different from Liu Shaoqi. Do not mention him in the report."[89]

Although the names of Liu and Deng were later linked for the purpose of mass criticism, Deng received much better treatment than Liu Shaoqi owing to Mao's protection. He was never forced to attend mass criticisms, and he received much less criticism from the masses, which meant less personal humiliation. In the 31 volumes of Red Guard publications at the Library of Congress of the United States, 653 items refer to the "crimes" of Liu Shaoqi, but only 30 to those of Deng Xiaoping. When the party expelled Liu permanently at the Twelfth Plenum of the Eighth Party Central Committee in December 1968, Mao himself saved Deng from being punished in the same way. "Some people also suggested Deng's expulsion from the party, but personally I disagree. He is somewhat different from Liu," Mao told the meeting.[90] After the Lin Biao incident, Mao indeed restored Deng to the position of vice-premier, as he had earlier told Wang Li he would. Only after Deng voiced his intention to stop the Cultural Revolution was he ousted again in April 1976. The charge against him then was his alleged effort to "overturn the verdict" (*fan an*) of the Cultural Revolution.

The fall of Mao's first designated successor, Liu Shaoqi, by no means solved Mao's succession problem. Despite the general argument that Communist countries never solved the problem of succession because of the totalitarian nature of their regimes, there were more profound social, cultural, and personal reasons behind each succession crisis. At least three sets of factors—systemic, traditional, and personal—have functioned in every succession crisis in China. Problems with the system derive from the ambiguous nature of Communist power. Neither from Marxist-Leninist theories nor from Communist practice in general did anyone ever devise a means for transferring power.[91] The People's Republic of China has never succeeded in drawing a line between the authoritarian rule of one person and the "collective leadership" of the party. It was always difficult to detect which policy was Mao's or Deng's and which was the party's collectively.

Chinese political tradition grants a leader the freedom to choose a successor. In Chinese history as well, emperors regularly designated their successors. Even now, few Chinese scholars question Mao's right to choose his successor.[92] Instead, they have criticized Mao for being unable to choose the right person. At the beginning of the Cultural Revolution when Mao designated Lin Biao to replace Liu as his successor, the whole party applauded the decision with much more sincerity than its leaders now admit.

The ambiguity regarding succession also led to the ill fortunes of Mao's designated successors. After Liu Shaoqi, Mao dropped one successor after another before he reluctantly transferred power to Hua Guofeng, who was clearly not the best choice but who was least likely to turn against Mao immediately after his death. We have learned repeatedly from history that the mightier a given leader, the more uncertain the fate of a designated successor. An heir apparent has to juggle the expectations of his overseer with goals of his own. Since the trusteeship rests on absolute obedience and loyalty, few designated successors survive any negative appraisal by their overseer, who often sees the successor as a potential usurper and a threat to his own remaining power. The so-called line struggles and the constant purge/rehabilitation cycle during the Cultural Revolution illustrated this ambiguous master-successor relationship.[93] Dittmer said Mao exhibited a Don Juan behavior toward his designated successors, "first embracing an heir apparent enthusiastically and with exaggerated expectations, only to grow disillusioned and finally to cast off the object of his previous ardor."[94] None of Mao's premortem arrangements for his successor worked out. Liu Shaoqi ended up "a traitor, a spy, and a scab" and died of exposure in a prison cell. Lin Biao was, in the end, a "careerist, conspirator, and double-dealer" who died in the Mongolian desert. After eight months as heir apparent, Wang Hongwen (formerly in charge of the Shanghai municipal government) was sentenced to life in prison after Mao's death. Hua Guofeng also lost his position to Deng Xiaoping after his unsuccessful defense of Mao's Cultural Revolution and disappeared from the political arena soon after Mao died.

4

Lin Biao and the Cultural Revolution

Disappointed in Liu Shaoqi as a successor, in 1966 Mao turned to Lin Biao, who was minister of defense. Although he had already had an accomplished political career, his name was little known in the outside world, partially because he kept a low public profile. Unlike other leaders such as Liu Shaoqi, Zhou Enlai, Deng Xiaoping, Chen Yi, Peng Zhen, and Luo Ruiqing, Lin seldom appeared in public. Despite his various party and governmental titles, he shared few responsibilities other than those for the armed forces. Why then did Mao choose him to replace Liu Shaoqi as his successor? Several considerations may account for Mao's decision. Mao understood from the very beginning that he would need the support of the PLA for a successful Cultural Revolution. Other high officials would likely accept Lin's leadership because of his contribution to the Chinese revolution as one of Mao's best generals and his lack of connection with any specific political power group due to his inactivity in public and governmental affairs. Above all, Lin was the person Mao trusted most. Apart from his record as an excellent military commander, Lin had been devoted to Mao throughout his career. One of Lin's biographers believes Lin was the only important figure who did not turn against Mao at one time or another in the years before 1949.[1] Another suggests that Mao may have fulfilled Lin's psychological need for a father figure.[2]

The Historical Relationship Between Mao Zedong and Lin Biao

The close relationship between Mao and Lin went back to the Jinggang Mountain period, during which Lin's military and political career advanced rapidly.[3] Lin participated in a series of battles that offered him opportunities to display his military talents. Within approximately four years, he rose from battalion commander to commander of the First Red Army Corps. In October 1928, Lin commanded the 28th Regiment. In January 1929 he was made commander of the First Column, the elite force of the Red Army.[4] In June 1930 he was appointed commander of the Tenth Division of the Fourth Red Army,[5] and in December 1930 he became commander of the Fourth Red Army in the First Front Army;[6] in March 1932, Lin was promoted to commander of the Red Army's First Army Corps.[7] By then, he was one of the most senior officers in the Red Army, having risen over many who were once his superiors. When Mao created a Revolutionary Military Commission sometime in 1931, Lin was its fourth-ranking member, after only Zhu De, Peng Dehuai, and Wang Jiaxiang.[8]

The reasons for Lin's rapid rise were twofold. First, he had earned distinction through his performance in many major battles. Lin and his troops fought in each of the five encirclement campaigns conducted by the Guomindang to annihilate the Communists, and in the first four campaigns his victories were instrumental in rescuing the Chinese Soviet Republic. When the fifth campaign ended in the defeat that forced the Communists to retreat from their revolutionary bases in Jiangxi, Lin's troops managed to avoid serious losses, although other Communist forces suffered heavy casualties.[9]

The second reason for Lin's rapid rise was his close personal relationship with Mao and Zhu De, especially with Mao. Lin owed his initial rise to Zhu, in whose army he became the best of all the company commanders.[10] He apparently grew closer to Mao, however, after the move to Jinggang Mountain. Lin's nomination as commander of the 28th Regiment in 1928, which was interpreted as a victory for Mao over Zhu, probably began the link between Lin and Mao.[11] Because of personality conflicts and differences over military strategy, Mao and Zhu were soon at odds at Jinggang Mountain. In order to gain control of the army, Mao had to make sure that the 28th Regiment, the best of his troops, had a reliable commander. Mao considered Lin the best candidate for the position and reportedly told Lin that when he nominated him for the post, Zhu had objected. Out of gratitude to Mao, Lin thereafter sided with Mao in his conflicts with Zhu.[12] Soon afterward Lin criticized Zhu at a CCP meeting, claiming that Zhu's "warlord habits" had caused the Red Army to lose a February 1930 battle.[13] Although Lin's role in the Zhu-Mao conflict may have been exaggerated, the period between the Seventh and the Ninth Party Congresses of the Fourth Red Army in 1929–30 marked a new phase in the Lin-Mao relationship. Lin became one of Mao's most trusted comrades, and Lin, for his part, faithfully supported Mao.[14] In June 1929, because of his disputes with Zhu, Mao himself was dismissed from the Red Army after the Seventh Congress, whereupon Lin sent a battalion of troops to western Fujian province to protect Mao.[15] Lin also demanded Mao's reinstatement in the Red Army, although his efforts were not immediately successful.

In December 1930, after his return to the Red Army, Mao presided at the Ninth Congress of the CCP in the Fourth Red Army, at which he purged his opponents in the army, whom he labeled "the A-B (anti-Bolshevik) Corps." He also wrote "The Resolution of the Gutian Meeting" for the Congress, in which he criticized "wrong ideas" in the Fourth Red Army. Lin once again stood out as Mao's most faithful supporter.[16] Zhu complained during the Gutian meeting that Lin was a "bad fellow" who "in the end turned against me publicly."[17]

There is other evidence of strengthening ties between Mao and Lin during this period. On January 5, 1930, Mao wrote Lin a letter, which Mao later retitled "A Single Spark Can Start a Prairie Fire" and placed in *The Selected Works of Mao Zedong*. After the Lin Biao incident in 1971, the party characterized the letter as Mao's critical response to a letter from Lin questioning the future of the revolution and used it as evidence against Lin.[18] In fact, it was a personal letter, which opened and closed with friendly remarks. In 1930, Lin was still an obscure officer in Zhu's command. To how many other such officers would Mao have written a personal letter discussing the political situation?

It is significant, however, that the available sources put little emphasis on Lin's participation in the political struggle within the party during the Jinggang Mountain period. As a junior military officer, Lin was more of an instrument of others' political ambitions than an independent political force.[19] No evidence suggests any direct involvement by Lin in the political struggles at that time between Mao's group and other factions, such as the party branches under Qu Qiubai.

In 1934 the CCP and the Red Army had to leave their revolutionary base in the Jinggang Mountain area and trek to northern China because of their defeat in the Guomindang's fifth encirclement campaign. The trek later became known as the Long March. Lin, as commander of the First Red Army Corps, contributed greatly during the Long March to the survival of the Red Army. His units were the vanguard; their primary function, according to Zhu, was "to clear the way for the rest of us."[20] They also had the task of protecting the political leaders of the CCP.

It was Lin's men who broke through the Guomindang's encirclement and enabled the Red Army to survive heavy losses.[21] Lin's units captured the Luding bridge over the Dadu River, enabling the main body of the

Red Army to escape from the Guomindang troops. "Had the Red Army failed there," Edgar Snow has speculated, "quite possibly it would have been exterminated."[22] In January 1935, Lin's troops captured Zunyi, a town in Guizhou province where the CCP held its first important meeting during the Long March. The meeting restored Mao to leading positions in the CCP and the Red Army.

On June 16, 1935, Mao's First Field Army arrived at Maogong in Sichuan province and joined forces with the Fourth Field Army led by Zhang Guotao. Immediately afterward, differences between the First and Fourth Field Armies over several fundamental matters erupted at the Lianghekou and Maoergai meetings.[23] Zhang and Mao reached a temporary compromise, reorganizing their troops into right and left columns. Mao kept Peng Dehuai's and Lin Biao's troops in his right column and sent Zhu De and Liu Bocheng to Zhang's left column. This compromise did not last long. Zhang Guotao, whose army was five times the size of Mao's and also better equipped, soon split with Mao. Mao virtually had to run from Zhang, turning his troops to the north while Zhang turned to the south. Mao reorganized his forces into three columns, which included Lin's First Army and Peng's Third Army.[24] Peng was commander and Lin deputy commander of this newly established force, named Shaangan zhidui (Shaanxi-Gansu Detachment).[25] The creation of the Shaangan zhidui was a personal victory for Mao, for he finally had an army of his own. It also showed Mao's preference for Peng and Lin over Zhu De and Liu Bocheng. At the crucial moment in the Mao-Zhang conflict, which Mao later described as "the darkest moment of my life," Lin again sided with Mao.[26] Throughout the Long March, Lin's forces helped save the Red Army from extinction. According to Snow, Guomindang armies sometimes turned and fled simply upon discovering that they were fighting the First Red Army Corps. Lin was also, in Snow's words, "one of the few Red commanders who was never wounded by the end of the Long March, although he had been engaged in more than a hundred battles."[27]

The Long March consolidated the relationship between Mao and Lin. On its way to northern China, the Red Army not only suffered the harassment of Guomindang forces, but also had to cross inhospitable grasslands and snow-covered mountains. There was also internal conflict between Mao, Bo Gu (also known as Qin Bangxian),[28] and Zhang Guotao. In these disputes from the Zunyi conference to the Maoergai meetings, Lin was always loyal to Mao. It should be noted that many of the materials published in the late twentieth century in the People's Republic offer biased comments on Lin because of his "crimes" during the Cultural Revolution. Wu Xiuquan, for example, asserts that at the Zunyi meeting, Lin "did not speak a word, having been a supporter of Bo Gu and Otto Braun and having come under criticism for this."[29] Hu Hua, a professor of CCP history at the People's University in Beijing, argues on the other hand that Lin supported Mao's call for the removal of Bo Gu and Braun. "Lin was said to have become openly critical of the pair after the Xiang River battle and the losses of the First Army Group," Hu wrote. "Now he became very vocal, very hostile."[30] Hu's comments are more reliable than Wu's, because there is little evidence that Lin had ties with either Bo Gu or Zhou Enlai.[31] In any case, after the Zunyi conference Lin maintained his position as commander of the First Red Army Corps, and Mao became its political commissar—further proof that Lin had sided with Mao during the meeting.[32]

By the end of the Long March in October 1935, Lin had become, in Harrison Salisbury's words, Mao's "darling." Although he did not always agree with Mao, Lin seldom failed to carry out Mao's orders.[33]

In June 1936, Lin Biao became president of the Anti-Japanese Military and Political University (*kangri junzheng daxue*, called Kangda, for short). Scholars have assessed this assignment variously. Thomas Robinson suggests that it was the result of an earlier disagreement between Lin and Mao and that the appointment was in fact a demotion for Lin, a blow to his career. Li Tianmin disagrees, saying he is unable to discover any basic disagreement between Mao and Lin during this period.[34] Li's argument is the more convincing because the presidency of Kangda was a very important position at the time.

According to Red Army regulations, every active commander or commissar was to spend at least four months of every two years of active service studying military affairs. The years 1936–37, when Lin was president of Kangda, were years of adjustment for the Red Army. Having lost 90 percent of his troops in the Long March, Mao wanted his men both to get some much-needed rest and to receive training. Mao himself was the political commissar of the university.

Lin did his work at the university conscientiously and benefited from his tenure there. He became "second to none in experience as a military educator and administrator" and a top Communist military leader in both knowledge of warfare and command experience.[35] He trained Red Army cadres, army and division commanders, and low-ranking officers, as well as students from various parts of China.

Lin's career in Kangda, however, was brief. In July 1937, when the CCP volunteered to cooperate with the Guomindang against the Japanese, the CCP reorganized its forces into two armies, the Eighth Route Army and the New Fourth Army, under Guomindang command. Lin was commander of the 115th Division of the Eighth Route Army, in which capacity he soon won national recognition for defeating Lieutenant General Itagaki Seishiro's Fifth Division as it advanced south through the Wutai Mountains in Shanxi province. He ambushed the Japanese at Pingxingguan Pass, inflicting 2,000–3,000 casualties.[36] The Pingxingguan campaign may not have halted the Japanese advance into central China, but it was the first Chinese defeat of the Japanese and hence was more important psychologically than militarily for the Chinese, giving them the confidence to fight the Japanese.

In March 1938, a severe injury removed Lin from military duty for several years until he resumed active command in 1942.[37] In the winter of 1939 he went to the Soviet Union for medical treatment, but his stay there is shrouded in mystery; it is not even clear where and for how long Lin stayed in the hospital. Li Tianmin believes that the purpose of Lin's stay in the Soviet Union was not just medical. Ten other military officers accompanied him, most of whom stayed at the Frunze Military Academy.[38] Some sources treat Lin as the Chinese representative to the Comintern and as such Mao's personal representative to Stalin. Mao did not trust Wang Ming, through whom the CCP normally communicated with the Soviets.[39] The only evidence from Soviet sources of Lin's presence is an article in the *Communist International* in August 1940 by a person named "Ling Pao."[40]

It is also not clear whether Lin had any contact with Stalin or whether Lin served in the Soviet army against the Nazis while in the Soviet Union. During the Cultural Revolution, the Red Guards reported that Lin had been involved in the Stalingrad Campaign, and that Stalin had been so impressed by Lin's military prowess that he gave Lin his own pistol.[41] This information, however, cannot be considered reliable because of the prevalence of propaganda in China during that period.

Lin returned to Yanan in January 1942, just in time to support Mao's "rectification" campaign against subjectivism and factionalism. Mao aimed this campaign at Wang Ming and his followers, who were known as "Internationalists."[42] It is not clear whether Lin's return was a coincidence or whether Mao called Lin back to support the campaign. In either case, Mao greeted him in person upon his arrival.[43] At the welcome meeting on February 17, 1942, Lin announced his support for the campaign, reportedly saying that the Communist Party in China should unite around Mao in order to make it a great party. He also endorsed Mao's basic reason for the Rectification Movement—to fight subjectivism and factionalism.[44] From Mao's perspective, Lin, freshly returned from the Soviet Union, would be helpful in his plan to oppose Wang and other Internationalists, many of whom were students returned from the Soviet Union. Lin reportedly declared he would not support Wang Ming's Internationalist faction, even though he himself had three years' experience in the Soviet Union. As Mao expected, Lin's cooperation undercut political support for the Internationalists.

Apparently, Mao and Wang Ming competed for Lin's support. Wang recorded an unpleasant incident between himself and Mao in the spring of 1939, when Mao reportedly asked Wang why he tried to woo Lin away from Mao by openly praising Lin as the "famous commander of Pingxingguan Pass." Wang denied this charge, but Mao was not convinced by the denial and warned him not to try to "undermine Mao's wall." "I tell you," Mao allegedly said, "I have engaged in military affairs for several years, and my one accomplishment is the training of Lin Biao. He is really my man, and among the units of the Eighth Route Army and the New Fourth Army, only the troops commanded by him are the troops I can rely on."[45]

Communist victories in the civil war were in fact closely associated with Lin Biao's name. The war gave Lin the opportunity to refine his military techniques, which he had worked on since his early years in the Red Army. In October 1945, Lin led 100,000 troops into northeastern China (Manchuria), which was then strategically important to the Communists for several reasons. It connected the Soviet Union and China and had remained a neutral area after Japanese forces in the region surrendered to Soviet forces in August 1945. If the Communists could occupy the area, they would have a solid base through which to secure aid from the Soviet Union and from which to mount a show of force in dealing with the Guomindang. But the Guomindang also realized the strategic significance of the area, which soon became the locus of a major confrontation.

Why did Mao choose Lin to command the fight against Guomindang forces in Manchuria? Of the Communist commanders, Lin was one of the most knowledgeable and experienced in conventional warfare and probably the most successful as well. While in the Soviet Union, he had received training in modern military warfare, and because of his recent stay there would probably be adept in dealing with his Soviet counterparts. But most important, Mao trusted Lin, not only because of Lin's personal loyalty but also because Lin's attitude toward the Soviet Union was, in Mao's eyes, "correct." Lin would never be an "intellectual captive" of the Soviets, as Mao considered Wang and many other returnees from the Soviet Union to be.

When Lin arrived in the Northeast, Communist forces there were inferior to those of the Guomindang in number and equipment. As a result, in April and May 1947 Lin's forces suffered several setbacks, especially the defeat at Siping, which cost some 40,000 casualties.[46] This was the first major defeat in Lin's career as a military commander. He attributed the loss to his own underestimation of Guomindang forces and to insufficient time to prepare properly. After this loss, careful planning became a hallmark of Lin's military style.

The turning point for the Communists in the Northeast began in 1948. In November, Lin concentrated his troops along the railway lines from Shenyang to Beijing and launched the Liaoshen campaign. He captured the city of Jinzhou first, then proceeded to Changchun and Shenyang, overcoming strong resistance from Guomindang forces. Within two months, the whole Northeast came under Lin's control.

Lin's experience in the Northeast proved pivotal for his military career. He refined his military style and also gained political and administrative experience. In 1946, Mao named Lin to replace Peng Zhen as general secretary of the Party Committee in the Northeast because Lin did not get along with Peng. This made Lin the most powerful man in the Northeast, responsible to the CCP for all political, administrative, and military activities there. Moreover, his army had developed into the most powerful force in the PLA.

After the Liaoshen campaign, Mao ordered Lin and his troops to central China. In cooperation with other PLA troops there, they were quickly embroiled in another major battle against Guomindang forces, the Ping-Jin campaign. The Communists soon captured Tianjin and, with the surrender of Fu Zuoyi's 250,000 Guomindang troops soon thereafter, in January 1949, Peiping (now Beijing) came under Communist control. Guomindang troops were in full retreat to the south of the Yangtze River.

The final stage of the civil war provided Lin further opportunities to demonstrate his prowess as a military leader. On April 21, 1949, after the breakdown of negotiations between the Communists and the Guomindang, Mao, then chairman of the Military Committee, and Zhu De, commander-in-chief of the PLA, ordered their Communist forces across the Yangtze River. Of the five field armies of the PLA at the time, Lin's Fourth Field Army was by far the biggest, numbering over a million troops, almost as many as the other four field armies combined.[47] In May, Lin's army captured the city of Wuhan, then Hunan province. On October 14, Lin's troops entered Guangzhou (Canton), and on November 22 they penetrated Guilin. On December 4, Nanning fell, and finally on April 26, 1950, the Fourth Field Army captured Hainan Island after an earlier futile effort by the Third Field Army that had cost 7,000 lives. Within a year, Lin's army had fought from the Northeast all the way to the Southeast, in the process capturing almost half of China.

Lin's military achievements also made him a key political figure in central China. Many of Lin's officers became provincial and local administrators after the war, and those areas taken by Lin's troops became Lin's "sphere of power" until after Lin died. By 1950 he was a member of the Central People's Government Council and the Standing Committee of the First Chinese People's Political Consultative Conference, commander of the Central China Military Region and of the Fourth Field Army, chairman of the Central-South Military and Administrative Committee, and first secretary of the Party Committee of Central-South China. It was very rare among the Communist leaders at the time for one person to hold simultaneously the positions of military commander, administrative governor, and party secretary of one region. For example, the commander of the Southwest China Military Region was He Long, the chairman of the Southwest China Military and Administrative Committee was Liu Bocheng, and the first secretary of the Party Committee was Deng Xiaoping. In June of that year, the Third Plenum of the Seventh Party Central Committee elected Lin Biao to the Politburo.

When the Communists took power in China, Lin was a rising star and among the most powerful members of the ruling elite. Because of his remarkable military record, in 1955 at the age of 47 Lin received the title of marshal, the youngest of the ten men in the PLA to hold the title. His future seemed bright and assured: he was still young, militarily brilliant, and loyal to Mao.

After the Communists formed a government in 1949, however, Lin Biao remained out of the national spotlight for several years. He did not participate in the Korean War, explanations for which have prompted controversy among scholars.[48] Even after the Korean War, Lin was invisible until 1956. He was reportedly absent from several important meetings the next year, 1957, including the third meeting of the Chinese People's Political Consultative Conference in October and the Supreme State Conference in November. The reason for Lin's absence seems to have been protracted illness. He may have been in the Soviet Union from 1953 to 1956 because of poor health.[49]

The Soviet interregnum, if that is what it was, did not hinder the advancement of Lin's political and military careers. In February 1950, he became chairman of the Central-South Military and Administrative Committee, which controlled the provinces of Henan, Hubei, Hunan, Jiangxi, Guangdong, and Guangxi. Also in the early 1950s, Lin was one of the ten state council vice-premiers under Zhou Enlai and one of the fifteen vice-chairmen of the newly established National Defense Council in 1954. In April 1955 the Fifth Plenum of the Seventh Party Central Committee reelected him to the Politburo, and in September he ranked third among the ten military marshals listed in the newspaper. In September 1956, when he made his first public appearance in five years, the Eighth Party Congress reelected Lin to the Central Committee, and the First Plenum of the new Central Committee reelected him to the Politburo. Significantly, of the seventeen members of the Politburo at that time, Lin ranked seventh, after Mao Zedong, Liu Shaoqi, Zhou Enlai, Zhu De, Chen Yun, and Deng Xiaoping. In February 1958, Lin became a vice-chairman of the CCP and a member of the Standing Committee of the Politburo.

Lin's political rise was clearly a result of his loyalty to Mao, given his relative inactivity in national affairs in the early 1950s. Lin's loyalty made a deep impression on Mao and allowed him to maintain a special relationship with him. According to Li Yinqiao, Lin Biao and Peng Dehuai were distinct among the military leaders for their frankness in front of Mao. Li remembered Lin's rigid, professional manner when he came to see Mao. Unlike others who may have felt intimidated by Mao, Lin voiced his opinion openly and even argued with Mao.[50]

Lin also enjoyed a good reputation among his military colleagues. In the 1950s, few high officials held low opinions of Lin. At the enlarged conference of the Central Military Committee in 1959, Liu Shaoqi insisted that he supported a cult of personality not only for Mao but for Lin Biao and Deng Xiaoping as well.[51] When Mao appointed Lin his successor in 1966, nobody in the leadership questioned the legitimacy of the appointment. Many leaders complimented Lin on his promotion much more heartily than they wanted to admit after Lin's fall. It was Zhou Enlai who first suggested using the expression Mao's "closest comrade-in-arms" to specify Lin's position as Mao's successor.[52] Zhou Enlai; PLA marshals Ye Jianying, Chen Yi, Nie Rongzhen, and Xu Xiangqian; and the members of the CCRSG repeatedly confirmed Lin's unique position among the nation's leaders.

On September 25, 1966, in a speech to representatives of the faculty and students of thirteen army colleges in Beijing, Marshal Ye Jianying made the following comments about Lin as Mao's successor:

> Recently, there has been another happy event in our party—that is, Chairman Mao has decided on his first successor. For several decades, the chairman has been considering the question of who should succeed him. . . . After a 40-year test of revolutionary struggle, Comrade Lin Biao, with his rich experience of revolutionary struggle, has proved to be a great politician and strategist. He has also mastered high-level leadership skills and is Mao's successor. It can be said positively that Mao's decision that Comrade Lin Biao, his closest comrade-in-arms, should be his successor will not

only guarantee a thorough victory for our Cultural Revolution movement, but also is a hopeful indication of victory in the Chinese as well as the world revolution. Comrade Lin Biao is in better health than any of us. We are convinced that Comrade Lin Biao will follow Chairman Mao's leadership for several decades.[53]

On October 5, Ye made another reference to Lin as Mao's successor in his speech to students from military schools:

> It is a most happy event for the Chinese and the people of the world to have Comrade Lin Biao as our vice-commander. . . . Among the party leaders, especially among the military leaders, Lin Biao has best mastered Mao Zedong Thought, and he is the youngest. He is only 59 years old this year and is the youngest among all the leaders. Doctors' examinations reveal that he is in good health. . . . So he is the best, the healthiest, the youngest, and the most capable person to lead us. We should propound not only Mao Zedong Thought, but also the healthiness of Chairman Mao and Comrade Lin Biao to the country and to the world. It is of tremendous political significance.[54]

Other marshals, including Chen Yi and Nie Rongzhen, expressed similar opinions in speeches on November 13 and 19.[55] Even after the Lin Biao incident, when it became politically necessary to denounce Lin, one of Lin's subordinates, Huang Kecheng, still defended Lin as one the best generals in the history of the PLA.[56]

The "Learn from the PLA" Movement and the Cultural Revolution

Mao's trust in Lin may not have been the only reason he decided to make Lin his successor. Mao had already worked out his grand plan for the Cultural Revolution before he made up his mind to replace Liu Shaoqi with Lin. Mao laid out his ideas about the Cultural Revolution as well as his opinion of Lin in a letter addressed to Jiang Qing dated July 8, 1966. This letter is one of the few available documents by Mao himself regarding the Cultural Revolution. On the eve of the Cultural Revolution Mao seems not to have fully made up his mind what to do next.[57] In this letter to his wife, he could discuss the issues without worrying about the political implications of his remarks. The letter conveyed several important messages, though vaguely. As Mao said, he wrote the letter in "dark words" and told Jiang not to publicize it because "publication of these words means pouring cold water on [the leftists], which will help the rightists."[58] Meanwhile, it was by no means a personal letter. Mao showed it to several other people, including Zhou Enlai and Wang Renzhong, a deputy leader of the CCRSG, and later Lin Biao.

When the party publicized the letter after the Lin Biao incident as supplementary material for the movement to criticize Lin Biao, Jiang Qing said it was evidence that Mao had had reservations about Lin Biao as his successor as early as 1966. Even party historians, however, have found this claim unconvincing.[59] A careful study of the letter suggests that it contained Mao's statement of the purposes of the Cultural Revolution and his strategic plan for implementing the revolution, as well as his expectation that Lin Biao and the military would remain his allies.

At the beginning of the letter, Mao made it clear that he was ready to permit the Central Committee to publish the speech Lin had given at the enlarged meeting of the Politburo on May 18, 1966, although he was not entirely happy with Lin's discussion of a possible coup d'état. Mao claimed this was the first time in his life he had had to go along with the ideas of another. Why did he have to do so? Mao's own explanation was that he needed allies in an impending confrontation with rightists. Mao used the word "rightists" with specific implications in mind. When he isolated himself in "a cave in the west" [Dishuidong at Shaoshan, his hometown] to draft his letter to Jiang Qing, China, in his view, faced an immediate showdown between leftists and rightists: "Ghosts and monsters jumped out by themselves."[60] Mao believed that his decision to launch the Cultural Revolution was not only justified but altogether necessary.

Mao also revealed how he would stage the impending revolution. "The Cultural Revolution this time is a large-scale and serious maneuver," he wrote, in which "the leftists, the rightists, and the wavering fence-sitters will absorb useful lessons." Mao anticipated and hoped for a nationwide upheaval, for only in that way, he believed, would China eventually achieve a great peace. To be successful, this process would have to be repeated every seven or eight years. Several months after writing this letter, Mao proposed a toast to "overall class struggle in China" after he discussed his notions of the Cultural Revolution in detail at his birthday dinner on December 26, 1966. The toast caught everyone present by surprise, including the members of the CCRSG, Mao's think tank for the Cultural Revolution.[61] Wang Li, for example, was totally stunned by this outrageous statement of Mao. He later interpreted Mao's words "overall class struggle" to mean "overall civil war."[62]

As we discussed before, Lin's speech on May 18, 1966, was a response to Mao's own concern of a possible military coup in 1964–65. Since Mao himself had first raised the possibility of an anti-communist, rightist coup in China, there was no reason for him to disagree with Lin's speech. In fact, during these years few people ever delivered important speeches without Mao's approval. One of Mao's later charges against Lin Biao was that he made a speech at the 1970 Lushan Conference without consulting him first. What perhaps made Mao uneasy was Lin's exaggerated rhetoric concerning the chairman's worry, and his remarks in the same speech regarding the cult of personality. As noted before, Mao seemed uncertain about the impact of the spreading idol worship of him and complained to Jiang Qing that he had been turned into the Zhong Kui of the Communist Party.[63] Mao used the Chinese expression "Old Lady Wang who bragged about the melons she sold" to describe the awkward position he would be in.[64] As a politician, however, he understood the political implications of the movement to create a cult of personality around him and the necessity to employ it to mobilize the masses. He decided to use it against his rightist enemies, even if the result were disappointing. "I am now prepared to be broken into pieces," Mao mentioned in the letter, "and this does not bother me." Despite all his self-doubt, which he attributed to the temperament of "a monkey," Mao was confident of his ability to lead a national war against rightists. "In me there is the air of the tiger which is primary," he said, "and also the air of the monkey which is secondary." He added confidently, "If there is an anti-Communist rightist coup in China, I am certain that it will not be peaceful and very probably will be short-lived." He would prepare the "leftists" to fight whenever an anti-Communist coup threatened, and in doing so would guarantee a revolutionary "Red" China forever.

On what forces could Mao rely for such a noble mission? When Mao referred to Lin as "my friend" (in contrast to the rightists), the answer seemed clear. Mao would make sure that the People's Liberation Army was on his side. From its beginning, the PLA had been a peculiar armed force because of its involvement in political affairs. In its history of more than 40 years, the army had always been more than a military institution. It was an "armed force of peasants and workers under the leadership of the Chinese Communist Party," and it performed diverse functions as "a fighting team, a work team, and a production team." Most political leaders of Mao's generation identified themselves closely with the army. In the first two decades of the PRC, the same elite group simultaneously held key positions in the party, the government, and the army. Lin himself was both defense minister and vice-chairman of the party. Marshal Chen Yi was the first foreign minister, and Marshal He Long was director of the State Commission of Sports. As a result, the line between party and army elites was never clear.

Mao was especially pleased with Lin's successful efforts to strengthen political and ideological work in the PLA after Lin replaced Peng Dehuai as defense minister. In October 1959, the newspaper *Jiefangjun bao* published an article under Lin's name, which avowed that the PLA would give priority to political work, and in doing so would become a "Great School of Mao Zedong Thought." From 1960 to 1965 the General Political Department of the PLA, with Lin's permission, made a series of efforts to achieve this objective.

In September and October 1960, an enlarged meeting of the Central Military Commission met in Beijing and adopted a resolution spelling out a detailed program for political and ideological work in the army.[65] It established the "Four First principles" as guidelines for political work in the PLA. The principles emphasized human factors over weapons, political work over military training, ideological over administrative work, and living ideology over previously published ideology. The resolution explained that by "living ideology" it meant that people should go beyond the words of books to put those words into practice. In other words, "It is what Mao often said of it: the unity of Marxism-Leninism with the concrete practice of the Chinese Revolution."[66] The resolution also detailed how to indoctrinate the masses, how to make party branches strong "bulwarks" for combat, and how a political director could accomplish political and ideological work.[67] In May 1960, Xiao Hua, the director of the General Political Department, issued a directive to cultivate the "Three-Eight work style" in the PLA, a tradition that could be summarized in three phrases and eight Chinese characters. The three phrases called for a firm and correct political orientation, a persevering and simple style of work, and flexible strategy and tactics. The eight characters meant united, alert, earnest, and lively. With all these purposes, the resolution served as a blueprint for revitalizing political work in the army.

One immediate effect of the resolution was the restoration of political organizations at the company level and below. By April 1961, party branches were in place in every company and party cells in every platoon.[68] In 1961, when this occurred, an estimated 230,000 new party members joined the PLA.[69] Mao's idea of and political and ideological work spread through the PLA when Lin advocated the study of Mao's works. The resolution just discussed included Lin's instruction to "read Chairman Mao's works, listen to his words, do as he instructs and become a good soldier of Chairman Mao," which later became a popular slogan of the Cultural Revolution.

In 1960, Lin wrote the introduction to the first edition of the four-volume *Mao Zedong zhuzuo xuandu* (*Selected Works of Mao Zedong*). In it he cel-

ebrated the victory of the Chinese Revolution as the victory of Mao Zedong Thought. In November 1961 the General Political Department of the
PLA provided copies of *Mao Zedong zhuzuo xuandu* to every company, and
over the next three years the number of copies distributed exceeded 150
million.[70] In May 1964 the General Political Department published the
first edition of *Mao zhuxi yulu* (*Quotations of Chairman Mao*), known as the
"Little Red Book" during the Cultural Revolution, and printed nearly a
billion copies over the next several years.[71]

By 1965, Lin's efforts to ideologically indoctrinate the PLA had succeeded. Politics dominated the army. In May 1965 the military abolished
its rank system in an effort to illustrate Mao's egalitarian principle that
"soldiers and officers are the same." The PLA had become "the Great
School of Mao Zedong Thought."

Lin Biao's accomplishments from 1960 to 1965 pleased Mao, as did
Lin's devotion to Mao's political work system. In a letter to Lin and other
PLA leaders on November 16, 1963, Mao wrote, "The ideological and political works of the PLA have become more theoretical and systematic
since Lin raised the ideas of 'the Four First principles' and the 'Three-
Eight work style.'" Through the Socialist Education Movement that got
under way at the end of 1963, Mao sought to extend Lin's achievements
in the army to the nation as a whole. "I have considered this question for
several years," he stated in the letter just mentioned. "Now that some
industrial departments suggest voluntarily learning from the PLA, and
we have gained positive results from the experiences of the Department
of Petroleum to convince people, it is time to implement it on a larger
scale."[72]

On February 1, 1964, *Renmin ribao* published an editorial initiating the
"learn from the PLA" campaign. The editorial praised the PLA as "an
army of extremely high proletarian and combat character."[73] One consequence of this campaign was the increased popularity and prestige of
Mao Zedong Thought. Mass adulation of Mao, which Lin had perfected
in the army, spread through the nation, fueled by the study of Mao's
works. The movement, which was "a new development of Mao Zedong's
thinking concerning socialist construction," aimed at pounding the values of Mao into the mind of everyone in the nation.[74] Through celebra-
tions of the revolutionary spirit of such model soldier-heroes as Lei Feng,
the whole country learned proper Maoist moral virtues and everyone was
to become "obedient tools" of the party in the "spirit of a nail."[75]

Some scholars have argued that because the "learn from the PLA"
movement was brief it had only limited impact on the nation as a whole.[76]
It is true that the high tide of the campaign lasted only four or five

months; however, the influence of the campaign was powerful and pervasive. It was not just a propaganda movement, but also a well-organized cultural force supported by both the party and the government. Zhou Enlai, the premier, applauded the movement in his speech at the Third National Congress in December 1964: "All our Party and government organs and the broad mass of our cadres should learn from the thoroughly revolutionary spirit and work style of the Liberation Army . . . and advance along the road to revolution."[77]

The influence of the movement continued in the first several years of the Cultural Revolution. In fact, the purpose of the "learn from the PLA" movement was not merely to improve political work at all levels. In a sense, the campaign was important preparation for the Cultural Revolution, which was to begin the next year. Mao used it as a test of the effectiveness of his methods of political education and of his idea of employing mass movements to fight the party bureaucracy. In doing so, he gained important experience in organizing and mobilizing the masses. More important, the campaign greatly enhanced both the cult of Mao and the prestige of the PLA and anticipated a full militarization of the country later in the Cultural Revolution. With Lin's help, Mao had turned the PLA into an "obedient and absolute tool" of the party and the whole country into a militarized institution. Without full confidence in the PLA and in his politics of the masses, Mao would probably not have felt comfortable initiating the Cultural Revolution, during which he had to rely heavily on the PLA to support the leftists. The "learn from the PLA" campaign convinced Mao that it was possible to mobilize the masses on a large scale.

Lin of course understood the meaning of Mao's July 8 letter to Jiang Qing. Zhou went to Dalian to show Lin the letter shortly after Mao had shown it to him in Wuhan.[78] In August 1967, Lin told Wuhan military leaders Zeng Siyu and Liu Feng that Mao had relied on two things in beginning the Cultural Revolution: the high prestige of Mao Zedong Thought and Mao himself, and the People's Liberation Army.[79] In her speech at the enlarged conference of the Central Military Committee in April 1967, Jiang Qing also revealed Mao's intention to ask help from "the god of the PLA" to attack the bourgeois representatives within the party.[80]

Despite these assurances, Lin felt uneasy in his new position as Mao's successor. Personally, Lin realized how vulnerable he was as Mao's designated successor, and institutionally he was concerned about the integrity of the PLA. According to his daughter, Lin was very reluctant to accept the position as successor, and even less willing to get involved in the Cultural Revolution. Despite his clear public record as Mao's loyal follower, Lin had his own opinions of Mao and what had happened in

China since the Great Leap Forward. After the Lin Biao incident it was revealed that Lin had made an uncomplimentary comment about Mao as early as 1949: "He will fabricate 'your' opinion first, then he will change 'your' opinion—which is not actually yours, but his fabrication. I should be careful about this standard trick."[81] In 1958, Lin Biao made another critical comment: "He [Mao] worships himself and has a blind faith in himself. He worships himself to such an extent that all accomplishments are attributed to him, but all mistakes are made by others."[82]

Like Mao, Lin had a good knowledge of Chinese history. He was especially interested in the theories and concepts of human relations in Confucianism, Legalism, and Daoism. On one occasion he asked a history professor to put quotations from the most revered Chinese philosophers, Confucius, Mencius, Han Feizi, and Lao Zi, on flash cards for him to study.[83] After the Lin Biao incident, the investigation group found boxes of such cards at Lin's residence. Some of them held transcripts of Lin's ideas made by his wife, Ye Qun, including his negative comments about Mao.[84] In 1974 these cards triggered a strange episode, the campaign to criticize Lin Biao and Confucius together, although many scholars now believe that the movement was actually targeted at Zhou Enlai.

Based on his understanding of Chinese history and of Mao, Lin knew that the position next to a powerful, charismatic leader would be a vulnerable one, especially after he saw what happened to Liu Shaoqi. In private, Lin often showed respect for Liu Shaoqi and sympathy for Liu and Deng Xiaoping. He told his daughter that Liu had "a better understanding of theory than Mao" and that it made no sense to oust Liu and Deng because both of them were "good comrades."[85] It seemed clear to Lin that Mao's dissatisfaction with the two men was the only reason for their fall. The ill fortune of Liu and Deng reminded Lin of an old Chinese proverb about court politics, "To be in the company of a king is to be in the company of a tiger." In fact, Lin was not the only person who understood the dilemma of Mao's successor. Zhou Enlai was always careful to distance himself from that position. Before the Eleventh Plenum of the Eighth Party Central Committee in 1966, Zhou crossed his name off the list of candidates for vice-chairman of the Communist Party. As a result, Lin Biao became the party's sole vice-chairman.

However, Lin could not refuse the appointment because Mao had made it a decision of the Party Central Committee. As a senior party official, Lin knew that once the party finalized Mao's decision he had no choice but to accept it. To reject it would violate a major party principle and jeopardize his political career. Still, Lin expressed his anxiety over the position in a speech on August 13, 1966, immediately after his appointment:

Recently, I have been quite heavy-hearted. Because of the incompatibility between the work assigned to me and my ability, I am afraid that I am not competent for such a job. I know I will make mistakes, although I will try my best to avoid them. . . .

I know that my knowledge and ability are not sufficient [for such a position]. Several times, I asked sincerely not to be given this post. But since the chairman and the Central Committee have decided, I have to accept the decision.[86]

When Lin expressed his desire to reject the position, he was not just being modest. He did not attend the Eleventh Plenum of the Eighth Party Central Committee in August 1966, when the move to criticize Liu Shaoqi and to name Lin as Mao's successor began. On August 8, after Mao publicized his big-character poster, "Bombard the Headquarters," Zhou Enlai made secret arrangements to bring Lin to Beijing from Dalian. After Lin's plane landed, Zhou and Wang Dongxing boarded it and talked with Lin for about half an hour. Lin was in a gloomy mood when he stepped out of the plane. Zhou took Lin directly to the Great Hall of the People, where Mao was staying for the summer.[87] There, Lin reportedly "begged" Mao not to appoint him his successor for the purposes of the Cultural Revolution.[88] But Mao was obviously unsympathetic to Lin's plea and sternly criticized him, likening him to Emperor Shizong in the Ming dynasty, who spent so much time looking for medicine to ensure his longevity that he left national affairs unattended to.[89]

Lin later sent a formal request to Mao asking him to rescind his appointment to the position of successor. Again Mao rejected the request. In his fury, Lin tore the returned report apart and threw the pieces in the garbage. Ye Qun later picked up the pieces and stuck them together. According to some scholars, the document is still kept in the central archives.[90]

"Passive, Passive, and Passive Again"

Since there was no way for Lin to refuse the appointment, he found the best way he could to protect himself—by following Mao unconditionally. He adhered closely to Mao's every decision and postponed making a decision on his own if he was unsure about Mao's opinion. To demonstrate Lin's loyalty to Mao, Lin's wife, Ye Qun, urged Lin's staff to make sure he always arrived minutes before Mao and was waiting for Mao whenever both men were to attend the same event. Lin encouraged people to believe he was Mao's closest follower. When one of his secretaries told Lin that he was well known as Mao's best student, he was very happy. "We should all follow Mao closely," he told the secretary, with a proud smile on his face. "I don't have any talent. What I know, I learned from Mao."[91]

Meanwhile, he adopted the Daoist strategy of "doing nothing." According to his former secretaries, he showed no interest in his new job. In sharp contrast to his public image as Mao's staunch supporter, Lin privately had no desire to promote the Cultural Revolution. He secluded himself in his residence and attended meetings only when Mao demanded that he do so. He managed his daily work peculiarly: he made no phone calls, had only minimal contact with his colleagues, and received very few visitors. His secretaries read documents for him, but he listened to only short summaries of selected documents for half an hour in the morning and half an hour in the afternoon. One of his secretaries complained that an hour a day was insufficient to do the work that had to be done. "As his secretary," Zhang Yunsheng stated, "I was at a loss as to how I could possibly fulfill my responsibilities of informing Lin of key decisions in such a short time span."[92]

Colleagues and staff members who knew Lin well noticed that except in public speeches he seldom expressed an opinion on issues related to the Cultural Revolution. Among his colleagues, he came to have a reputation as "reticent and mysterious." He seldom spoke his mind, and when he did speak, he did so as briefly as possible. When one of his long-term subordinates, Tao Zhu, was in trouble with the CCRSG and facing an impending purge, Lin tried to warn him about the danger. Lin's words to Tao were, "You should be passive, passive, and passive again." Despite the value of this message, Tao probably never figured out what it meant.[93]

As head of the PLA, however, Lin was deeply concerned about the security of the military, in particular, keeping the PLA out of the Cultural Revolution. He was worried that the PLA could not meet Mao's requirements without damaging itself. In speeches throughout 1966 and 1967, Lin repeatedly expressed his anxiety over threats to the integrity of the PLA. In August 1966 he warned army officials to avoid political mistakes. "It will be the worst scandal," he said, "if someone among the military officers turns out to be opposing Chairman Mao."[94] In an address to military commanders in the spring of 1967, Lin again reminded his subordinates to avoid political errors. The danger of doing so just then, he felt, was especially great because the People's Liberation Army had never been engaged in such a large intervention in national affairs.[95]

Lin's concerns about threats to the integrity of the army were warranted. From the beginning of the Cultural Revolution, it was difficult for the army to maintain internal discipline. In fact, Mao launched the Cultural Revolution in such a way that nobody save Mao himself understood what was going on. Mao wanted a mass movement against rightists that would achieve "ultimate peace in the country through a great chaos." With his personal encouragement, the Red Guards did soon throw the whole country into chaos.[96]

The first Red Guard organization appeared on the campus of the middle school attached to Qinghua University on May 29, 1966. A group of students there decided they wanted to join and intensify an ongoing campaign to criticize the Beijing municipal government. They put up big-character posters around campus, identifying themselves as Hongweibing (Red Guards). Students from other schools followed suit, and similar organizations soon sprang up on other campuses in Beijing. This movement, however, perhaps would not have lasted long had it not caught Mao's attention and received his personal endorsement. On July 28, Red Guards from the Qinghua University middle school asked Jiang Qing to forward two of their posters to Mao. To everybody's surprise, Mao responded with a letter supporting the Red Guards and their activities.

On August 1, Mao circulated his letter and the two posters from the Red Guards at the Eleventh Plenum of the Eighth Party Central Committee. The party and the central government, however, were less impressed than Mao had been, and the committee did not affirm the legality of the Red Guards at the Eleventh Plenum. It did adopt a document known as the "Sixteen Items," which contained an outline of the Cultural Revolution but did not officially recognize the Red Guard movement. Mao therefore decided to act on his own. As a charismatic leader, he felt no need for anyone else's endorsement to implement his own ideas. He was confident that he could rely on the forces outside the regular institutions to stage the Cultural Revolution, namely the CCRSG and the Red Guards.

On August 3, Wang Renzhong, a deputy leader of the CCRSG, told the Red Guards from Qinghua University middle school of Mao's endorsement.[97] To further encourage the students, Mao decided to receive the representatives of the Red Guards in public. On August 18, 1966, the first Red Guard rally was held at Tiananmen Square. When Mao, Lin Biao, Zhou Enlai, and others appeared on Tiananmen in PLA uniform and with the armband of the Red Guard, no one doubted that Mao had legitimized the Red Guard movement. Soon afterward, the movement spread across the country. Most of the Red Guards were teenagers who were thrilled to be chosen to carry out Mao's mission to "smash the four olds"—old ideas, old culture, old customs, and old habits—nationwide. On the evening of August 19, a group of them took their first action, breaking into a well-known Beijing restaurant, smashing the signboard, and tearing down the decorative paintings and pictures. They then put Mao's picture and quotations from his writings on the wall to "revolutionize" the place. In the following days, other Red Guards swarmed into hospitals, hotels, theaters, department stores, public parks, and historical sites, destroying whatever was viewed as old, even revolutionizing "old" names. For example, Xiehe Hospital, which Americans had established in the 1920s, was renamed Fandi (Anti-imperialism) Hospital; "Dongan Market" became "Dongfeng (East Wind) Market."[98] Even their schools received new names, many of them some variation of "Red Guard Fighting School."[99] As their revolutionary enthusiasm rose, Red Guards began targeting people on the street, harassing anyone who dressed or otherwise appeared bourgeois or Western. They stopped individuals with long hair or permanent waves and cut their hair on the spot. They also targeted miniskirts, suits, leather shoes, and tight jeans as "bourgeois" and therefore unacceptable. For the rest of the year, the nation suffered under the red terror of these "little generals."

This violent and irrational behavior provoked no interference from the authorities. Instead, the official propaganda organs, now controlled by the CCRSG, gave the green light to students to do whatever they wanted. On August 21 the General Political Department of the PLA issued a "hands-off" order to troops not to interfere with the movement. The next day, Mao approved a directive of the Public Security Department strictly forbidding policemen to interfere with the students. In his speech at a Central Working Meeting on August 23, Mao expressed his approval of the turmoil. "In my opinion, we should let it be like this for several months," he said. "I do not think the chaos in Beijing was that bad. [The students] are still too civilized in their behavior."[100]

Although the Eleventh Plenum had not acknowledged the legitimacy of the Red Guard movement, central newspapers and journals, including *Renmin ribao, Jiefangjun bao*, and *Hongqi*, encouraged and applauded its anarchical behavior, making it impossible for local authorities to challenge its legitimacy. *Renmin ribao*, for example, saluted the Red Guards and editorially labeled some of their atrocities as "achievements of our Red Guards." "They [the Red Guards] truly have shaken the whole society and the old world," stated one editorial. "The Red Guards exposed 'blood-suckers' and the enemies of the people one by one." The CCRSG received a constant stream of Red Guard representatives and instructed them how to carry out their revolutionary mission. Xie Fuzhi, head of the Public Security Department and deputy chief of the CCRSG, asked in one of his speeches, "Should the Red Guards who beat someone to death go to jail? If someone is dead, he is dead. I do not think we can do anything about it at all. . . . You will make a big mistake if you arrest the person who beat others up."[101] On September 7, Mao wrote to Lin Biao, Zhou En-lai, Tao Zhu, Chen Boda, Kang Sheng, and Jiang Qing, asking them to have the Central Committee issue a directive to the provinces against interference with the Red Guards. "It is wrong to provoke workers and peasants against students," Mao said.[102]

Encouragement from Mao and the CCRSG rationalized the irrational behavior of Red Guards. The radicals soon realized that changing the names of streets and destroying the "four olds" were only minor parts of their mission. They came to see themselves as what Mao said they were: chosen rebels against institutional authority, instruments of the class struggle, and enforcers of Mao's theories. From the very beginning, the reputation of the Red Guards rested on the idea that the Red Guard organizations consisted of youths from "good" family backgrounds—that is, from families of workers, poor and lower-middle-class peasants, and revolutionary and military cadres. Among the people from "bad" backgrounds were members of the "black classes," including intellectuals. These conceptualizations reflect the ambiguity of the concept of class itself in Communist China, where there were no easy answers to the question of whether class was a factor of economic status, as Marx suggested, or of political consciousness, or both.[103]

The students, however, had no time for social complexities. They simplified the matter of social class with a popular saying that everyone understood: "If one's father is revolutionary his son is a hero, and if one's father is reactionary, his son is a bad egg."[104] Such slogans justified ransacking the households of people with "bad" backgrounds and humiliating, torturing, and even killing the occupants.

As early as June 18, 1966, students at Peking University created new ways to humiliate professors they considered "demons and evil spirits." In one incident the students gathered eighteen objectionable professors and administrators, poured ink on their faces, put paper hats on their heads, and hung signs with humiliating words around their necks. They also shaved half the head of each victim, man or woman, making it easy to identify them as "bad." This was the first of many cases of the physical abuse of people relegated to "black gangs" (*heibang*).[105] Although the work team on the campus stopped the students and criticized them for the incident just described, physical torture later became the most standard form of Red Guard punishment for everyone from high school teachers to the state chairman.

Statistics on the overall human and material cost of the Red Guard movement are still not available. The following list illustrates the damage done by the Red Guard movement in Beijing between August and September 1966.[106]

On August 23, Red Guards burned a huge pile of opera costumes they had confiscated from opera troupes in Beijing.

On August 24, Lao She, author of *Rickshaw Boy* and one of China's best-known contemporary writers, committed suicide after several humiliating beatings by Red Guards.

On August 27, Red Guards broke into the houses of several former generals of the Guomindang, humiliated the men, and ordered them to clean up the street every day thereafter. Few non-Communist celebrities escaped punishment of some sort from Red Guards. Even Madame Song Qinglin, the 74-year-old widow of former Chinese statesman and revolutionary leader Sun Yat-sen, was harassed from time to time. Red Guards "ordered" her to change her hair style and destroy her pet pigeons.

During this two-month period, the Red Guards beat more than 1,700 people to death in Beijing. In Daxing county alone, they killed 325 people from "four black categories" within a single week. The oldest victim was 80, the youngest one month old. In 22 households, the Red Guards killed everyone. During the same period, they ransacked 33,695 households and expelled 85,198 residents from the city. They also destroyed 4,922 of the 6,843 historic sites and relics in Beijing, sent more than 3.2 million tons of books to paper mills, including more than 2 million copies of classic, ancient, and rare books. No institution remained untouched. In late August various democratic parties closed their offices, and every school, from primary grades to universities, closed for the semester.

Mao had not expected this when he supported the Red Guard movement in mid-August. From October 9 to 28, Mao chaired a Central Working Meeting in Beijing. In a speech to the conference on October 25, 1966, he appeared to be apologetic:[107]

> I brought trouble [when I decided] to broadcast the big-character poster [from Peking University], [when I] wrote a letter to the Red Guards of Qinghua University middle school, and [when] I myself wrote a big-character poster.
>
> Even I did not expected that [the Red Guard movement] would develop on such a large scale in such a short time. Once the big-character poster (the poster from Peking University) was on the radio, it created agitation throughout the country. Red Guards were organized across the country even before I sent out my letter to them.[108]

Although Mao voiced reservations about the movement, he had no intention of ending it, even if most of his comrades disagreed with his decision. "The movement has been on the stage for five months," Mao told his comrades at the meeting. "It probably needs twice as much time as this, and maybe more." Instead of restricting the movement, Mao decided to make another move to further encourage the radicals' challenge of various authorities, especially those of the central government. While continuously encouraging the student movement, Mao called on workers, peasants, and others to join the students' revolt. Mao believed that by September 1966 the development of the Cultural Revolution was far from satisfactory but that the basic problem was his colleagues' "misunderstanding" of the movement. Many of them were still under the influence of Liu Shaoqi's "wrong line," which referred to Liu's handling of the Cultural Revolution between June and July 1966. After the Red Guard organizations had appeared on campus and caused trouble in the schools, Liu Shaoqi and Deng Xiaoping, who were in charge of the routine work of the Central Government, had sent work teams to schools to maintain order. Most of the work teams had sided with school authorities, trying to discipline rebellious students. In doing so, they met resistance from the radical student groups backed by Jiang Qing and Kang Sheng. The conflicts between the rebellious students and the work teams had brought bloody collisions in some schools, and many revolting teachers and students had ended up in prison.

Mao was not in Beijing when these incidents developed on campus. In several subsequent working meetings, Mao angrily criticized Liu and Deng for "suppressing the student movement" and asked them to make self-criticisms.[109] Liu and Deng did so and asked the work teams to withdraw. Liu's attitude toward the Cultural Revolution seemed to be the last straw in the Mao-Liu relationship, which had already become very fragile during the Socialist Education Movement in 1964.[110] Mao subsequently announced his split from Liu Shaoqi by reading his big-character poster "Bombard the Headquarters" at the Plenum. Liu and Deng were asked to "step aside" (*kao bian zhan*) after the meeting.[111]

Mao believed that Liu might still have strong influence among his colleagues, since many of them showed reluctance to accept the Cultural Revolution—to accept criticism from the masses and to criticize themselves before the masses. In late September, Mao publicized his big-character poster "Bombard the Headquarters" across the country. This meant that Mao deliberately made public his criticism of Liu Shaoqi, which was an obvious violation of the usual pattern of an "inner-party struggle"—to keep different opinions only within the party. Meanwhile, Mao came out with the new idea of criticizing "the bourgeois reactionary line" and asked Lin Biao to mention it on National Day, which celebrates the establishment of the PRC. This made many of his close colleagues uneasy. Before National Day, Tao Zhu, Wang Renzhong, and Wang Li each suggested to Mao the inappropriateness of using the word "reactionary" to refer to an inner-party struggle, but Mao turned a deaf ear to their suggestion. Zhou Enlai also questioned the use of the expression "bourgeois reactionary line." He told Wang Li that he would speak to Mao about this because in the past the "wrong" side in inner-party struggles was referred to as leftist or rightist opportunists, but never as "bourgeois reactionaries." Zhou did not understand why Mao now insisted on the terms "bourgeois" and "reactionary" to refer to a difference of opinion within the party. Mao would not listen to Zhou, either.[112] Mao asked Chen Boda, Wang Renzhong, and Zhang Chunqiao to draft Lin's speech, and also asked Wang Li to call for mass criticism of "the bourgeois reactionary line" in his draft of the *Hongqi* editorial for the month of October.

These decisions by Mao, together with his other decisions about the Cultural Revolution, threw the country into a state of anarchy. After the October Central Working Meeting and the publicizing of the slogan "criticize the bourgeois reactionary line," the situation everywhere became increasingly chaotic. By October 1966, workers, peasants, and other people had joined the Red Guards to rebel against various authorities. People organized against the leaders of administrative organizations. Local radicals (*zaofan pai*) kidnapped many ranking provincial cadres as they returned from the conference in Beijing. In response, many local government agencies created conservative mass organizations (*baohuang pai*) to counter the radicals and to protect local leaders. As a result, mass organizations everywhere divided into different factions and fought one another. After January 1967, when the revolution entered a new stage characterized as a general "seizure of power from capitalist roaders"—the overthrow of party and administrative institutions and their reorganization under radical supervision—anarchy prevailed throughout the country.

Factional controversies, especially over who should exercise power after the breakdown of formal institutions, soon developed into armed conflict, as every faction bid for a share of power. In some areas, radicals broke into military garrisons and seized PLA weaponry. In the Northeast, the winning radical factions even patrolled the streets in captured army tanks. This was probably what Mao expected when he made a birthday toast to an "overall class struggle" in December 1966. In Lin's words, the Cultural Revolution had become an "armed revolution."[113]

Mao finally realized that he had to call in the PLA to stabilize the situation. On January 23 he received a report concerning the use of troops in the Anhui Military Region to keep order at a rally to criticize and denounce the secretary of the provincial party committee, Li Baohua. Mao wrote on the report:

[We] should send the PLA soldiers to support the leftist revolutionary masses. From now on, if the real revolutionary masses ask the army for assistance, it should agree. The so-called "noninterference" [policy] is a fiction, for [the PLA] has already gotten involved. [We] should issue a new order and declare the previous order null and void. Please consider this.[114]

Mao's order left Lin no way to keep the PLA out of the Cultural Revolution, which was a key point of controversy between the CCRSG and the military. As defense minister, Lin was responsible for maintaining order in the military for the sake of national security. He did not want the PLA involved in the Cultural Revolution, and he especially wanted to keep the military away from local radicals. The Central Military Committee under his supervision had worked arduously to keep order within the PLA when everything else was in chaos. When Liu Shaoqi sent work teams to schools, the PLA also dispatched work teams to military schools to maintain order. After the Red Guard movement began, the Central Military Committee issued several documents requiring students at military schools to remain on campus to receive "positive education" (*zhangnian jiaoyu*). These documents emphasized party leadership at military schools after the withdrawal of work teams and established rules to keep students from displaying posters on campus and from contact with local radicals. Until October 1966 the Central Military Committee had managed to make the Cultural Revolution in the PLA less violent and chaotic than it was elsewhere. The students in military schools were relatively easy to control because of the PLA's tradition of stern discipline.

Lin was in an awkward position. As Mao's successor, he was supposed to be actively assisting Mao in the Cultural Revolution. He also had to cooperate with the CCRSG headed by Madame Mao. Because Jiang Qing was Mao's wife, Lin and others in high places felt obliged to maintain good relations with her and her group. Since the beginning of the Cultural Revolution, Jiang Qing had pressed the military to start a revolution within itself, and Kang Sheng had accused the PLA of "staying idle outside the overall war" that was the Cultural Revolution. Chen Boda likewise insisted that in the Great Proletarian Cultural Revolution, which was a general class struggle, the PLA had no right to remain uninvolved and could not hope to do so.[115]

In a sense, Chen Boda was right. It was impossible for the PLA to remain immune to the social chaos created by the Red Guards. It was more and more difficult to control the military students, especially after Mao encouraged Red Guards across the country to make contact with one another by going to Beijing to be received by Mao. In August 1966, the students demanded to go to Beijing and called for the rehabilitation of radical army students whom the work teams had previously criticized as "counter-revolutionaries." When their complaints reached the CCRSG, Jiang Qing pressured Lin to encourage the Cultural Revolution within the PLA. On October 1 a group of military students who had traveled to Beijing raised the issue with Mao and Lin at Tiananmen. Lin was probably embarrassed by the incident because it appeared as if the PLA did not support Mao's Cultural Revolution. Students from the Second Military Medical School in Shanghai also sent a coat "stained with blood" to Lin, demanding that he give military students permission to come to Beijing.[116]

To ease the pressure on himself, Lin asked Ye Jianying to preside over an enlarged conference of the Central Military Committee called to discuss the issue. Although the officials at the meeting were reluctant to grant the students' request, nobody could find an appropriate excuse to prevent military students from going to Beijing to see Mao. The students' other request, for the "rehabilitation" of the radicals in military schools, was an especially sensitive issue because Mao had insisted that whoever suppressed a student movement was carrying out a "bourgeois reactionary line." The Central Military Committee finally decided to compromise with the students, with three conditions: students must return to their schools immediately after attending a rally to see Mao; they must observe military discipline while in Beijing; and they must not make contact with local Red Guards or interfere with the local Cultural Revolution. After the meeting, the Military Cultural Revolution Small Group (MCRSG) drafted a document outlining the implementation of the Cultural Revolution in military schools.

However, when the draft of a directive implementing these orders reached the CCRSG for endorsement,[117] Liu Zhijian, the head of the MCRSG and also a deputy chief of the CCRSG, encountered opposition from Chen Boda, Jiang Qing, and others. The latter rejected the basic idea behind the directive, namely that the party organizations should maintain the right to supervise the Cultural Revolution in military schools. Chen Boda edited the entire document, sentence by sentence, completely changing its original meaning.[118] As a result, the document, titled "An Urgent Instruction regarding the Cultural Revolution in Military Schools," became just another document the CCRSG used to promote the Cultural Revolution. After Ye Jianying described the "Urgent Instruction" to army students at a rally on October 5, Zhang Chunqiao announced at a mass rally the following day that the "Instruction" enabled students in military schools to join the Cultural Revolution on the same basis as other students.[119]

The "Instruction" produced chaos in military schools as well as at military headquarters in Beijing. Military students swarmed into Beijing to see Mao and refused to leave. They resented having been "suppressed" and kept out of the movement for so long. By November, the number of military students in Beijing exceeded 100,000, and assisted by Red Guards they began assaulting the Defense Ministry, the National Defense Science Committee, and military headquarters. On November 8, more than 600 army students broke into the Defense Ministry, wounding guards who tried to stop them. They demonstrated around and within the building, demanding that Deputy Chief of Staff Li Tianyou accompany them to a "struggle meeting." Lin was surprised when he learned of this and asked Ye Jianying and Liu Zhijian to handle the matter. Lin told them to persuade the students to withdraw, but not to punish them and to avoid direct confrontation with the radicals. After several rounds of negotiation with the students, they were finally persuaded to leave.[120]

While the crisis in the Defense Ministry was temporarily resolved, the poor handling of the situation brought unexpected consequences. Lin's "nonpunishment policy" resulted in increased rebelliousness among the students. Between late October and the end of the year, radical students crowded into all military headquarters buildings in Beijing. At the end of October, approximately 3,000 students took over the air force headquarters and demanded self-criticisms from leading air force officers at student rallies. In order to evade the students' assault, many senior officials stayed away from their homes as well as their offices. Whoever fell into the students' hands would be humiliated and perhaps even tortured. Wu Faxian, commander of the air force, later gave the following account of the difficulties:

> The students took over all the offices and disrupted our routine work at headquarters. They wanted the leading officers to attend their meetings and demanded that we make self-criticisms. Under these circumstances, there was no way for us to keep up with our daily work. I was worried to death. There were so many planes in the air every day that we might have plane crashes if things continued out of control like this. As the commander-in-chief of the air force, I would have to take full responsibility if any accidents occurred. I asked Yang Chengwu, the acting chief of staff, for help. He, however, had his own difficulties in dealing with radical students. He fled from his home and his office in order to evade the students' assault. He told me to seek help from Ye Jianying, the secretary of the Central Military Committee. After Ye consulted Zhou Enlai, he told me that I could take refuge in his house. I could not stay for long, however, because I was worried about what was happening back at headquarters.
>
> As soon as I returned to the compound, the students came to demand that I attend their meeting to be criticized. They prepared a spittoon as a

hat to be put on my head and ink for my face. It was said that they even planned to shave off half my hair. Again, I reported this to Ye, who told me to stay away from the students and leave the compound immediately. Otherwise, the students might kidnap me, as they did many other high officers. Again I was on the run. The students got several cars to follow me everywhere, seeking an opportunity to catch me. As a last resort, Ye told me to move to the Jingxi Hotel, which the students felt hesitant to break into because it was guarded by troops from the Beijing garrison. Meanwhile, the students kept breaking into my house at night and harassing my wife and children if they could not find me there. Thus I remained a "refugee" for at least several months until Jiang Qing referred to me as a "good comrade" in one of her receptions for the students, upon Lin's request. At that time, if you were lucky enough to get direct "protection" from "proletarian headquarters," you would be spared students' harassment.[121]

Other branches of the military fared no better than the air force. Qiu Huizuo, director of the General Logistics Department, was among the initial victims of the students' attack. Students took him from his home and held him for several weeks to make sure he would be available for their "criticism meetings." At one meeting they forced Qiu to crawl from one end of the stage to the other while they beat him. If Ye Qun had not come in person to rescue him it is unlikely that Qiu would have survived the Cultural Revolution.[122]

Qiu was lucky that Lin Biao and Ye Qun went out of their way to help him because of his long-term special relationship with Lin.[123] He ended up with only a few broken ribs and missing teeth. Other generals and civilians victimized by the students were not so lucky. To give just a few examples, on September 19, 1966, Wan Xiaofang, party secretary of Tianjin, died after students kidnapped and abused him; on January 8, 1967, Yan Hongyan, first political commissar of the Kunming Military Region, committed suicide after Chen Boda refused his plea for help; on January 21, 1967, the commander of the East Sea Fleet, Tao Yong, died mysteriously after a "criticism meeting"; and on January 22, 1967, Zhang Linzhi, minister of the Coal Industry, was beaten to death.[124]

The radical students did not confine their activities to military headquarters in Beijing. They subjected military officers all over the country to attack. Students from military schools in the area, for example, assaulted eight military commanders in the Nanjing Military Region. Xu Shiyou, commander of the region, threatened to open fire if students assaulted him. Students kidnapped and tortured Tan Zi'an, vice-commander of the Shenyang Military Region. Commander Han Xianchu of the Fuzhou Military Region complained to Lin's secretary that a radical Red Guard faction in Beijing called "the Third Headquarters" had sent members to Fuzhou to encourage local radicals to assault military establishments there. "If this continues, I will go up to the mountains and engage in guerrilla war," Han shouted angrily over the phone. "I believe that Chairman Mao is surrounded by bad people. Be warned of that!"[125]

Lin adopted a Daoist strategy of passive involvement and provided only limited help to local troops assaulted by radicals. In fact, Lin handed over the problems in the military to the CCRSG. This worked to a degree, because people "protected" by the CCRSG were thereby exempt from students' harassment and could return to their routine work. In the long run, however, Lin's concession to the CCRSG increased the group's hold over military students at the expense of the military's own authority. As a result, radical students listened to the CCRSG rather than to their military superiors. Thus, Lin provided an opportunity for Jiang Qing and her colleagues to interfere in military affairs and made it more difficult for the Central Military Committee to control the PLA.

It is difficult to understand why Lin, the defense minister, tolerated this situation, which put many of his long-term subordinates in danger. Of course his options were limited, even if he had exercised his responsibilities more actively. Mao often refused Lin's suggestions when he offered them. One day in October 1966, for example, Lin learned that radicals in Shanxi province had broken into army garrisons there and grabbed arms. He brought the incident to Mao's attention, attaching a note to the reports, which he sent to Mao, asking Mao to pay attention to the turmoil in the Northwest. Mao promptly returned the reports with a written comment: "Comrade Lin Biao, this is a very good thing. The leftists should be prepared to sacrifice thousands of lives in exchange for tens of thousands of the rightists.'" Mao criticized Lin for making a fuss over something so trivial.[126]

In January 1967, when conditions in the military worsened, Lin's office received "private instructions" from Mao that the basic strategy for the time being was still to "let it go" instead of acting to curb the movement.[127] Between late 1966 and August 1968, Mao rejected several suggestions from Lin that he forbid mass organizations to take arms from the military. In a letter to Jiang Qing, he criticized Lin's proposal that he issue orders to keep radicals from seizing arms from the military on the grounds that the central strategy of the Cultural Revolution at the moment was to arm the leftists. Mao believed that 75 percent of the regional military organizations were supporting the rightists. He later even ordered the PLA to issue arms to the leftists, which resulted in widespread armed conflict in mid-1967.[128] Lin realized by that time that he had no

influence with Mao on matters concerning the Cultural Revolution because Mao was determined to reach "an ultimate harmony under heaven
through a great chaos" (*tianxia daluan dadao tianxia dazhi*). Mao's subordinates now had only two choices, to follow or to perish. Lin, like many
others, chose the former and thus later told Tao Zhu to "be passive, passive, and passive again."

After these episodes, Lin became even more reluctant to assume responsibility in leading the Cultural Revolution. Using poor health as an
excuse, he avoided reading documents and attending meetings, and his
position as Mao's successor exempted him from Red Guard assaults. Lin
was probably the only person, apart from Mao and the CCRSG, able to
protect himself in this way during the Red Guard stage of the Cultural
Revolution. He could easily find scapegoats among his subordinates, who
were in much more vulnerable positions than he was. None of the other
military leaders holding executive positions had the liberty to do the
same. They had to pass Mao's tests, which were carried out by the Red
Guards.

The PLA Cannot Be in Disorder: Resistance from
the Other Marshals

The Cultural Revolution put the PLA through its worst ordeal since 1949.
Although Lin protected himself by taking as little responsibility as possible, the Central Military Committee under Ye Jianying, the General Political Department under Xiao Hua, and the MCRSG under Liu Zhijian were
responsible for leading the Cultural Revolution in the military. Not one
of them survived the test politically in the initial chaos of the Cultural
Revolution.

As the leader of the MCRSG, Liu Zhijian was the liaison between the
CCRSG and the military. This was an almost impossible job because the
CCRSG, which sided routinely with radical students, and the Central Military Committee, which was concerned with discipline in the PLA, rarely
agreed on anything. Often caught in the resulting crossfire, Liu could do
nothing to improve the situation. In early October 1966, when military
students crowded into Beijing, Liu, on the instruction of several marshals,
drafted a telegram ordering the military regions to prevent their students
from traveling to Beijing in large groups. Chen Boda rejected the order,
however, and it was not issued. In November, Liu drafted another order
prohibiting mass organizations in the army, but Chen Boda again over-
ruled him. Subsequently, Chen withheld approval of two other orders of

Liu's. In one, Liu wanted to forbid students to interfere with the regular work at military headquarters for reasons of national security and to punish those who disobeyed the prohibition. In the other, Liu wanted to instruct military hospitals to provide shelter for local leaders assaulted by radicals. At a CCRSG meeting to consider these orders, Chen accused Liu Zhijian of trying to "suppress the revolution."[129]

In an attempt to discipline army students in Beijing, the General Political Department invited the marshals of the armed forces to speak to the students at rallies on November 11 and 29. Marshals Ye Jianying, Chen Yi, Xu Xiangqian, and He Long criticized the students' disruptive behavior and urged them to go back to their schools immediately.[130] But the radical students merely jeered, and some even questioned the legitimacy of the rallies, asking whether the CCRSG and Lin had approved them.

After the meetings, several students complained to the CCRSG. Jiang Qing, who was already upset with the marshals' attitude toward the Cultural Revolution, claimed at a meeting of the group that the purpose of the rallies was to "suppress the masses." "It was wrong for the marshals to make such speeches," Guan Feng, a member of the CCRSG, added; "so they should go to the masses to make self-criticisms and be educated by the masses." With support from the CCRSG, the radical military students scheduled a rally to criticize and "educate" the marshals. They invited members of the CCRSG to chair the meeting and local Red Guards to attend. They demanded that Chen Yi, Ye Jianying, and other marshals and generals attend the meeting to "be educated." The invitations to the marshals and generals were on paper of different colors, red or white. The students intended to criticize those who received white invitations.

Approximately twenty of those who received white invitations gathered at Ye Jianying's house to discuss how to handle the matter. Ye Jianying suggested that they attend the meeting, but most opposed doing so because no one knew what the students might do. The meeting continued until midnight with no solution.[131] When Zhou Enlai finally heard about this, he brought the issue to Mao, who agreed with him that the students had gone too far. Mao criticized Jiang Qing for organizing the meeting to criticize the marshals, but the CCRSG did not cancel the meeting until 100,000 students had been waiting all day at the amphitheater for it to start.

Embarrassed and resentful, Jiang Qing insisted that the marshals make self-criticisms before a smaller group of students in order to pacify the furious crowd. At the smaller meeting in the Jingxi Hotel, Ye Jianying could hardly finish his self-criticism, prepared for him by Liu Zhijian, because of student jeering. In addition to the 2,000 students present at the meeting, many more had gathered outside and threatened to break in. Concerned about the safety of the marshals, Liu Zhijian and the other generals in charge directed Marshal Ye and the others to leave the hall through the back door.

When Lin Biao reported this to Mao, Mao became doubly angry because Jiang Qing had not informed him of the smaller meeting beforehand. To deflect Mao's criticism, Jiang Qing blamed Liu Zhijian, who, on Zhou Enlai's advice, agreed to make a self-criticism. While he was doing so, Kang Sheng suddenly interrupted him and shouted, "Liu Zhijian, you are not an 'eclecticist' [one who takes a middle road]. You yourself represent the Liu-Deng bourgeois reactionary line in the military. If this meeting is being held to criticize and assault, it is you, Liu Zhijian, who should be criticized and assaulted." Liu Zhijian thus lost his position after the meeting. It became known only later that Kang Sheng had denounced Liu on instructions from Mao. On January 8, 1967, on the advice of Jiang Qing and with the approval of Mao, Lin appointed Guan Feng deputy director of the General Political Department to replace Liu, and three days later Xu Xiangqian became the leader of a reorganized MCRSG. Jiang Qing took charge of personnel changes in the new MCRSG. Even before the reorganization of the MCRSG was announced, Yang Chengwu told Xu Xiangqian that Jiang had suggested to Mao that Xu Xiangqian head the new group, and Mao had accepted her suggestion. Then, Jiang sent the list of new group members to Xu for his "advice." She also went to Lin's residence to suggest that he appoint Guan Feng deputy director of the General Political Department and she herself as adviser to the new MCRSG. She told Lin that Mao had agreed to this arrangement. When Lin asked Mao about it, Mao said he had indeed agreed.[132]

In early January, with permission from the Party Central Committee, the Central Military Committee held an enlarged conference in Beijing. Among the participants were the commanders of the military regions and the heads of military headquarters in Beijing. In addition to reaching policy decisions about the Cultural Revolution in general, the conference participants adopted several policies designed to alleviate tension within the PLA. For example, attacks on military establishments were outlawed. For some time, the participants in the meeting had shared the leadership of the Cultural Revolution with Zhou Enlai and the CCRSG, who regularly attended the meetings. After the collapse of various institutions, the PLA, for all its difficulties, remained the only institution that could still function.

But the removal of Liu Zhijian had not eased the tension between the CCRSG and the military. On the contrary, the conference intensified the dispute since now the army was sharing the leadership of the Cultural Revolution with the CCRSG. After Liu's dismissal, Jiang Qing had turned her eyes to Xiao Hua, her next target. Lin and Ye, however, did not support Jiang's idea to remove Xiao Hua because Xiao was one of Lin's longtime subordinates. Lin told Jiang that since Xiao Hua was director of the General Political Department he would have to ask Mao about her proposal.

On January 19, Jiang Qing went to Lin's residence to discuss the issue with Lin and Ye. After she left, Ye told the secretaries that Mao had decided to remove Xiao Hua from office. At Jiang's request, Ye immediately left to attend a meeting at the Jingxi Hotel.[133] When Ye arrived at the hotel, the meeting, which was to discuss the Cultural Revolution in the military, had already begun. Chen Boda was criticizing the PLA for its arrogance and for putting too many restrictions on the Cultural Revolution. Even members of the CCRSG, he claimed, were intimidated by the idea of going to Sanzuomen, the MCRSG office. Chen himself was disgusted every time he passed by the place. "The military," he added, "has actually moved within the boundary of revisionism." Chen concluded by accusing Xiao Hua of abusing his position as head of the General Political Department.

Chen's speech enraged many military commanders. Xiao Hua tried to speak in self-defense, but Chen rudely interrupted him. "If you want to say something, say it at the mass rally this evening." Ye Jianying burst out in anger, "Chen Boda, you talk nonsense! To find fault with Xiao Hua is to tarnish the reputation of the PLA. The country is in a mess because of you, and now you want to bring disorder to the military!" Ye pounded his fist on the table so hard that he broke a finger. As the leader of the MCRSG, however, Xu Xiangqian was obliged to join Chen in criticizing Xiao Hua and the General Political Department, which brought a direct confrontation between the two marshals. Everyone at the meeting, including Chen Boda, was uncomfortable watching the conflict between Marshals Ye and Xu, and the meeting soon adjourned for the day.[134]

At midnight, radical students surrounded Xiao Hua's house, though Xiao managed to escape. The students broke into Xiao's office, pried open his safe, and removed top secret documents. Mao ordered an immediate investigation and asked Jiang Qing to see that the students left the house promptly.

Lin was outraged by the incident and asked Jiang Qing for an explanation. He was especially incensed by Chen's comment on revisionism within the army. He yelled at Jiang, reprimanded the CCRSG for its reckless disruption of the army, and threatened to resign. "You have no respect for the Central Military Committee," Lin shouted. "Who would ransack the house of the director of the General Political Department and steal documents like this without permission from the Central Military Committee?" When Ye Qun tried to calm him down, Lin asked her to send Jiang away because he could not stand her anymore. Lin also asked Ye to get his car ready because he wanted to go see the chairman right away. "I will resign, for I am unable to perform my duty anymore," Lin continued his tirade. Ye was so frightened and worried by Lin's outburst that she begged him to calm down. A secretary recalled later that he had never seen Lin so angry.[135] Lin was among the few people who ever dared raise his voice to Jiang Qing, and the event left a permanent scar on his relationship with her. Thereafter, Lin tried to avoid Jiang and prohibited Ye from seeing her as well.

On January 20, Lin asked Marshals Ye and Xu to chair an enlarged meeting of the Central Military Committee to announce Mao's positive comments about Xiao Hua. Out of embarrassment, no one from the CCRSG except Guan Feng attended the meeting. With the clear intention of excusing Jiang Qing from responsibility, Guan blamed Chen Boda for everything, saying that Chen had been drunk the day before and thus had not known what he was saying. With support from Mao and Lin, Xiao Hua and others disputed the criticism of the CCRSG. One after another, the generals condemned the group's activities since the beginning of the Cultural Revolution. Huang Yongsheng was particularly outspoken. To everyone's surprise, he even accused Jiang Qing of not listening to Mao. (Most people shared Huang's opinion but dared not say so.) Guan Feng immediately accused Huang of opposing the work of the CCRSG and trying to protect Jiang. Jiang Qing later claimed that the purpose of the meeting had been to oppose Mao and the CCRSG. She demanded an apology from Xu, chief of the MCRSG, who in his distress asked Huang to make a self-criticism instead because he had provoked Jiang Qing. Lin, however, was on Huang's side. He told Huang not to back off and not to make a self-criticism. Lin promised that he would report directly to Mao if anything happened to Huang.

In the increasing tension between the military and the CCRSG, Mao probably felt obliged to support his comrades in the military. On January 22, Mao received 40 military leaders who were participating in the enlarged conference mentioned above. After all of them complained about their predicament, Mao patiently explained the necessity of the Cultural Revolution but promised he would help maintain order in the PLA.[136] This meeting may have been part of Mao's preparation for having the PLA intervene in the Cultural Revolution on a large scale.

On January 23, Mao informed Lin of his decision to employ the PLA to support the leftists. The military asked Mao to first guarantee the stability of the PLA. Lin, together with Ye Jianying, Xu Xiangqian, Nie Rongzhen, and Yang Chengwu, had already worked out a nine-point command to implement Mao's decision. Lin asked the marshals to bring the draft to the enlarged meeting for further discussion. After some difficult bargaining with the CCRSG, Ye told Lin that only seven points in the original draft were agreeable to the CCRSG. Ye suggested that Lin ask Mao to resolve the disagreement. On January 28, Mao immediately ratified the seven points and added an item about the education of the children of senior officers. "These eight points are very good," Mao wrote on the document, "issue it as it is." Lin was relieved when Mao returned the document to him. "Long may you live, Chairman. [You deserve it] because you have approved this document," said Lin gratefully.[137]

This document, known as "The Eight-Point Order from the Central Military Committee," ordered the students to stop disrupting army headquarters and facilities, stop breaking into houses of military officials, and stop kidnapping, torturing, and insulting military officials. In addition, PLA soldiers and officers were to remain at their posts; military students in Beijing were to return at once to their schools; and field armies were not to participate in the Cultural Revolution.[138]

For a while, the orders helped protect military leaders and facilities. The radical students who brought most of the chaos to military establishments gradually left Beijing. However, the "Eight-Point Order" did not and could not achieve what Lin had desired in the long run. The chaos in the country as well as in the PLA was too profound to whisk away by decree. Radicals at military headquarters continued to cause problems after the students left Beijing. Moreover, after Mao ordered the PLA to support the leftists, local tensions between the military and the radicals continued and even increased.

In February the first serious debate regarding the Cultural Revolution at the central level got under way. Following the breakdown of most government institutions, the so-called Occasional Meetings (*pengtouhui*), presided over by Mao, Lin, Zhou, or members of the CCRSG, conducted daily routine work and made policy decisions. Regular participants were Politburo members, vice-premiers, and military commanders, as well as members of the CCRSG. The participants varied according to the agenda. In many cases, Mao himself decided who would attend, and he occasionally consulted with Zhou Enlai, Kang Sheng, and others. Regularly using his poor health as an excuse, Lin Biao seldom attended these meetings. At several February meetings, the marshals criticized the CCRSG's management of the Cultural Revolution. These criticisms came to be known as the "February Adverse Current."

In retrospect, the key issues were whether responsibility for the Cultural Revolution belonged with the party or the CCRSG; whether all cadres, including military officers, should be subject to assaults and criticism by the Red Guards; and whether stability in the PLA should take precedence over the Cultural Revolution.[139] When Mao launched the Cultural Revolution in the second half of 1966, most members of the Politburo had supported his decision or were at least willing to give him the benefit of the doubt out of respect for Mao. As events unfolded, they tried their best to understand and support the Cultural Revolution despite their growing doubts about its value. They accepted the Cultural Revolution as another effort to help the party solve the problems of bureaucracy and corruption. As staunch Communists, none of them opposed the noble mission ascribed to the revolution by Mao—to make sure that China was forever under the control of the Communist Party. It was their understanding that the Cultural Revolution would end within a few months. Ye Jianying said in an address on October 9, 1966, that according to the chairman's tentative plan, the movement would last until January 1967.[140] Xiao Jinguang, commander of the navy, also recalled in his memoirs his naive belief in October 1966 that the Cultural Revolution would end in a few months.[141]

What high officials saw by February 1967, however, was completely beyond all expectations. Red Guards and radicals were rebelling against all party and state establishments. Factories had closed, and peasants had left the fields to take part in the revolution. Only Mao, Lin, Zhou, and members of the CCRSG were exempt from the radicals' assaults. Most participants in the February meetings had been criticized and harassed by the Red Guards. Many senior officials had been especially upset by two developments in the Cultural Revolution in January 1967: the overthrow of the Shanghai municipal Party Committee in the "January Revolution," and the fall of Tao Zhu, who had been in charge of the Cultural Revolution and the CCRSG since June 1966.

In that "January Revolution," radical groups headed by Wang Hongwen had taken over the two major newspapers in Shanghai, *Wenhui bao* and *Jiefang ribao*, both of which were controlled by the municipal Party Committee. This was the first time in the Cultural Revolution that power had been seized from former local officials who were labeled "bourgeois capitalist roaders." The CCRSG, with Mao's support, immediately approved the action. On January 4, the group sent Zhang Chunqiao and Yao Wenyuan to Shanghai to direct the movement. Zhang and Yao delivered Mao's recent directive to leaders of the radicals in Shanghai, "[It is necessary] to start an overall class struggle nationwide," the directive read.

"Beijing, Shanghai, Tianjin, and the Northeast are crucial areas [for the success of this struggle]."[142] On January 6, several radical groups in Shanghai held a mass rally to criticize Governor Cao Diqiu and other municipal leaders. In flyers circulated at the end of the meeting, the radicals announced they would no longer acknowledge the leadership of the Shanghai municipal government and Party Committee led by Cao Diqiu. On January 8, Mao congratulated the Shanghai radicals in a speech to the members of the CCRSG. He described the events in Shanghai as a revolution in which one class overthrew another class, and suggested that the central presses in Beijing issue editorials in support of the Shanghai radicals. Thus, radicals in Shanghai set the example for the "seizure of power" from local party organizations. After serious internal disputes among themselves, the leading radical organizations in the city announced on February 5 that the "Shanghai Commune" would take over the duties of the municipal government and Party Committee. Senior officials in Beijing understandably had serious doubts about allowing mass organizations to overthrow party establishments.

The second development in January was the fall of Tao Zhu. In June 1966 he had transferred from Guangzhou to Beijing to replace Lu Dingyi as director of the Central Propaganda Department. In August 1966, Tao became a member of the Standing Committee of the Politburo and adviser to the CCRSG at the Eleventh Plenum. However, he never relished the job of directing the Cultural Revolution and could not get along with Jiang Qing and other members of the group. As with veteran cadres, Tao Zhu's acceptance of the Cultural Revolution rested on his trust in and respect for Mao. Tao, Vice-Premier Li Xiannian, and others often met at Li Fuchun's house to discuss and come to an understanding of Mao's directives, but the discussions only added to their confusion. Tao never understood what Mao actually wanted from the Cultural Revolution or what it was supposed to achieve.[143] Working on the basis of his own instincts, he often found himself opposing Jiang Qing.

When the conflict between Jiang and Tao intensified, the chairman adopted his usual strategy of detaching himself from both sides and watching developments. In late December and early January, Mao still favored Tao; he told him on December 29, 1966, that Jiang Qing was "narrow-minded" and "intolerant" and asked Tao not to take what she said seriously. Mao also instructed Tao to travel to the provinces after New Year's Day. Before Tao left Mao's residence, Mao handed him a list of more than twenty provincial leaders and said: "These people should be 'put into the fire,' but do not 'burn' them."[144]

Several days later, however, in speeches to the Red Guards, the CCRSG suddenly labeled Tao "the biggest conservative" in China, linking Tao with Liu Shaoqi and Deng Xiaoping and alleging that he had tried to protect them. The Red Guards took this as permission to bombard Tao with criticism. When they hung big-character posters proclaiming "Down with Tao Zhu" on the streets, Tao was in a meeting with Zhou and others attempting to solve the problems of the Cultural Revolution. The sudden assault on Tao puzzled even the members of the Standing Committee of the Politburo. When Li Fuchun asked Mao about the matter, Mao claimed to know nothing about it.[145] It is still not clear whether Mao had prior knowledge of the criticism of Tao Zhu, which was made chiefly by Jiang Qing and Chen Boda. At least one source indicates that Jiang reported the incident to Mao immediately after the speeches.[146] Another source indicates that Mao discussed his disagreements with Tao Zhu on several important matters at his birthday party on December 26 in the presence of members of the CCRSG.[147]

Tao learned of the Red Guard posters when he returned home after midnight on January 3. When he checked with Zhou Enlai about Mao's response to the criticism, Zhou told Tao only that Mao wondered whether Tao had suppressed the mass movement. Zhou, who was unsure of Mao's thinking at the moment, told Tao to "stop working" and "rest at home for a few days." Several days after this informal suspension, Mao's attitude toward Tao Zhu became clear.[148] On January 8, at the same meeting at which he approved the January Revolution, Mao recalled that it was Deng Xiaoping who had introduced Tao Zhu to Beijing. Mao, however, shunned responsibility for Tao's fall by attributing it to the Red Guards. "I could not solve the problem of Tao and you could not either," he said. "Only after the Red Guards came, they solved the problem."[149] Mao therefore approved Tao's dismissal.

To many senior officials, the ouster of Tao was a serious violation of party principles. Tao was a member of the Standing Committee of the Politburo, secretary of the General Secretariat, and minister of the Central Propaganda Department. In theory, at least, no single person could decide the removal of anyone from such high posts without formal approval from the party. Although these principles had never stopped Mao from getting rid of individuals he disliked in the past, he had at least gone through the motions that "legitimized" the removal. Usually Mao brought up such matters at party conferences as subjects for "discussion." Previous dismissals of leaders such as Peng Dehuai and Liu Shaoqi had thus appeared to be party decisions rather than Mao's personal decisions. This time, however, Mao made no attempt to legitimize the dismissal of Tao. Speeches to the Red Guards by Chen Boda and Jiang Qing, who held no position higher than Mao's secretary and head of the CCRSG, became the final verdict on Tao Zhu. In theory, this was a serious violation of party principles.

Mao himself may have realized this soon after he confirmed Tao's ouster. On February 10, Mao suddenly blamed Chen Boda and Jiang Qing for Tao's removal. "You [Chen Boda] were only a member of the Standing Committee, but [you] decided the fall of another member of the Standing Committee," Mao told Chen Boda angrily. "You never came to me for advice unless you yourself were in trouble." Mao also rebuked Jiang as "ambitious but with little talent." He instructed the CCRSG to hold a meeting to criticize both of them, but the group permitted no outsiders to attend.[150] Chen Boda, who dreaded being criticized by Mao, told Wang Li after the meeting that he was so despondent over always being caught between Mao and Jiang that he wanted to commit suicide. He had checked and found no proof that committing suicide was against Communist Party rules. Wang Li reported this to Zhou Enlai, who was able to calm Chen down.[151]

Chen's dilemma was understandable. Like Liu Zhijian's job as liaison between the CCRSG and the army, Chen's job as chief of the CCRSG was an impossible one. He was in a better position than Liu had been to figure out what Mao had in mind, but there was no guarantee that he could always fathom Mao's whimsical moods. On August 12, 1966, the CCRSG headed by Chen drafted a plan to ask provincial administrations to prevent local students from coming to Beijing in large numbers and to advise students already in Beijing to return to their homes.[152] However, these instructions were never published or issued. At Mao's direction, Chen had to change his opinion once again, and four days later he made a speech encouraging students to come to Beijing to establish "revolutionary connections" and "grow up in a revolutionary storm."[153]

Chen also had to change his public stance on the Shanghai Commune the following January. Early in January 1967, Chen criticized Shanghai radicals, saying that what was happening in Shanghai was "a new form of the capitalist line." He said that the radicals should "supervise" local administrations rather than "seize power" from them. Chen later suffered criticism for this stance after Mao decided to support the Shanghai radicals. Constantly changing his own position to follow Mao's ideas, however, did not always help Chen's political career. Part of Chen's problem was that neither Mao nor Jiang Qing had any respect for him. Wang Li recalled an occasion on which Mao scolded Chen in front of others, telling him to "get out of here" unless he was prepared to do whatever Mao told him to do.[154] From time to time, Chen also had to take responsibility for

Jiang Qing's errors. Chen told Wang Li that he had no prior knowledge of the rally at which he had criticized Tao Zhu. He was awakened by a call from Jiang Qing only minutes before the meeting, asking him to accompany her to receive Red Guards. At the meeting he had repeated what Jiang Qing told him to say. Later, when Mao was angry at Chen and Jiang and asked them to make self-criticisms, Chen was the only victim at the meeting. Jiang Qing excused herself from attending because of poor health. "Jiang Qing had pushed me into a corner and left me no room to live," Chen told Wang Li when he spoke to Wang about contemplating suicide.

Lin Biao was among the few who understood Chen's problem because he and Chen faced the same dilemma. But because Mao and others respected Lin, Chen's position was even worse than his own. Like Lin, Chen had also privately expressed his sympathy for Liu Shaoqi. Chen had first sensed Mao's intention to get rid of Liu Shaoqi when he helped Mao draft the "Twenty-three Items" in 1964. He told Wang Li: "Liu Shaoqi is an authentic Marxist. What shall we do?" Chen had asked Wang, who later suggested to Liu that he make a self-criticism to Mao.[155] After Mao criticized Chen Boda, Lin was probably the only person who let his colleagues know of his sympathy for Chen. Lin told Wang Li that Chen was only a *shusheng* (intellectual), and "it is not easy for a *shusheng* to shoulder such heavy responsibilities." Chen was grateful to Lin, which may explain why Chen later allied himself with Lin against Jiang Qing and Zhang Chunqiao at Lushan.[156]

Although Mao did not want to criticize Jiang Qing and Chen Boda in public, several senior officials soon learned that he had done so in private. Ye Jianying and Li Xiannian were present when Mao gave vent to his anger at Chen and Jiang. Tan Zhenlin and others also heard Mao criticize Chen and Jiang at Li Fuchun's home on February 10.[157] Several marshals and vice-premiers took the opportunity to add their own criticism of the CCRSG at other meetings, perhaps because the CCRSG excluded them from its own closed meetings to criticize Jiang and Chen.

On February 11, Zhou Enlai chaired a meeting to discuss how to "promote production by encouraging revolution." It was at this meeting that Ye Jianying, Xu Xiangqian, and others publicly blamed Chen for the chaos in the party, the country, and the army. Before the meeting, the marshals had learned that Mao objected to using the name "Shanghai Commune" for the new administrative body in Shanghai. They angrily demanded to know why Chen had not brought an issue as important as the "Shanghai Commune"—which indicated a change in the nation's political system— to the Politburo for discussion. They also questioned whether it was right to carry out the Cultural Revolution without party leadership and the participation of the PLA. This discussion, however, did not last long, for Zhou cautiously interrupted the marshals and changed the subject.

On February 16, the veteran cadres and the CCRSG had a more serious confrontation at another Central Working Meeting. This second confrontation involved Chen Pixian, party secretary of Shanghai. After Mao gave Tao Zhu a list of provincial leaders to be protected, Zhou arranged for those on the list to come to Beijing to avoid harassment by local radicals. Chen Pixian was on the list, but the Shanghai radicals refused to let him go. Vice-Premier Tan Zhenlin wanted to protect Chen, who was one of his long-term subordinates, and asked Zhang Chunqiao at the Central Meeting to do so; but Zhang refused, saying he first had to discuss the matter with the radicals. The veteran cadres at the meeting could no longer contain their anger at the CCRSG and the Cultural Revolution and turned the meeting into a forum for their grievances.

Mao was not surprised by their anger or complaints. He knew the Cultural Revolution had brought personal humiliation and other difficulties to most of his subordinates. He had intended that all along. "Do not take it too seriously if these old comrades complain about the Cultural Revolution," Mao had told Wang Li, Zhang Chunqiao, and Yao Wenyuan with a smile. His smile disappeared, however, when he learned the details of the complaints. Xu Xiangqian attributed the harassment of veteran cadres to a *Hongqi* editorial in October 1966, which had publicized Mao's injunction to "thoroughly criticize the bourgeois reactionary line." What alarmed Mao even more was that Zhou Enlai agreed with Xu's complaint and claimed that he had not had an opportunity to read the editorial before it was published. Mao interrupted Wang Li's report at this point to state that the party constitution did not stipulate that an editorial should be submitted for Zhou's approval.[158] Statements by Chen Yi and Tan Zhenlin irritated Mao even more. Chen Yi had said little, but what he said touched three especially sensitive points for Mao: Khrushchev, Stalin in his last years, and the Yanan Rectification Movement. Next to the Lushan Conference of 1959, the final years of Stalin was the last topic Mao wanted to discuss. Also, Mao was unwilling to accept criticism of the Yanan Rectification Movement against the "Internationalists" because he suspected that some of his comrades still had sympathy for their leader, Wang Ming.[159]

Among the participants, Tan Zhenlin was the most outspoken and emotional. "Your purpose is to get rid of all the veteran cadres—to finish off each and every one of them." Tan shouted at the CCRSG. "This is by far the cruelest struggle in party history."[160] In his excitement, Tan made an assertion Mao later made him regret. Tan ascribed his own miseries in the Cultural Revolution to three things he regretted having done—participating in the early stages of the Chinese Revolution, following Mao during those stages, and living to the age of 65.[161] In short, Tan suggested that if he were not one of the veteran cadres he would have been better off in the Cultural Revolution. After the February 16 meeting, Tan was still so angry that he wrote letters to Mao and Lin Biao repeating his grievances against the Cultural Revolution. In one he referred to Jiang Qing as a "latter-day Empress Wu Zetian," who usurped power after her husband died to become the only empress in the Tan dynasty.[162] According to Wang Li, it was understandable that Tan hated Jiang Qing, Zhang Chunqiao, and Yao Wenyuan most of all. Tan believed that they were responsible for what was happening in Shanghai and eastern China, which was Tan's power base. Most provincial and military leaders in the area were Tan's long-term subordinates.[163]

As Roderick MacFarquhar has noted, the February meetings were not unlike those that took place at the Lushan Conference in 1959 during the Great Leap Forward.[164] On the earlier occasion, senior officials had stepped forward to expose the disruptive consequences of one of Mao's mass movements, and Mao had responded accordingly. Now, however, an angry Mao could no longer tolerate defiance—or even criticism—of his personal authority. He not only disregarded opposing opinions, but also dismissed those who offered them as enemies of his leadership. This was not the last time Mao used his veto power to suppress opposing opinions of the Cultural Revolution.[165] A few years later, in 1970, Mao crushed another revolt against the Cultural Revolution—or, rather, against the members of the former CCRSG—at Lushan, a revolt led by Lin Biao himself.

Mao decided to confront the challenge posed by his comrades among the senior cadres. Around midnight on February 18, Mao summoned Zhou Enlai, Kang Sheng, Ye Qun, Ye Jianying, Li Fuchun, Li Xiannian, and Xie Fuzhi for a meeting. There, he reprimanded the marshals and vice-premiers for their speeches at the February meetings. Mao insisted that no one could deny the achievements of the CCRSG; whoever opposed the group opposed Mao himself. "Comrade Ye Qun," Mao called out, "You tell Lin Biao that his position is not stable at all, for somebody wants his power. Tell him to get ready. If this Cultural Revolution should fail, I will take him out of Beijing and go up to Jinggang Mountain to start guerrilla warfare again." Mao then berated the marshals. "You said that Jiang Qing and Chen Boda are not capable [of doing the job]," he told them, "then, let you, Chen Yi, head the CCRSG. Arrest Chen Boda and

Jiang Qing and execute them. Send Kang Sheng into exile, too. I will also step down and you can invite Wang Ming back to chair the party. The whole party will not agree if you, Chen Yi, want to negate the case of the Yanan Rectification Movement."[166] After this speech, Mao suspended Chen Yi, Tan Zhenlin, and Xu Xiangqian from their jobs and forced them to make self-criticisms.

From February 22 to March 18, the Politburo held seven meetings to criticize veteran cadres who had spoken against the CCRSG.[167] Zhou Enlai chaired these central meetings. Li Fuchun was also criticized because Mao learned that the marshals and vice-premiers often got together in his home, where, according to Kang Sheng, they had founded a "black club," or undesirable faction.[168] As a result, most of these senior officials actually "stepped aside," and the CCRSG gradually superseded the Politburo and the State Council, both of which could no longer function because most of their members had been ousted or similarly stepped aside. In March 1967, Mao granted the CCRSG the right to organize Occasional Working Meetings, which replaced the working meetings of the Politburo and the State Council. Although Zhou was one of the organizers of these meetings, he had effectively lost power to the CCRSG.[169] Jiang Qing was so carried away by her victory that she once said to Zhou, mockingly, "You, Zhou Enlai, also have to come over to our meetings, because your meetings do not work anymore."[170]

At the outset of the Cultural Revolution, Mao probably had no intention of ousting so many marshals, vice-premiers, and other senior officials; he probably just wanted to force them to accept criticism from the masses, which was part of his agenda for the revolution. But after the February meetings Mao was disillusioned by his comrades' rejection of the Cultural Revolution. As the movement got out of control, Mao did not want to risk imperiling his impending victory in his last revolution. He decided to teach the marshals and other senior cadres a lesson. As Deng Xiaoping put it later, "Whoever did not listen to him, [Mao] would punish in some way. However, he knew to what extent the person should be punished."[171] Later, paranoid about his marshals' response to his criticism of the February Adverse Current, Mao asked a vice-commander of the air force to move to Xishan, where most of the marshals and vice-premiers lived and secretly report his findings to Mao.[172] Meanwhile, at Mao's instigation, Kang Sheng found new ways to harass the senior cadres. In addition to encouraging Red Guards and radicals to criticize these men in public, Kang turned to their family members and staffs, including secretaries, bodyguards, chefs, and chauffeurs, to hold regular meetings of criticism in the cadres' own homes. During Mao's time, a party branch was organized in each of the residences of the high officials, consisting of party members among the staff and the family members. Now Kang Sheng asked the secretary of the household party branch to be in charge of these meetings. This was all for the purpose of "teaching a lesson" to the veteran revolutionaries. After several months of harassment of this kind, Lin Biao suggested that Mao "liberate" the seniors because of their poor health and old age. After Mao agreed, Lin sent Huang Yongsheng and Wu Faxian to the homes of the cadres to inform them of their freedom. But Mao exempted Tan Zhenlin from the decision, because he was still angry about what Tan had said about him.[173]

One consequence of the repression of the February Adverse Current was that the party lost another opportunity to end the Cultural Revolution in early 1967. But even if Mao and the party had wanted to end it then, they might not have been able to do so. After Mao's counterattack on the February Adverse Current, Mao found that he had bound himself tightly to the chariot of the Cultural Revolution. He had no alternative but to carry on with it for the foreseeable future. By the summer of 1967, Mao at last achieved his goal of creating "great chaos under heaven" (*tianxia daluan*), but there was still no "ultimate harmony under heaven" (*tianxia dazhi*) in sight.

Lin Biao (left) and Mao Zedong (right), 1930s. *Renmin huabo* (*People's Pictures*), October 1971, p. 17. Courtesy of the East Asian Collection, Hoover Institution, Stanford University.

Lin Biao, president of Anti-Japanese Military and Political University (*Kangri junzheng daxue*), addresses the students, Yanan, 1937. *Renmin huabo*, October 1971, p. 28. Courtesy of the East Asian Collection, Hoover Institution, Stanford University.

Left to right, Lin Biao, Zhou Enlai, and Mao Zedong, 1967. *Renmin huabo*, March 1968, p. 32. Courtesy of the East Asian Collection, Hoover Institution, Stanford University.

Lin Biao and General Wu Faxian, Tiananmen Square, October 1970. Generals Qiu Huizou (center) and Li Zuopeng (obscured) stand in the background. Yang Kelin, ed., *Wenge bowuguan* (*Cultural Revolution Museum*), p. 410. Courtesy of the Library of the Center for Chinese Studies, University of California, Berkeley.

Lin Biao and Jiang Qing (Madame Mao), Tiananmen
Square, possibly late 1966. *Wenge bowuguan* pt. 2, p. 428.
Courtesy of the Library of the Center for Chinese Studies,
University of California, Berkeley.

Lin Biao (left) on an inspec-
tion tour with his son, Lin
Liguo (center), and Air
Force General Wang Bing-
zhang (right), July 23, 1970.
Wenge bowuguan, pt. 2,
p. 422. Courtesy of the
Library of the Center for
Chinese Studies, University
of California, Berkeley.

Ye Qun and Lin's generals on the Great Wall, July 1970. *Left to right,* Li Zuopeng, Qiu Huizuo, Ye Qun, Wu Faxian, and Huang Yongsheng. *Wenge bowuguan,* pt. 2, p. 422. Courtesy of the Library of the Center for Chinese Studies, University of California, Berkeley.

Lin Biao and his wife, Ye Qun, Tiananmen Square, ca. 1969–70. *Wenge bowuguan,* pt. 2, p. 414. Courtesy of the Library of the Center for Chinese Studies, University of California, Berkeley.

Above, the aftermath of the plane crash of September 13, 1971, Mongolia. *Left*, the document identified by the Chinese government as Lin Biao's handwritten order for a coup d'état. According to the official interpretation, the document reads, "Please follow the message passed on by Liguo and Yuchi." *Wenge bowuguan*, pt. 2, p. 430. Courtesy of the Library of the Center for Chinese Studies, University of California, Berkeley.

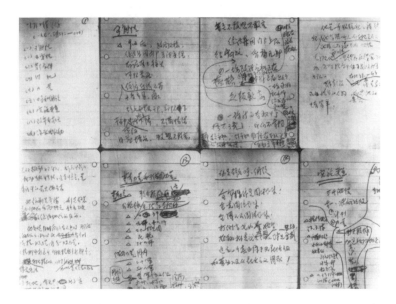

Portions of "Project 571," Lin Biao's alleged coup plan. *Wenge bowuguan*, pt. 2, p. 427. Courtesy of the Library of the Center for Chinese Studies, University of California, Berkeley.

Defendants at the open trial of the Lin Biao and Jiang Qing counter-revolutionary cliques, 1980–81. *Left to right*, Qiu Huizuo, Wu Faxian, Jiang Qing, Huang Yongsheng, and Chen Boda. *Wenge bowuguan*, pt. 2, pp. 594–95. Courtesy of the Library of the Center for Chinese Studies, University of California, Berkeley.

5

The Conflict Between Power Groups

In 1967–68 two power groups emerged from the chaos of the Cultural Revolution: Jiang Qing and her Central Cultural Revolution Small Group (CCRSG), and Lin Biao and his generals. Chinese officials now lump them together as "counter-revolutionary cliques" responsible for the disastrous consequences of the Cultural Revolution. In the "Indictment of the Special Procurator Under the Supreme People's Procurator of the People's Republic of China," the two groups were accused of acting "in collusion during the 'great cultural revolution' and, taking advantage of their positions and the power at their disposal, framed and persecuted Communist Party and state leaders in a premeditated way in their attempt to usurp party leadership and state power and overthrow the political power of the dictatorship of the proletariat."[1] This accusation is misleading, however, because during much of the Cultural Revolution the two groups had little in common and were often in conflict. Ross Terrill quotes a Chinese intellectual who said, "The Cultural Revolution became nothing more than a struggle for power between Jiang and Lin."[2] Many events in the Cultural Revolution related directly to the friction between the two groups. In fact, what happened at the Second Plenum of the Ninth Central Committee in 1970, which marked the beginning of the rupture between Mao and Lin, was the result of accumulated tension between the two.[3]

The Rise of Lin Biao's Generals

After most marshals had "stepped aside" during the February Adverse Current, Yang Chengwu and Xiao Hua remained in charge of routine work at the Central Military Committee. At the time, military leaders became subordinate to the CCRSG because of the removal of many reputed marshals and generals from their positions. Xiao Hua was under constant assault from radicals, and chaos continued at military headquarters in Beijing. This disarray lasted until after "the May 13 incident," an episode in the armed conflict (*wudou*) between military conservative factions (*bao-huang pai*) and radical factions (*zaofan pai*), in which the latter enjoyed the support of local Red Guard organizations all the way up to military headquarters in Beijing.

By May 1967, officers in military headquarters found themselves divided into factions based on their attitudes toward leading officers at headquarters. In the air force, the dispute revolved around Commander Wu Faxian and Political Commissar Yu Lijin. In the navy, the struggle focused on Political Commissar Li Zuopeng, and in the General Logistics Department on Qiu Huizuo, the director. Both factions refused to budge. Conservatives were under increasing pressure from military and local radicals, who charged that the conservatives did not respond to Mao's call to rebel against authorities. More and more officers joined radical organizations and the conservatives became a minority, especially in such units as military hospitals, schools, and performing arts troupes.

In desperation, conservatives in the various military headquarters decided to hold an artistic performance on May 13, 1967, as a show of their determination and strength. Army radicals, with the support of one of Jiang Qing's right-hand men, Kuai Dafu, leader of the local Red Guards, promised to disrupt it. Worried that armed conflict might occur, Xiao Hua refused to approve the performance. Several women from the conservative faction in the performing arts troupe of the air force went directly to Mao for support, taking advantage of Mao's intimate relationship with some of them. Mao then referred them to Lin Biao. Since it was Mao who sent the women to him, Lin felt obliged to approve the performance.

The performance took place the evening of May 13 at Zhanlanguan Theater. As soon as it began, radicals from within and outside the military rushed into the theater to harass the performers, confident that the CCRSG would support their action. The theater soon resembled a battlefield, and many conservatives were wounded.

As soon as the leaders at military headquarters learned of the melee at the theater, they sent help for the conservatives. Xiao Jinguang, commander of the navy, Li Zuopeng, and a group of navy officers rushed to the theater to rescue the them. As they left, Li Zuopeng called Wu Faxian, commander of the air force, to ask him to guard the navy compound, which was next door to the air force headquarters. Wu immediately announced a state of emergency at air force headquarters, requiring all officers to stay in their offices ready to go to the aid of the conservatives at the theater if necessary. He also reported to Lin Biao and Zhou Enlai.[4]

When the naval officers arrived at the theater, they joined the fight and helped evacuate the wounded from the theater. As more partisans on both sides arrived, the fight threatened to get completely out of control. The confrontation lasted several hours, until Chen Boda, sent by the CCRSG, and Xiao Hua, sent by Lin Biao, arrived at the theater. The two men succeeded in restoring order and then criticized the conservatives for not canceling the performance.

The following evening, May 14, Zhou Enlai held a meeting at the Great Hall of the People to discuss the problem. Zhou supported Xiao Hua in blaming the conservatives; the conservatives resented being so criticized and reported the incident to Lin Biao.

In responding to the report, Lin Biao for the first time revealed his opinion about a Cultural Revolution issue, because of its possible consequences to the stability of the armed forces. He believed that if chaos spread at the military headquarters in Beijing the whole military institution might collapse. By so stating he ran the risk of open confrontation with the CCRSG, but it seemed to him that he had little choice.

On the morning of May 15, Lin asked Ye and several leading military officers to go to the hospital to express his sympathy for the conservative victims of the fight. On May 23, the conservatives staged another performance, this one at Tiananmen Square. Lin Biao asked Ye to attend and ordered troops from the Beijing garrison to maintain order for the show. After Lin had thus openly supported the military conservatives, Zhou Enlai and the CCRSG changed their positions. On June 9 the conservatives gave a third performance at the Great Hall of the People. This time, not only Lin Biao, but also Zhou Enlai, Chen Boda, Kang Sheng, Li Fuchun, and Li Xiannian attended the show, thereby demonstrating their support for the conservative faction in the dispute. With open support from Lin Biao, and now also from the CCRSG, the military conservatives achieved a complete victory over their radical rivals and the local radical students formerly aided by the CCRSG. After this show of support, the military finally restored stability at its Beijing headquarters under the supervision of Generals Yang Chengwu, Wu Faxian, Li Zuopeng, and Qiu Huizuo, all of whom were Lin's longtime subordinates. Gradually the military regained its independence from the CCRSG.

There are still differing interpretations of the May 13 incident. Some party historians use it to support their argument that Lin took the opportunity to enhance his personal power and thus to form a "Lin Biao clique" by appointing his generals to important military positions. Others disagree, believing that the decision actually came from Mao.[5] Whatever the case, the decision to restore control of the PLA to Lin's generals was an important one. By the summer of 1967, the chaos in the nation had become a virtual civil war. Even Mao no longer maintained his optimistic fantasies about the Cultural Revolution. He admitted to Edgar Snow that "the conflict during the Cultural Revolution developed into war between factions—first with spears, then rifles, then mortars."[6] The restoration of order had to begin at military headquarters in Beijing. Once that was done, the military could help bring the country under control. The urgent need to restore national order may explain why Lin gained the upper hand and managed to grant power to his generals. It may also be assumed that Mao approved of this development.[7]

In June 1967, Mao toured the South to check on the progress of the Cultural Revolution. To guarantee Mao's security, Yang Chengwu, Yu Lijin, and Li Zuopeng accompanied him on the tour. Because Yang Chengwu was the acting chief of staff, Zhou Enlai suggested that Lin Biao appoint an ad hoc committee to run the military in Yang's absence, which would last several months. Lin agreed, and designated Wu Faxian, Qiu Huizuo, and Zhang Xiuchuan (Zhang was deputy political commissar of the navy) to the committee, with Wu as the ranking official.[8]

The ad hoc committee reported to the Occasional Meeting of the CCRSG and also participated in the Occasional Meetings. When Yang Chengwu returned from the South in September, the ad hoc committee disbanded and control of the military reverted to the Working Group of the Central Military Committee headed by Yang Chengwu. The members of the ad hoc committee as well as Ye Qun and Li Zuopeng joined the newly established Working Group. Later, in March 1968, Huang Yongsheng replaced Yang Chengwu as head of the group; Wu Faxian was the deputy chief. Although Ye Qun was a member of the Working Group, she never attended meetings. The other members of the group were Xie Fuzhi, Liu Xianquan, Wen Yucheng, Zhang Caiqian, Li Desheng, and Ji Dengkui, though not everyone worked with the group at the same time. Until the Lin Biao incident in 1971, the Working Group and not the Central Military Committee continued to direct the military.[9] However, the Working Group was only in charge of routine work. It issued all orders under the name of the Central Military Committee, or under the joint names of the General Political Department, the Department of the General Staff, and the Department of General Logistics.

Since the Cultural Revolution was still raging, it was impossible for the PLA to achieve complete internal stability. Startling events continued to take place in the military, among the most mysterious of which was the simultaneous fall of Yang Chengwu, the acting chief of staff; Yu Lijin, political commissar of the air force; and Fu Chongbi, commander of the Beijing garrison. On March 22, 1968, the Central Military Committee unexpectedly announced the dismissal of the three men from their posts, denouncing them for having "made mistakes" and charging Yu with treason.[10] Why these men suddenly lost favor with Mao and Lin is still unclear. One possibility is that they were victims of the conflicts between the competing power groups headed by Lin and Jiang Qing.

Yang Chengwu had been Lin's subordinate since the Red Army period, and the two had always gotten along well. After the fall of Luo Ruiqing in 1965, Lin suggested that Yang be made acting chief of staff. When he appointed the Working Group in September 1967, Lin made Yang its chief. The two families were also close. Ye Qun had helped arrange for Yang's daughter, Yang Yi, to work at the air force press with her own daughter, Lin Doudou (also known as Lin Liheng).

During the Cultural Revolution, however, Yang Chengwu also won the trust of Jiang Qing, who often asked him for personal favors and in whom she confided her political problems. For instance, Jiang even asked Yang to help her to handle a box of "black," or secret, materials about her early life in Shanghai. In the 1930s, before marrying Mao, Jiang Qing had been a movie actress in Shanghai, a not altogether reputable profession. During the Cultural Revolution, information about her life in Shanghai fell into the hands of Red Guards and radicals when they ransacked the municipal archives and libraries. Jiang was much worried that her political opponents would use these materials against her. Jiang asked Wu Faxian to help her find these materials using local air force units and brought everything to Beijing. Later, Jiang asked Yang Chengwu to store the materials and then to burn them in the presence of Xie Fuzhi and Qi Benyu.

Jiang also put Yang in charge of another of her projects, drafting "An Outline of the History of the Two-Line Struggle," a new version of the party history. Yang organized a group of more than 30 writers from the armed services, including his daughter, but at Jiang's insistence the finished party history mentioned only three names: Mao Zedong, Lin Biao, and Jiang Qing. When Jiang brought the finished history to Mao for approval, Mao angrily threw it to the ground and ordered her to burn all copies and send everyone in the writing group back to their original work units.[11]

Yang gradually fell out of favor with Mao and Lin by the end of 1967. The first indication of this concerned Yang Chengwu's article "Establishing the Great and Absolute Authority of Mao Zedong Thought." The article was drafted by Yang's subordinates at the Department of the General Staff. Before its publication, Yang sent a draft to Mao, which Mao passed on to Chen Boda and Yao Wenyuan without reading. After Chen Boda approved the draft, Yang Chengwu published the article on November 13, 1967, under his own name. Yang, who was very proud of it, told Wu Faxian excitedly that after Luo Ruiqing had read the article, which included the criticism of Luo Ruiqing, Luo immediately confessed that he had never formally joined the party. However, on December 17, 1967, Mao publicly criticized the article on the ground that the title was inappropriate. "All authority is relative," Mao asserted. "Authority is established through the practice of revolutionary struggle, not through certain announcements."[12]

For Yang Chengwu, misfortunes came in pairs. His relationship with Lin Biao was also deteriorating. One day, the CCRSG viewed an opera rehearsal in order to decide whether it was suitable for public release as a "model opera." During the Cultural Revolution, Jiang was especially keen on "reforming" Beijing operas. She personally helped direct eight operas, honoring them as "model operas."[13] For a while, only the CCRSG, and Jiang Qing in particular, could decide which new operas or movies should be released to the public. Jiang Qing invited Lin Biao to attend the rehearsal of one model opera that night. Yang Chengwu, however, had not reconfirmed Lin's plan to attend the rehearsal, and as was his habit, Lin took his sleeping pills at 8:00 P.M. and was in bed before his office was notified of Jiang's invitation. Jiang insisted that Lin be present and delayed the performance until he arrived. Once the performance started, Ye Qun called Yang Chengwu and Wu Faxian to the lobby and scolded them. "You two ungrateful men! As soon as you become acting chief of staff and deputy chief of staff you snub Commander Lin. What are you up?" Wu was puzzled because it was unusual for Ye to lose her temper over such a trivial matter. The situation was awkward but nothing more, and Lin himself said nothing about it afterward.[14]

Thereafter Yang became very cautious and often avoided meetings of the Working Group and the Occasional Meetings of the CCRSG. But another seemingly trivial matter triggered a chain of events that finally led to Yang's dismissal. One day in March, Wang Fei, director of the General Office of the air force, and Zhou Yuchi, Wang's assistant, reported to Wu Faxian that the wife of one of Yu Lijin's secretaries believed that her husband was having an affair with Yang Chengwu's daughter.[15] During the Cultural Revolution, everyone except Mao and a very few others in high places was punished severely for any extramarital affair that became known. In this instance, the two people involved were the secretary of the air force commissar and the daughter of the acting chief of staff. Wu told

Wang and Zhou to do nothing until he looked into the situation. They could talk to Yu's secretary, but should do or say nothing to harm the reputation of Yang Chengwu's daughter.

Yu's secretary insisted on his innocence, but Wang and Zhou took him into custody anyway. Wu became angry when he learned of this because he thought it was inappropriate to detain Yu's secretary without consulting Yu first. In addition, Wu was already unhappy with Wang Fei and Zhou Yuchi, because he thought they had behaved arrogantly since becoming friendly with Lin Biao's son, an air force officer. They often made false accusations against their colleagues, and Wu suspected that the accusation against Yu's secretary was another one.[16] Wu therefore criticized Zhou Yuchi for his imprudence.

To Wu's surprise, Ye Qun called him the evening after he reprimanded Zhou Yuchi to ask why he was accusing Liguo of usurping his power. "If you think it is no good for Liguo to stay in the air force, he can leave," Ye shouted angrily. Confused, Wu tried to explain that the incident had nothing to do with Liguo. Ye, however, would not listen to Wu's protestations. "What are you afraid of?" Ye continued. "Even Commander Lin said that it was right to detain Yu's secretary. It was a move to protect Acting Chief of Staff Yang's reputation."[17]

As soon as Wu put down the phone, he received a call from Zhao Zizhen, Yang Chengwu's wife, demanding that Wu free Yu's secretary immediately. Wu was thus caught between conflicting pressures from two powerfully connected women: the wife of Lin Biao on the one hand and the wife of Yang Chengwu on the other, neither of whom he could afford to offend.

The next day, Zhao Zizhen and Yu Lijin visited Ye Qun. Zhao cried and asked her to report the matter to Lin. "Wu Faxian tried to ruin the reputation of Acting Chief of Staff Yang," Zhao claimed. "Please ask Commander Lin to criticize Wu." By now, the alleged affair between Yang's daughter and Yu's secretary had developed into a confrontation between the acting chief of staff and the air force commissar on the one side and the air force commander on the other. Lin was therefore forced to choose sides. After careful consideration and probably under Ye's influence, Lin decided to back Wu. Lin told Wu that Zhao Zizhen and Yu Lijin had accused Wu of opposing Yang Chengwu. "They are seeking control of the air force," Lin told Wu. "Don't be afraid. You shouldn't shrink from challenging Yang Chengwu."[18]

Although Lin sided with Wu on this matter, there was not yet any other indication that he had decided to oust Yang. The decision to dismiss Yang Chengwu was Mao's, not Lin's. When Lin Biao announced the dismissal of Yang Chengwu as well as Yu Lijin and Fu Chongbi on March 24, 1968, he said that Mao had held four discussions of the issues involved before making the decision.[19] At 1:00 A.M. on March 23, 1968, Wu received a call from the Central General Office asking him to come immediately to the Great Hall of the People. When Wu arrived, he saw among others Mao, Lin, Zhou Enlai, Chen Boda, Kang Sheng, Jiang Qing, Zhang Chunqiao, Yao Wenyuan, Xie Fuzhi, Ye Qun, and Wang Dongxing. As soon as Mao saw Wu, he told him, "You are right and I support you." Then, Mao checked with Lin concerning a replacement for Yang Chengwu as chief of staff and accepted Lin's suggestion that the job go to Huang Yongsheng. Even Wu was surprised by the decision to dismiss Yang and Yu. If it was because of Yang's daughter's affair, the punishment was too severe. As for Yu Lijin, Mao said that Commander Xu Shiyou of the Nanjing Military Region had sent him information that Yu Lijin had once betrayed the revolution during the war. Mao ordered Yu arrested and the charge investigated.

The real reasons for the fall of Yang Chengwu, Yu Lijin, and Fu Chongbi are still not clear. The three cases had no direct connections. Information revealed later suggests that Fu Chongbi's fall was the work of Jiang Qing, who personally disliked him. One Chinese writer assumes that Jiang Qing was angry with Fu Chongbi because Fu chanced upon the information about Jiang's early life in Shanghai.[20] In retrospect, it seems that Lin had become unhappy with Yang for two reasons. First, Yang did not get along with Lin's other generals. In his speech denouncing Yang, Yu, and Fu, Lin reproached Yang for being too ambitious and for being unable to get along with other military leaders such as Xie Fuzhi, Han Xianchu, and Huang Yongsheng.[21] With the army's stability still precarious, Lin did not want disputes among his generals.

Yang may also have offended Lin by his close association with Jiang Qing. According to Wang Nianyi, Yang had annoyed Lin by writing several admiring letters to Jiang. When Mao toured the provinces in the summer of 1967, Yang had accompanied him. According to Wang, Yang had refused to report to Ye Qun the content of Mao's discussions during the tour.[22] Whatever the reasons, it was Mao who made the decision to dismiss Yang. In a speech delivered after Lin's fall, Mao blamed Lin for deceiving him in the case of Yang Chengwu and for causing him to make a wrong decision. Wang also suggests that although Lin made the speech denouncing Yang on March 24, he failed to explain why Yang, Yu, and Fu should be ousted. The reason for that, according to Wang, was that Lin had not known how to explain their dismissal until Ye Qun brought him Mao's instructions on what he should say. According to Lin's secretary, it was Ye Qun who called Lin's staff from Mao's quarters after 7:00 P.M. on

March 24—two hours before the meeting—and told them how to prepare Lin's speech in accord with Mao's instructions.[23] One by-product of this event was that Huang Yongsheng, who had been one of Lin's major supporters, became chief of staff.

From the Ninth Party Congress to the Lushan Conference of 1970: Increasing Tension Between the Two Power Groups

The conflict between the two power groups intensified after Yang Chengwu's ouster. The major problem was that Lin's generals could not get along with Jiang Qing, whose behavior was capricious and unpredictable. She was difficult to work with because of her "subjectivism, theatrical ways, and sensitive ego."[24] She reveled in using her position as Mao's wife to force other people to do her bidding. For Jiang, the Cultural Revolution had a personal meaning—it was the instrument she used to enhance her personal reputation and power. Ross Terrill suggests that Jiang Qing's personal quest is the key to understanding the Cultural Revolution.[25]

Unlike Yang Chengwu, Huang Yongsheng did not think much of Jiang Qing as a political leader, and he believed that she did not always represent Mao. Despite their growing irritation with Jiang's subjectivity and imperiousness, however, the generals were still awed by Jiang because she stood in the reflection of Mao's glory. And one never knew when an issue would became personal. After Huang became head of the Working Group of the Central Military Committee, he and the generals decided to "stay at a respectable distance" from Jiang Qing and the CCRSG.

Meanwhile, Jiang Qing became increasingly discontented with the members of the Working Group because of their reluctance to accede to her wishes. Two months after Huang became the PLA chief of staff and head of the Working Group, Jiang Qing complained to one of her colleagues that Huang did not appear to be ideal for his position. Then one day in May 1968, Jiang suddenly charged the Working Group with usurping her power and withholding information from her. She demanded that Huang Yongsheng and Wu Faxian be suspended from the Occasional Meetings of the CCRSG and that they make self-criticisms. What angered her was a recent decision by the Working Group. At the beginning of the Cultural Revolution, the central government had decided that the PLA must report all decisions on troop maneuvers, even down to the platoon level, to Mao, Lin, Zhou Enlai, and the CCRSG. After Huang became chief of staff, Mao decided that it was no longer necessary to send such decisions to the CCRSG and wrote on his copy of one such decision, "From now on, reports like this should be sent only to Mao, Lin, and Zhou." When Jiang Qing found out that she was being left out of decisions on military affairs, she accused Huang and Wu of "blocking her access to information."

As usual, Zhou Enlai was caught in the middle. After considering the matter, Zhou, together with Kang Sheng and Yao Wenyuan, asked Huang and Wu to make self-criticisms to Jiang Qing. Lin Biao, however, told his generals not to back down, because it was Mao who had decided to leave the CCRSG out of the routing of military decisions. As a result, Huang Yongsheng and Wu Faxian refused to make self-criticisms.

The Party Central Committee had decided earlier that Huang Yongsheng would head a delegation to Albania in late 1968. Jiang Qing, however, announced that Huang Yongsheng's upcoming visit would be canceled if Huang refused to make a self-criticism. This put the Foreign Ministry in an awkward position. The ministry had already informed the Albanian government of Huang's visit, and it would be difficult to explain a change in the head of the delegation. After Zhou reported this flap to Mao, Mao criticized Jiang Qing and said that Huang would head the delegation and that the Working Group would continue its routine work.[26] Thereafter, the relationship between the two groups became even more strained.

By late 1968, Jiang Qing was already working to oust Huang Yongsheng. In a report to Mao and Lin on the Cultural Revolution in Guangdong, she included a long comment about how the conservatives were taking power in the South with support from "someone in the central government." Obviously, this someone was Huang Yongsheng, who had been in charge of the Guangdong area before going to Beijing. Jiang suggested that the report, together with her comments, be released to the country. Neither Mao nor Lin responded to her request.[27] Jiang then suggested that Lin appoint Zhang Chunqiao director of the Department of General Politics of the PLA, but Lin refused. In retaliation, Jiang rejected one candidate after another that the Working Group selected for the position, and the position remained unfilled until Li Desheng was appointed in April 1970.[28]

The tension between the armed forces and the CCRSG grew as the Ninth Party Congress, scheduled for April 1969, approached. As the split between the two groups became clear, more people joined the military group because they could not get along with Jiang Qing. By the end of 1968, only five members remained in the CCRSG—Chen Boda, Jiang Qing, Kang Sheng, Zhang Chunqiao, and Yao Wenyuan. Zhang and Yao had become Jiang's right-hand men, and Kang had long been Jiang's adviser. The relationship between Jiang and Chen, however, was deteriorating.[29] At several Occasional Meetings, Jiang initiated criticism of Chen and encouraged the military group to join her. But the generals refused because Lin had voiced his support for Chen. Ye Qun reassured Chen Boda of this support later on, when Chen called her to complain about his difficulties with Jiang Qing.[30]

Chen Boda moved still closer to Lin Biao after the dispute over the drafts of the report to the Ninth Party Congress. Mao had decided at the Twelfth Plenum of the Eighth Central Committee in December 1968 that Lin Biao would give a report to the Ninth Party Congress and ordered Chen Boda to help Lin draft it.[31] After several discussions, Lin and Chen decided that the theme of the report would be "Strive to Build China into a Great Socialist Country," which would also be the title of the political report. In fact, the title of Lin and Chen's draft of the political report to the Ninth Party Congress was very similar to that of Zhou's report to the first meeting of the Fourth People's Congress several years later, on January 13, 1975, "March Toward the Glorious Objective of Four Modernizations," which to many indicated a national transition from focusing on the Cultural Revolution to emphasizing economic policies. Also, according to Cheng Qian, as early as January 28, 1968, Chen Boda wrote Mao to suggest enhancing the development of the electronics industry.[32]

In a draft of the first section of the report, Chen wrote that the purpose of the Cultural Revolution was to promote socialist production and raise the people's living standard, both materially and culturally. In a meeting called to discuss Chen's draft, which was chaired by Mao, Jiang Qing, Zhang Chunqiao, and Yao Wenyuan objected to the theme, claiming that it incorporated the theory that "the forces of production alone will be decisive for social development" (*wei shengchanli luan*). Mao agreed with them and rejected Chen's draft, saying that it emphasized economic development at the cost of revolution and class struggle. Mao then asked Kang Sheng, Zhang Chunqiao, and Yao Wenyuan to produce another draft.[33]

Chen, however, continued to work on his own draft, hoping that Mao would in the end prefer his version. After all, over the years Chen had drafted many important documents for Mao and made important contributions to the development of Mao Zedong Thought. The competition between the two groups intensified as the Ninth Congress approached. When Chen sent Mao a second draft, the envelope was returned several days later, unopened. Chen could not believe that Mao would not even bother to open the envelope before returning it. "I cried when I found this out and I had never cried so hard," Chen told Ye Yonglie, his biographer. "I was hurt, I was really hurt."[34]

As Lin Biao once said, Chen Boda was only a *shusheng* (intellectual). This means that Chen lacked the shrewdness and flexibility of a politician and stubbornly insisted on using facts if he believed they were right. At another meeting Mao called to discuss the report drafted by Kang, Zhang, and Yao, Chen clung to his own version when no one else dared to venture a differing opinion. "It is better to concentrate on developing the economy," he insisted. "If we focus only on the [Cultural Revolution] movement, it will remind people of E. Bernstein's statement that 'a movement is everything and no specific purpose is needed except the movement itself.'" Most of the people at the meeting feared for Chen and watched carefully for Mao's reaction. Mao indeed was angry at the comment. "You, Chen Boda, just could not wait," Mao said angrily. "It has been only half a month and you come back to seek revenge. You will never change your nature, just as both imperialism and Marxism cannot change."[35]

After Mao criticized Chen Boda, Jiang Qing and Kang Sheng took the opportunity to organize several meetings to continue the criticism. Lin's generals, however, remained silent at these meetings. While Ye Qun occasionally expressed her support for Jiang Qing, Lin Biao had his own way of showing his dissatisfaction with the version of the report drafted by Zhang Chunqiao and the others.[36] He detached himself from the preparation of the report after Mao rejected his ideas, ideas that Chen had incorporated into his own draft. When Zhang sent the finished report to Lin Biao, Lin refused to sign it, and Zhang had to find someone to forge Lin's signature. Lin did not touch the report before he presented it to the Ninth Party Congress.[37] It is no wonder that Jiang Qing complained afterward that Lin's presentation was poor and that he stuttered during his speech.

Wang Dongxing also gradually identified himself with the military group.[38] For many reasons, Wang was a key figure in the central power struggle, not simply because of his position as head of Unit 8341 (the military unit of the Party Central Committee's Regiment of Guards) but also because of his close relationship to Mao. He was in charge of Mao's personal staff and was one of the few who had free access to Mao. Others, even Zhou Enlai and Lin Biao, did not. Usually, he was in a better position than anyone else to approach Mao and ascertain his thinking. Wang had secret information about many high officials, including Mao, which he could use either to protect himself or to undermine his opponents. He told Ye Qun in private that he kept a record of everything he did for Mao and Jiang Qing in case anything went wrong.[39] Despite this caution, Wang was often caught between Mao and Jiang. Once, Jiang asked Wang to fire one of Mao's nurses, of whom she was jealous. Knowing that the nurse was one of Mao's favorites, Wang refused Jiang's request. She was infuriated and scolded him harshly. Her daughter, Li Na, also joined in the criticism of Wang. When Wang turned to Lin for help, Lin told Wang to tell Jiang Qing that Mao had the right to choose his own staff without interference from anyone. Wang was grateful for Lin's help because he knew Lin was among the few people who could intimidate Jiang Qing. Mao was pleased too.[40]

What finally pushed Wang over to Lin's side, however, was not Jiang Qing's capriciousness but Mao's treatment of Wang. Before the Ninth Party Congress, Wang was seriously ill with a bleeding ulcer and had to be hospitalized. Zhou Enlai took Dr. Li Zhisui, Mao's personal physician, and Nurse Wu to Mao to break the news to him. Although the three expressed grave concern about Wang's condition and even shed tears, Mao remained impassive, saying only, "If Wang is sick, get him the treatment the doctor suggests. We can do nothing else." As they left the room, they heard Mao make a derisive remark about their tears. According to Dr. Li, Mao even suspected that Zhou and Li were colluding with Wang Dongxing against him.[41] Such things happened repeatedly during the years of Wang's service to Mao and greatly hurt Wang's feelings. During Wang's stay in the hospital, neither Mao nor Jiang Qing went to see him. When Ye Qun took her daughter, Doudou, to see him at Lin's request, Wang's wife told Ye, "They want Wang to die because he knows too much."[42]

Even Zhou Enlai, who was "obsequious before Jiang Qing" in Li Zhisui's eyes, made gestures toward Lin's group, although he did so cautiously and only to a limited degree. After the Lin Biao incident, Li came to believe that Lin and Zhou were closer than Zhou wanted to admit.[43] Lin understood Zhou's awkward position and often told his subordinates they should respect Zhou because no one, not even Mao or Lin himself, could handle national affairs as effectively as Zhou. He warned Wu Faxian not to listen to Jiang Qing and Kang Sheng, who had said that Zhou Enlai was responsible for a previous anti-military slogan. "I don't think that Kang Sheng can handle the work of a premier," Lin told Wu, believing that Kang aspired to replace Zhou.[44] Whenever Jiang Qing initiated criticism of Zhou, Lin's group remained silent. This is perhaps why Zhou placed more trust in Lin's generals than in members of Jiang's group. After Wang Dongxing became too ill to work, Zhou asked Wu Faxian to help him prepare for the Ninth Party Congress.

Although the Ninth Congress elected all the major members of both groups to the Politburo, these seeming victories did not heal the rift between them. Before the vote for Party Central Committee members, Ye Qun told the generals to persuade several military delegates not to vote for Jiang Qing and her men. In the voting, Jiang Qing and her supporters, including Kang Sheng, Zhang Chunqiao, and Yao Wenyuan, received fewer votes than Lin's group. Jiang felt humiliated and demanded an investigation.[45]

To retaliate against Ye Qun, Jiang Qing openly turned against Lin Biao after the Ninth Congress. At one Politburo meeting, Jiang criticized Lin's reading of the report to the Party Congress. At another, Jiang suddenly suggested that Lin's speech at the Twelfth Plenum of the Eighth Central Committee, in which he had compared the Cultural Revolution to the European Renaissance, should be criticized. After the meeting, Jiang asked Yao Wenyuan to write an article criticizing the ideas of the Renaissance in order to deprecate Lin. Jiang raised the same issue at six subsequent Politburo meetings, demanding that Yao's article be published as a government document. On each occasion, only Kang Sheng, Zhang Chunqiao, and Yao Wenyuan supported her; all the others, including Zhou Enlai, Chen Boda, Li Xiannian, Wang Dongxing, Ye Qun, and Lin's generals, opposed her. Jiang continued to push her idea until even the long-suffering Zhou could stand it no longer. "Comrade Jiang Qing," Zhou told her, "you should understand the basic principle of collective leadership, that is, the principles of democratic centralism. Only three or four of you agreed on this issue, but the majority opposed it. Yet you still raise the issue again and again. If you insist on issuing the article as a party document, we have to get the chairman's approval." Jiang knew Mao would not approve it, so she gave up the idea of criticizing Lin for the time being.[46]

The Second Plenum: The Beginning of the Mao-Lin Rupture

It was against this background that the Second Plenum of the Ninth Central Committee was held from August 23 to September 6, 1970. On the evening of May 8, 1970, Wang Dongxing had returned to Beijing from Hangzhou, where Mao was staying, with Mao's instructions on the upcoming Fourth People's Congress. Wang Dongxing told the Politburo that Mao wanted the Politburo to discuss ways of summing up the experience of the Cultural Revolution, restoring government institutions to their regular functioning, developing the economy, and preparing for war. In addition, Mao wanted the Politburo to set up groups to draft a new state constitution, prepare reports for the forthcoming congress, and discuss whether the new constitution should retain the position of state chairman. Mao himself preferred to eliminate the position. "I, Mao Zedong, do not want to be chairman," Wang read Mao's own words. "If [the Politburo] decides to maintain such a position, it is Lin Biao who should hold the position."[47]

After the meeting, Wang Dongxing wanted to go to Lin's home to report Mao's instructions in person, but Lin had already gone to bed. Wang Dongxing then invited Ye Qun, Huang Yongsheng, Wu Faxian, Li Zuopeng, and Qiu Huizuo to his residence for a late dinner. When their conversation turned to the topic of the state chairman, Wang repeated what Mao had said—that if there were to be such an office, Lin Biao should hold it. Everybody present was pleased that once again Mao trusted Lin.

At the Politburo meeting on May 9, Zhou decided that Kang Sheng should head the group to draft the new constitution. The other members of the group were to be Chen Boda, Zhang Chunqiao, Wu Faxian, Li Zuopeng, and Ji Dengkui. On the matter of the state chairmanship, the group would report its decision to the Politburo. Mao himself had already worked out a brief outline for the new constitution, and all the group actually did was fill in the details.

On the afternoon of July 17, the Working Group of the Central Military Committee went to Lin's residence to report on their recent work. After they told Lin of Mao's instructions concerning the state chairmanship, Lin made the following statement:

> I will not take the position of state chairman. It is not appropriate. Chairman Mao should hold this position as state chairman and it is perfectly justifiable. China is such a big country, it will not be appropriate if this big country has no symbolic head to represent it. Chairman Mao should be the only candidate for state chairman. Of course, Mao is in his old age now and may have difficulty going abroad to visit other countries. We can have several vice-chairmen, who can visit other countries in Mao's place. I am not fit for the position of vice-chairman because of my poor health. I will be unable to attend public activities or visit other countries. In a word, Mao should be the state chairman.[48]

This was not the first time Lin had expressed himself on the subject of the state chairmanship. In mid-April, Lin had asked his secretaries to compose a written statement of his views and send it to the Party Central Committee. China, he believed, should have a state chairman and Mao should hold the office. It did not matter to him whether there was one vice-chairman or more than one, but he himself would not take the job.[49] This statement by Lin, especially the last point, was later used as proof that Lin harbored ambitions to become state chairman because he implausibly claimed he did not want to be a vice-chairman.[50] Soon thereafter, Mao's secretary Xu Yefu called Lin to convey Mao's latest opinion, that the new constitution could keep the position of state chairman. Mao wrote Lin, "As to the state chairman, I will not hold the position, and neither will you. Let Old Dong [Dong Biwu] be the state chairman and, at the same time, put several younger people in the position of vice-chairman."[51]

Because of the persisting conflicts between the military and the CCRSG, the task of drafting the new constitution under Kang Sheng did not go smoothly. The group soon split, with Kang Sheng and Zhang Chunqiao on one side, Chen Boda, Wu Faxian, and Li Zuopeng on the other. Ji Dengkui remained neutral, perhaps because he had only recently joined the central government from Henan province and was still uninformed about the issues that divided the others. The disputes focused on two issues: whether the new constitution should maintain the office of the state chairman, and whether it should contain the sentence, "Mao Zedong Thought is the guiding principle of the country." Wu Faxian and Li Zuopeng supported both ideas, and Kang Sheng and Zhang Chunqiao opposed them. Kang suggested that instead of keeping the state chairmanship the constitution should create a new position, "director of the Committee of the People's Congress."

Only four people attended the August 13 meeting, Kang Sheng, Chen Boda, Zhang Chunqiao, and Wu Faxian. When they finally agreed that they could not agree on the issue of state chairman, Kang Sheng proposed that they leave the matter to the Politburo. On the issue of the State Council, Wu suggested writing that Mao Zedong Thought should be the guideline for the work of the State Council. Kang Sheng and Zhang Chunqiao opposed the suggestion, insisting that Mao himself would not agree to it. What Zhang said after this, however, annoyed Wu. "Some people mention Marxism and Mao Zedong Thought all the time," Zhang said to Wu, "but it does not mean that they are real Marxists. Someone claimed that [Mao] 'creatively' developed Marxism, but even Khrushchev had 'creatively' developed Marxism." Wu took Zhang's remarks as an assault on Lin Biao, because everyone knew that it was Lin who said that Mao had "creatively" developed Marxism.

Both Wu and Chen Boda believed that Zhang's statements referred to Lin. Wu immediately reported Zhang's remarks to Zhou Enlai and Huang Yongsheng, who expressed support for Wu's stand. Huang also told Wu he would ask Li Zuopeng to return to Beijing to help Wu in subsequent group meetings.[52]

The next day, August 14, Wu asked Ye Qun to report Zhang's remark to Lin Biao. An hour later, Ye called Wu to tell him that Lin approved and wanted Wu to stand firm on the issue. "This is very good," Ye added excitedly, "Zhang Chunqiao has at last given us an excuse to get at him."

It was in this context that the Second Plenum of the Ninth Central Committee met in August 1970 at Lushan. In retrospect, this Lushan Conference, in the middle of the Cultural Revolution, had much in common with the previous Lushan Conference of 1959, which met in the midst of the Great Leap Forward. Party comrades had become increasingly discontented with the disturbing results of mass movements initiated by Mao. At both conferences, someone from the military, Peng Dehuai in 1959 and Lin Biao in 1970, voiced the concerns of most participants. And on both occasions Mao took the criticism as a challenge to his power and crushed the challengers.

Like the Lushan Conference of 1959, the Second Plenum of the Ninth Central Committee began calmly. Before it began, Ye Qun took generals Wu, Li, and Qiu sightseeing around Lushan. She told them that the impending meeting was of little importance and that they should take the opportunity to relax for several days after a long period of hard work. As to the dispute with Kang Sheng and Zhang Chunqiao over provisions of the new constitution, Ye Qun told the generals that the issue might not even surface. Lin himself had prepared no speeches for the conference.

At the opening session on August 23, Mao unexpectedly announced that Lin Biao would give a speech, surprising even Ye Qun. The reason for this unexpected development is not altogether clear. According to Wang Dongxing, Mao had received members of the Standing Committee of the Politburo for a final discussion of the agenda just before the conference began. When Mao had asked the members who wanted to make a speech, Lin expressed his desire to say a few words, and Mao granted Lin's wish.[53] Ye Qun later told Lin's generals that Lin Biao actually told Mao that he would say a few words about the new constitution because someone had objected to the idea of adding the statement affirming Mao's genius. Lin then told Mao of the dispute just described between Wu Faxian and Zhang Chunqiao. Zhou Enlai then added his agreement with Lin's remarks when Mao asked Zhou's opinion. Mao instructed Lin to criticize Zhang Chunqiao, but without mentioning Zhang's name. "It must be Jiang Qing who backed Zhang Chunqiao," Mao told Lin.[54]

According to the written record of Lin's speech at the opening session, Lin emphasized the importance of the new constitution's confirming Mao's position as a "great leader, head of state, and supreme commander." By saying that, Lin revealed his opinion that there should be a state chairmanship and that Mao should hold the office. Lin also suggested that the constitution acknowledge Mao Zedong Thought as the guiding principle of the country. Further, he stated that it could not be denied that Mao was a genius, which was a reply to Zhang's previous speech at the constitution preparation meetings. Lin, however, did not mention Zhang's name, as Mao had requested.[55]

Delegates received Lin's speech favorably, especially those who knew of the conflict between Lin's group and the CCRSG. Most of the delegates had suffered during the Red Guard stage of the Cultural Revolution, and still resented the treatment they had received. When they learned that Zhang Chunqiao was the individual Lin had criticized for opposing the idea that Mao was a genius, many of them took pleasure in Zhang's misfortune. Most of them preferred Lin's group to Jiang Qing's because it was less radical about the issues of the Cultural Revolution. Military representatives constituted about 40 percent of the membership of the Ninth Party Central Committee, and most could identify with Lin and his generals because of their common experiences in the war. After the speech, many of them and other senior cadres shook Lin's hand to show their support.

At the enlarged Politburo meeting that evening, Zhou Enlai decided, upon the suggestion of General Wu Faxian, that the participants would discuss Lin's speech at the subsequent sections of conference. Wang Dongxing chaired the meeting when the recordings of Lin's speech were played twice, and Zhou Enlai, Chen Boda, and Kang Sheng were all present. Some delegates suggested that Lin's speech be printed, and Mao consented, on the condition that Lin should see the final draft before it was issued.[56]

Group discussions were organized by region—there was a Central China Group, a South China Group, and a North China Group, for example. Delegates from the central government were assigned to various groups. Over the next two days, Lin and his men gained the upper hand over Jiang Qing and Zhang Chunqiao. According to the conference minutes, Chen Boda, Ye Qun, and the generals took the lead in criticizing Zhang Chunqiao, although no one mentioned his name. "Someone wanted to take advantage of the chairman's great modesty to disgrace Mao and Mao Zedong Thought," Chen Boda claimed in a meeting of the North China Group. "Comrade Lin Biao had mentioned many times that Mao is a great genius," Ye Qun similarly said at the Central China Group, "Should he take all this back? Never!" At the same time, Wu Faxian was telling the Southwest China Group, "During the discussions in preparation for the new version of the state constitution, someone opposed the idea that Chairman Mao had ingeniously and creatively developed Marxism and

Leninism and described this idea as 'ridiculous.'" Qiu Huizuo and Li Zuopeng expressed similar ideas at the Northwest Group and the South Central Group.[57]

When participants learned that the "someone" alluded to by Wu and others was Zhang Chunqiao, they erupted in anger. Many who blamed the CCRSG for their personal agonies during the Cultural Revolution took the opportunity to settle personal scores with the group. In their speeches, they demanded that the "someone" referred to "make a self-criticism at the conference" and "be expelled from the Central Committee immediately to receive re-education from the workers and peasants." Chen Yi, for example, discussed Mao's genius in detail and insisted that it would be a serious matter for "someone" to deny it.[58]

Yang Dezhi, who became chief of staff of the PLA in 1983, recalled the second Lushan Conference this way:

> Everyone hated Zhang Chunqiao, so we criticized him severely. Zhang Chunqiao was so nervous and frustrated that he smoked one cigarette after another. Every day the ashtray in front of him was filled with cigarette butts. Watching him in such an awkward plight, we were extremely delighted. For the first time since the Cultural Revolution began we finally got a chance to vent the anger in our hearts as never before.[59]

The general opinions against Zhang Chunqiao and the CCRSG also produced the following passage from Briefing no. 6 of the Second Plenum (also known as Briefing no. 2 of the North China Group):

> Many felt that their understanding of Vice-Chairman Lin's speech was enhanced after they listened to Comrade Chen Boda's speech at the group meeting. They expressed the greatest and strongest anger when they learned that some people within the party tried to deny that the great leader Chairman Mao is the greatest genius of our time. It is a very serious problem that within the party there are some members with such reactionary ideas. These people are power-hungry conspirators, reactionaries in the extreme, and authentic counter-revolutionary revisionists.[60]

Popular support for Lin's position was further evident when many members and supplementary members of the Party Central Committee wrote a joint letter on behalf of their provinces, cities, and autonomous regions to Mao and Lin Biao suggesting that Mao hold the position of state chairman.[61] Zhang Chunqiao might have faced an immediate purge as a counter-revolutionary had the conference continued in this vein. The tension grew so palpable that Mao, who did not attend the group discussions, had to make a decision.

Mao reacted quickly. Around noon of August 25, Wang Dongxing received a message that Mao wanted to see him immediately. When Wang arrived at Mao's place, Mao asked him whether he had read Briefing no. 6.

"Yes, I just read it," replied Wang, " I read it on my way here."

"They [Jiang Qing, Zhang Chunqiao, and Yao Wenyuan] had just left," Mao said. "They said that Briefing no. 6 spread enormous influence." Mao proceeded to criticize Wang Dongxing for supporting the notion that Mao should be the state chairman.

"I was angry when I heard from Chen Boda that some people became excited when they learned that Chairman Mao would not be the state chairman," said Wang, trying to defend himself. "When the masses discussed the revisions of the constitution," Wang added, "all supported the notion that you should be the state chairman."[62]

Mao, however, would not listen to Wang and continued to reproach him. Wang began to realize that the tide was about to turn. Other accounts also provide evidence that Jiang Qing came to Zhang's defense. She brought Zhang Chunqiao and Yao Wenyuan to Mao's residence to complain about what was happening at the conference. Lin and his generals wanted to "throw someone out," she allegedly said.[63] Jiang and others tried to convince Mao that the critique was actually directed at Mao and the Cultural Revolution. Their strategy succeeded. "They [Lin Biao, Chen Boda, and Lin's generals] only used their criticisms of Zhang Chunqiao for an excuse," Mao said later in August 1971. "They actually opposed me."[64]

After his talk with Wang Dongxing on August 25, Mao called an urgent meeting of members of the Standing Committee and the Politburo, where he spoke in Zhang's defense and voiced his discontent with Lin's group. He then adjourned the plenum and collected all the copies of Briefing no. 6. Mao later stated that he would not be state chairman and would advise Lin Biao not to be either. That seemingly innocuous statement was the first signal that Lin had begun to lose Mao's favor.

The conference was adjourned on August 26. On August 27, Wang Dongxing, on Zhou's advice, made a quick move to compromise and submitted his first self-criticism to Mao. In his letter, Wang expressed his deep regret for "not having listened to Mao" and for "violating the party discipline." He promised Mao that he would "learn a lesson" and would "follow Mao's instructions in the future without any reservations." Meanwhile, Zhou Enlai and Kang Sheng were asked to urge General Wu to make a self-criticism, too. When Wu went to see Lin Biao for advice on the evening of August 28, Lin, however, told him not to back down.[65]

On August 31, Mao issued a letter entitled "Some Opinions of Mine" to the reconvened Lushan Conference. In it he unexpectedly denounced

Chen Boda as a "political fraud" intent on deceiving the Central Committee. Chen had supported Lin Biao and was one of the authors of the second briefing of the North China Group, quoted above. At an enlarged Politburo meeting on September 1, Mao bid Chen Boda to make a self-criticism and indicated that he would give a second chance to those who had made "erroneous speeches" if they did so as well.[66] At Mao's instigation, the conference then proceeded to criticize Chen, Wu Faxian, Ye Qun, Qiu Huizuo, and Li Zuopeng.

As at the previous Lushan Conference of 1959, where Peng Dehuai's political career had ended, Lin Biao and his military men were the losers in the confrontation with Jiang's group at the Lushan Conference of 1970. Lin failed to win Mao's support in his effort to discredit Zhang Chunqiao. Instead, Mao made clear his discontent with Lin Biao. What is difficult to determine is why Mao suddenly turned against the man who had been his "closest comrade-in-arms" since the beginning of the Cultural Revolution. Perhaps their disagreement on the issue of the state chairmanship was the reason. Mao came to believe that Lin wanted to be the chairman himself, despite his protestations to the contrary. After the Lushan Conference, Mao's criticism of Lin and his generals became increasingly strong. In August 1971, one year after the conference, Mao began to accuse Lin and his lieutenants of plotting an "unaccomplished coup," which referred, bizarrely, to Lin's suggestion that Mao was a genius, that the new constitution should acknowledge his genius, and that the new constitution should maintain the position of state chairman and reserve the position for Mao.[67] Back in the summer of 1970, these two ideas had constituted Lin's strategy to defeat Zhang, not to offend Mao. Would he have been better off if he had denied Mao's talent?

Obviously, the key issue was still the Cultural Revolution and the fact that Mao trusted Jiang Qing and the CCRSG despite their weaknesses and limitations, rather than Lin and his generals. Lin's strategy of challenging Jiang's group during the conference had not succeeded. Lin and his generals probably did not realize that, given Mao's concerns, the course of events had turned against the military now that they had saved the country from total anarchy. Mao may have been worried that the military would become disproportionately powerful. Through the nationwide proliferation of "revolutionary committees," which consisted of representatives of the military, the masses, and the cadres, military officers had become heavily involved in administrative work at all levels, from the ministries of the central government to the smallest local district. Instead of civilian officials, military officers were in actual charge of most of the "revolutionary committees." After the restoration of national order in early 1970, it seemed unnecessary for military personnel to remain on the civilian posts. Military control of the governments seemed to have become an obstacle to rebuilding an effective civilian administrative system. It was time for the PLA to hand power back to the civilian administration. This might have affected Mao's decision to side with the Cultural Revolutionaries against the military.

On the issue of the state chairmanship, there is no evidence to support Mao's suspicion that Lin actually wanted the job himself. It is widely noted in the recent literature that Ye Qun had asked Wu Faxian what position Lin should take if there were no state chairman. However, according to Wu himself, it was Wang Dongxing, not Ye Qun, who raised the question with Cheng Shiqing, the commander of the Jiangxi Military Region, who in turn told Wu about it.[68] If the question was Wang's, not Ye Qun's, it can be considered a piece of evidence that Wang actively supported the idea of establishing the position of state chairman. Although Wang Dongxing has since denied Wu's allegation and maintained that it was Ye Qun who asked that famous question, he revealed details about his activities at Lushan.[69] The following is Wang's account of how he supported Lin Biao and Chen Boda at the conference:

> Chen Boda's provocative speech at [the meeting of] the North China Group made those who had no idea what was going on very excited. After Chen's speech, many other comrades made speeches to support [Chen's] stand on the issue and all suggested that the section of state chairmanship be established in the new constitution. I also spoke out at the meeting. Not having been able to see through Chen's conspiracy, I lent verbal support to Lin Biao's speech. "When the staff of the General Office of the Party Central Committee and soldiers of Unit 8341 discussed the issue of the new constitution," I said, "[All] expressed a sincere desire that Chairman Mao be the state chairman and that Vice-Chairman Lin Biao be vice–state chairman. . . . It is the desire of all the staff of the General Office of the Party Central Committee, of the entire Unit 8341, and of myself as well that [we] establish the section of state chairmanship in the constitution."
>
> I was so excited at the time that I *forgot* Mao's repeated suggestion to the Central Committee that he did not want a state chairmanship to be established in the Constitution.[70]

Despite his obvious efforts to support Chinese officials' (or Mao's) explanation of the events at Lushan, Wang's argument and defense add little credence to the official version. In the years of the Cultural Revolution, few dared or could afford to "forget" Mao's instructions about important issues. Wang's memory of the events at Lushan actually supports the argument that Mao's own opinion about the issue was not especially clear.

Otherwise, it is unlikely that Wang would have "forgotten" Mao's opinion. Mao soon let Wang Dongxing off the hook because Wang initiated his own self-criticism and "admitted his mistakes with sincerity."[71]

There are reasons to believe Lin had no interest in being state chairman or vice-chairman. In poor health and introverted by nature, Lin disliked public appearances and activities. According to his daughter, Doudou, Lin often had to be injected with imported medication before appearing in public during the Cultural Revolution. The medication kept him "up" for the duration of his public appearance but left him sick for weeks thereafter. In my interviews with two other secretaries of Lin, both of them agreed with this account.[72] No one seems to know, however, what exactly the "medicine" was. Lin's son-in-law told me that usually the bottle was labeled "Vitamin C."[73] Doudou later described an occasion on which Ye shut herself in her room crying because she could not stand to see Lin suffer as he did after a public appearance.[74]

Lin Biao abhorred receiving foreign guests, and a secretary has described several occasions on which he refused to do so. Once, Lin refused Mao's repeated requests that the two of them receive an Albanian delegation until Ye begged him to behave sensibly for the sake of his family. He later remarked to his bodyguard how much he hated doing such things.[75] Although these anecdotes may not fully explain why Lin did not want to be state chairman himself, they are evidence that Lin was not interested in carrying out the duties of the position. The new party constitution had already legalized Lin's position as Mao's successor, so there was no reason for Lin to further pursue a position with no real power and whose duties he detested.

Moreover, Lin must have known that any state chairman other than Mao would be in a vulnerable position. Mao did not want the chairmanship established because he himself had no interest in the title, yet he was reluctant to see anyone else claim it. He would have considered any person in such a position to be a potential competitor; this was the lesson Mao drew from his problems with the former state chairman, Liu Shaoqi.[76] In criticizing Lin Biao, Mao drew an analogy to the classical story of Sun Quan and Cao Cao. Sun Quan had urged Cao Cao to become emperor, a position of no use to Cao Cao. "Sun Quan wanted to put Cao Cao on a stove to burn him," Mao said, "and Lin Biao was doing the same thing to me." If Mao's reasoning was valid, why then would Lin choose to put himself on a stove?

Lin may have realized, however, that it was time to restore formal state institutions as a first step toward ending the Cultural Revolution and allowing the armed forces to return to their normal duties. Lin was in no position himself to make such decisions, but he had reason to see that they were made. Even before the Ninth Party Congress, Lin and Chen Boda had suggested in their version of the report to the Congress that it was time to focus on the national economy, which would have meant ending the Cultural Revolution. Later developments proved that Lin and Chen were right in their arguments for economic development and that Lin was also right about the state chairmanship. In 1982, China did restore the position of state chairman. "In terms of the state system, it is compulsory to have a state chairman to represent the country both inside and outside the state," declared Zhang Youyu, the state spokesman, in 1982. "To reestablish the position of state chairman is both truly necessary and wish-fulfilling for the Chinese people."[77] Why then was Lin Biao considered so wrong to propose the same idea in 1971, and why does the Chinese government still criticize him for doing so?

In more personal terms, Lin may have believed that a state chairman would relieve Lin himself of his awkward position as Mao's successor. Whoever became chairman or vice-chairman would assume the routine responsibilities that Lin was then shouldering, and Lin would be able to retreat from the public activities he hated so much. Vice-chairman of the Communist Party was a much more powerful, convenient, and safe position for him. But his wife and his followers did not necessarily agree, and each wanted him to become chairman for one reason or another.

The most interesting of Lin's supporters was Wang Dongxing, who pushed hard for Lin's nomination as state chairman. If Wang had missed Mao's point as he maintained, it was even more likely that Lin Biao, Chen Boda, and Lin's generals, who did not have the direct access to Mao that Wang had, were also ignorant of Mao's true wishes. Lin's generals might have mistaken Wang's position for Mao's own because of Wang's closeness to Mao. Wang's enthusiastic support for Lin during the Lushan Conference made some scholars wonder whether Mao had made the state chairmanship a test of Lin's loyalty.[78] As noted above, Mao did tell Lin, through his secretaries, that Mao was thinking of making Dong Biwu state chairman. And Lin was not the only one to support keeping a state chairmanship in the new constitution. The draft approved by the Politburo contained a section regarding the election and responsibilities of a state chairman.

In the end, Mao chose to save the political careers of Zhang Chunqiao and Yao Wenyuan and to criticize Lin's group at Lushan; in so doing he spurned one more opportunity to end the destructive Cultural Revolution and restore the country's formal state institutions. For the largely personal reasons discussed in Chapter 4, Mao stubbornly persisted in the

Cultural Revolution at the expense of the country and the people. Mao was angry because Lin's dispute with the CCRSG had led to an outpouring of criticism among the delegates toward the Cultural Revolution, and Lin's group won enough support at Lushan, in Mao's words, "to level Lushan or stop the earth's rotation."[79]

But Lin and his generals were no match for Mao in political maneuvering. In disappointment, Lin told his generals before he left Lushan, "We are generals, and we only know how to fight wars." Later, after the Lin Biao incident, party historians purposely interpreted this remark as evidence that Lin had already decided to plot a military coup against Mao. Frustrated by the events at Lushan, General Li Zuopeng also said, "There is no room for us [generals] in complicated political struggles."[80]

Lin was obviously angry at Mao when he left Lushan and told his generals not to make any self-criticisms.[81] General Wu did not submit his first self-criticism until September 29, and the other generals did not criticize themselves until March 1971.[82]

Interestingly, not a word was mentioned about Lin's "coup attempt" at Lushan during the 1980–81 open trial of the Lin Biao and Jiang Qing counter-revolutionary cliques. The "judges" may have realized that such an accusation would not have reinforced the underlying assumption of the trial—that Lin Biao and Jiang Qing had cooperated closely during the Cultural Revolution. Bringing public attention to the conflict at Lushan would only have undermined the strategy of putting the two groups on trial together.

Mao in Action

The events of the Second Plenum are important to understanding Lin's fall. In fact, the Lin Biao incident in its broadest sense consists of events that began at the Second Plenum and culminated in his flight from China in September 1971.[83] After the Second Plenum, Lin and his generals had increasing difficulties. By October 1970 a movement to criticize Chen Boda was under way within the party. Soon, Huang, Wu, Li, and Qiu also found themselves criticized at central meetings, although the criticisms had been implicit from the beginning. When Lin, who went to Beidaihe directly from Lushan after the Second Plenum, returned to Beijing in mid-September for National Day on October 1, Mao called him in for a chat. After the conversation, Lin summoned Wu Faxian and directed him to go to Mao and make a self-criticism. "In the past I told you not to make self-criticisms," Lin told Wu, "but now, I think you should go directly to Mao to report your dispute with Zhang Chunqiao and your work in the air force so that Mao will know you better." In telling Wu this, Lin was warning him that Mao was thinking of removing him from his position.[84]

Taking Lin's advice, Wu immediately had his secretaries draft a self-criticism for him. However, when he asked Mao's secretary for an appointment, he was told that Mao was too busy to see him before National Day. Mao also refused Wu's subsequent requests for an interview until the following May. Thus Wu decided to submit a written self-criticism to Mao on September 29. On October 14, Mao commented on Wu's self-criticism: "In the history of our party, there has never been such a thing as several people making trouble and trying to deceive over 200 committee members."[85] On October 12, Ye Qun had also submitted a written self-criticism to Mao, on which Mao's comment was even more severe: "When [someone] became a member of the Party Central Committee, [she] got carried away, as if [she] was the number one in the world."[86] According to Chinese political tradition, in criticizing Lin's wife Mao was demonstrating his dissatisfaction with Lin Biao as well.

Meanwhile, Mao initiated a series of movements to criticize Chen Boda and to tighten his political control. In October 1970, Mao proposed, in his comments on a report from Guizhou province, to educate the members of the party and the military about the ideological and political "lines" (*luxian*). On November 6, the Party Central Committee issued a circular urging the senior officials to study Marxist and Leninist works. On November 16, the Party Central Committee, under Mao's instruction, issued a document, "The Directives of Relaying Chen Boda's Anti-Party Activities [to the Whole Party]," which initiated a movement called "Criticizing Chen [Boda] and Rectifying the Party" (*pi Chen zheng feng*).

On December 18, Mao told Edgar Snow that he was disgusted by the expression "the Four Greats" (i.e., Great Teacher, Great Leader, Great Commander, and Great Helmsman), which served as another indicator that Mao was angry with Lin. Everybody knew during the Cultural Revolution that it was Lin Biao who first used the expression to refer to Mao.[87]

From December 22, 1970, to January 26, 1971, the Party Committee of the Beijing Military Region held meetings to criticize Chen Boda, which were later known as the *huabei huiyi* (North China Conference). Chen Boda had his strongest working relationship with the Beijing Military Region, which was in charge of northern China. All Politburo members attended the meeting. The military leaders who gathered for the meetings of the Central Military Committee in early January also joined the meetings later. By the time these meetings ended, critics had labeled Chen Boda "a traitor, a spy, and a careerist." Chen thereupon disappeared from the political stage. On January 8, 1971, Mao issued another directive to emphasize the need for an overall rectification movement to clear up misleading ideas. Under his instructions, the Central Military Committee began to hold enlarged meetings, beginning on January 9, with criticizing Chen Boda as the primary topic.

Despite all this, Mao himself became increasingly frustrated. He was not satisfied with the outcome of the strategies he had used against Lin and his generals, which he described as "mixing sand," "throwing stones," and "digging up the corner of the wall." On November 13, Mao had decided to add Li Desheng and Ji Dengkui to the Working Group of the Central Military Committee. This was what Mao meant by "mixing sand." In order to further weaken Lin's group, on January 24 Mao had dismissed Li Xuefeng, the chief of the North China Group during the Second Plenum at Lushan and commander of the Beijing Military Region, and Zheng Weishan, who was political commissar of the Beijing Military Region, because of their close working relationship with Chen Boda. These were instances of what Mao called "digging up the corner of [Lin's] wall."[88]

All this, to Mao's disappointment, did not break Lin's military group. Although Wu Faxian was increasingly worried about his political future, the other generals, especially Huang Yongsheng, still refused to make self-criticisms. According to Wang Dongxing, Mao was upset by the results of the North China Conference and the enlarged meetings of the Central Military Committee, because neither one criticized Chen as Mao had expected.[89]

The military group's failure to criticize Chen Boda convinced Mao that Lin's generals had not accepted his criticisms against them. He attempted to guide the movement to criticize not only Chen Boda but also the Working Group of the Central Military Committee headed by Lin's generals. In his February 19 instruction concerning how to promote the movement to criticize Chen Boda, Mao warned the party and the military not to follow the example of the Working Group, which had deliberately shied away from making criticisms of Chen Boda. On February 20, Mao repeated this warning in commenting on a self-criticism the Working Group had written in response to Mao's earlier critiques. When Generals Huang, Li, and Qiu finally submitted their personal self-criticisms to Mao at the end of March, Mao again criticized them sharply. On March 30, he wrote on the self-criticism of Liu Zihou, who was in charge of Hubei province, "[They] had boarded the pirate ship (*zeichuan*) of Chen Boda for so long that [they] did not speak of truth until March 19."[90] Mao was so determined to make issues out of the events of the Second Plenum that even Wang

Dongxing felt increasingly insecure about his political future, despite Mao's promise to forgive him. On April 18, Wang submitted his third self-criticism.

Meanwhile, Mao waited for Lin to make a self-criticism. But Lin stayed away from Beijing and refused to do so. In May 1971, Mao suddenly summoned Zhou Enlai, Kang Sheng, Huang Yongsheng, Wu Faxian, Li Zuopeng, Qiu Huizuo, Li Desheng, Ji Dengkui, and Wang Dongxing and told them that the self-criticisms of Huang, Li, and Qiu were good but that those of Wu and Ye Qun were not. "Go back and write another one," Mao told Wu. "Then I will protect you again." Mao then asked Zhou to take the members of the Working Group to Beidaihe and "report" their work to Lin Biao. This was to be Mao's last test of Lin's response to what had happened at Lushan the year before.

As usual, Lin uttered only one sentence to Zhou and others concerning the problems of his generals during the whole conversation: "One often harvests what he did not sow." When Zhou and others reported to Mao on their trip, the first thing Mao asked was whether Lin had criticized the generals. To protect Lin, Wu assured Mao that Lin had done so, and Zhou Enlai confirmed that Lin had criticized Wu and others. Only then did Mao smile with relief. "That is good. Now you can go prepare for the central working conference."

That conference met in May 1971 to continue the criticism of Chen Boda and Lin's generals. Lin Biao, however, did not attend the meeting. Mao circulated the self-criticisms of Wu and others and asked the participants to criticize Chen Boda as well as Lin's generals. However, unlike the conference at Lushan, at which Zhang Chunqiao had been showered with criticism, this meeting went relatively well from Lin's standpoint, because many of the participants still had respect for Lin's generals. Only Kang Sheng and others promoted since the Cultural Revolution began offered severe criticisms. Senior officials, such as Zhu De, Li Xiannian, and Nie Rongzhen, said little at the meeting.

Halfway through the meeting, however, something unexpected happened that almost put an end to Wu Faxian's political career. Some of his air force colleagues exposed his "underground activities" at Lushan. At Lushan, Wu had encouraged several air force officers to criticize Zhang Chunqiao and Yao Wenyuan during the group discussion of Lin's speech at the opening session. As had happened to Peng Dehuai and others at the Lushan Conference of 1959, critics of the generals interpreted this as an "organized anti-party activity," but Zhou Enlai downplayed the significance of the event.

When Lin Biao learned of this, he immediately returned to Beijing to protect his generals. He did not go to the meetings himself, though he did send Ye there from time to time. Mao probably expected Lin to make a self-criticism at the meeting, or at least to express regret over what he had said at Lushan. "It would be much better if Vice-Chairman Lin made a self-criticism speech," Zhou told Wu Faxian after Lin had returned to Beijing, trying to pass the message to Lin. Lin, however, remained silent.[91]

By July 1971, Mao had decided to get rid of Lin Biao and his generals. One day that month, Mao had a surprising conversation with Xiong Xianghui, Zhou Enlai's longtime subordinate who at the time held a position in the Department of the General Staff of the PLA. Xiong, accompanied by Zhou, went to see Mao for what Xiong thought was to be a discussion of the international situation after Henry Kissinger's secret visits to China. To Xiong's surprise, Mao began by asking about a meeting held by the General Staff to criticize Chen Boda. Mao wanted to know in detail what Huang Yongsheng had said to his staff about the plenum at Lushan the previous year. Mao learned that Huang had said only that if Mao and Lin had not pointed out the problem with Chen Boda he too would have been deceived by Chen. This convinced Mao that Lin's generals did not really accept Mao's criticism of them. "Their self-criticisms are nothing but fake," Mao said, suddenly raising his voice. "What happened at Lushan is not over, for the basic problem has not yet been solved. They have someone behind them."

Zhou tried to mitigate Mao's bitterness by saying that the generals had made self-criticisms and would correct their mistakes. Mao, however, did not agree. "Their mistakes are different from your past mistakes because they were conspirators," he said. Mao spent the next hour criticizing Lin Biao, Ye Qun, and the generals. This was probably the first time Mao had ever criticized Lin Biao in front of subordinates other than his own staff. After their talk with Mao ended, Zhou warned Xiong that he must not tell anyone what Mao had said.[92]

From August 15 to September 12, 1971, Mao made an inspection tour of southern China, during which he began to whip up public opinion against Lin Biao, his generals, and even his family. In speeches to local cadres, Mao expressed his dissatisfaction with Lin clearly:

> At that [Lushan] Conference they engaged in surprise attacks and underground activities. Why weren't they brave enough to come out in the open? It was obvious they were up to no good. First they concealed things, then they launched a surprise attack. They deceived three of the five standing members and the majority of comrades in the Politburo, except for the big generals. The big generals, including Huang Yongsheng, Wu Faxian, Ye Qun, Li Zuopeng, and Qiu Huizuo, and also Li Xuefeng and Zheng Wei-

shan, maintained airtight secrecy and suddenly launched a surprise attack. Their coup didn't just last a day-and-a-half, but went on for two-and-a-half days. . . .

I thought that their surprise attacks and underground activity were planned, organized, and programed. . . .

Comrade Lin Biao did not consult with me about or show me that talk of his. . . .

The struggle at the 1959 Lushan Conference with Peng Dehuai was a struggle between two headquarters. The struggle with Liu Shaoqi was also a struggle between two headquarters. The struggle at this Lushan Conference was again a struggle between two headquarters. . . .

This time, to protect Vice-Chairman Lin, no conclusions concerning individuals were reached. But of course, he must take some of the responsibility. . . .

When I return to Beijing, I will again seek them out to talk things over. If they won't come to me, I'll go to them. Some can probably be saved; some not—we must observe their actions. There are two future possibilities: one is to reform; the other is not to reform. Those who have made serious mistakes of principle, of line, and of direction, and who have been the leaders in this, will find it difficult to reform. . . .

I have told Comrade Lin Biao that some things he said aren't particularly proper. . . .

I just don't believe that our army would rebel. I just don't believe that you, Huang Yongsheng, could lead the Liberation Army to rebel! . . .

I have never approved of one's wife heading the Administrative Office of one's own work unit. At Lin Biao's place, Ye Qun is the director of the Administrative Office. . . . In work one should rely on one's own effort—read reports yourself, endorse reports yourself. You shouldn't rely on secretaries and allow secretaries to get such enormous power. . . .

But there should be no flattery—what good is there in praising someone in his twenties as a "super genius"?[93]

These were unmistakable signals that Mao considered Lin Biao to be a "problem." But even this and Mao's other moves against Lin's group do not completely account for what happened to Lin Biao later. The key to a plausible explanation is the most likely reaction of Lin and his generals to Mao's challenge. Was that a military coup d'état? In the words of Wu Faxian, "I was a member of the Chinese Communist Party, and everything I have is given by the party. If the party wants me to die, I would give my life to it."[94] When he said that, nobody doubted that Mao was the party.

6

Families in Chinese Politics

As the previous chapters have hinted, family ties played a peculiar role in Chinese politics during the Cultural Revolution. The Lin Biao incident itself can be considered the result of the problems in Lin's family. Without the active participation of Lin's family members in Chinese politics, the Lin Biao incident in its narrow sense probably would never have happened.[1] And without an understanding of the role of family in politics in Communist China, we might never fully understand or believe what happened to Lin Biao in September 1971, even with all the evidence in hand.

In Confucian China, the family, rather than the individual, was the basic social and economic unit of society. Confucian doctrine put great emphasis on a strong family structure. According to Mencius, the state itself was rooted in the family.[2] An individual properly raised in a family that valued Confucian doctrine would learn to respect authority, to carry out duties responsibly, and to remain a loyal member of the family. Such a person would also be loyal to the state, which replicated the hierarchical structure of an extended family. The relationship between rulers and deputies was analogous to that between fathers and sons.[3]

Within this Confucian structure, the state consciously cultivated the family as the primary unit of social organization, and this structure persists in contemporary China.[4] Respect for family remains a defining feature of Chinese civilization. Family members follow strict hierarchical rules. In nuclear families, which consist of parents and children, the ideal is an authoritarian husband and father, an obedient wife and mother, and filial children. In extended families of more than two generations living in the same household, the oldest male holds the highest authority.

Confucian doctrine, however, does not fully account for the importance of the family in traditional Chinese society. The state strengthened

Confucian values through social administration and legislation. In addition to its vital economic functions, the family performed equally important administrative functions in imperial China, where social administration was built around the household. The bureaucratic hierarchy of the Qing dynasty, for example, rested upon the *pai*, or ten households. Ten *pai* equaled one *jia*, and ten *jia* equaled one *bao*. The heads of these organizations were also the heads of families within them and were responsible for the moral and political conduct of their members.[5] Through such organizations, the government made family members socially and politically responsible to one another. If one became prosperous, all became prosperous; likewise, if one was in trouble, all were in trouble. Punishment could be extended to the members of a *jia* or a *bao*, under the assumption that this would make a person think twice before engaging in any form of crime. The concept of "guilt by association" (*zhulian*) may have originated partly in that assumption.

In China, therefore, the stability of the state was predicated on the stability of the family. Confucius put so much emphasis on proper family structure that three of the five relationships that formed the core of Confucian teaching concerned establishing a strict hierarchy in the family, in which the father rules the son, the husband rules the wife, and the elder brother rules the younger. Anyone who violated these principles was not just morally and ethically wrong, but legally wrong as well. A son who struck a parent committed a capital offense; the punishment for striking an elder brother was imprisonment.[6] Chinese rulers even extended a criminal's punishment to his family members as a powerful deterrent to the commission of crimes.[7] There are numerous instances in Chinese history in which entire families were punished, even put to death, because of the crime of a single member.

Family ties, however, had positive as well as negative consequences for the individual. Nepotism was an important factor in the economy of traditional China. Chinese customs and ethics insisted family members and relatives help one another. A person who did not use a position to help family members and kinsmen, regardless of their capabilities, was considered immoral.[8] Even in modern China it is not unusual to conduct business through family members and networks based on kinship.

Families cultivated with these traditions bore specific features. Confucian doctrine requires the perfection of the individual not for his own sake but for the sake of the family and the state. In this sense, the individual was subordinate to the family and clan. The primary responsibility of a male was to maintain a "continuum of descent," which, as Hugh Baker has suggested, was analogically similar to a rope that "began somewhere back in the remote past and which stretches on to the infinite future." The family and its individual members were strands or fibers of the rope.[9] Parents chose spouses for their children on the basis of what they believed was best for the family. Love was not necessary for a good marriage. The traditional wife was obedient to her husband and acted according to his wishes. All these traditions remained more or less unchanged in Chinese society, even under Communist rule.

Confucian ideas about strong personal loyalty to family was a mixed blessing for the state. According to Baker, the great inward pull of the family was achieved at the cost of indifference toward extrafamilial affairs. When the interests of the family and those of the state conflicted, the individual's fundamental loyalty was often divided. In many cases, family interests prevailed over those of the state. In a comparative study of Chinese and Japanese kinship, John Pelzel found that the tensions between loyalty to kin and loyalty to the state in Chinese society were stronger than in Japan, where "task-oriented organizations that fall somewhere between family and nation are relatively numerous."[10] In neglecting the non-kin social community, Confucian doctrine created something of a vacuum between the state and the family. One question that continues to puzzle scholars is whether a "civil society," as defined by Western ideas, has ever existed in the long history of China. Some have even concluded that China is "a state without a society."[11]

Wives of the Leading Revolutionaries

The Communists changed some features of the traditional Chinese family but preserved many others. The men who led the Chinese revolution, including Mao Zedong, Zhou Enlai, Deng Xiaoping, and Zhu De, rebelled against Confucian family norms and rejected traditional ideas of family and marriage. The young Mao was well known for his defiance of a tyrannical father. As an eldest son, Mao had to fight for permission to leave home and pursue an education. His father had demanded that Mao remain at home and carry on the family business. Throughout his life, even in his later years, Mao remembered his father's strict treatment.[12] The young Zhou Enlai proclaimed that he would remain celibate throughout his life, a state that Confucian doctrine condemned as extremely unfilial and even immoral. The tendency to rebel against tradition was also common among women revolutionaries, who had to be exceptionally strong-minded and defiant to leave home and join the revolution. Most of them either ran away from their families or grew up in nontraditional families.

What were the general characteristics of the families of leading revolutionaries? As with the changes these revolutionaries introduced to the family elsewhere in communist society, the most noticeable feature was the position of women. Marriage was the result of personal choice, usually based on love. In communist theory, at least, wives enjoyed equal rights with husbands and thus had an equal say in family decisions. In many cases, wives exercised considerable power in family affairs because their husbands were preoccupied with the revolution. Even in traditional Chinese society, it had not been uncommon for educated wives to have relatively more power in the family than their uneducated counterparts.

However, certain traditional assumptions concerning the family remained untouched by the Communists. As Ross Terrill has observed, even in the revolutionary world of Yanan between 1936 and 1947, two basic principles guided sexual practice—the party ruled the bedroom, and men ruled women.[13] The party, in fact, played a role "reminiscent of that of a family head in feudal China."[14] All marriages required party approval, and the party intervened whenever it concluded that a comrade's sex life would "affect" his political career. Even Mao had difficulty convincing the Party Committee to approve his marriage to Jiang Qing, his fourth wife. Those who indulged in extramarital affairs were reprimanded or punished, but the punishment varied according to the miscreant's position and influence. In most cases at Yanan the woman was sent away and the man was allowed to stay. Mao's affair with Lili Wu, who came to Yanan as the interpreter for American journalist Agnes Smedley, ended that way. In fact, both Lili Wu and He Zizhen, Mao's third wife, left Yanan.[15] Frustration over their husbands' constant affairs was typical among the women who made the Long March.

In the male-dominated world of Yanan, the wives, especially those who were veterans of the Long March, were victims of the chauvinist attitudes of their husbands, and many of their marriages became shaky under the conditions at Yanan. When younger and mostly better-educated women began arriving at Yanan after 1936, the older women lost much of their appeal in the eyes of their husbands. Li Min, the daughter of Mao and He Zizhen, admitted later that her biological mother was no match for Jiang Qing in beauty, intelligence, or demeanor. With her training and experience as an actress in Shanghai before she came to Yanan, Jiang stood out as exceptionally beautiful and intelligent. Jiang could speak and read English, which was rare among women revolutionaries at Yanan, and her calligraphy was outstanding. She soon caught the attention of Mao, who often voiced his admiration of her in public.[16] Mao was also impressed by her political insight and later told Tao Zhu's wife, Zeng

Zhi, "He Zizhen was not of any help to me politically, but Jiang Qing could provide help."[17] When He Zizhen left Yanan for the Soviet Union for a rest, Jiang soon became Mao's de facto wife. In 1939, Mao wrote to He Zizhen in Moscow that their marriage was over. Similarly, the marriage between He Long and his first wife, Jian Xianren, ended after he met Xue Ming; he too wrote a letter from Yanan to his wife in Moscow, declaring that he was divorcing her. According to Harrison Salisbury, divorce was easy in Yanan. All that was needed was a simple statement from the husband.[18]

Following Mao's example, many others married or remarried during the Yanan period. It was not unusual for leading revolutionaries to divorce their wives to marry young female intellectuals. Since few women survived the Long March of 1935–36, a group of younger and better-educated women who came to Yanan to join the revolution in the 1940s caught the eye of the leading revolutionaries. Jiang Qing, Ye Qun, Wang Guangmei (Liu Shaoqi's wife), Zhang Qian (Chen Yi's wife), Zhuo Lin (Deng Xiaoping's wife), Lin Jiamei (Li Xiannian's wife), Xue Ming (He Long's wife), and Pu Anxiu (Peng Dehuai's wife) all belonged to this group. The age difference between these husbands and wives was often substantial. Mao Zedong was 21 years older than Jiang Qing, Liu Shaoqi 25 years older than Wang Guangmei, Deng Xiaoping 12 years older than Zhuo Lin, Lin Biao 14 years older than Ye Qun, Chen Yi 21 years older than Zhang Qian, and Peng Dehuai 14 years older than Pu Anxiu.

The wives of leading revolutionaries had to make considerable adjustments in their lives. There was a significant gap between the revolutionary ideal they pursued and the realities of "the wife of a cadre" role they found themselves playing. Much like traditional Chinese wives, they were expected to devote themselves to their husbands. Both He Zizhen, Mao's third wife, and Jiang Qing, his fourth wife, served as Mao's secretary, which meant that their revolutionary career was to take care of their husband. It was therefore difficult for them to draw the line between family matters and party affairs when disobeying their husband was tantamount to disobeying the party. Part of the reason He Zizhen left Mao was that she could no longer handle the imbalance between her own desire to be a revolutionary and the role she had to play as a loyal supporter of her husband's career and the mother of his children.

Moreover, frequent pregnancies under harsh living conditions destroyed the health of many of the women. He Zizhen, for instance, had six pregnancies within ten years. At the time, there were few effective methods available of birth control or abortion. Women revolutionaries who became pregnant therefore were frequently abandoned and left to survive

on their own when the army had to move. Pregnancy was not just a physical ordeal for the women, but led to mental torment as well. In most
cases, for the safety of both the troops and the children, they had to abandon their babies shortly after they were born. To avoid pregnancy and its
painful consequences, many of the women chose to undergo sterilization.
Among those who did were Deng Yingchao, Zhou Enlai's wife, and Zeng
Zhi, Tao Zhu's wife.[19] Wang Xingjuan, He Zizhen's biographer, describes
He's decision to leave Mao this way:

> She felt very depressed. She had sacrificed so much for Mao. The result [of
> this marriage] was that she lost her chance to be promoted to a position
> [appropriate to her own abilities] and her health collapsed. [As Mao's sec-
> retary], she spent ten years reading newspapers and collecting clippings.
> To her extreme dismay, she found out, at this time of depression, that she
> was pregnant again. This destroyed her final hope of starting a new life [as
> an independent person]. To be pregnant meant that she would have to stay
> idle for another year. The more she thought about it, the more frightened
> she felt. She wanted to separate from Mao temporarily in order to avoid
> another pregnancy.[20]

Wang Xingjuan mentions elsewhere that it was impossible for He to seek
sterilization. As Mao's wife, she had the responsibility of producing heirs
for the revolutionary leader.[21] Even though her marriage had ended, she
lived in Mao's shadow for the rest of her life. She could not hold a job or
start a new life of her own. Because her identity as Mao's ex-wife had a
negative impact on Mao's political image, her existence was to be known
to as few people as possible.[22] After she left Yanan, she stayed in the Soviet Union until the end of 1946. When she finally returned to China, she
had to remain anonymous and was kept under "protection" wherever she
went. She was not allowed to visit Beijing until after Mao's death and
Jiang Qing's arrest in 1976. She even had trouble seeing her daughter, the
only one of her children who survived the harsh war years, but who lived
with Mao. He Zizhen lived alone in Shanghai, struggling through a lonely
life without family or work. Under such conditions, she could not recover
from the emotional problems that began when she was in the Soviet
Union in the 1940s and continued for the rest of her life. According to one
of her friends, He Zizhen used to spend time staring at Mao's picture,
sometimes for hours.[23] Interestingly, people began to remember her after
Mao's death and the fall of the "Gang of Four," headed by Jiang Qing, in
1976. The name He Zizhen reappeared everywhere as Mao's former wife.
"Many people believed," stated Wang Xingjuan, "that if He Zizhen had
not left Mao, Jiang Qing would not have had the chance to become Mao's
wife. Nor would the Cultural Revolution have happened, during which

so many veteran revolutionaries were purged."[24] Wang was not the only one with this opinion.

He Zizhen was not the only woman who became the wife of a leading revolutionary at the cost of personal identity. Deng Yingchao, who belonged to the earliest group of women revolutionaries, emerged from the shadow of her husband, Zhou Enlai, only after his death. In 1978, two years after Zhou's death, she was elected to the Politburo, an office she could never have aspired to while Zhou was alive.[25] Zeng Zhi, the wife of Tao Zhu, was another revolutionary wife who had difficulty pursuing her own career. A Red Army veteran herself, Zeng wanted a public career, not that of a housewife. In order to demonstrate her independence, Zeng moved out of the house she shared with Tao Zhu and found a residence of her own after she was appointed to a leading position in the Guangzhou municipal government. Once she wrote directly to Mao, with whom she had maintained a good personal relationship since the late 1920s, complaining that Tao Zhu had crossed her name off the list of candidates for the First National Congress simply because she was his wife. Since it had been a party decision that she represent Guangdong province at the First National Congress, how, she asked Mao, could Tao alone cancel her candidacy? On another occasion, she even considered divorcing Tao Zhu, who, she claimed, always "suppressed" her with his "male chauvinist" attitude and ignored her opinions on public affairs.[26]

Of course, wives also benefited from their husbands' power and fame. Jiang Qing and Ye Qun, the two female villains supposedly responsible for the Cultural Revolution, had reputations for being especially adept at exploiting their husbands' power and parlaying it into an extravagant lifestyle. Jiang Qing was extremely particular about what she ate and was very demanding of her staff. According to Dr. Li Zhisui, few people in "Group One" (a code name for Mao and his staff) got along with her. Her nurses, who endured her constant scolding, frequently ran to Dr. Li in tears. From time to time, Mao apologized to his staff for Jiang Qing, asking them to be tolerant of her for his sake.[27]

Despite these acknowledged facts, there is another side to the story of these women. Like He Zizhen, they suffered emotionally from the constant struggle to keep their own identity and at the same time maintain something like a normal husband-wife relationship with their spouses. When the Communists triumphed in China in 1949, Jiang Qing was only 35 years old. With her beauty, talent, intelligence, and above all her status as Mao's wife, she probably had great ambition and expectations for her future. From the very beginning, however, something had been wrong with her marriage to Mao. Because of Jiang's past as an actress in Shanghai, the Party Central Committee considered her unsuitable to be Mao's wife. Because Mao had insisted on marrying her, the committee exacted from her a pledge that she would devote herself to taking care of Mao and not interfere in political affairs for the next 30 years.[28] Thus, Jiang was kept out of politics until just before the Cultural Revolution. The highest position she had held until then was section chief in charge of artwork in the municipal government of Beijing.

In the mid-1950s, Jiang seemed to be repeating He Zizhen's tragedy. In 1956 she almost collapsed physically and mentally and went to the Soviet Union to be treated for cervical cancer. According to Dr. Li, Jiang became hysterical when she learned about her cancer and after she returned became "obsessively hypochondriacal." She often accused her nurses of trying to "poison" her.[29] Dr. Li believed that her condition was the result of a life without meaning and her constant fear of being abandoned by Mao.[30]

Mao understood Jiang's problem. "What really bothers her is that she is afraid that one day I might not want her anymore," Mao told Dr. Li. "I have told her many times that it is not true and that she should stop worrying about it." Mao's promises did little to reassure Jiang Qing, since she knew Mao had affairs with numerous young women. According to Dr. Li, Mao in his later years did not even bother to hide his affairs from Jiang Qing. Once, Dr. Li caught Jiang crying on a park bench just outside Mao's compound in Zhongnanhai. She begged him not to tell anyone and told him that Mao's womanizing was becoming so flagrant that she feared he would eventually abandon her.[31]

In 1957, Dr. Li reported Jiang's mental condition to Mao and Zhou Enlai. They did nothing about it, however, because, in Deng Yingchao's words, it would not have been "fair to the chairman" to say that Comrade Jiang Qing had mental problems since Mao had already suffered so much from the loss of family members. Beginning in the late 1950s, Jiang Qing and Mao lived separately. Mao continued his active sex life with numerous female partners, but there was no possibility of Jiang Qing's finding a lover. Even after the Cultural Revolution, when Jiang became notorious throughout China, her biographers found no credible evidence that she had had love affairs with anyone else. According to Dr. Li, to do so would have provided Mao with an excuse to get rid of her. Her fear of abandonment was too strong to give Mao such an opportunity.[32]

Jiang Qing's devotion to Mao was unquestionable. Even Mao knew this, which was why he constantly defended her during the Cultural Revolution. Most of Mao's criticism of Jiang, which was widely quoted later as proof that Mao had decided to part company with her, was actually prompted by his concern for her future. Although contemporary Chinese writers now typically portray Jiang as a dragon lady who took advantage of her husband's power to play her own political role, Mao probably could not have found a more appropriate wife. Despite all her problems, Jiang remained absolutely loyal to Mao for reasons of her own. Not only was she a help to Mao politically, as Mao himself confirmed, but she finally came to tolerate Mao's frequent affairs and even tried to maintain a civil relationship with the women involved.[33]

If Jiang Qing suffered from Mao's infidelities, Ye Qun's problem was just the opposite; her husband had little interest in intimacy because of his health problems. Like Jiang Qing, Ye belonged to the group of young students who went to Yanan to join the revolution. With her beauty and intelligence, she soon caught the eye of Lin Biao, one of the most powerful men at Yanan, and married him in 1943.[34] Before 1949 she remained a housewife, taking care of Lin Biao and their two children. She held no public position and remained off the political stage until the beginning of the Cultural Revolution.

In the eyes of many Chinese, Ye Qun was also a malicious woman, greedy, capricious, and mean. Some members of Lin Biao's staff, however, described Ye as benign and caring, something no one has said of Jiang Qing. Ye had more control over Lin than Jiang had over Mao.[35] This was not because Ye had a stronger personality than Jiang, but because Lin was in poor health for much of their marriage and thus more vulnerable and submissive. Few people know for sure what was wrong with Lin, and his medical records have never been released. It is clear, however, that in the later years of his life he was in very fragile physical and mental health. Dr. Li believed Lin suffered from neurasthenia and was a hypochondriac. Lin became seriously ill whenever he perspired and had phobias about water, wind, and cold.[36] He was even said to be nervous at the sight of the rivers and oceans in traditional Chinese paintings and got diarrhea at the sound of water. As early as the 1950s, a Soviet doctor diagnosed Lin's problem as manic depression, but Ye rejected the diagnosis and sent the Soviet specialist back to the Soviet Union. Chinese doctors are said to have later confirmed the diagnosis. One source suggests that Lin's medical records indicated as early as 1953 that he had been suffering from manic depression.[37]

There are numerous incredible stories about Lin Biao's health problems, though they almost certainly contain elements of truth. There is little reason for the authors of the stories to have lied about Lin's health. One of the strangest stories originated with a former member of Lin's staff, Guan Weixun:

My friend Zhang, who was Ye's literature tutor, witnessed one event. In the summer of 1971, when he was watching a movie with Ye Qun and other people after swimming, one of Lin's staff approached Ye and said, "The Commander says that he has phlegm in his mouth and he does not know whether he should swallow it or spit it out. He sent me here to ask you," Guan recorded. "Tell him to spit it out," Ye said impatiently. The staff in Lin's office was quite accustomed to things like this, so no one felt that this was strange or even amusing.[38]

According to the manager of a guest house for high officials in Guangzhou, Lin Biao's poor health was the result of his wartime experience. One summer when Lin arrived at Guangzhou, the manager noticed that there was an old-fashioned motorcycle in Lin's house with its muffler sticking outside the house through the wall. Another day, a member of Lin's staff reported to the manager that Lin was ill. When the manager arrived, Lin entered the room where the motorcycle was standing. He was supported by his bodyguards, and he looked pale and weak and held his head with both hands. At Ye Qun's direction, the manager started the motorcycle. "More gas, more . . . ," Lin told him, sitting beside him in the motorcycle's sidecar. The manager opened the throttle to its maximum, and the motorcycle roared, filling the room with the fumes of diesel gasoline, which Lin inhaled the way a smoker inhales tobacco smoke. After about fifteen minutes of this, Lin's color returned and he opened his eyes. When he finally recovered from his pain, he thanked the manager with a grateful smile.[39] On another occasion, one of Lin's bodyguards said to the same manager, "The commander has been away from war for too long." He meant that war had so affected Lin that he could no longer feel comfortable in a peaceful environment. It seems that he constantly needed a warlike environment to revive his energy.

Dr. Li, who treated Lin Biao for the first time in August 1966, gave this description of the experience: "When we were escorted into his room, Lin Biao was in bed, curled in the arms of his wife, Ye Qun, his head nestled against her bosom. Lin Biao was crying, and Ye Qun was patting him and comforting him as though he were a baby. In that one moment, my view of Lin Biao changed—from bold and brilliant military commander to troubled soul unfit to lead." The experience led Dr. Li to conclude that Lin was "obviously mentally unsound." But when he told Mao about Lin's problems, Mao was "expressionless and silent." Li dared not tell others of Lin's condition because to do so would be to commit the political crime of revealing privileged information about a high official.[40] In fact, Dr. Li was not the only one whose opinion of Lin Biao changed as a result of Lin's medical condition. One of Lin's staff members was so shocked by the discrepancy between Lin's public image and his actual condition that he wept after meeting Lin for the first time.[41]

Lin Doudou is the source of another story that illustrates how Lin's disorders affected his work. When Lin announced the ouster of Yang Chengwu, Yu Lijin, and Fu Chongbi at a meeting in March 1967, Doudou was away from Beijing. When she returned, she asked her father what was wrong with Yang Chengwu. "Yes, what was wrong with Yang Chengwu?" Lin answered, seemingly puzzled himself. "But it was you who gave the speech, which was passed on to the troops as a document from the Party Central Committee," Doudou reminded him. "Why don't you remember what was wrong with Yang Chengwu?" "Is that so?" Lin seemed more confused. "What did I say? Call Ye Qun over and let her tell us what on earth was wrong with Yang Chengwu."[42]

Whether or not these stories are exaggerations, it is clear that Lin was indeed often ill, and nobody knew what was wrong with him or how to cure him. According to Dr. Fu Lianzhang, who headed a group of medical experts who gave Lin a physical checkup in the 1950s, the doctors "could find nothing functionally wrong" except for "a plenitude of symptoms of psychological disorientation and plain evidence of drug usage."[43] However, Lin clearly had a disorder of the central nervous system probably because of a war wound near his spine. It became Lin's hobby to read medical books, especially those about Chinese medicines, and he began to experiment with ways to ease his own pain. His experiments included concocting his own Chinese medicines and riding on a motorcycle or in a jeep when he was in pain. Because of his poor health, Lin cared little about what was happening around him and even to him. He did not want to disturb others or to be disturbed himself. Ye Qun thus became the master of the house. Whatever was reported to Lin had to be reported to her first. Many of Lin's staff later admitted that Ye sometimes made decisions for Lin behind Lin's back and asked them to help her keep the information away from Lin.[44] Meanwhile, Ye Qun's dissatisfaction with Lin Biao as a husband increased. "My marriage was a political one," Ye said to Lin's secretaries several times.[45]

Wives in Politics

Without the Cultural Revolution, Jiang Qing's and Ye Qun's lives and marriages would have remained private matters. Despite their lack of political experience, however, both Jiang Qing and Ye Qun were elected to the Politburo at the First Plenum of the Ninth Party Central Committee in

April 1969. Ye disappeared from the political arena two years later, in the plane crash in the Mongolian desert, and Jiang was arrested after Mao died in 1976 and committed suicide while serving a life sentence. Today, conventional Chinese interpretations of the Cultural Revolution blame the two women for its disastrous results. Some writers even suggest that the Cultural Revolution should be understood as a time of "wives in politics" (*furen zhengzhi*).[46] To a certain extent, that is a valid understanding.

After 30 years of political "exile," Jiang Qing suddenly appeared on the political stage in 1966. The only reason she could do so was that she was Mao's wife, and Mao entrusted her with the responsibility of leading the Cultural Revolution. "I was Mao's dog. What he said to bite, I bit," Jiang Qing said later of her role in the Cultural Revolution.[47]

When Mao appointed Jiang first deputy chief of the Central Cultural Revolution Small Group in May 1966, most party and government officials did not take her seriously. In their understanding, the Cultural Revolution was to be another rectification movement, one mainly concerned with cultural matters, as its name suggested. If that had been the case, Jiang Qing's appointment as one of the leaders of the CCRSG would have been justifiable since she had long been in charge of an office of cultural affairs in the Beijing municipal government. Party and government officials agreed to Jiang's appointment because of their respect for Mao.

Their expectations of the Cultural Revolution and of Jiang Qing's role in it soon proved to be completely wrong. The Cultural Revolution became a "revolution to touch people's souls" (*chuji linghun*), during which all the veteran cadres except a select few were "held to the fire."

In Chinese Communist political culture, the family was treated as a unit, which meant that the wife enjoyed the same status as her husband. To offend the wife or other family members was an insult to the husband, the head of the family. Jiang Qing tapped this source for her own purposes. She regularly appeared in public as Mao's wife, always beginning her speeches with the announcement, "I come to see you on behalf of Chairman Mao." Once she established herself as the guiding force at the CCRSG, the Red Guards and the radicals listened to no one else. And she and her group caused trouble for most of the leading revolutionaries at Zhongnanhai, including Liu Shaoqi, Zhou Enlai, Deng Xiaoping, and Tao Zhu.

In the eyes of party and government officials, there were thus two Jiang Qings: Jiang Qing as Mao's wife, and Jiang Qing as herself. Most of the officials had little personal respect for Jiang as herself, but all of them had a great deal of respect for her as Mao's wife. They usually had no way of knowing for certain, however, whether Jiang was speaking for herself or for Mao, and they were in no position to make a mistake. During the Cultural Revolution, which was also the last decade of Mao's life, Mao isolated himself from the public and from his comrades. Even Lin Biao and Zhou Enlai had only limited access to him. After 1969, Mao also forbade Jiang Qing and other family members to see him without prior permission.[48] For example, in 1976, before Mao died, Mao's elder daughter, Li Min, was allowed only three visits with her father. The second time was in August 1976, one month before Mao's death, after she had read about Mao's critical condition in a CCP document. Mao isolated himself even further in the last few years of his life. Nobody but two women had free access to his room. Those who wanted to see him usually had to inform these women, who in turn reported to Mao and brought back his response.[49]

Mao's self-imposed seclusion gave Jiang freedom to push her own agenda in his name. Because her own problems with Mao were known to few, people respected her as Mao's wife. For the last several years of the Cultural Revolution, Jiang Qing acted as a liaison between Mao and other leading officials. By the time she became a Politburo member in 1969, even Mao was losing control of her. In 1975, when Mao learned from Zhu De's letter that Jiang Qing had provided personal information to an American scholar, Roxane Witke, and had asked Witke to write her biography, Mao angrily wrote on Zhu's letter, "Little knowledge and stupid. [She] has not changed her bad habits for 30 years. Expel [her] from the Politburo immediately and go different ways." When this letter reached Zhou Enlai, Zhou decided not to pass it along, and the matter was dropped.[50] Jiang was able to exploit her position as Mao's wife, but the source of her power disappeared with Mao's death, and her political career ended as well.

During the Cultural Revolution, Ye Qun played a role no less important than Jiang Qing's, though less public. Because of Lin's poor health and his distaste for socializing, Ye became the indispensable link between Lin and the outside world. She decided not only what he should know, but also what others should know about him. Mao actually encouraged Ye to act on Lin's behalf and gave her an unusual amount of responsibility. It was Mao who asked Ye to participate in the Shanghai Conference in December 1965, during which Luo Ruiqing was purged. Mao also asked her to make a long speech at the Party Central Committee meeting to criticize Luo Ruiqing on Lin's behalf, although Ye Qun was not even a member of the committee at the time. According to their daughter, Lin scolded Ye afterward for making such a speech at a meeting she had no right to attend in the first place. In her defense, Ye told Lin that she had had no choice but to follow Mao's instruction.[51]

Lin frequently used his poor health as an excuse to avoid Politburo meetings. Lin's absences angered Mao, and once Jiang Qing told Lin and Ye that "the chairman said that Comrade Lin Biao had to shoulder the responsibilities, no matter what." "If the deputy commander [Lin Biao] is ill, why does Comrade Ye Qun not attend meetings, either? Is she also ill?"[52] After the February Adverse Current, when most Politburo members were suspended from their work, Mao decided to make Ye a regular participant in Politburo meetings. This put Ye in a special position—though she held no formal position in the party, she nonetheless attended Politburo meetings as Lin's wife and representative. Mao may have deliberately involved Ye in political matters so that Jiang Qing would not be the only wife to hold an important position because of the power of her husband. And Ye enjoyed the publicity, for it brought power, fame, and new meaning to her life.

Lin, however, became increasingly distraught over his wife's increasing involvement in politics. To remind her of her proper position, Lin wrote Ye a couplet that he asked her to hang above her bed. It said, "Focus on morality, education, and physical exercise instead of seeking fame, position, and power."[53] Instead, Ye began to hide most of her outside activities from Lin in order to avoid his criticism. On many occasions, she asked Lin's staff to lie if Lin inquired after her whereabouts while she was attending to her political activities. The more active Ye became on the political stage, the less she informed Lin of her activities outside the household.

This attitude of Lin toward Ye Qun's political involvement gradually changed, however. He began to realize that Ye's talent for handling human relations could be of great help to him. To ensure his "political correctness" in public, Lin often told his secretaries to show Ye documents he had approved before they were circulated to others. Among other things, Ye reminded Lin to take the "Little Red Book" with him to public appearances and made sure he arrived on time for meetings with Mao.

When Zhang Yunsheng worked as a secretary in Lin's office, he came to understand that Ye's opinion counted for even more than Lin's own on many issues. In October 1967, Jiang Qing sent two documents to Lin, asking his permission to issue them as central government documents. One was a letter to the party, in which Jiang Qing criticized cultural work in China before the Cultural Revolution, and the other was Jiang Qing and Yao Wenyuan's criticism of the European Renaissance. When Zhang asked Ye whether to give the documents to Lin, Ye told him to hold them until she had time to find out through "back" channels what Jiang was up to. Several days later, she told Zhang she had learned from Zhou Enlai and Wang Dongxing that Mao had already rejected the two documents. Zhou told Ye to make sure that Lin did not approve the documents, and especially that he did not send them to the Politburo. Only then did Ye allow Zhang to report on the matter to Lin.

When Lin asked Zhang what Ye's opinion was, Zhang replied that Ye wanted Lin to make the decision. Without much thought, Lin told Zhang to shelve it. "That will not do," said Ye Qun, who had just come into the room. "You have to make comments on it and send it back to Zhou Enlai, although he does not want it," Ye continued. "We have to throw the ball back to him: if someone has to be blamed by Mao, let it be Zhou Enlai."[54]

This episode was one of many such events. Zhang Yunsheng offers another example of how things worked in Lin's office during the Cultural Revolution. One day Ye Qun asked to see a document Lin had just endorsed. Ye wanted to make sure that Lin had mentioned the "two-line struggle" (*luxian douzheng*) in his comments on the document. During the Cultural Revolution, it had become a symbol of political correctness to do so. If one emphasized the importance and the victory of Mao's revolutionary line, it indicated that one listened to Mao attentively and followed Mao closely. Ye was careful to follow these unwritten rules so that Lin's political opponents would not have a chance to find fault with him.

When the secretary told her that Lin had not done so, Ye delayed sending it out. "No need to be in a hurry," Ye told the secretary, "we can wait a few hours." On second thought, Ye asked again, "How will you report to the commander after he gets up?" "I will just tell him that the Director [Ye] suggested mentioning *luxian* in his comment," the secretary answered. "That will not do," Ye yelled. "I am the wife of the commander, and I do not want people to think that I am the backstage boss of the commander." "But if we do not mention you, how can mere secretaries take on the responsibility for holding up the document?" the worried secretary asked. "Why don't you just lie to him, tell him that the chairman is taking a nap, so you had to wait until the afternoon?" replied Ye Qun. Still, the secretary was not convinced, "How can I say such a thing without proof?" he asked. "All right, whatever," Ye said angrily and left the room. Later, Ye came up with another idea. She called Chen Boda and convinced him that Lin's comments had to mention *luxian douzheng* and that it would be better if Chen, instead of Ye, made the suggestion to Lin. "I simply do not want people to say that I am the one who runs this house," Ye told Chen. After she hung up the phone, she told the secretary to tell Lin that Chen Boda had made the suggestion.[55]

In the prologue to his book, Zhang Yunsheng answers questions about

Ye Qun that had been raised by readers of his manuscript. He writes as follows:[56]

> *Question:* You made many comments about Ye Qun in your book. It seems that many of Ye's activities were conducted behind Lin's back. Is this true?
>
> *Answer:* Ye Qun was the director of Lin's office, and I was a secretary. I had many contacts with Ye in the course of my work. That was why I often mention Ye Qun in my memoirs. Ye did hide many of her activities from Lin Biao, but at the same time she made full use of Lin's name. I have presented many examples of this in my memoirs. I can add still more if necessary. It was, however, not true that everything Ye did was behind Lin's back. The problem was that Ye often told lies. It was difficult to tell to what extent Ye Qun was telling Lin Biao the truth.
>
> *Question:* Why, then, didn't Lin's staff expose her to Lin?
>
> *Answer:* Who dared to do so at that time? Ye often threatened that whoever opposed her opposed Lin Biao, and whoever opposed Lin Biao opposed Mao. . . . Who was willing to be condemned as a "counter-revolutionary? At Maojiawan [Lin's residence], only the courageous Lin Doudou was an exception. Several times she exposed Ye Qun in front of Lin Biao, which only resulted in her drawing fire on herself. Ye Qun punished her severely afterward.[57]

"The Princes' Party": Children of High Officials

Contemporary Chinese writers refer to the children of high officials as the "princes' party" (*taizidang*). The expression not only refers to the privileges the children enjoy because of their family, but also suggests that they form a political subgroup because of their social status and personal experiences. Although in theory hereditary social and political status disappeared in China with the fall of the Qing dynasty, in practice it never happened, before or after the Communist revolution. Some Chinese even assumed that the death of Mao's eldest son, Mao Anying, during the Korean War was one of the tragedies of contemporary Chinese history. They believe that if Mao Anying had outlived his father, Mao might not have felt so desperate about the succession problem and been so determined to launch the Cultural Revolution.

Very few studies, however, provide information about this political subgroup beyond brief biographical sketches.[58] To better understand the Lin Biao incident as an instance of family involvement in high politics, we turn now to Lin's children, who epitomize certain aspects of the princes' party.

THE TRAGEDY OF LIN DOUDOU

Both of Lin Biao's children, Lin Doudou and Lin Liguo, were born during wartime. Doudou, the older, was born in 1944 and had an especially difficult early childhood. When Ye Qun was pregnant with her, she tried several times to abort the fetus but failed. When Doudou was born, two months prematurely, she weighed less than five pounds, and Ye was so weak that she had no milk to feed her. As an infant, Doudou was very frail and often ill. As an adult, she recalled that Luo Ruiqing had told her to eat raw turnips to make herself stronger.[59] When she was eleven months old, Ye gave her away to a villager, believing Doudou had no chance to survive the harsh environment in which Ye had to live.[60] Ye later asked for Doudou back when she found out that Doudou's adoptive family might not be politically reliable. On another occasion, Ye abandoned Doudou on a battlefield because she could no longer carry her. Fortunately, one of Lin's bodyguards went back to get her. In the words of Luo Ruiqing, Doudou had nine lives.[61] When Doudou learned of her mother's attempts to abandon her, she began to suspect that Ye was not her biological mother.

Being the daughter of a high official proved to be a mixed blessing. On the surface, Doudou was a member of an elite who enjoyed many privileges—nice living quarters, nannies, the best schools and medical care, and modern conveniences—all of which were rare luxuries in Mao's China. Still, Doudou's childhood was not easy. Lin Biao was not an uncaring father, but he was too busy to spend much time with his children. Similarly, Ye Qun was not an unfit mother, but she wanted to control her daughter's life, and Doudou resisted her efforts to do so. When Doudou became defiant, Ye punished her, sometimes with beatings. Doudou eventually found that silence was the most effective way to show her disobedience.

The most sensitive point of conflict between Ye Qun and Doudou concerned Lin Biao himself. Because of his poor health, Lin was isolated, and Doudou became one of the few people Lin counted on to tell him the truth about events inside as well as outside the house. According to some of Lin's staff, Doudou seldom lied to Lin and often told him what Ye Qun did behind his back. These reports made Lin angry, and he often scolded Ye for what she had done. Ye, in turn, vented her anger at Doudou, berating her with foul language. After several such episodes, Doudou became more careful about what she told Lin and sometimes asked him not to tell Ye what she had told him. But this strategy no longer worked after Lin's short-term memory began to deteriorate.[62] Doudou became very cautious after repeated episodes in which she was caught between Lin and Ye, and eventually Doudou tried to avoid seeing Lin. When she did visit, she kept the visits short or arranged to have someone else present so that Lin would not ask her anything.

Ye Qun sometimes did desperate things to try to control her daughter. In 1966, for example, Ye sent photographs of pages of Doudou's diary in which she had made negative remarks about Mao, perhaps under the influence of her father, to the Security Bureau and then burned the diary itself.[63] Ye burned the diary to protect her daughter, but Ye also wanted to demonstrate her power so that Doudou would obey her.

Because Ye Qun treated her so badly, and especially after Yan Weibing, Lu Dingyi's wife, sent her anonymous letters saying that Ye was not her real mother, Doudou neared the point of total collapse, for which she had to seek medical treatment.[64] Doudou became more and more cynical and detached from her family. Like her father, she too may have suffered from manic depression.[65]

Life became even more difficult for Doudou when Ye interfered with her marriage plans. In 1967, when Doudou was 23, Ye became concerned about her marriage prospects but refused to allow Doudou to find her own spouse. When Ye found out that Doudou had fallen in love with an air force officer with whom she worked, without explanation Ye asked Wu Faxian to send the officer to faraway Xinjiang so Doudou would never see him again.[66] In response, Doudou tried to kill herself, only to be thwarted by her mother. Ye told everyone on the house staff to keep Doudou's suicide attempt from Lin Biao, and apparently he never learned of it.[67] So strong were the tensions between Ye and Doudou, however, that even Mao knew of them. After the Lin Biao incident, Mao passed the word to Doudou through the Central Investigation Group for Special Cases that he knew about the two "parties" in Lin's family, her father's party and her mother's party, which meant that Mao knew about Doudou's problems with her mother and brother.[68]

Among the children of high officials, Doudou was not the only victim of a distorted family relationship. Because of the strength of tradition, Ye may not have realized that her desire to control her daughter's life actually ruined it. She may well have believed that what she did was for Doudou's benefit, especially when she insisted on choosing Doudou's husband. Mao's three surviving children, Li Min, Li Na, and Mao Anying, all had problems similar to Doudou's.[69] All of them may have suffered some degree of depression in response to the pressures associated with being Mao's offspring.

LIN LIGUO AND HIS COLLEAGUES

If Doudou was a victim of family circumstances, her brother, Lin Liguo, used family connections to his own advantage. Liguo, born in 1946, was less sensitive than Doudou, and he likely received much better treatment from Ye Qun, though little biographical information is available about Liguo except for the last few years of his life. Even the memoir of Zhang Ning, Lin Liguo's former fiancée, gives few clues about Liguo. People who knew him in his school years remember him as a quiet and timid person. Zhang Ning says that Liguo "seldom spoke on public occasions" and was an introvert, like his father.[70] When the Cultural Revolution began, he was a student at Qinghua University. When the revolution closed all schools, Ye Qun arranged for him to join the PLA, one of the best careers for young men during the Cultural Revolution. Most high officials arranged for their children to join the armed forces, where they enjoyed social prestige and established their careers. The air force became a favorite career starter for children of high officials. Mao Yuanxin, Mao's nephew, was an air force officer in a missile unit in the Northeast. Both Lin Doudou and Lin Liguo joined the air force in Beijing. Children or relatives of other high officials, including Zhou Enlai, Zhu De, Dong Biwu, Liu Bocheng, Li Fuchun, Li Xiannian, Yang Chengwu, Xu Shiyou, Han Xianchu, Wang Dongxing, and Yang Dezhong, all entered the air force through "special arrangements" (*teshu guanxi*).

When Lin Liguo arrived at air force headquarters in Beijing, he immediately became a center of attention. The air force commander, Wu Faxian, saw to it personally that Liguo received the best care. He chose Zhou Yuchi, a secretary in the general office where Liguo worked, to be Liguo's partner and to make sure that all Liguo's needs were met. Unlike Lin Doudou, who behaved cautiously and seldom asked for special favors, Liguo quickly learned to take advantage of his special status to have things done his own way. Ye Qun, who seldom showed special concern for Doudou, often called Wu to make special arrangements for Liguo. She wanted Wang Fei, director of the General Office of the Air Force Party Committee, to take care of Liguo politically and demanded that Wu recruit Liguo into the party. "It will also help the work of the air force to put Liguo there," Ye told Wu. "He can report directly to Commander Lin about your work." Wu felt flattered, believing that Lin and Ye's decision to have Liguo enter the air force showed their trust in him and would later bring honor to the air force. Out of loyalty to Lin Biao, Wu acceded to Ye's every demand. He personally recommended that Liguo be enrolled in the party organizations of the air force.[71]

But things did not turn out as Wu expected. With Ye protecting him, Liguo soon began acting on his own. He gathered a group of mid-ranking air force officers around him, most of whom were his colleagues in the General Office of the Air Force Party Committee. Liguo, like many children of high officials, believed he was superior to other people in intelligence and ability. Because of their family connections, children of the elite had access to privileged information and were also in positions to influence their parents. They belonged to a new generation that was qualitatively different from their parents' generation: they were better educated and less intellectually rigid, but they were also more self-servingly ambitious and politically naive. Probably only a few of them genuinely respected their parents, and probably most of them believed they could do better than their parents if given the chance.

Ambitious young officers flocked to Liguo, hoping that a close association with the son of so exalted a man would open up opportunities for them. During peacetime, promotion was slow and limited in the armed forces, especially for men who worked in offices. China did not develop a system of civilian employees in the armed forces until the mid-1980s. If these young officers were lucky enough to be chosen as secretaries for commanders or vice-commanders, they might have a brighter future. Otherwise they would remain junior officers until released from the armed forces, which seldom brought better opportunities in the Maoist era. Zhou Yuchi was one such officer. He had been chosen as secretary to the former commander, Liu Yalou, but was sent back to the General Office for neglecting his duties. If he had not met Lin Liguo, he probably would have remained an anonymous junior officer, awaiting his turn to be released from the service. Association with Liguo, however, brought him fame and power, as it did to Liguo's other close associates. Gradually, they formed a de facto faction at air force headquarters.

After he settled into his career in the air force, Liguo professed to be unhappy at always being treated as only Lin Biao's son. He was eager to prove himself and wanted a career of his own. As noted earlier in the discussion of the fall of Yang Chengwu, Yu Lijin, and Fu Chongbi in early 1968, Liguo and his colleagues, with Ye Qun's backing, had behaved arrogantly and defiantly toward Commander Wu. Those who would not associate themselves with this group at air force headquarters were the objects of their constant harassment. Commander Wu, however, did nothing to restrain their conduct since one of them was Lin Biao's son.

Bored with his job as a secretary in the General Office of the air force headquarters in Beijing, Liguo decided to create a more exciting assignment for himself elsewhere. In the summer of 1968, Wang Fei and Zhou

Yuchi approached Wu Faxian, asking permission for Liguo and a group under his command to inspect troops outside Beijing and gather firsthand information for policy makers at headquarters. When Wu agreed to the proposal, Liguo and his colleagues gained license to travel to Guangzhou, Shanghai, Nanchang, and wherever else they wanted to go. Few people knew what they were doing, and no one cared to find out. Made careless by the presence of Liguo at their helm, the young officers went overboard. They had special buildings built or designated for themselves and set up "investigation groups" in Shanghai and Guangzhou, which the Party Central Committee labeled a counter-revolutionary "small fleet" after the Lin Biao incident. The label, however, was political rather than factual. There is no evidence that the groups engaged in any counter-revolutionary activities. Liguo and his colleagues may have abused their powers and squandered funds, but their almost juvenile antics were not really associated with anti-party or anti-government motivations.[72]

In October 1969, Ye Qun pressed the air force to promote Liguo. She called Wu Faxian to suggest that Liguo could do more for the air force than he was doing in the General Office. Wu took this as another opportunity to do something for Lin Biao. At the time, Li Na, Mao's daughter, was deputy chief editor of the *Jiefangjun bao* (*PLA Daily*), and Mao Yuanxin, Mao's nephew, was deputy director of the Liaoning Province Revolutionary Committee. It seemed appropriate to Wu to promote Lin's children as long as they did not outrank Li Na and Mao Yuanxin. On October 17, Commander Wu and Political Commissar Wang Huiqiu appointed Lin Liguo deputy director of the General Office and deputy minister of the Department of Operations of the air force. Lin Doudou became deputy chief editor of *Kongjun bao* (*Air Force Daily*). Since Ye Qun had raised the subject of promotion, Wu believed that it was Lin's idea, too. In fact, Lin knew nothing of the promotions for a year because Ye was afraid he would oppose the special treatment she had arranged for Liguo.[73]

At Ye Qun's instigation, Liguo became actively involved in politics. By 1970, he and his colleagues were pushing hard to further Liguo's career. Young and politically inexperienced, Liguo became more and more ambitious and hotheaded with each new advancement. Even the secretaries in Lin's office noticed the changes in Liguo. Unlike Doudou, who became more and more cynical and uninterested in politics, Liguo grew increasingly keen about anything with implications for his new career. He acted as if he were a special channel between Lin and the air force, making important decisions on his own without consulting his superiors. For example, after his trips to the South to inspect local troops, Liguo recommended several changes to improve military technology in the air force.

Taking advantage of his special status and without approval from his seniors, he carried his reports directly to Lin, which violated every rule for processing documents of this kind. Later, Lin sent one of Liguo's reports to Mao, and Mao responded with complimentary comments on Liguo's "achievement." Encouragement from Mao fueled Liguo's willingness to act on his own.[74]

In the summer of 1970, Liguo and his friends at headquarters prepared a report on Liguo's "achievements" since joining the air force. Ye Qun arranged for Liguo to rehearse the presentation of the report in front of Lin's staff before Liguo read it at an air force conference chaired by Political Commissar Wang Huiqiu. Commander Wu did not attend the conference but sent his wife there to show his support. Afterward, Wu called Ye Qun to offer his congratulations on Liguo's performance. The flattering compliments to Lin Liguo from air force leaders resulted in a new movement to have Lin Liguo instruct the air force on how to accomplish its mission. The situation was soon out of control. Liguo's colleagues made full use of the praise Liguo's report had garnered, especially Wu's exaggerated statement that "Liguo could command the entire air force." Wu was carried away by his eagerness to please Lin Biao and Ye Qun and did not realize that Liguo's colleagues were taking advantage of his words until it was too late. Liguo's comrades began acting as if Wu had actually yielded command of the air force to Liguo. "I truly regretted that I accepted Liguo into the air force," Wu recalled many years later. "I never expected that he would bring so much trouble."[75]

The exaggerated compliments on Liguo's report and Liguo himself soon had negative results at air force headquarters. His colleagues insisted that the air force print the report and distribute it to the troops, even though Commander Wu had not endorsed the idea.[76] Wu was worried that these antics would catch the attention of party leaders and cause him trouble. His worries soon became reality. At the Second Plenum at Lushan in August 1970, Zhou Enlai told Wu that Liguo's report was good, but that the air force should not praise it so uncritically. When someone on Mao's staff expressed a similar opinion to Wu, he became even more nervous. Wu reported the criticisms to Ye Qun, who also agreed that caution was necessary since Mao had just issued his criticisms of Chen Boda and Lin's generals. Wu immediately asked his wife in Beijing to go to headquarters and confiscate and destroy the copies of Liguo's report.

But it was already too late to stop Liguo and his colleagues. Liguo, who had little respect for his father's generation, was determined to go his own way. In the summer of 1970, he went to Lushan with Ye Qun to observe the Second Plenum and concluded that Ye Qun and Lin's generals were no match for Mao and Jiang Qing's group. Because of his own family experience, Liguo knew too much to respect the first-generation revolutionaries. He therefore decided to mobilize his own allies and establish a power base of his own.

After the Lushan Conference, Commander Wu recognized that he was losing control of Liguo and his colleagues, as well as other junior officers at air force headquarters. Liguo's colleagues visited the various air force units in the military regions, spreading the word that Wu had "made mistakes" at Lushan.[77] In the summer of 1970, Wu's office received repeated reports from the regions that something "abnormal" was afoot. Zhang Yonggeng, the political commissar of the air force in the Shenyang Military Region, told Wu that one of his junior officers was spreading the word that Lin Liguo was a genius and that whoever opposed the "learn from Liguo" movement was politically out of step. The officer also reportedly told his young colleagues that when they went to Beijing they should contact He Dequan in the Department of Intelligence and Lu Min in the Department of Operations, both of whom were believed to be members of Liguo's group, and no one else.[78]

In the summer of 1971, Wu's office received more reports on the factional activities of Liguo and his colleagues. Even one of Wu's former secretaries, who had been transferred to the Guangzhou Military Region, reported to Wu that he was spied on and was treated as a "dissident" at Guangzhou because he had come from Wu's office. In the Beijing headquarters, Liguo and his colleagues made lists of the officers on their side, as distinct from those they considered loyal to Commander Wu. Their list of men loyal to Liguo contained the names of at least 64 officers at air force headquarters. All the people on the list were arrested after the Lin Biao incident. One section chief of the Department of General Staff of the air force related to me later that he was the only section chief in his department who was not on the list of men loyal to Liguo. He was therefore isolated at the time from his colleagues and treated as a dissident.[79]

The split between Liguo and Wu was not just a personal dispute. On the contrary, the split indicated a wide generation gap between first-generation revolutionaries and their children's generation. Liguo and his group represented a younger generation in the military, ambitious and better educated than their seniors. So far, there is little information available about the ideas and activities of Liguo's group, but in interviews with several group members I learned that they were not simply ambitious, power-hungry, and even malicious as they have been depicted by most Chinese writers. They struck me as open-minded and possessed of more political insight into and understanding of the Cultural Revolution than other officers I interviewed. It is not totally surprising that the officers around Liguo believed that they deserved more power and space to practice Liguo's ideas and their own. The best written illustration of their thinking is perhaps the "Outline of Project 571," the alleged plan for the coup. Most of it is concerned with the political situation during the Cultural Revolution and reads more like a political proclamation than a plan for a coup. The following excerpts from the "Outline" are typical:

> Since the Second Plenum of the Ninth Party Central Committee, the political situation has been unstable; a split has shattered the ruling group and the rightists are getting the upper hand; the military is being suppressed. The national economy has been stagnant for over ten years, and the living standard of the masses, basic-level cadres, and middle- and lower-ranked military officials is falling. Dissatisfaction is spreading. They are angry but dare not speak, and they have even come to the point of not daring to be angry, let alone speak. The ruling group is corrupt, muddled, and incompetent. The masses are in rebellion and friends are deserting.
>
> (1) A political crisis is in the making.
>
> (2) A struggle for power is in progress.
>
> (3) The object of opponents is to change successors.
>
> (4) China is in the midst of a gradual, peacefully evolving political coup.
>
> (5) This kind of coup was his [Mao's] old trick.
>
> (6) He [Mao] employed the same old tricks.
>
> (7) The coup is developing in a way that will benefit the "pen" instead of the "gun."[80]
>
> (8) Therefore, we should make violent, revolutionary, and rapid change to block this evolving peaceful, counter-revolutionary change. Otherwise, if we cannot use "Project 571" to stop peaceful evolution, once they succeed, who knows how many heads will fall and for how many years the Chinese Revolution will continue to be conducted?
>
> (9) A new power struggle is inevitable. If we do not gain power, it will fall into the hands of others. . . .
>
> The Trotskyite clique that wields the "pen" willfully tampers with and distorts Marxism-Leninism in order to deceive and mislead the Chinese people.
>
> Their present theory of continuing revolution is the same as Trotsky's theory of permanent revolution.
>
> The target of their revolution is, in fact, the Chinese people, and above all the armed forces and those whose opinions do not agree with theirs. Their socialism is in essence social fascism.
>
> They have turned China's state machine into a meat grinder for mutual slaughter and strife.
>
> They have turned political life in the state and the party into a feudal, dictatorial, and patriarchal system. . . .

Cadres who were rejected and attacked in the course of the protracted struggle within the party and the Cultural Revolution are angry but dare not speak.

The peasants lack food and are short of clothing.

The sending of young students to the mountains and the countryside is really a disguised form of unemployment.

During the early stages, the Red Guards were cheated and used, and they served as cannon fodder; during the later stages, they were suppressed and made into scapegoats.

Administrative cadres were cut back and sent to "May 7 cadres' schools," which amounted to reform through labor.

Workers (especially young workers) had their wages frozen, which amounted to disguised exploitation. . . .

Is there a single political force that has been able to work with him [Mao] from beginning to end? His former secretaries have either committed suicide or been arrested. His few close comrades-in-arms or trusted aides have also been sent to prison by him. Even his own son has been driven mad by him.

He [Mao] is a paranoid and sadist. His philosophy of liquidating people is either do not do it or do it thoroughly. Every time he liquidates someone, he does not desist until he puts them to death; once he hurts you, he will hurt you all the way, and he puts the blame for everything bad on others.

Frankly speaking, all of those who have been forced from the scene in his merry-go-round style have in fact been made scapegoats for his own crimes.[81]

From these excerpts, one can see that the "Outline of Project 571," written in 1971, anticipated many criticisms of Mao and the politics of the Cultural Revolution that have been widely accepted in the post-Mao era. During the Cultural Revolution, however, probably only a person like Lin Liguo, who knew the "inside story" of the ruling elite and who combined that knowledge with a sense of superiority, could speak this way—or would have dared to do so. Liguo's thinking had obviously influenced his colleagues; unfortunately, the thoughts of anyone who reasoned that way while Mao lived were unacceptable.

The experiences of Doudou and Liguo illustrate two different results of being the children of Chinese high officials. Some children had identity problems and lived in the shadow of their families, but many made the most of their privileged lives, becoming involved in politics and enjoying their fathers' reflected glory. While most people had only limited chances for upward social mobility, these children of high officials used their family connections to emerge as a privileged social group. They connected with each other through elite educational networks off-limits to the children of common families. School connections were a major source of "networking" power for those in important positions in government and business. When they went too far in pushing their privileges, they created problems not only for their families but in many cases for the country as well.

Political developments after Mao provide even more evidence of the connection between a national crisis and the behaviors of this privileged group. Despite brief setbacks and some personal suffering experienced by the "children" of the Cultural Revolution, many nonetheless reappeared later as an even more highly privileged group than they had been during the Cultural Revolution. Today, many of them, now in middle age, hold important government and military positions or have become the nouveaux riches of China. In fact, the general anger toward this privileged group was one of the elements that triggered the students' protests in early 1989, which led to the showdown at Tiananmen Square on June 4, 1989. Still, because of the traditional Chinese emphasis on family and family ties, this group, now collectively known as the "princes' party," will probably continue to influence China's future policies more than any other social group. Liguo's role in the Lin Biao incident, which we turn to next, sheds new light on the mystery of Lin's death and shows how problems in the family of a high official triggered a national crisis.

7

The Lin Biao Incident

The Lin Biao incident in the narrowest sense was what happened to Lin Biao on September 12 and 13, 1971. Here I try to reconstruct what really happened that night. The following account is based on a careful study of the literature recently published in the PRC, in-depth interviews with many of the people involved in the incident, and careful readings of the official documents. An overall explication of the incident depends on one's interpretations of the activities of four groups: Lin's family at Beidaihe between September 6 and 12; Lin Liguo and his air force colleagues in Beijing; Lin Biao's generals, Huang Yongsheng, Wu Faxian, Li Zuopeng, and Qiu Huizuo; and most important, Mao and Zhou Enlai before and after they received reports of problems at Beidaihe.

Beidaihe, September 6–11, 1971

By September 1971, a split between Mao and Lin was inevitable and impending. Mao went on an inspection tour in the South in mid-August for the purpose of preparing provincial and military officials for the downfall of Lin and his generals.[1] At the same time, Lin Biao, who was in very poor health, was spending the summer at the seaside resort of Beidaihe.

On September 6, Lin Doudou, who was in Beijing at the time, received a phone call from Beidaihe asking her, her fiancé, Zhang Qinglin, and her brother's fiancée, Zhang Ning, to join Lin and the rest of Lin's family there. They arrived at Beidaihe around noon the next day. After a brief exchange of greetings, Ye took them to see Lin Biao. Zhang Ning was surprised to see that Lin Biao looked even sicker than he had two months earlier. His face looked thinner and pale, his eyes were sunken, and he was unshaven. Li Wenpu, Lin's chief bodyguard, told Doudou and Zhang

Ning, however, that Lin Biao had been in a good mood when he saw them and that their visit had pleased him.[2]

That afternoon, Liguo, who was by then deputy chief of the Department of Operations and deputy director of the General Office of the Party Committee of the air force, took Doudou away for a conversation. The exact content of their conversation is not known, but there is evidence that Liguo tried to persuade Doudou to go along with his plan to "protect" their father from Mao's challenge. Doudou apparently disagreed with her brother on the need for aggressive action and urged him instead to consult their father before making any important moves. Their conversation lasted a couple of hours, which suggests that both siblings considered it important. The following is the conversation between Lin's children, Liguo and Doudou, as reconstructed by Liguo's fiancée, Zhang Ning:

> At 3:00 P.M. [September 7], Lin Liguo asked Lin Doudou to come over to Building 57 alone for a talk. Liguo said to her, "Since the Lushan Conference, Group One will not let the director go.[3] She made several self-criticisms, but still could not satisfy him. Now, he is on an inspection tour to the South and has meetings with provincial leaders along the way, taking advantage of Shou Zhang's convalescence at Beidaihe.[4] In several of his speeches, he openly discussed his problem with Shou Zhang, spreading his negative opinions of Shou Zhang. His purpose is to get rid of Shou Zhang eventually. Being in such poor health, how can Shou Zhang survive if Group One decides to purge him? There were the examples of Liu Shaoqi and Peng Dehuai in the past.[5] What is worse is that Shou Zhang refused to give in and to admit that he had done anything wrong [i.e., he refused to make a self-criticism]. Group One has sent a very clear message that he has lost his trust in Shou Zhang, which indicates that he will purge Shou Zhang soon. It is better for us to risk everything on a single venture and to wage a struggle than to wait for our doom."
>
> Doudou did not know much about what had happened after the Lushan Conference, since she did not live at home. She could hardly believe what Liguo told her and was even more shocked when she heard Liguo's plan to fight back.
>
> "What kind of struggle do you want to wage?" She asked Liguo. "The chairman has such high prestige that Shou Zhang will be in an even more disadvantageous position if we do not act with great caution."
>
> "After all, we are already in a very disadvantageous position," Liguo replied. "Better to strike actively than to sit there awaiting the worst. We may have a chance. Who knows! Of course I can wait to see what happens in future. As a last resort, we may either wage a "hard" struggle against Group One or go to Guangzhou in the South to set up another central government, or we may go to the mountains to start a guerrilla war. Shou Zhang has been a military commander for so many years and enjoys very

high prestige in the armed forces. When the time comes, we will expose the two-faced behavior of Group One and make public all the evil things he did in the past. Then, we can call on the whole country to condemn him. We will find a way."

Believing that it was very dangerous for Liguo to think along that line, Doudou tried to discourage him. "Do not just listen to what the director says. She always exaggerates and also lies to Shou Zhang. Do not be so hot-headed as to mislead Shou Zhang. . . ."

Sensing that Liguo had not told her everything, Doudou was eager to find out what was really in Liguo's and Ye Qun's minds. She asked again, "Are things really as bad as you described? What is Shou Zhang's opinion? Does he know anything?"

"No," Liguo replied. "Shou Zhang does not know anything yet. I cannot tell him something like this before I have considered it carefully."

Doudou immediately sensed that things were serious. "You cannot cooperate with the director to deceive Shou Zhang," she warned Liguo. "You must not do anything radical, no matter what, without Shou Zhang's consent. You must not believe what the director says. You will not be able to escape responsibility if anything happens. Shou Zhang will not forgive you."

"In your opinion, is it best that we do nothing but await our doom?" Liguo shouted at Doudou.

Because Doudou disagreed so completely with his idea of taking radical action, Liguo complained, "I just cannot take it like that. Group One can simply make the sky clear and then make it dark. He purges whoever he wants to and nobody dares wage a struggle against him. But I will not take it. Shou Zhang has restrained himself for so many years but still cannot be spared a purge. Can you just stand idly by and see Shou Zhang be purged?"

"I will return to Beijing tomorrow," Liguo then said firmly.[6]

The conversation between sister and brother continued the next day, September 8. They still could not agree on what to do if Mao took action against their father. Before Doudou left her room in Building 56 around noon to talk to Liguo, she told Zhang Qinglin, her fiancé, part of her conversation with Liguo the day before. She asked him to be careful and to seek protection from the guards if she failed to return by 6:00 P.M. Qinglin did not know exactly what was going on and became very nervous. Nothing happened that day, however, and Doudou returned early. Without telling Qinglin everything she knew, Doudou nevertheless told him that *Laohu* (the tiger), a nickname for her brother, was planning to take action against Mao and probably would take Lin Biao away from Beidaihe. She did not agree with Liguo's plan because she was primarily concerned with protecting Lin Biao, who was suffering from a chronic illness and had been in isolation from the outside world for a long time.

Lin Liguo left for Beijing that evening, telling Lin Biao he was going to see his dentist. Lin Biao seemed to disapprove of Liguo's returning to Beijing, so Liguo told Li Wenpu that if Lin Biao asked about Liguo's whereabouts Li should tell him that Liguo had gone swimming.[7] According to one of Lin's secretaries who had remained at Maojiawan, Lin's residence in Beijing, Liguo did see a dentist while in Beijing. The secretary made the appointment for Liguo at Hospital 301, the General Hospital of the Military.[8] However, Liguo did not stay at Maojiawan all the time because it was being renovated in preparation for Lin's return before October 1, National Day, on which he was to give a speech at Tiananmen.

After Liguo left Beidaihe, Doudou and Zhang Qinglin warned some of the staff members of Liguo's possible plan to take Lin Biao away from Beidaihe. Doudou first told Liu Jichun, one of Lin's two chief bodyguards, about her conversation with Liguo and asked him to alert Li Wenpu about the problem. She then talked with Lin's attendants and medical orderlies, few of whom believed her, however.[9] Doudou seldom lied to the staff, but what she told them was too astonishing for them to believe. They seemed to believe that this just was another episode in the family feud. They asked Doudou what evidence she had for such an accusation against her mother and brother. "It's no joke to exaggerate your family problem to such an extent," they pointed out. Li Wenpu, who was in charge of Lin Biao's security and daily life and a key figure in subsequent events, was especially suspicious about Doudou's account, claiming that nothing unusual had happened in the previous several days.[10] In fact, of the two siblings, Liguo was more popular than his sister among the staff because of his easygoing nature. If Doudou was wrong about her brother, it was the staff who would be punished. Not knowing whom to trust or what to do, everyone in the household staff watched carefully instead of taking substantive action to counter a possible "plot." This stance among the staff members continued until late on the night of September 12.

Doudou was confused, too. She knew that she had every reason to believe her father was in trouble, because it seemed that Liguo completely sided with Ye Qun, whom she had never trusted, and that together they might do something radical to "protect" Lin. Things like that had been happening in the family for years, and Doudou had known Ye to lie to Lin many times before. Doudou tried hard to persuade Liguo not to return to Beijing, but Liguo would not listen to her and left anyway. Doudou was not sure, however, that she knew everything about Liguo's plan; she did not even know whether Liguo was serious about what he had said. Challenge Mao? Nobody dared to think of such a thing during the Cultural Revolution! She still hoped that what Liguo had told her was nothing more than another complaint against Mao, though this one struck her as more serious than others. In any event, Liguo had mentioned before he left that he would wait until after National Day and see what happened. By that time, Doudou hoped, Liguo might change his mind.

For the first several days after Liguo left, Doudou was torn over what to do. If she went to her father directly but was wrong about her mother and brother, they would never forgive her. The only person she could confide in was her fiancé, who had come into her life only a few months earlier and was still unfamiliar with the complexities and subtleties of Lin Biao's family life. In desperation, Doudou isolated herself from others, including Zhang Ning, who was housed in the same building with her. Meanwhile, she and the few people who shared her concern paid close attention to what happened around Lin Biao. Each morning, she and Zhang Qinglin walked around the area, trying to determine the regular route of Lin Biao's morning car ride. Otherwise, Lin Biao seldom left the house.[11] After that, Doudou would shut herself in her room, refusing to see anyone, especially Ye Qun. Once, she even had Zhang Qinglin eavesdrop on Ye and Lin Biao from the roof, but Zhang had not been able to hear anything. Between September 9 and 11, nothing out of the ordinary happened, and Doudou began to relax a bit. On the afternoon of September 10, she, Qinglin, and Zhang Ning went sightseeing at Shanhaiguan, a famous historic spot near Beidaihe. Upon their return around 5:00 P.M., they went to see Lin Biao, taking him gifts they had bought on the excursion. Lin was happy to see them and impressed by the gifts, especially a toy soldier that performed military exercises.

Ye Qun seemed to lead a quiet life at Beidaihe, enjoying swimming, reading, and attending history lectures. She was seen reading a Chinese translation of *Le Père Goriot* and a biography of Richard Nixon and regularly attending lectures given by Zhang Zhan, her history tutor.[12] Each evening, she invited Doudou, Qinglin, and Zhang Ning to watch movies with her until midnight. On the evening of September 9, Ye asked Zhang Ning to stay after the movie, and the two chatted until early the next morning about details of Ye's life. Zhang Ning told me years later that after the incident she had been forced to write about this talk repeatedly, because the Central Investigation Group for Special Cases could not believe that Ye would have spent so much time talking about such trivial things only three days before the incident. She was supposed to have been busily engaged in plotting a "profound" struggle against Mao.[13]

The Lin family was also preparing a wedding at Beidaihe. Ye had telephoned General Wu Faxian on the afternoon of September 9 to inform him of Doudou's upcoming marriage to Zhang Qinglin. Ye had asked Wu to choose movies for the wedding celebration, since Doudou was an officer in the air force. Despite his annoyance at being asked to attend to such a trivial matter, Wu had his wife borrow some movie magazines and went through them in order to find appropriate movies for the wedding.[14] Hu Min, the wife of General Qiu Huizuo, telephoned Ye on the afternoon of September 11 to congratulate Doudou and Qinglin. She also talked directly with Qinglin for a while. Zhang Qinglin told me years later that he had wanted to tell Hu Min what was happening at Beidaihe but could not because Ye was present. "Things might have been totally different if I could have gotten the message across to the generals," Zhang told me.[15]

Around 5:00 P.M. on September 12, Ye Qun took Doudou and Qinglin to Lin's quarters, where she announced suddenly that their wedding would be held that evening. Taken by surprise, both Doudou and Qinglin refused to get married so suddenly. In a compromise, they agreed to celebrate their engagement instead. Liguo brought them gifts when he returned from Beijing later that evening. The celebration of Doudou's engagement continued until around midnight, when Ye abruptly decided to leave for the airport.

BEIJING: LIN LIGUO AND HIS COLLEAGUES

In retrospect, it seems certain that what Liguo and his colleagues did in Beijing between September 8 and September 12 is crucial to understanding the incident. Most of the official charges against Lin Biao, including the alleged attempts to assassinate Mao, stage a military coup, and establish a rival government in the South, point directly to the activities of Liguo. The following reconstruction of the activities of Liguo's group over those four days is largely based on evidence provided by the CCP documents about the Lin Biao incident and the publications of the official investigation for the open trial of Lin's group in 1980–81.

After Liguo left Maojiawan on September 8, he and Zhou Yuchi, one of his air force colleagues, had gone to Xijiao airport, a military airport in the suburbs of Beijing.[16] There they met several other air force officers, including Jiang Tengjiao and Li Weixin.[17] According to a CCP document, Liguo showed the other officers a "handwritten order from Lin Biao," which said, "Please follow the message passed on by Liguo and Yuchi." The order was signed by Lin Biao and dated September 8.[18] Liguo then told Jiang Tengjiao to take action against Mao—that is, to assassinate Mao in Shanghai, and they then discussed how it might be accomplished.[19] Later that night, Liguo went to the air force academy, where he showed Lin's "written order" to Liu Peifeng and Cheng Hongzhen, secretaries of the office of the Party Committee of the air force. "Confessions" detailed in the CCP documents and testimony by Liguo's colleagues during the 1980–81 "open trial" of Lin Biao and Jiang Qing claim that Liguo and Zhou Yuchi continued constructing their plot the next day, September 9. According to Cheng Hongzhen, Zhou Yuchi had asked him that morning to sketch a map of Diaoyutai, where Madame Mao and her colleagues were staying. After Cheng finished the map, he gave it to Zhou between 4:00 and 5:00 P.M. that day. Zhou also asked Cheng to get information concerning new chemical weapons and explosives being experimented with by the State Commission for Science and Technology in National Defense (*guofang kewei*) and the Science Department of the air force.[20]

Jiang Tengjiao testified during the 1980–81 trial that he met with Liguo, Zhou Yuchi, and Wang Fei, deputy chief of staff of the air force, on the evening of September 8 and again on the morning of September 9 at the Xijiao airport to discuss the assassination plan, but that they could not reach an agreement at either meeting.[21] The following is an excerpt from Jiang's testimony concerning this discussion:

Judge: Jiang Tengjiao, Article Forty-one of the indictment accuses you of the following: that after reading Lin Biao's personal instructions on September 8, 1971, you did specifically, until September 11, plan and conspire with Lin Liguo and Zhou Yuchi to assassinate Chairman Mao Zedong, and did accept Lin Liguo's commission to act as commander of the front line in the Shanghai district.

Jiang: Uh!

Judge: Where did you see Lin Liguo on September 8?

Jiang: At Peking West airfield [Xijiao airport]. . . .

Judge: What command did Lin Liguo bestow on you?

Jiang: He wanted me to go to Shanghai as commander of the front line.

Judge: To command what?

Jiang: The implementation of the plot to kill Chairman Mao. . . .

Judge: [to Jiang Tengjiao] What course of action did you plan?

Jiang: On the evening of the eighth, after Lin Liguo showed me Lin Biao's counterrevolutionary instructions and I had committed myself to their side, we sat down and he said they had thought up three courses of action. One was to attack the special train that Mao was traveling in with flamethrowers and bazookas. The second was to use 100mm anti-aircraft guns to fire point-blank at the train. The third was for Wang Weiguo to go see Chairman Mao, take a pistol along, and shoot him on the train. [Wang Weiguo was the political commissar of the Fourth Air Force Army in the Nanjing Military Region.]

Judge: Did you go on and discuss any other ideas?

Jiang: We couldn't reach an agreement that evening and didn't come to a conclusion. On the ninth, we went on discussing it, and the question of bombing a bridge was raised—that was Zhou Yuchi's idea. In the afternoon we discussed other suggestions.

Judge: Did you discuss blowing up fuel tanks?

Jiang: That was brought up on the previous evening, after the other three ideas. We ate—it was getting overlate. Everybody left the room to eat; only Zhou Yuchi and I stayed behind . . . Zhou Yuchi asked me whether the fuel tanks could be bombed, and I said I wasn't sure, but anyway they could be set alight. The ensuing confusion would be splendid, because in the conflagration we could seize the opportunity to act, and assassinate Chairman Mao. We planned that when Chairman Mao's train came into the station. We would say there had been an accident involving the fuel tanks, and troops were guarding him. But that plan wasn't approved that evening either.

Judge: Did you give this plan to Zhou Yuchi, and did he give it to Lin Liguo?

Jiang: As soon as they saw it, they agreed to this course of action. But later on I said the plan was no good, because after the fuel tanks were bombed the guards on the Chairman's train would come to take over.

Judge: Did you really plan to bomb the fuel tanks? Had you drawn up a plan to this effect, and had they then agreed to it? [without waiting for the reply]. . . . Did you go into the question of code words and passwords to be used between Shanghai and Peking?[22]

Little is known about the activities of Liguo and his colleagues for the next two days, between the evening of September 9 and the afternoon of September 11. It seems that after the initial contact with his colleagues in Beijing and several fruitless meetings, Liguo took care of personal matters, including a visit to the dentist, and relaxed for a while until the afternoon of the eleventh when he and his colleagues met again. By then Liguo had received the contents of Mao's speeches to the provincial leaders, and Mao was on his way back to Beijing to implement his plans against Lin Biao.[23]

In response to Mao's challenge, Liguo and his colleagues held two key meetings in Beijing that day.[24] The first meeting began at Xijiao airport in the afternoon and continued into the evening. Wang Fei, Zhou Yuchi, Jiang Tengjiao, and Yu Xinye were present when Liguo told them of his decision to assassinate Mao in the South.[25] Lu Min, director of the Department of Operations of the air force, joined them at the airport in the evening. They still could not agree on exactly what to do, apparently because few among them were really serious about the plan to assassinate Mao. For instance, one of them told me later that he himself dared not participate in a plot to assassinate Mao. However, because Lin Liguo was Lin Biao's son, he did not think that he was in any position to confront him, either. So, he deliberately proposed something outrageous during the discussion in order to discourage Liguo from taking any action. After the meeting, he was so nervous about the possible consequences that he deliberately hurt himself and was hospitalized, using this as an excuse for not participating in any further meetings with Liguo. After much hesitation, he tried to report to the central government on September 12 before learning what had happened at Beidaihe. The accusations against Lin Biao in the first group of CCP documents issued after the Lin Biao incident were largely based on his and other colleagues' confessions. Because none of Liguo's colleagues knew anything about "Project 571" at the time, accusations that Lin had planned a coup were not included in the CCP documents issued in September–October 1971, but appeared in documents after November 1971 after the Special Case Group discovered the notebook on which the alleged plan was written.[26] Even if Liguo and his colleagues had agreed on a course of action against Mao, the plan would have had to be canceled later that night when Wang Weiguo called to tell them that Mao had left Shanghai for Beijing.[27]

The next day, September 12, when Liguo learned that Mao had returned to Beijing, he and his colleagues came up with another plan in desperation—to take Lin Biao as well as Generals Huang, Wu, Li, and Qiu to Guangzhou on the next day, September 13. Lin Liguo left for Beidaihe that evening, leaving Zhou Yuchi to work out the details. After Liguo left, Zhou called a meeting at the air force academy. When Jiang Tengjiao arrived, Zhou Yuchi told him, "We have decided that at 8:00 A.M. tomorrow Lin's plane will take off from Beidaihe and fly directly to Shati airport in Guangzhou."[28] Zhou then proceeded to explain in detail what Wang Fei, Yu Xinye, and Jiang should do in Beijing the next day: After arriving at Xijiao airport, one of them would call General Huang Yongsheng, telling him that Lin Biao had returned from Beidaihe and wanted to see him at the airport. Then they would ask Huang to call Generals Wu, Li, and Qiu to the airport, giving the same reason. Upon the generals' arrival, at least two persons from Liguo's group would force each general onto waiting planes. Then, the group would fly together to Shati airport in Guangzhou. When Jiang asked what Lin Biao would do in Guangzhou, Zhou asserted that Lin would first call a meeting of military cadres to tell them what had happened, and then would address the people nationwide over the radio.

At the end of the meeting, Zhou asked Wang Fei and Yu Xinye to gather enough men from air force headquarters to carry out the mission the next day. Wang and Yu, consequently, held another meeting at the major office building with seven people present, including Lu Min, Liu Shiying, He Dequan, Zhu Tiezheng, and Zheng Xinghe.[29] They decided which air force officers should be in charge of which general and who should be on which plane and made a list of people they could trust and should bring to Guangzhou.[30] However, everything was again called off around 11:00 P.M. At that time, Zhou Yuchi passed word to the people at the meeting that Zhou Enlai had suddenly checked the whereabouts of Trident 256, the plane designated for Lin's use.[31] This indicated that Zhou may have known about the plan, and thus the plan had to be canceled. Before everybody returned home, Wang told them to forget what had happened and not to mention a word of it to anyone.

One other point should be mentioned here. The most dubious bit of official evidence in the CCP documents is "Lin's handwritten order," which was the *sole* direct link connecting Lin Biao to the "plots." Lin Doudou and her husband always insisted thereafter that the handwriting on the order was not Lin's at all. During the trial, the prosecutors provided a document of determination by the Department of Security of the General Political Department of the PLA, No. 226, to prove that the handwriting was Lin's. However, they refused Doudou's request to show her either the handwriting or the document.[32] She knew that Liguo had practiced imitating Lin's handwriting for a long time, and Liguo had even encouraged her to do so, assuring her that someday the ability would prove useful. Zhang Yunsheng, a former secretary to Lin Biao, provided another piece of evidence to support Doudou's notion. He revealed in his book that Lin himself had endorsed Ye's idea that several of Lin's secretaries should be capable of imitating Lin's handwriting in order to write comments on documents for Lin Biao.[33] However, even if the handwriting was really Lin's, the order was so vague that it could have meant anything.

In fact, one of Lin's former secretaries who had seen "Lin's order" and was familiar with Lin's handwriting told me that he believed at the time that the note was actually written by Lin. He later provided written testimony on this point at the request of the Central Investigation Group for the Special Case of Lin Biao. However, after learning years later of Liguo's ability to imitate his father's handwriting, he felt much less sure about his earlier testimony. Regardless of whether the handwriting was Lin's, the secretary is sure that the note had nothing to do with the alleged coup attempt.[34] Even though he testified that the order was Lin's and was one of the few who had seen it, he was not accused of helping Lin or Liguo to stage a coup. To him, this meant that the order had nothing to do with the alleged coup attempt.

Beidaihe, September 12

Everything remained calm at Beidaihe until Liguo returned between 8:00 and 9:00 P.M. on September 12. First, he hurriedly went to talk to Ye Qun. Later he met Doudou and Qinglin in Lin's room and congratulated them on their engagement. As they were leaving the room, Doudou asked Liguo what his next step was. "Leave," Liguo told her. "To where?" "Dalian, or Guangzhou, or Hong Kong. Anywhere, depending on the situation."[35] He also told Doudou that the situation was tense in Beijing. Mao had decided to get rid of Generals Huang, Wu, Li, and Qiu, as well as Ye Qun. Then Liguo went to Ye's office again.

A moment later, a medical orderly, Little Zhang, arrived to tell Doudou that he had overheard Ye talking to Lin Biao about going to Guangzhou or Hong Kong, if necessary, but that Lin had remained silent. Doudou told Little Zhang to return to Lin's room immediately and try to find out Lin's own opinion about leaving.

Doudou's nightmare had at last come true: Liguo and Ye were going to take Lin Biao to Guangzhou, and perhaps some other place after that. Until then, she had felt reasonably sure that leaving would be against Lin's wishes. From all she had gathered in the past few days, Lin himself knew nothing about Liguo's plans. Several days earlier, Little Zhang had told her that Lin had said firmly to Ye, "I will, at least, remain as a patriot to the country. If I am going to die, I will die here at Beidaihe." Li Wenpu, who had been with Lin for more than twenty years and whom Lin trusted even more than he trusted Ye Qun and Liguo, also assured her that Lin knew nothing about what Liguo had told her on September 7 and 8. Doudou now realized that to save her father from trouble she had to act promptly. As long as she could keep Lin at Beidaihe, she would be able later to explain to her father what had happened. In her desperation, Doudou decided to turn for help to Unit 8341, the troops guarding the villa in Beidaihe.

Unit 8341, also known as the Party Central Committee's Regiment of the Guards, was under the command of the Beijing garrison and the General Office of the Central Committee of the CCP. For years, it had been under the direct control of Wang Dongxing and Zhang Yaoci, both of whom, but especially Wang, were known for their close relationship with Mao. In a sense, Unit 8341 performed the function of secret police, and Wang was its head. In retrospect, nothing could have been worse for Lin than Doudou's hasty revelation of Ye and Liguo's plan to these guards, for Unit 8341 was under the direct control of Lin's political opponents. Doudou's decision to report Liguo's plan, like her brother's action in Beijing, left Lin Biao's family no choice but to leave Beidaihe that night. Of course, Doudou's decision to go to Unit 8341 was due more to her own sense of desperation than to her trust of Wang Dongxing and Zhang Yaoci. She personally mistrusted both men. Later on she realized how naively she had dealt with the political crisis, but by then it was too late.

Before she went to Unit 8341, Doudou consulted Lin's bodyguards Li Wenpu and Liu Jichun.[36] Liu agreed with Doudou's concerns, but Li still questioned her interpretation of the situation.[37] Doudou asked the two guards whether Lin Biao knew what Liguo had told her. "There was no way for Shou Zhang to know this," Li firmly assured her. "I was with Shou Zhang all the time, and I am absolutely sure that he knows nothing." Then, Li told Doudou something that to Li himself seemed strange: sometime earlier, Ye had instructed Li to be ready to go to Guangzhou at 6:00 the next morning and told him not to inform Unit 8341 of the planned departure. This made Li Wenpu take Doudou's warning more seriously, because in the past, whenever Lin and Ye went somewhere, Ye had informed Zhou Enlai first, then the leaders of Unit 8341. Afterward, when Li asked Lin about going to Guangzhou, Lin told Li he did not want to go because the hot weather there was not good for his health. Later, Ye assured Lin that the building they would stay in in Guangzhou was air-conditioned, so it would not be as hot as he imagined. Lin did not comment further.

Thus, convinced that Lin knew nothing about why Ye and Liguo wanted to go to Guangzhou, Doudou decided to act on her own to protect her father. She asked Li if he had authority to issue direct orders to Unit 8341. Li told her that he had: several years before, Wang Dongxing and Zhang Yaoci had suggested that Li assume a leadership position in Unit 8341 while he continued to guard Lin, but Lin and Ye had rejected the suggestion. However, the Party Committee of Unit 8341 later decided to grant Li Wenpu the right to command the unit if it became necessary for Lin's safety. However, Li still was unsure that Doudou was right about Liguo's plot against Mao. "The director told me to get ready to go to Guangzhou, and so did Liguo," Li said hesitatingly. "In my opinion, they are just going to Guangzhou. If nothing like you mentioned happens, who will bear this responsibility?" Thus Li refused to go to Unit 8341 with the excuse that he was not sure what was going on.[38]

Around 10:00 P.M., Doudou and Liu Jichun went to Building 58, the office of Unit 8341 in Beidaihe. Zhang Hong, the deputy regiment commander, and Jiang Zuoshou, the head of the subunit (*dadui*), received them. Zhang Yaoci later recalled that Doudou told the officers of Unit 8341 that

Ye Qun and Liguo had a plan to kidnap Lin and force him to leave Beidaihe. They also planned to send planes to bomb Zhongnanhai (where
Mao's residence was located) in order to kill Mao.[39] She assured the officers repeatedly, however, that Lin himself knew nothing of the plan. In
order to convince them, Doudou asked them to contact Li Wenpu immediately; and since there were still about seven hours before the planned
departure to Guangzhou the next morning, she suggested that troops sur-
round Building 57, where Liguo resided, and Building 96, Lin and Ye's
residence. Zhang Hong, however, insisted on reporting the matter to
Wang Dongxing and Zhang Yaoci in Beijing before giving any orders.
This was the last thing Doudou wanted. She knew that a report to Wang
Dongxing meant a report to Mao and Zhou Enlai, for Wang would never
keep such important information from them. However, what was most
crucial at the moment to Doudou was preventing Liguo from taking Lin
away. Without the help of the guards, it would be impossible for her to do
that. But the guards would not listen to her or Li Wenpu without permission from their superiors. Doudou tried in vain to convince Zhang and
Jiang that it was unnecessary to report the matter to Beijing.

Doudou left the regimental office hoping that Unit 8341 would help
her protect her father. She felt reasonably certain by then that she could
save him from trouble, since Lin's staff as well as the officers at Unit 8341
seemed willing to help her. When Doudou returned to Building 96, the
movie at her engagement celebration was still on. She told Zhang Qinglin
that she had gone to Unit 8341. A moment later, a member of Ye's staff
summoned Doudou to see Ye. Uncertain what was about to happen,
Doudou told Zhang that if she did not return he should go to Unit 8341
and report her absence.[40] However, Ye Qun wanted only to tell her to be
ready to leave the next day; Shou Zhang was taking her and others to
Dalian.[41]

After Doudou returned, she again asked Li Wenpu about Lin. Li told
her Shou Zhang had already gone to bed after taking sleeping pills; as
was his habit, he went to bed before 11:00 P.M. All those I interviewed
agree that Lin had taken sleeping pills that night. While Doudou and Li
were talking, Ye sent for Li. When Li returned, he told Doudou that Ye
had told him to make arrangements to go to Guangzhou immediately. At
the same time, Little Zhang came to tell her "they" would leave soon.[42]
Then, Ye suddenly appeared in the corridor where the movie was being
shown, shouting, "Stop the movie. Go back to pack and get ready to go to
Dalian tonight." Alarmed by this sudden change, Doudou made Li promise to make sure that Lin was not taken to the car, and then she, with Yang
Sen of the family staff and Qinglin, took a car down to the office of Unit

8341 to ask again for help. On the way there, Doudou dropped Qinglin off at Building 56, telling him to confront Liguo if he arrived. Zhang Qinglin told me later that he was very nervous that night because he knew that if Liguo came over they would probably exchange fire. He hoped he would be able to get the upper hand on Liguo and then incapacitate him, perhaps by injecting him with a medication to make him sleep for several days.[43]

When she reached the office of Unit 8341, Doudou again asked Zhang Hong to send troops to Building 96 to help officer Jiang, who was already there. To her surprise, Zhang did nothing but walk back and forth in the room. Then, he stepped out. When he returned, Doudou repeated her request, begging him to rush troops over, but she still got no response from Zhang. In desperation, she beseeched him to call Li Wenpu, but still Zhang did nothing.

Meanwhile, Zhang Qinglin in Building 56 received a phone call from Little Zhang, telling him to hurry if he wanted to stop Liguo from taking Lin away. Ye and Liguo had entered Lin's room and helped him dress. "Hurry up, the car will come down in ten minutes," Zhang cried nervously. It was around 11:30 P.M. Hanging up the phone, Qinglin dashed toward the office of Unit 8341, where he repeated to Zhang Hong and Doudou what Little Zhang had told him and urged Zhang to act immediately. Doudou began yelling at Zhang Hong, unable to hold her anger any longer, "I informed you two hours ago what would happen. Why on earth have you still not gotten troops ready? You can lead troops up there yourself!"

It is still unexplained why Zhang changed his attitude after Doudou's first report to him. Zhang still refused Doudou's request and simply left the room without saying anything. When he reappeared, he picked up the phone in front of everyone in the room and asked the operator to connect him with Beijing. On the phone he said, "They said just now that the car would leave in ten minutes," and then he repeated "Yes, sir" several times. Then, the most unexpected thing happened. As he hung up the phone, Zhang Hong said to Doudou and Qinglin slowly but clearly, "Now, the directive from the Party Central Committee is that you should get on the plane and go with them."

Doudou could hardly believe her ears! What?! Get on the plane and go with them?! She collapsed onto a chair and, for the first time, cried. She knew she had lost the battle. But why? "Who on earth asked us to go along with them? Who said so?" Doudou burst out.

"This is a directive from the Party Central Committee," replied Zhang Hong.

"Who represents the Party Central Committee to give directives like this to you? I would rather die here than get on the plane. I will simply stay here and go nowhere! If you want to get on the plane, go yourselves."

Yang Sen, who had accompanied Doudou to the office, pleaded with Zhang Hong, "The plane is about to leave. Who knows where it will go!" Zhang Qinglin waved his fists and shouted at Zhang Hong, "You cannot keep hesitating like this at such a crucial moment. The car will be there in a moment. If you let the car leave, the party and the people will not forgive you. You must take full responsibility if you don't stop the car right now!"

"Please don't issue orders to us like that," said Zhang Hong angrily. "We only obey orders from the Party Central Committee."

"Which Central Committee do you submit to?" Doudou yelled, still crying, "Shou Zhang's safety is in jeopardy, but you would rather do nothing. Should you not do something for the party and the country? Do something, for God's sake! I beg you to stop the car, please!"

More and more soldiers had gathered around the office, many of them holding guns in their hands, obviously waiting for orders to stop the car. Zhang, however, said nothing. Not willing to give up, Doudou asked Zhang Hong repeatedly who had ordered them to get on the plane. "The Party Central Committee" was the only answer Zhang gave.

"Who did you talk to over the phone?" Doudou asked. "It was Zhang Yaoci, wasn't it?" Reluctantly, Zhang nodded in the affirmative.

Doudou demanded that Zhang call Beijing again. If he did not, she would call Zhang Yaoci herself. Zhang Hong called and reported to Zhang Yaoci that Doudou refused to get on the plane. Doudou suddenly grabbed the phone and started to explain to Zhang Yaoci what had happened. She pleaded with him to order the troops to stop the car. However, the answer was the same refrain: Zhang Yaoci needed permission before he could do anything. This was the fourth time Doudou had asked Unit 8341 to stop the car.

Shortly thereafter, a big black car drove by the building at high speed, leaving behind the armed troops gathering around Building 58. In desperation, Zhang Qinglin grabbed a pistol from one of the officers and rushed out. Suddenly, the car came to a screeching halt 500 meters from the office, and Li Wenpu was seen to jump out. Gunshots rang out, and the wounded Li Wenpu ran toward the building. While Zhang Qinglin, who was an army doctor, attended to Li's wound, Li kept murmuring, "Lin Liguo, the traitor."

We still have only a tattered picture of what happened in Building 96 once Doudou and Zhang Qinglin left around 11:00 P.M. Even Doudou and

Zhang Qinglin do not know exactly what happened in Lin's building between 11:00 P.M. and midnight, for neither one of them returned to the building. Some of the key witnesses, such as Li Wenpu, still choose to remain silent. The following account is based on the "reminiscences" of some key witnesses to the events. Caution should be exercised in reading these "reminiscences," most of which probably are excerpts from the "confessions" of these people collected by the Special Case Group, which is well known for its ability to force people to make false confessions.

After Lin had gone to bed, his two medical orderlies, Little Zhang and Little Chen, went in turn to take their snack break. Sometime after 11:00 P.M., Lin called Little Zhang over, telling him, "I cannot fall asleep tonight anyway, so get ready to go to Dalian immediately. No need to bring too much luggage, we will only be staying there for a week." Little Zhang informed Doudou of this immediately.[44]

Around 11:30, Lin called Little Zhang in again, telling him to tell Ye that there was no need to bring the two nurses who took care of him at Beidaihe along to Dalian. When Little Zhang arrived at Ye's quarters, he was stopped by Liu Peifeng, who had come to Beidaihe with Liguo. Ye, Liu Peifeng told Little Zhang, was talking with Liguo.[45] Around 11:40 or 11:50, Ye, Liguo, and Liu Peifeng appeared in Lin's room. After a moment, Lin called Little Chen in, telling him, "We are going to Dalian immediately. I cannot rest anyway. No need to bring too much luggage. We will come back in a few days and then go to Beijing on National Day." When Lin told him this, Liu Peifeng was the only other person still in the room.[46]

As Little Chen came out, he saw Ye and Liguo busy packing; Lin's car was being brought to the building. Both Little Zhang and Little Chen tried to contact Doudou to tell her what was happening, but neither succeeded before Lin left the building.

Li Wenpu was a key witness to this critical night of September 12–13. He must have seen Lin several times. He was seen with Liu Jichun trying to telephone Dalian to make arrangements for Lin there.[47] Their calls to Dalian, however, were cut off by Liguo, who told them not to contact anyone, including Unit 8341.[48] Eventually, Li got word that Lin was leaving, or at least Li believed that Lin wanted to leave, for Dalian. He even told Doudou it would be better to get on the plane and then fight if something happened.[49]

According to Li Wenpu, Ye asked him around 11:40 that night to go see Lin.[50] Ye went into Lin's room first, telling Li to wait outside. When Li entered the room later, Lin told him, "I cannot get to sleep tonight anyway. Get my things ready and let's leave now." Lin made it clear to Li that he was going to Dalian. However, when Li came out of the room, he got a different message from Ye and Liguo, both of whom told him to hurry up, for someone was coming to arrest Shou Zhang. Confused, Li called Hu Ping, the former commander of the 34th Air Force Division who was in charge of all Lin's flights, to check whether Liguo had told him what their destination would be. In response, Hu Ping told Li not to ask any more questions and not to call Beijing.[51] The only option left for Li was to carry out his orders as an army officer. He had no more time to find out what was going on. He called Lin's and Ye's chauffeurs, Yang Zhengang and Little Mu respectively, and asked them to bring the cars to Building 96 immediately. At that moment, Zhang Hong of Unit 8341 called to ask what was going on. Pretending ignorance, Li told him only that they would be leaving soon.

In Li's account, he did not realize that the Lins were going to "betray the country" until he heard Lin himself ask Liguo in the car on the way to the airport, "How far away would Irkutsk be?"[52] During the next few seconds, Li was torn over what to do. Finally, he realized what was happening; everything Doudou had told him was suddenly clear, and he realized that the group was heading for the Soviet Union. Torn between loyalty to his master and the well-being of his own family, Li asked himself what would happen to his wife and children if he were labeled a traitor to the country. He dared not think along that line.

The car continued at high speed, approaching Building 58, the office of Unit 8341. By his own account, Li decided to side with his family instead of his master the moment he saw troops lining up beside the road at Building 58. He suddenly ordered the chauffeur to stop the car and jumped out before anyone in the car could stop him. It was at this point that gunshots rang out and Li was wounded. Nobody knows who fired the shots, though some eyewitnesses insist that Li shot himself. Zhang Qinglin, who attended to Li Wenpu on the spot, also insists that Li shot himself.[53] In any case, the car stopped for only a second and then rushed ahead again.

We know little about the rest of Lin's story. Unit 8341 dispatched troops to the airport before Lin's car left his residence, but when Lin's car passed, nobody intercepted it. Several carloads of soldiers pursued Lin's car to the airport. Officer Jiang of Unit 8341 took soldiers with him in one car, while Liu Jichun and other members of Lin's staff rode in another. When the soldiers arrived at the airport, however, Lin's plane had already taken off. Zhang Hong, the highest-ranking officer of Unit 8341 at Beidaihe, also arrived at the airport, but only in time to report to Beijing that Lin's plane was already airborne.[54] A truckload of soldiers commanded by deputy officer Yu of Unit 8341 had managed to get to the airport at the same time as Lin's car, but without orders the soldiers stopped a hundred meters away from the plane, where they watched the Lins and their entourage climb aboard. Yu ran to the control tower to ask the officials there to prevent the plane from taking off, but time ran out.[55] In the confusion at the airport, the plane carrying Lin Biao and eight other people took off and disappeared into the dark sky.

Little is known about what happened to the plane next. We probably will never know why it flew to the Mongolian Republic instead of Dalian or Guangzhou or how it crashed. When Doudou learned that the plane was airborne, she did not cry again. Instead, staring in the direction the plane had disappeared, she murmured to herself, "Where can they go?"

Beijing: Lin's Generals

On September 24, two weeks after Lin's escape, four of the ranking generals in his command—Huang Yongsheng, Wu Faxian, Li Zuopeng, and Qiu Huizuo—were placed under house arrest and then imprisoned. A document issued by the Party Central Committee immediately after the incident announced their removal from their posts because "they were deeply involved in the factional activities of the "Lin Biao and Chen Boda counter-revolutionary clique."[56] After the arrests, not even their families knew what had happened to them until late 1980, when they appeared at the trial of the "Lin Biao and Jiang Qing counter-revolutionary cliques." At the end of this show trial, the generals received sentences of sixteen to eighteen years in prison. Despite these verdicts, the basic questions remain: Were the generals involved in the events of September 12 and 13? If so, how and to what extent? The following narratives rest largely on the generals' own accounts.

GENERAL WU FAXIAN

At 8:00 P.M. on September 11, 1971, General Wu Faxian attended a Politburo meeting chaired by Zhou Enlai.[57] During the meeting, Zhou announced Mao's directive that the Third Plenum of the Ninth Party Central Committee should meet soon. At the plenum, several members would be added to the Party Central Committee, among them the foreign minister, Ji Pengfei. The membership of the Standing Committee of the Politburo would also be enlarged. When the meeting ended, it was 2:00 in the morning, September 12. After the meeting, Wu returned to his residence at West Mountain and told Chen Suiqi, his wife, about the upcoming Third Plenum. Wu told her, too, that because of his "mistakes" at the Second Plenum at Lushan he would probably have to make another self-criticism, which they had better get to work on. He also told Chen to prepare to move back to their residence at the air force compound, since all their papers, including the drafts of Wu's earlier self-criticisms, were there. After lunch on September 12, Wu returned to the compound, where he read the draft of Zhou's report to the Fourth People's Congress, which the Politburo would later discuss. Meanwhile, Chen looked for materials related to Wu's previous self-criticisms. After reading Zhou's report, Wu decided to spend time on air force affairs. At the time, the air force was holding a conference on the work of the aviation schools. Wu asked one of his secretaries to arrange a meeting with the dean and the political commissar of the Eighth School of Aviation at 8:00 P.M. to discuss their problems. After that, he met with six political instructors who had just transferred from other units to the performing arts troupe of the air force.

During Wu's meeting with the political instructors, Zhou Enlai called around 11:00 P.M. to ask whether he had ordered a plane to fly to Shanhaiguan airport at Beidaihe. "No," Wu answered. Zhou repeated the question, "Was there such a plane at Shanhaiguan after all?" "Absolutely not," Wu replied. Zhou asked Wu to check into the matter and report back to him. After hanging up the phone, Wu immediately called the commander of the 34th Air Force Division, who was in charge of the "designated planes" (*zhuanji*) for high officials. To Wu's surprise, the division commander, Shi Niantang, told him there was indeed a plane at Beidaihe. "It was Hu Ping who ordered the plane to fly to Beidaihe," Shi told Wu.[58] Wu immediately realized that something was wrong. Usually, flights of "designated planes" required his authorization, but this time he had been kept in the dark. More important, why was Premier Zhou personally checking into the matter?

"Where is Hu Ping?" Wu asked when he learned of the problem. Shi told him Hu was at Xijiao airport. Wu immediately demanded to speak to Hu Ping. "That was a test flight after repairs," Hu told Wu. "That was why I did not report to you." "Then why did the plane fly to Shanhaiguan instead of somewhere else?" Wu asked Hu over the phone. Hu had no answer to this question, so Wu ordered Hu to get the plane back to Beijing immediately. Hu agreed to do so but called Wu five minutes later to report that "something is wrong with the engine, the plane is undergoing repairs now." Wu ordered Hu to get the plane back to Beijing immediately after the repair was completed. After the conversation with Hu, Wu immediately reported to Zhou Enlai and told him that he had ordered Hu to get the plane back to Beijing as soon as possible. Zhou approved of what Wu had done and told him that no passengers should be allowed on the plane when it flew back to Beijing. Wu promptly relayed this order to Hu Ping.[59]

A moment later, Zhou called Wu back, "Ye Qun called me just now," Zhou said, "and told me that the deputy commander [Lin Biao] wants to go to Dalian." Zhou told Wu that when he asked Ye whether there was a plane at Beidaihe, Ye answered no, but added: "I haven't asked for planes to fly here yet, but I will call Wu Pangzi [Wu Faxian's nickname] in a moment to ask him to send planes over." Zhou told Wu that Ye probably would call him soon. If she did, Wu should tell her that he had to ask Zhou's permission. Indeed, Ye called Wu a moment later. "Commander Lin wants to go to Dalian," she said. "Send Hu Ping here, and if you have time, come too." "Hu Ping has been in the hospital for medical treatment recently," Wu responded. "Also, his flying skill has not been very good lately. Better use Shi Niantang instead." "I don't know Shi well," Ye insisted, "Better send Hu over. He is not seriously ill, anyway." Then, Wu told Ye what Zhou had told him to say, "I cannot send planes over now. I have to ask the premier." After hanging up, Wu reported Ye's call to Zhou Enlai. He told Zhou that he would go to Xijiao airport to look into the matter in person. Zhou agreed. Wu then went to Xijiao airport, taking with him Zhang Shuliang, a secretary, and Xue Pangxi, a bodyguard.

It was about midnight on the night of September 12 when Wu got to the airport. Hu Ping, who had not returned to the hospital, was talking to the deputy chief of staff of the 34th Air Force Division, who left when Wu approached. Wu asked Hu again about the plane, but Hu repeated what he had told Wu earlier over the phone. At this point, Zhou reached Wu at Xijiao airport, informing him that Lin Biao, together with Ye Qun and Lin Liguo, had left their compound at Beidaihe by car and that they had wounded a bodyguard on their way to the airport. Wu suddenly realized that something terrible was afoot. Figuring that it would take about an hour for Lin's party to get to Shanhaiguan airport, Wu had his secretary call Pan Jingyin, deputy commander of the 34th Air Force Division and captain of the Trident at the Shanhaiguan airport. Wu instructed Pan not to fly the aircraft under any circumstances: "You must remain absolutely loyal to Chairman Mao. The plane must not take off under any circumstances, no matter whose order it is." Pan assured Wu that he would obey the order. However, when Wu finally reached Zhou Enlai at about 1:00 in the morning on September 13 to report his conversation with Pan, Zhou told him that Lin Biao and Ye Qun had boarded the plane and that it had already taken off.

Zhou asked Wu to track the plane and report where it landed. Zhou wanted to go talk to Lin Biao in person. Wu suggested that he get planes ready for Zhou's use, and Zhou agreed. Wu immediately asked the 34th Air Force Division to get two planes ready for Zhou and his troops. Meanwhile, Wu kept Zhou informed about the location of Lin's plane.

After taking off, the plane first flew west, but then turned northward. Wu immediately informed Zhou of the change in direction. When the plane neared Chifeng northwest of Beijing, Wu asked Zhou whether he should order nearby fighters to intercept it. "Don't be so hasty," Zhou said sternly, "I have to ask Mao about this." Shortly thereafter, Zhou called back to say that Mao did not agree, saying, "Rain will fall, widows will remarry. What can we do? Let him go."

When the plane again changed course to head west, Wu asked Hu Ping to contact the plane through the control tower of the 34th Air Division and order the pilot, Pan Jingyin, to return to Beijing. Hu tried for about fifteen minutes, but Pan did not reply. At 2:00 A.M. on September 13, Zhou called Wu again to ask about the location of the plane. "It is about to fly out of the country. It is only 100 kilometers from the Sino-Mongolian border," Wu reported. "The altitude of the plane is only about 300 meters, almost below the reach of our radar."

Zhou soon called again, "From now on, absolutely no plane is to be allowed to fly to Beijing. Otherwise, both of us will lose our heads," Zhou said to Wu sternly. "Please trust me, Premier," Wu replied. "I will absolutely guarantee it. I will order an interception if any plane flies toward Beijing. I will shoot it down." Wu immediately issued orders to Li Jitai, commander of the air force of the Beijing Military Region, to ground all planes in the region, to turn on all radar screens, and to make sure that no plane flew into Beijing. If a plane approached Beijing, it was to be shot down. Then, Zhou issued an order grounding all planes nationwide. Zhou also ordered Wu to allow no plane to take off without an order endorsed jointly by Zhou, Huang Yongsheng, Wu, and Li Zuopeng. Wu immediately relayed Zhou's order to Li Jitai and to Zhang Yonggeng, commander of the air force in the Shenyang Military Region. The officer on duty in the control center at air force headquarters then passed the order to the air forces of other military regions. However, Wu could not reach Liang Pu, chief of staff of the air force, who was away from his command post making arrangements for the National Day parade. Wu ordered the deputy chief of staff on duty to relay the order to Liang.

Wu then ordered Shi Niantang of the 34th Air Force Division to ground all the planes under his command. No plane was to take off from any of the three airports—Xijiao, Nanyuan, or Shahe—under the division's control. At 2:30 A.M., Zhou called Wu again and told him he was going to send Yang Dezhong, the commander of Unit 8341, over to "help" him. By the time Yang arrived, Wu realized that he had lost Zhou's trust. He felt confident, however, that he had done nothing wrong.

GENERAL LI ZUOPENG

Of the four generals arrested, Li Zuopeng was the only one charged with direct involvement in the incident.[60] In 1980–81, Li stood trial on charges of attempting to facilitate Lin's escape by changing one of Zhou's orders, a charge Li repeatedly denied.[61] Shanhaiguan airport, from which Lin's plane took off, had been under navy control. On the night of September 12, Zhou called Li Zuopeng after he talked with Wu, to ask if there was a Trident at Shanhaiguan airport. After checking with the airport at 11:05 P.M., Li told Zhou that there was.[62] Around 11:30, Zhou called Li again to tell him that the Trident was not to take off without specific permission from Zhou himself *and* Generals Huang, Wu, and Li. Zhou explained to Li that it was concern for Lin's safety that prompted the order, because night flight was not safe for Lin Biao. Li called the airport twice, repeating Zhou's order at 11:35 and again at 12:06 A.M. However, there was a difference between what Zhou said he told Li and what appeared on the record of phone calls at the control tower. According to the record, the plane was not to take off without the approval of *one* of the four people mentioned above. After the incident, Zhou corrected the airport record. "What I said," Zhou corrected, "was that the plane could not take off unless an order was endorsed by the *four jointly*."[63] It is not clear why Zhou made such an issue of this point, or why (or if) Li changed Zhou's order when he relayed it to the airport. Or the mistake in the record may have been inadvertent. However, after the incident, Li changed the telephone record to conform to Zhou's version, which made the matter more complicated.[64] It does not seem to make much difference whether the order required authorization by all four men or only one of them. In any case, neither General Huang nor Wu seemed to be aware of Zhou's order at the time. Whether it was caused by miscommunication or calculation, the entry in the phone log became a key piece of evidence that Li facilitated Lin's escape that night by changing Zhou's order. Li, however, never admitted this charge. He claimed instead that if he had done anything wrong in handling the matter, it was because Zhou did not make it clear to him what was really happening at Beidaihe.

Li also denied another charge—that, without authorization, he had told Huang what Mao had said about Lin Biao in talks with provincial leaders during Mao's secret inspection tour. According to the official charge, Li's "unauthorized" report to Huang about Mao's remarks provided the motivation for Lin's final actions against Mao because Huang, in turn, had passed Li's words along to Ye.[65] Li admitted that on September 6, after returning to Beijing from Wuhan, he told Huang what he had learned in Wuhan of Mao's talks. He denied, however, that he did so as part of any plot against Mao: "I believed that it [Mao's talk] was very important, because Mao referred to Lin Biao many times. I felt that it was necessary to inform Huang of this. Huang was chief of staff, my superior. Also, I trusted Huang at the time. I told him to make sure not to tell this to Ye and Wu Faxian as well."[66]

Li then described his response when he heard about Mao's talk:

> First, I felt that what happened at Lushan [the Second Plenum of the Ninth Party Central Committee] was not over yet. Second, I believed that Mao took things more seriously now and had raised the problem to the higher plane of principle. At Lushan, Mao had talked about the problem of the party line. Now he changed by emphasizing three issues: i.e., to maintain a Marxist line or to hold a revisionist line; to unite or to split; to be honest or to be conspiratorial. So, it was no longer just a problem of the party line. Third, I felt that this was pointing to Lin. Mao mentioned that he did not agree with having one's own wife as director of one's office. It was well known that Lin's wife was the director of his office. Consequently, Mao's talk was directed at Lin Biao. After I realized this, I became very nervous, believing that things were now getting worse.[67]

GENERALS HUANG YONGSHENG AND QIU HUIZUO

Little is known about the involvement of Generals Huang and Qiu in the incident. On September 12, Huang spent the day at home. From 8:00 P.M. until midnight, he attended a Politburo meeting to discuss Zhou's forthcoming report to the Fourth People's Congress. When Zhou received the first report from Beidaihe that evening, he asked Huang if there had been any problems in Lin's family recently, and specifically whether Doudou had been at odds with Ye Qun again. Huang said no, and after the meeting Zhou asked Huang to stay with him for a while.[68] Zhou told Huang he needed Huang's help to clear up the situation caused by reports that Lin intended to leave Beidaihe.[69] After this, the only thing known of Huang's activity was that he was with Zhou until another Politburo meeting was convened, around 3:00 A.M. on September 13.

Of the four generals, Qiu Huizuo had the least involvement in the incident. He was caught completely by surprise when he was awakened by a phone call around 3:00 A.M. on the thirteenth, summoning him to the Politburo meeting just mentioned. He was dumbfounded when Zhou announced at the meeting that Lin had escaped the country.[70] Qiu had no idea how that could have happened. The night before, Qiu's wife and Ye Qun had discussed Doudou's wedding. On the morning of the twelfth, Qiu had held several meetings in his office and had had an appointment with General Wu in the afternoon. That appointment was canceled, however, at Wu's request. Around midnight, Qiu took sleeping pills and went to bed. As far as Qiu knew, General Huang Yongsheng had been at home all day and General Li had gone to the Summer Palace for sightseeing with his family until 5:00 P.M. To this day, Qiu still expresses puzzlement over what happened to Lin Biao on September 12 and 13.[71]

It should be mentioned that although all four generals were charged in the CCP documents with helping Lin Biao to conspire against Mao, none was found guilty during the reinvestigation of Lin's case in 1980–81. Because of political concerns at the time, however, Chinese officials kept a low profile on this issue, and most people, including Wang Dongxing, did not note that the generals were exonerated. In his 1997 memoir, Wang stuck to the version created by the Special Case Group under his charge. The only public evidence partially redeeming the generals was the defense lawyers' statements on their behalf. For example, General Wu's lawyer pointed out that since there was no evidence provided in court to prove that Wu "knew about Lin Liguo's activities in preparation for a military coup d'état," Wu "should not be directly responsible for the crime."[72] It was clear that without official approval such a revelation would never be allowed in the newspapers at the time. But charges connected with any "conspiracies" by the Lin family were eliminated from the generals' verdicts. All the generals were released from prison soon after the trial for health reasons.

Beijing: Mao Zedong and Zhou Enlai in September

Zhou, with Mao behind him, probably held the most crucial pieces of this puzzle. However, not much is known about the activities of Zhou and Mao on the night of September 12–13. Around 9:20 P.M., while he was holding a meeting at the Great Hall of the People, word came to Zhou from Wang Dongxing that Lin Doudou had asked Unit 8341 to protect her father from a possible plot by her brother.[73] It is difficult even to speculate what went through Zhou's mind when he learned this. One of Zhou's biographers, Lin Qing, described Zhou's reaction this way:

Zhou could hardly believe his ears. It was something out of the clear blue sky. He already knew that Mao and Lin were at odds, that there was even the possibility of a split. But now, Lin was escaping from the country? He could not believe that it was actually true. . . . Handling this matter involved incredible responsibility. What if something went wrong?[74]

According to Lin Qing, Zhou hesitated because the source of the information was Doudou. Zhou tried to understand her actions. She should know what was going on in her own family, but why would she report on her brother? Out of a sense of "justice"? Or because of a family feud? Zhou had known of the problems in Lin's family for years. Once he himself had to talk to Ye and Doudou separately to mediate one of their quarrels. If the report tonight was mere caprice on Doudou's part and the information she provided misleading, who would bear the responsibility for lodging a false accusation against Vice-Chairman Lin?

There is probably much truth in Lin Qing's speculations along these lines, although his account of the content of Doudou's report is not credible. Doudou repeatedly denied that she ever said to Zhang Yaoci, Zhou Enlai, or anyone else that Lin planned to escape from the country.[75] Zhou's consultation with Huang about the possibility of a family problem added credibility to Doudou's claim. However, Zhou had to look into Doudou's report, since he had himself received it. Zhou left the meeting to concentrate on the developments at Beidaihe. Zhou had told troops there to watch carefully and report any further developments, but not to take any action without consulting Beijing. Meanwhile, he asked Wang Dongxing to stay by the phone to make sure that the communication with Beidaihe was clear. He then called Generals Wu and Li to ascertain the whereabouts of Trident 256, because Doudou had mentioned its presence at Shanhaiguan airport at Beidaihe. What was more important, however, was Zhou's phone conversation with Ye around 11:30 on the night of September 12. There is still some doubt about who telephoned whom first. According to Wang Dongxing, who was among those in charge of the investigation of the Lin Biao incident, it was Zhou Enlai who called Ye Qun. Wang even revealed part of the conversation between the two:

Around 11:30, Premier Zhou called Ye Qun in person. "How is Vice-Chairman Lin?" Premier Zhou asked Ye Qun.

"Vice-Chairman Lin is fine," answered Ye.

Premier Zhou then asked Ye Qun whether she knew about the "designated plane" (Trident 256) at Beidaihe. Ye Qun tried to lie to Zhou at first, saying that she did not. After a while, however, Ye Qun said again, "Yes, there is a 'designated plane' at Beidaihe. My son brought that plane back. His father said that if it is fine tomorrow, he would like to fly around."[76]

"Are you going someplace else?" Premier Zhou asked again.

"Actually [we want] to go to Dalian," replied Ye Qun, who was quick to respond to the situation. "It is getting cold here."

"It is not safe to fly at night," said Zhou.

"We are not going to fly at night," said Ye Qun. "We will wait until to-morrow morning, if the weather is fine. [Then] we will leave by plane."

"Do not fly, it is not safe. [We] must take the weather into considera-tion," said Zhou.

"If it is necessary, I will go to Beidaihe to see Comrade Lin Biao," Zhou said again.

Ye Qun became alarmed over Premier Zhou's idea of coming to Bei-daihe. . . . "It would make Lin Biao very nervous. Lin Biao would feel more uneasy if you come to Beidaihe," said Ye, trying to discourage Zhou from coming.[77] "Anyway, do not come here, Premier."[78]

This conversation was one of the pivotal events of that dramatic night. According to official accounts, including Zhou's own recollection, it was this conversation that convinced Zhou that what Doudou had reported about Ye and Liguo was true.[79] In any case, immediately after the conver-sation, Zhou ordered Li Zuopeng to ground the Trident.

However, there is another side to this story. At Beidaihe, Ye and Lin Liguo decided to leave immediately after the conversation. Suspicious about the real purpose of Zhou's proposed trip to Beidaihe, Ye called General Wu to ask him to send more planes to Beidaihe. To her surprise, Wu was not his usual obedient self and claimed that he could not do so without Zhou's permission. This indicated to Ye that Zhou had probably already gained control of Lin's generals. Ye was even more panicked when she later discovered that Doudou had disappeared. Believing that Doudou had probably informed Zhou Enlai of their plan to leave Bei-daihe and that Zhou was trying to prevent their departure, Ye and Liguo rushed to get Lin ready to leave. While doing so, they yelled at Lin's staff, "Hurry up, someone has come to get Shou Zhang." A more dramatic ver-sion of this event pictures Ye telling Lin when she got to his room, "Hurry up, we have to leave now. Huang, Wu, Li, and Qiu were arrested. We will not be able to leave if we do not go now."[80]

Doudou later said she had been angry with Zhou about his conversa-tion with Ye. She believes he betrayed her by informing Ye of Doudou's re-port to Unit 8341. Around 9:00 on the morning of September 13, Zhou had a long telephone conversation with Doudou about exactly what had hap-pened and why Lin wanted to leave. The conversation lasted over an hour. From the fragments of it Doudou revealed, Doudou believed that Zhou knew nothing of Mao's criticism of Lin Biao in the South.[81] According to Doudou, Zhou had not seemed to doubt her claim that Ye and Liguo had got Lin onto the plane by deception. Zhou even told her that her father was in poor health, that he had not been in touch with the outside world for a long time, and that the matter of Lin's flight should be looked at objectively. In the CCP document issued after the incident, Doudou was actually portrayed as a heroine who had provided a great service to the party and the state by exposing "at the critical moment Lin Biao, Ye Qun, and Lin Liguo's ordering of the plane [to Beidaihe] without permission and their plot to betray the country and surrender to the enemy."[82] Doudou did not know about the document until October 6. When she learned about it, she accused the Party Central Committee of "[borrowing] her name to deceive the world," because she had never described what happened at Beidaihe as Lin Biao's attempt to "escape from the country."[83] After this, she repeatedly requested and was denied permission to see Zhou to explain what had really happened at Beidaihe. Eighteen months later, however, when Zhou finally agreed to see Doudou in person, together with Wang Dongxing, Ji Dengkui, Li Desheng, Zhang Caiqian, Tian Weixin, and Yang Dezhong, he denied Doudou's version. Instead, Zhou told Doudou to acknowledge her own "mistakes" and to concur with the central government's version of the incident. At the end of the meeting, Li Desheng announced the Politburo's decision that Doudou should go back to the air force to receive "reeducation," which was a euphemism at the time for "house arrest." Doudou lost her freedom until late 1975.[84]

Mao played the most obscure role of all in the events of September 12 and 13. All we know for certain is that Mao uttered the famous sentence about letting Lin go *after* Lin's plane had taken off. But what did Mao do in the two and a half hours *before* that? For now, we have only conflicting answers to the questions concerning Mao's involvement in the incident. One key issue is *when* Mao learned about what was happening at Beidaihe. Some, including Dr. Li Zhisui, believe that Mao moved to the Great Hall of the People for security purposes around 11:00 P.M.[85] Others maintain that Zhou reported to Mao around midnight September 12 and then asked Mao to move the Great Hall of the People.[86] According to Wang Dongxing and Zhang Yaoci, they went together with Zhou to inform Mao what had happened after Lin's plane took off.[87] Another question is who told Zhang Yaoci at Unit 8341 to tell Doudou and Zhang Qinglin to get on the plane with Lin and his family, and why.

In comparison with the ambiguity of Mao's response to Zhou's report about Lin's leaving Beidaihe, Mao's early speeches to the provisional leaders during his fall 1971 inspection tour were a definitive sign that he planned to dismiss Lin. The details of Mao's trip and his talks with provincial leaders became available only recently. According to Wang

Dongxing, who accompanied Mao on his tour and was in charge of Mao's schedule and security, Mao had at least fourteen talks with more than 25 local leaders in Wuhan, Changsha, Nanchang, Hangzhou, Shanghai, and Beijing. The following are only brief summaries of what was discussed.[88]

In Wuhan between August 16 and 27, Mao had four talks with the local leaders, including Zeng Siyu (commander of the Wuhan Military Region, also in charge of Hubei province), Liu Feng (political commissar of the Wuhan Military Region, also in charge of Hubei province), Liu Jianxun (in charge of Henan province), Wang Xin (also in charge of Henan province), Hua Guofeng (formerly in charge of Hunan province and transferred to Beijing shortly before). On August 17, Mao criticized Lin's generals, stating that the events at Lushan were "planned, organized underground activities with an agenda to oppose the [party] line established by the Ninth Party Congress." Although Mao did not mention Lin's name, it would not have been difficult for the people present to figure out whom he referred to when he said, "someone believes that I am getting old and am about to go the 'Western Paradise.' He is desperate to become state chairman, to split the party and to usurp power."[89]

On August 25, Mao made a similar comment about the 1970 Lushan Conference to Hua Guofeng and Wang Dongxing. His criticism of Lin and his generals went even further: "They appeared to oppose Zhang Chunqiao, but in fact they opposed me. . . . They wanted to blow up Lushan, and only the air force could do so."[90]

Liu Feng later told General Li Zuopeng, who had accompanied a North Korean military delegation to Wuhan, about Mao's talks on September 6. When Li returned to Beijing, he informed General Huang Yongsheng about this, and Huang, in turn, alerted Ye Qun.

In Changsha between August 27 and 30, Mao had four talks with Hua Guofeng, Bu Zhanya (political commissar of the Hunan Military Region), Ding Sheng (commander of the Guangzhou Military Region), Liu Xingyuan (political commissar of the Guangzhou Military Region), and Wei Guoqing (commander of the Guangxi Military Region and also in charge of Guangxi Autonomous Region). Wang Dongxing was present at all the talks. On August 29, Mao told Wang that he should pass his major points on to the Politburo at an appropriate time.[91]

In Nanchang between September 1 and 2, Mao had two talks with Xu Shiyou (commander of the Nanjing Military Region), Han Xianchu (commander of the Fuzhou Military Region), and Cheng Shiqing (commander of the Jiangxi Military Region). In these talks, Mao repeated his criticisms of Lin and his generals.

In Hangzhou on September 3 and 10, Mao had two talks with Nan

Ping (political commissar of the Zhejiang Military Region and in charge of Zhejiang province), Chen Liyun (political commissar of the Fifth Air Force Army), Xiong Yingtang (commander of the Zhejiang Military Region), and Bai Chongshan (commander of the Fifth Air Force Army).

In Shanghai on September 10 and 11, Mao had another two talks with Wang Hongwen (in charge of the Shanghai municipal government), Xu Shiyou, and Wang Dongxing.

Finally, in Beijing on September 12, Mao asked Ji Dengkui and Li Desheng (both new members of the Central Military Working Group), Wu De (in charge of the Beijing municipal government), and Wu Zhong (political commissar of the Beijing garrison) aboard his train for talks.

What did Mao say to these local leaders and how did they respond to Mao's speeches?

Wang Dongxing, who was present for most of Mao's talks, recorded Mao's speeches and his impressions as follows:

> The chairman emphasized many times in his speeches that [we should] "practice Marxism and not revisionism; unite, and don't split; be open and above board, and don't intrigue and conspire." [Mao mentioned that] someone desperately wanted to be state chairman, split the party, and usurp power. [Mao said that] Lin Biao neither consulted with him nor showed him [the content] before his speech (at the Second Plenum at Lushan). They had something to say but would rather not say it until they believed that they would win. Once when they spoke out but did not get [what they wanted], they became panicked. . . . [Mao said that we] should still protect Lin. He would talk to them once he returned to Beijing. However, [Mao believed] those who had made serious mistakes of principle, line, and direction, and who had been the leaders in this, would find it difficult to reform.
>
> I realized at the time that the purpose of Mao's speeches was to help the local leaders of the party, the government, and the military to understand the conflicts at the Second Plenum of the Ninth Party Congress at Lushan.[92]

Bu Zhanya provides another look at Mao's speeches to him and others at Hunan:

> On the afternoon of [August] 29, Mao told us to come over as a group. All together there were seven of us, including Chairman Mao, Hua Guofeng, Wang Dongxing, Liu Xingyuan, Ding Sheng, Wei Guoqing, and me. Secretaries and other staff were not allowed to join. This time the talk lasted longer, for about three hours. It also touched on a wide range of the topics: the party line, the party history, the Second Plenum of the Ninth Party Congress, strengthening the work of the armed forces, and the problem of Lin Biao. . . .

"Huang Yongsheng was originally from the Guangzhou Military Region and both of you are his long-term subordinates," the chairman said to Ding Sheng and Liu Xingyuan when he talked about how Huang Yongsheng, Wu Faxian, Ye Qun, Li Zuopeng, and Qiu Huizuo were engaged in the anti-party activities of Lin Biao and Chen Boda. "What are you going to do if Huang is ousted?" [asked Mao].

"Are you going to welcome Zhong Chibing's coming to work at Guangzhou?" Mao asked again. Ding Sheng and Liu Xingyuan, however, were so shocked at the time that they did not reply. . . .

After Chairman Mao left Changsha, we believed that the chairman's "testing-the-wind" (*chuifeng*) speeches were very important. So Hua Guofeng, Ding Sheng, Liu Xingyuan, Wei Guoqing and I went to Dishuidong at Shaoshan[93] and spent three days recalling the major points of Mao's talks and printing them out.[94]

On September 5 we transmitted [the major points of Mao's speeches] to the members of the standing committees of the party committees of the provincial government and the provincial military region respectively.[95]

In the same article, Bu mentioned that he had transmitted the major points of Mao's talk to the local cadres above the county and regimental levels on September 9 after he learned that the Guangzhou Military Region had already provided the information to military officers above the army commander level on September 5.[96]

Ding Sheng, commander of the Guangzhou Military Region, also revealed his responses to Mao's talk:

When the chairman asked Liu Xingyuan and me during his talk in Changsha what we would do if Huang Yongsheng were ousted, we could not figure out what was going on. We were briefly at a loss for words and did not know how to respond to the question, because [the question] was incredible and because we sensed at the same time that it indicated something very serious. . . .

"Chairman, you have said so much about so many important things, should we transmit your opinions [to our subordinates]?" I asked. "You can go back and test the wind," the chairman said. After that, we went to Dishuidong at Shaoshan to write down what Mao had said. Then we returned to our provinces to transmit the major points of Mao's talks.[97]

Li Desheng, whom Mao transferred from the Shenyang region to Beijing to be a member of the Central Military Working Group, also gave us a glimpse of Mao's talk to him and others at Fengtai (the railroad station) in Beijing:

"The 'black hand' was not just one Chen Boda," Mao said. "There are other 'black hands.'" This actually meant Lin Biao. Finally, Mao gave me a mission: to transfer one division to Nankou. At that time, Mao not only became very alert but also had a concrete plan already. . . . After I left the chairman['s train], I immediately set out to transfer one division.[98]

Finally, let us examine how Wu De, who was in charge of the Beijing municipal government and later joined the Central Investigation Group for the Special Case of Lin Biao, remembered Mao's talk:

> On the afternoon of September 12, 1971, we (Li Desheng, Ji Dengkui, Wu Zhong, and I) boarded Mao's designated train at Fengtai. When Mao talked to us, Wang Dongxing was present as well.
>
> Mao included various topics in his talk, such as the numerous struggles over the party line in the party history, the problems of the Lushan Conference last year, his strategies of "throwing stones," "mixing sand," and "digging up the corner of the wall," the Huabei Conference, and so on. . . .
>
> The Chairman criticized the practice of making one's wife the director of one's own office. Although [he] did not mention a name, it was obvious that he meant to criticize Lin Biao.
>
> Mao criticized Huang Yongsheng in particular.
>
> Mao mentioned in the conversation that Briefing no. 6 of the Lushan Conference was a counter-revolutionary document.
>
> When Mao mentioned this, I immediately made a self-criticism. "Chairman," I said, "I also signed my name on the Briefing no. 6 before it was issued. Briefing no. 6 was a reactionary briefing, and I made a political mistake."
>
> "You had nothing to do with it," said Mao, waving his hand. "You Wu De have De.[99]
>
> It seemed that Mao also mentioned something about the counter-revolutionary clique or reactionary activities afterward. However, I was too nervous to hear it clearly. . . .
>
> We returned to downtown Beijing by car. Getting out of the car, Ji Dengkui could not help but tell me that the problem was getting worse. All of us were very nervous.
>
> I went to Wu Zhong's house and had a long conversation with him after we came back from Fengtai. I exchanged my opinion with Wu Zhong. . . . I mentioned that although Chairman Mao did not mention Lin Biao's name, it was already very clear who he meant was the person behind Chen Boda. So, should not we "test the wind" to the members of Standing Committee of the Party Committee of the municipal government or the secretaries so that they would be prepared when something happened? However, what should we say? Chairman Mao did not mention Lin Biao's name after all!
>
> We discussed this until 1:30 A.M. but still could not figure out how to transmit Mao's talk.[100]

Not long after Wu De went to bed, however, he was awakened by a phone call around 3:00 A.M. and asked to go immediately to the Great Hall of People to see Zhou Enlai. When he got there, he learned that Lin Biao, together with his wife and son, had fled in the direction of the Mongolian Republic.

Two final questions about the Lin Biao incident remain unanswered: Why did the plane eventually turn north toward the Soviet Union? And how did the plane crash? Before Lin's family left Building No. 96 for the airport, Ye Qun and Lin Liguo had mentioned going to Dalian, Guangzhou, and even Hong Kong, but no one had heard them say a word about going to the Soviet Union. People sympathetic to Lin Biao have indulged in much speculation. Some believe that the reason Lin's plane turned northward had much to do with Zhou's order to ground all planes, for the order effectively closed all airports. It was thus impossible for the plane to land in China, even if the pilot had intended to return to Shanhaiguan airport.[101] According to two air force officers I interviewed, however, Captain Pan made no attempt to contact an airport. The pilot shut off the communication system after the plane took off.[102]

As to the second question, we can rule out the possibility that the plane was shot down by Chinese missiles. No proof has ever been found that Zhou or anyone else issued an order to shoot it down. In his speech to the leading officials of the Guangzhou Military Region, Zhou Enlai himself made the following explanation:

> I will say, once again, that I gave no order to shoot down Lin Biao's plane. It exploded during its forced landing. It was a self-destruction. Consider that Lin was vice-chairman of the CCP Central Committee, but I am only a member of the Executive Committee. In the armed forces, he was vice-commander, but I have no official position. How could I order the troops to shoot down [the plane of] the vice-chairman of the CCP Central Committee and the vice-commander of the armed forces? And he was the designated successor, which had been made clear by the party regulation adopted by the Ninth Party Congress! What could I have said to the whole party, the whole country, and the whole population if I had ordered the troops to shoot him down?! . . .
>
> Of course, I reported to the chairman when Lin Biao's plane was on its way abroad. This is the basic principle that a party member should observe! But the chairman said that rain would fall and widows would remarry. Let him go if he wanted to go. If the chairman could be tolerant to Lin Biao, why should I, Zhou Enlai, stop him? The chairman also said during his inspection tour to the South that [he would] still protect Lin Biao. If he could admit his mistakes, [the chairman] would still keep him in the Politburo. If the chairman could forgive Lin Biao, why should I put him to death?"[103]

Zhou's account is reasonable. The actual causes of the plane crash thus remain unknown. It is not clear whether the plane ran out of fuel, as the official documents claim, or the crash resulted from a mechanical problem or a fight inside the plane. Interestingly, the Chinese government awarded the title "Revolutionary Martyr" to Pan Jingyin, the captain of the plane, several years after the crash. The award rehabilitated Pan and the other crew members, absolving them of any involvement in the "plot." But what about Lin Biao? Is it possible that someday he will be so honored and absolved?

Conclusion: What Happened to Lin Biao

How much does this version of the incident differ from previous accounts? The following points distinguish this from most of the literature published previously.

1.   The Lin Biao incident narrowly defined as Lin's flight from Beidaihe was accidental. Lin's hasty departure from Beidaihe was a result of unexpected events that developed over the several hours preceding the flight. Neither Mao Zedong nor Zhou Enlai expected that Lin Biao would attempt to "flee."[104] Lin's family had not agreed to leave Beidaihe before their sudden departure late on the night of September 12. There is no evidence that Lin was previously involved in any plots against Mao. There seemed no reason for Lin to leave Beidaihe hastily unless he thought that he or his family was in danger. It is possible, as Doudou insisted after the incident, that Lin was totally ignorant about the events of that night, including Liguo's plans, Doudou's report, and Ye Qun's talks with Zhou Enlai.

There is no evidence to support the official claim that Lin had been actively involved in planning a final escape to the Soviet Union. Until 11:00 P.M., Ye was still talking about going to Dalian or Guangzhou the next morning. Lin himself never mentioned anything to anyone about going anywhere besides Dalian. Even Li Wenpu, Lin's trusted bodyguard, believed Lin was going to Dalian or Guangzhou until the car left for the airport around midnight. If he had not, Li would have stayed out of the car rather than getting in and then jumping from it seconds after it started moving. Without Li's help, Lin would not have been able to leave the house. According to Zhang Ning, in the last years of his life, Lin never got into a car without the help of Li Wenpu. Each time before Lin left his residence, Li helped him dress and get ready. It is also said that for security reasons, Lin refused to get into a car if he did not see Li inside.[105] Li's later report to the Special Case Group that Lin had asked in the car about the distance to Irkutsk is the sole piece of evidence indicating that Lin knew they were going to the Soviet Union. There is no other evidence to cor-roborate Li's testimony on this point. It is difficult to believe that Li could have reached a decision to desert his master of 40 years during the sec-onds between the car's starting and his jumping out of it.

There is some evidence that Li testified falsely under pressure from the Special Case Group, which was not uncommon during the investigation of Lin's case. According to Zhang Ning, who was under house arrest with other members of Lin's staff, the Special Case Group had difficulty gath-ering evidence from Lin's staff about Lin's plotted "escape." The staff of Lin's office were forced to rewrite again and again their reports to the CCP Central Committee exposing Lin's crime according to guidance given by the Special Case Group.

When other members of Lin's staff learned that Li had provided the key piece of evidence that Lin intended to betray the country (the ques-tion about the distance to Irkutsk) only after being separated from the rest of the group, few professed to believe Li's testimony. Instead, many be-lieved that Li made up the evidence in exchange for better treatment for himself and his family. If this was his purpose, he achieved it. While most other staff members were expelled from the party, dishonorably dis-charged from the military service, and assigned to places far away from Beijing, Li remained a party member and a military officer, and his family was allowed to stay in Beijing.[106] Years later, when Doudou finally had a chance to see Li Wenpu, she said that Li seemed apologetic.[107]

Moreover, there is no reason to assume that Ye and Liguo would have excluded Li from their plans, if they had any plans at the time. Both of them knew how much Lin trusted Li and that without Li's cooperation it would have been impossible to get Lin to leave the house. Finally, if Lin himself had had any calculated plan to leave Beidaihe, he would never have left his daughter, Doudou, behind.

2.   Lin's unexpected death was largely a result of the disagreement among the family members about how to meet Mao's challenge. The offi-cial charges focused on the activities of Lin Liguo, especially his discus-sions with his air force colleagues in Beijing between September 8 and 12. Each member of the family—Lin, Ye, Liguo, and Doudou—had his or her own agenda for dealing with Mao's challenge. Lin's inclination was to re-main silent and do nothing: "be passive."

Lin was heard to have told Li Wenpu on September 2 that there was no need to build a new residence for him at Beidaihe, for "I do not have much time to live." On September 8, some of Lin's staff overheard a discussion between Lin Biao and Ye Qun, during which Ye cried, telling Lin that "[Mao] said that I was a spy, and how can I survive in the country-side without sleeping pills? I wanted to leave, but you said no."[108] Lin probably did not believe Mao would purge him in the same way that he had Liu Shaoqi, for to do so would jeopardize the success of the Cultural Revolution, in the making of which Lin had been his number one assis-tant. Also, Lin was one of the first-generation revolutionaries who had followed Mao loyally for more than 40 years. To those revolutionary vet-erans, to oppose Mao was to oppose the party, and to oppose the party was to deny something they had been fighting for most of their lives. This was probably why Lin Biao chose to face Mao's challenge passively.[109] In retrospect, Lin was probably right, because a successful Cultural Revolu-tion was psychologically important to Mao.

Lin Liguo, however, had other purposes. Young, ambitious, and inex-perienced, he believed he could save his family, even the whole country, from Mao's schemes. Loyalty to Mao and to the party meant little to him if his or his family's future was in jeopardy. In facing Mao's challenge, it was possible for him to devise radical plans. Authentic as those plans seem to be, however, there is no evidence that Liguo and his colleagues actually carried any of them out, including their plan to assassinate Mao. Ye Qun may not have known about all her son's schemes, but she was in-volved in at least the last-minute decision to leave Beidaihe in haste.

The most difficult judgment is what to make of Doudou's disagree-ment with her brother and mother and her report to Unit 8341. Her re-port, which soon reached Wang Dongxing and Zhou Enlai, was one of the things that sent her family to their death, although she had no idea that would happen. Her motivation, as she later described it, was under-standable, but it is difficult to explain why she thought she could better help her father by going to Unit 8341 than by going to him. Her own ex-planation—that Lin had for years been out of touch with reality because of his illness—is plausible only if Lin had lost the ability to make rational judgments—that is, lost the ability to protect himself.

3.   None of Lin's generals had anything to do with the incident of September 12–13 or with any of the alleged plots to assassinate Mao. In fact, Lin Liguo's group had planned to kidnap the generals and take them, with Lin Biao, to Guangzhou. Thus the generals were purged for undisclosed reasons. Given Mao's earlier behavior, it is clear that he would have purged Lin and his generals even if nothing had occurred on the night of September 12–13. Mao had promised to solve the problem of Lin at the upcoming Third Plenum and had talked about dismissing Gen-erals Huang Yongsheng and Wu Faxian. However, the fate of Lin's family

and others associated with Lin might have been wholly different without the incident. Mao probably intended to gradually deprive Lin of power, in which case Lin might have been rehabilitated later, as Deng Xiaoping was. As Zhou revealed in one of his speeches, Mao still intended to keep Lin Biao in the Politburo if Lin admitted his "mistakes." Mao would not have risked tarnishing the Cultural Revolution by taking radical measures against Lin Biao, whose name was so closely associated with it. In other words, Mao would, in the long run, have purged Lin and his generals for political reasons, but the purge would have taken a very different form had the incident never happened.

4.   The one political event most directly tied to Lin's departure was Mao's inspection tour in the South between mid-August and September 12. Mao undertook the tour for the purpose of undermining Lin's support among provincial military commanders and to prepare them and other high officials in the provinces for his future actions against Lin Biao. Mao made it clear to the provincial leaders that he had taken the issues at Lushan personally and seriously, referring to what happened at Lushan as another struggle about the party line, a description that Mao had employed to describe conflicts with his previous political opponents. Not only did he openly criticize Lin Biao and his generals, he also told the military commanders of the Guangzhou Military Region that he intended to dismiss Huang Yongsheng. While Mao repeatedly asked his addressees to keep his words confidential, he did not actually care if Lin knew his opinions. Mao himself asked the provincial leaders to transmit his opinions to their subordinates and told Hua Guofeng and Wang Dongxing to inform Zhou Enlai and the Politburo members in Beijing about his intention to solve the "problem of Lin Biao." As early as September 5 to 8, the Guangzhou and Hunan Military Regions had already transmitted Mao's criticisms on Lin Biao and his generals to the mid-ranking officers. It would not have been difficult for Lin Biao and Ye Qun at Beidaihe to learn what Mao had said about them, especially since Liguo had already set up his own network around the country.

What Mao and Zhou Enlai did after they learned of Doudou's report remains among the missing pieces to the puzzle. There is still no plausible explanation for Zhang Yaoci's suggestion that Doudou get on the plane with her family. It must have originated with Mao or Zhou, however. Probably neither Zhou nor Mao was in a position to "protect" Lin, even if they believed Doudou's claim that Lin was innocent. Zhou's position, as he repeatedly emphasized later, was inferior to Lin's, and Zhou would certainly not have acted without the facts in hand and, more important, without knowing what Mao's views were. Mao, however, may have seen Doudou's report as providing him with a perfect opportunity to take advantage of an opponent's mistake.

Lin had no choice but to leave Beidaihe that night, regardless of whether he wanted to do so. When his family became involved in politics, Lin's choices grew more limited. It was too dangerous for all of them to stay at Beidaihe, where he was under the direct control of Mao's Unit 8341. However, Lin probably would not have suffered such a miserable fate if his family had not interfered to protect him from imminent purge by Mao.

8

Conclusion: The Tragedy of Lin Biao

One of the "best and the brightest" of his generation of CCP veterans, Lin Biao had the intelligence and courage to lead the million-man Fourth Field Army in triumph from the Northeast to South China. Perhaps none of his peers exceeded him at strategic planning or commanding troops on the battlefield. After 1949 he began a promising political career in which he rose to become defense minister in 1959. Only a dozen years later he died a mysterious death in the Mongolian desert at the age of 64, and he was posthumously the target of severe criticism and was even tried as a "counter-revolutionary" in 1980–81.

Lin's tragedy, however, was not just a personal matter. As a ranking member of the national leadership, he cannot escape all responsibility for the disaster of the Cultural Revolution, which ruined or ended the lives of millions of people. From the perspective of that leadership, the Cultural Revolution was largely the result of the personal and political problems of Mao and a few other members of his ruling clique, including Lin Biao.

But the profound movement that was the Cultural Revolution had deep roots. This study has emphasized extra-institutional factors in Chinese politics to help explain the origins of the Cultural Revolution, but other approaches may be equally helpful. Every study of the Cultural Revolution should take into consideration the dynamics of the interaction between leaders and circumstances.[1] In fact, one way to fill in the gaps between two seemingly disparate levels of analysis, the institutional and the extra-institutional, is to study the interaction between the leaders and the led.

Mao was a frustrated man over the last decade of his life. In his later years, he was unable to see his personal limitations and could not have overcome them even if he had recognized them. Gradually, his personal preoccupations and senile paranoia created a predicament he finally escaped only in death. Mao possessed in abundance the qualities needed by a revolutionary leader. To his revolutionary comrades, he was an inspired man who promised them and the people of China a utopian future, a transcendence of the hopelessness that had defined their lives. With the sacrifice of six members of his immediate family, including his second wife, his son, and his brother, Mao set a personal example of commitment to the revolution. A politician with many of the qualities of Machiavelli's prince, Mao knew how to maintain his power by love if possible, by fear if necessary. When the Communists took power in 1949, Mao had already established his personal authority within the party and the army.[2] He became the personification of the party. Among the CCP elite, loyalty to Mao *was* loyalty to the party.

But things changed after 1949. Thereafter, the major tasks for the ruling party were state-building and economic development. In theory, the new tasks presupposed a change in leadership if the will of the followers were taken into consideration. Thus, the CCP and Mao faced new challenges. To consolidate his power, Mao had to inspire the Chinese people as he had the revolutionaries. He had to convince tens of millions of people that the road they were being asked to follow was first promising and then rewarding. When Mao repeatedly emphasized the "Mandate of the People," he acknowledged the importance of providing inspirational leadership. This, however, was no easy task. Complicating it was the "geographic separation, social distance, and sheer size" of the population Mao had to convince; as Neil Smelser has suggested, these things made direct, efficient communication between leaders and followers impossible.[3] When channels of direct communication are limited and controlled, a leader has the opportunity to create a public image that may differ from—and even contradict—the realities of his actual behavior. This probably explains why Dr. Li's book about the private life of Mao was an astonishing revelation to many Chinese and an embarrassment to the CCP. At the same time, the lack of direct communication between followers and the leader makes it difficult for him to correctly evaluate political and economic actualities and thereby reduces his ability to take appropriate action. Both these circumstances applied to Mao, and they ultimately contributed to the collapse of his leadership.

In addition, Mao experienced difficulties with his followers within the party, especially those in the highest circle of leadership. The process of creating institutions weakened Mao's position as a charismatic leader because it required the division of power and responsibility. Although leadership in the party remained in the hands of the same group of people after 1949, Mao's task thereafter was to inspire bureaucrats rather than enthusiastic revolutionaries. He never convinced his comrades that he was as great a leader of government as he had been a leader of revolution. The failures of the Great Leap Forward and the calamitous famine that followed shattered the myth of an infallible Mao. At the first Lushan Conference in 1959, Mao's immediate followers openly criticized his leadership for the first time since the establishment of the People's Republic. Thereafter, bureaucrats gradually excluded Mao from basic economic policymaking. As a charismatic leader, Mao found it difficult to accept this change. To prove his indispensability, he fought back by resuming ideological leadership and guidance for the party and by devising theories to facilitate the consolidation of proletarian power. Thus, by maintaining his charismatic appeal to his comrades, especially those who had been with him long before 1949, Mao could ignore their differing opinions on the Cultural Revolution and still launch it without their active support.

In this sense, the Cultural Revolution was a result of Mao's precarious hold on leadership. One important indication of this was the breakdown of trust between Mao and his older colleagues. Even his closest supporters in the leadership began to question his position as an invincible and indispensable leader. He felt an increasing, and personally frightening, alienation from his close comrades, who fit more easily into bureaucratic structures. The more alienated he felt, the more imperative was his need to reassert his leadership, even if it meant punishing his oldest colleagues. The series of purges against almost all these men during the Cultural Revolution was the result of Mao's personal frustration over his inability to control everything the government was doing. The purges of his own comrades, however, only added to his frustration. Indeed, Mao collapsed physically after Lin Biao, his last "closest comrade-in-arms," deserted him in 1971.[4] Until the end of his life, he never completely recovered from that desertion and collapse.

Thus, what we see in Mao at the time of the Cultural Revolution is a frustrated elderly man, full of contradictions. He cared for his people and the state and wanted what he thought was best for them. But he was psychologically unable to relinquish his personal power or to adjust to a position other than that of charismatic leader. He was sensitive and compassionate, with the temperament of a poet, but at the same time he was a ruthless politician, willing to destroy his opponents when he thought it necessary. He was always at ease in battle, but found no place for himself in the processes of institution-building and modernization his party launched after 1949. He never admitted that he was ill suited to lead the new China his fellow Communists were creating. Frustrated and lonely, he isolated himself from almost everyone, including his own family, and surrounded himself with pretty young women and poorly educated bodyguards, from whom he received absolute loyalty. By that time he trusted no one, not even those who had been his closest followers for three decades, against whom he took action before they had a chance to destroy him. Mao's personal tragedy, however, was China's as well because Chinese traditions allowed Mao to project his personal agony onto the country and its 1 billion people. The party and the government became miserably impotent in the face of this onslaught. Mao and the party had become identical. To dispute Mao's authority was to dispute the party's claim to power, hence shaking the foundations of the party's legitimacy and its continued right to rule. This issue still haunts the CCP today.

A puzzling question remains, however. Why did China's leaders follow Mao unconditionally even after they realized his actions were seriously damaging the country? If Lin Doudou and Lin's former staff members are right, Lin Biao never agreed with Mao that China needed a Cultural Revolution. Contrary to his public image, apparently Lin often expressed concern over Mao's decisions in private. But in public, Lin always appeared to be a devoted supporter of Mao's revolution.

There is no easy answer to this question. Almost all the CCP leaders who survived the wars and the early purges developed total loyalty and obedience to Mao. This personal loyalty may have arisen from a combination of many elements—respect, fear, the need for self-identification, belief in a common cause, and personal benefits. In retrospect, Mao finally established his position as an unchallengeable party leader in the mid-1940s, after he finally managed to expel Wang Ming from leadership in the Yanan Rectification Movement. As early as 1943, the CCP media started an intensive propaganda effort to present Mao as a great leader. Several important CCP figures published articles in *Jiefang ribo*, a CCP newspaper, attributing the major successes of the CCP to Mao personally. In 1944 the Party Central Committee published the first *Selected Works of Mao Zedong*. In the foreword to the book, Deng Tuo, the chief editor, claimed that "to achieve the victory of the Chinese Revolution, all party comrades must unanimously unite under the guidance of Mao Zedong's thought."[5] In his speech at the Seventh Party Congress the following year, Liu Shaoqi completed the introduction of Mao:

> Our party has become a party with its own great leader. This great leader is no other than Comrade Mao Zedong, who is the organizer and the leader of our party and the modern Chinese Revolution. Our comrade Mao Zedong is an outstanding representative of the brave proletarians of our country and a superb representative of the excellent tradition of our great nation. He is a talented and creative Marxist, who combined the universal

truth of Marxism—the highest ideal of mankind—with the practice of the Chinese revolution.[6]

Nearly all Mao's colleagues joined in the endeavor to promote Mao's cult of personality. At the time, the party needed an established leader to hold its members together in order to compete with the Nationalists under Jiang Jieshi (Chiang Kai-shek) for national power. Many of Mao's colleagues believed that establishing Mao as the rightful leader of the party was the first step toward establishing his legitimacy as ruler of China, and thereafter the right of the party and their own right to rule. Lin Biao's later efforts to promote Mao's personality cult was simply a continuation and repetition of the practice that had started long before. The party needed to personify its claim to power. Mao later described this role as a means "'to scare off ghosts with the help of Zhong Kui,' and I became a party Zhong Kui of the twentieth century."[7] All those who advocated the elevation of Mao's personality cult gained or consolidated their own power and reputation in the process. Nobody, including Liu Shaoqi, Lin Biao, Zhou Enlai, and others who were purged by Mao during the Cultural Revolution, expected the powerful leader they helped to create to turn against them and plunge the party and the country into a ten-year disaster.

The complicated relationship between the leaders and the led, however, needs further exploration. It seems that Lin, like many others, was caught between personal loyalty to Mao and the dynamics of the political process. Their loyalty to Mao had been the source of their political power. It was Lin's ability to demonstrate continuously his loyalty to Mao that finally gained him the position of Mao's designated successor. At the same time, Lin's loyalty put him at the center of the power conflict. Personal loyalty to a mighty and capricious leader does not guarantee a successful political career in the modern era. As Mao's successor, Lin was involved in many political processes fraught with conflict and compromise. Once the political process starts, however, it gains a dynamic of its own. In other words, many elements other than personal loyalty come into play, during which the participants have to follow the "rules of the game" in order to win. A good politician is a master of these rules, knowing how and when to use them to his advantage. In many cases, compromise plays an important role. When compromise and other mediating means fail, a showdown becomes inevitable. In fact, many of the purges within the CCP resulted from the failure of compromise, with the participants finally being forced to choose sides. During Mao's rule, even Mao was forced to choose between conflicting groups. The best examples of this are the purges of Yang Chengwu and Chen Boda at the Second Plenum of the Ninth Party Central Committee. Nonetheless, we still need to study each individual case carefully to determine which elements were in play. Were the central issues of an institutional or extra-institutional nature? Were they formal or informal? When and how did the process start, and what contributed to its evolution? For many events during Mao's rule, we still lack answers to these questions.

Lin Biao was an outstanding military leader but a mediocre politician. When Lin told his generals after the Lushan Conference of 1970 that they knew how to maneuver on the battlefield but not in the political arena, he was apparently aware of his own and his generals' limitations. Although Lin disagreed with Mao at times, he was unable to provide—or even to imagine—a political alternative to Mao. When he and his generals were caught up in the Cultural Revolution, a tragic end to their political careers was more or less inevitable. What finally brought about Lin's fall, however, was his unyielding attitude toward Mao's criticism after the Second Plenum at Lushan. Mao waited almost a year for Lin's self-criticism, but Lin refused to give in. A frustrated Mao finally decided to move against Lin in July and August 1971.

We still know too little about Lin Biao as a person. Like the incident that caused his death, his life remains shrouded in mystery. Although we know that Lin was constantly ill after 1949, and that his chronic illness impaired his political functioning, we do not know exactly what ailed him. The effects of his poor health made Lin cynical and withdrawn. He increasingly avoided public activities, at least partly because of the physical toll they took. Lin remained interested only in military strategy and technology. Contrary to the general belief that Lin opposed rapprochement between China and the United States, he actually had a keen interest in meeting with the Americans, from whom he expected to learn about advanced military technology. One of his secretaries told me that during Lin's stay at Beidaihe in the summer of 1971 the only reports he wanted to read were concerned with the upcoming visit of President Nixon. Lin told the secretary that he wanted to meet the Americans—a departure from his usual reluctance to meet with foreigners.[8] Although this type of personal information is difficult to collect and to evaluate, the discrepancy between the public and private Lins appears to be great.

Zhou Enlai is another enigmatic figure among the PRC leaders. The public and private Zhou were also different, although not as dramatically so as the two Lin Biaos. As premier, Zhou contributed greatly to the political and economic development of the country, and he still enjoys a good reputation among the Chinese people. Of all the PRC leaders, he has received the least critical treatment from Chinese scholars. Despite their personal grievances about the Cultural Revolution, many Chinese still hold positive views of Zhou's role in that revolution, believing that the situation would have been worse without his restraining influence on Mao and his running of the country while Mao was distracted.

Zhou's political career, however, especially his relationship with Mao, badly needs examination. It is difficult to understand why Zhou, as a sophisticated student of politics and an accomplished statesman in his own right, always supported Mao's ideas unconditionally and implemented them with absolute loyalty, in many cases at a cost to his own integrity. Li Zhisui believed that Zhou Enlai remained more loyal to Mao than any of China's top leaders. Zhou was not just loyal, but "subservient, and sometimes embarrassingly so."[9]

Also according to Cheng Qian, Zhou was the first member of the Standing Committee of the Politburo to endorse Mao's ideas for a Cultural Revolution.[10] By doing so, however, Zhou put himself in a difficult position. He survived politically during the Cultural Revolution thanks only to his political shrewdness, a quality Lin Biao obviously lacked, and his organizational ability, which made him indispensable to Mao.

On July 14, 1967, Mao commented to Wang Li on his chief associates, including Deng Xiaoping, Lin Biao, and Zhou Enlai. Mao said he had disagreed with the ouster of Deng, whose political talents ranked with those of Liu Shaoqi and Zhou Enlai, and whose military talents ranked with those of Lin Biao and Peng Dehuai. When Lin's poor health finally rendered him unable to work, Mao said he would rehabilitate Deng Xiaoping and let him shoulder Lin's responsibilities. However, Mao added, Zhou Enlai was indispensable among the leadership, no matter who was in charge of the country, be it Mao, Lin, or Deng.[11] Lin Biao said much the same thing about Zhou. On many occasions, Lin told his generals to respect Zhou, because it was Zhou who turned Mao's ideas into reality and who made the party and the country function.[12]

If this was so, why did Zhou Enlai accept what amounted to the position of Mao's housekeeper, or, in Li Zhisui's words, Mao's "obedient servant," rather than seeking an independent political role? Zhou personally looked after Mao's family and was especially effective in dealing with Mao's difficulties with individual family members. According to one of Mao's bodyguards, it was Zhou Enlai who decided that He Zizhen, Mao's third wife, should not be allowed to come to Beijing.[13] And when Jiang Qing was ill, Lin Biao and Zhou Enlai saw to it that she received the best medical care.[14] On more than one occasion when Jiang was having problems with her nurses, Zhou adjourned Politburo meetings to attend to Jiang's problems.

One explanation for Zhou's subservience to Mao and his family is that

Zhou had a total or blind commitment to Mao as a person, which is not uncommon among followers of a charismatic leader. The bases for such commitments vary from person to person, from expectations of personal reward to individual psychological needs, and the common manifestations of such a commitment are demonstrated public loyalty, willingness to follow faithfully, and devotion to the person of the leader.[15] Both Lin Biao and Zhou Enlai fit this pattern in their relationships with Mao.

When weighing the loyalty of Chinese leaders to Mao and the party, one must always remember the depth of the commitment the old leaders had to the Chinese revolution. Many had joined the revolution as teenagers and risked everything, including their lives, for the cause they pursued. Most lost close relatives, and nearly all were wounded in battle at one time or another. According to Downton's theory of commitment, when the sacrifices and costs of a commitment become overwhelming, a decision to "end [the] commitment become[s] impossible, or at least, traumatic," even after one becomes disillusioned with the object of the commitment.[16] This may help explain the enigma of Zhou Enlai. He may have cared so much for his reputation that he was unable to face the consequences of losing what he had already achieved. Or he may have cared too much for his political career, without which he would have had no identity. When he learned that he was dying of cancer, he refused to enter the operating room, from which he might not come out, until he finished a letter and had it sent to Mao along with evidence that he had never betrayed the party.[17]

Like Zhou Enlai, many of Mao's colleagues were prepared to sacrifice everything to protect their reputation as faithful party members and revolutionaries, even after Mao had them purged. Their "revolutionary mentality" required that they be willing to sacrifice personal interests for the integrity of the party. If Mao's decision was also a party decision, they had to accept it. Liu Shaoqi's handling of his disagreements with Mao over the Cultural Revolution is an illuminating example of this. Instead of challenging Mao's decision, he decided to resign.[18] Liu Yuan, Liu Shaoqi's son, who had respect and affection for his father, later said his father's biggest mistake as state chairman was not stopping the chaotic Cultural Revolution.[19] A story told about Luo Ruiqing by his daughter, Diandian, illustrates the same point. After Mao had him purged in December 1965, Luo Ruiqing attempted suicide but survived. When he was finally released from prison in 1974, the first thing he did was to go to Tiananmen, where he saluted Mao's picture with obvious sincerity. Even his daughter could not help but wonder why Luo did this, especially after he had suffered so much at the hands of Mao.[20]

Although the basis for such devotion needs further study, the loyalty of the first generation of revolutionaries to Mao, the party, and the revolution is unquestionable. This loyalty makes it unbelievable that Lin Biao and his generals would plot a military coup against Mao. In my opinion, only members of the second generation of revolutionaries, who shared the glory of the first generation but not the loyalty and commitment to the party, could have contemplated a plan to topple Mao. This fundamental fact constitutes perhaps the strongest argument that Lin Biao could not have plotted a coup.

To understand the nature of Chinese politics in Mao's era, we have to understand Mao and his lieutenants. Who were they, and why did they behave the way they did? What were the political and cultural restraints on their thinking and performance? To what extent did their personal lives influence Chinese politics? A better understanding of these factors will go far toward answering many questions about Chinese politics under Mao. This book is one modest step on the road.

REFERENCE MATTER

—

■ Notes

For full titles and publication data on works cited in short form in these notes, see the Bibliography. CCP documents on the Lin Biao incident are cited by the abbreviation ZZB (Zhonggong zhongyang bangongting) and a bracketed number (e.g., ZZB [1]). Unless otherwise indicated, translations from the Chinese are by the author of this book.

CHAPTER 1. *Introduction*

1. By this statement, Mao probably meant that the issue of Taiwan was still unresolved and that the Cultural Revolution was ongoing.

2. Wang Nianyi, *Dadongluan*, pp. 600–601; see also Hu Sheng, "Mao Zedong yisheng suo zuo de liangjian dashi."

3. "On Questions of Party History," in Liu Suinian and Wu Qungan, eds., *China's Socialist Economy*, p. 598.

4. In 1967, when the Cultural Revolution was still in its initial stage, Tang Tsou had already predicted its future negation. See Tsou, "The Cultural Revolution and the Chinese Political System."

5. Roderick MacFarquhar, for example, has finished three volumes on the origins of the Cultural Revolution and has not gone beyond 1966, when the Cultural Revolution started. See MacFarquhar, *The Origins of the Cultural Revolution 1*; *The Origins of the Cultural Revolution 2*; and *The Origins of the Cultural Revolution 3*.

6. There are some excellent studies on the Cultural Revolution by both Western and Chinese scholars. See, for example, Dittmer, *Liu Shao-ch'i and the Chinese Cultural Revolution*; Lee, *The Politics of the Cultural Revolution*; MacFarquhar's three-volume work *The Origins of the Cultural Revolution*; Perry and Li Xun, *Proletarian Power*; L. White, *Policies of Chaos*; Wang Nianyi, *Dadongluan*; and Wang Shaoguang, *Failure of Charisma*.

7. Barnett, *Cadres, Bureaucracy, and Political Power in Communist China*; Schurmann, *Ideology and Organization in Communist China*; Barnett, *Chinese*

Communist Politics in Action; Johnson, *Ideology and Politics in Contemporary China*; and Harding, *Organizing China*.

8. See, for example, Lewis, *Party Leadership and Revolutionary Power in China*; Scalapino, *Elites in the People's Republic of China*; Whitson, "The Field Army in Chinese Communist Military Politics"; Nathan, "A Factionalism Model for CCP Politics"; Tsou, "Prolegomenon to the Studying of Informal Groups in CCP Politics"; "Andrew Nathan Replies," *China Quarterly* 65 (January 1976): pp. 114–17; Pye, *The Dynamics of Factions and Consensus in Chinese Politics*; and Lee, *From Revolutionary Cadres to Party Technocrats*.

9. For example, in addition to numerous biographies of Chinese high officials, the 1994 biography of Mao by Li Zhisui, Mao's longtime personal physician, includes a large amount of information about Mao's personal life. Li Zhisui, *The Private Life of Chairman Mao*.

10. Other scholars have also included informal dimensions of politics in their inquiries into Chinese politics. See, for example, Dittmer, "Chinese Informal Politics" and the responses to his arguments from other scholars.

11. For a detailed analysis of the official charges against Lin Biao, see Jin Qiu, "The Fall of Lin Biao: A Reappraisal," pp. 110–24.

12. During the Cultural Revolution, *Mao zhuxi yulu* (*The Quotations of Chairman Mao*) was known as the "little red book."

13. Chen Lisheng, *Zhongguo "wenhua geming" he zhengzhi douzheng*, p. 264.

14. See Uhalley, *A History of the Chinese Communist Party*, p. 167. *Hongqi* (*Red Flag*) was the journal controlled by the Central Committee of the Chinese Communist Party.

15. See Li Tianmin, "Lin Piao's Situation," p. 74. In Communist China, an official usually disappears from public media immediately after his or her political career comes to an end. China watchers in the West often read this as the signal of a major personnel change within the Communist Party.

16. For example, Chen Yi, a member of the Central Military Committee, did not get word of Lin Biao's death until September 21. Huang Yongsheng, the chief of staff of the People's Liberation Army, did not announce Lin's death to his bureau chiefs until September 22. Xiong Lei, "'9.13' shijian qianhou de Mao Zedong," in Xiong Huayuan and An Jianshe, *Lin Biao fangeming jituan fumie jishi*, p. 85. See also the CCP document ZZB [2].

17. ZZB [3].

18. Some people in the provinces maintained that they did not learn about Lin's death until summer 1972. See Liang Heng's words quoted on p. 6.

19. ZZB [8].

20. Liang Heng, "Room at the Top," p. 35.

21. ZZB [12] and [19].

22. John Burns, "Mao Confirms Lin's Death in Crash," *Washington Post*, July 28, 1972; and C. P. Chang, "The Death of Lin Piao," *Issues and Studies* 8 (September 1972): 8.

23. Yao Ming-le, *The Conspiracy and Death of Mao's Heir*. The other publishers were Collins in the United Kingdom, Australia, and Canada; Laffont in

France; Bertelsmann in Germany; Garzanti in Italy; Teden in Sweden; Veen in Holland; and Bungei Shunju in Japan.

24. For discussions of the book, see Uhalley and Jin Qiu, "The Lin Biao Incident," pp. 392–98; Uhalley, "A Compelling but Unlikely Account of Lin Biao's Death"; "The Conspiracy and Death of Lin Biao by Yao Ming-le"; Leys, "The Death of Lin Biao," pp. 141–51; Shapiro, "Wild History"; and Liang Heng, "Room at the Top," pp. 35–36.

25. Yan Jiaqi and Gao Gao, *Wenhua dageming shinian shi*, vol. 1, pp. 493–542; Wang Nianyi, *Dadongluan*, pp. 368–434; Barnouin and Yu Changgen, *Ten Years of Turbulence*, pp. 199–246; MacFarquhar, *The Politics of China: 1949–1989*, pp. 256–78, and n. 78; Kau, *The Lin Piao Affair*, introduction; and Wu Tien-wei, *Lin Biao and the Gang of Four*, pp. 15–21.

26. Oksenberg, "Source and Methodological Problems in the Study of Contemporary China."

27. One such example can be found in an early study of the Beijing government's policies on the Vietnam War. One scholar detected different factions among the top Chinese leaders by reading the texts of their public speeches. He found that Luo Ruiqing had referred to the United States as "the main *source* of aggression and war," while Peng Zhen had claimed that the United States was "the main *force* of aggression and war." Based on this reading, he concluded that there were different opinions, even factions, among top leaders in the 1960s. Little evidence, however, has surfaced since then to support his observation. See Ra'anan, "Peking's Foreign Policy Debate," p. 41. Other examples can be found in Zagoria, "The Strategic Debate in Peking." For arguments about the problems of Kremlinology, see Hoffmann, "Methodological Problems of Kremlinology," p. 145; and Yahuda, "Kremlinology and the Chinese Strategic Debate."

28. Some of the documents about Lin Biao's "crimes" are available in both Chinese and English. See, for example, Yuan Yue, *Lin Biao shijian yuanshi wenjian huibian*; Kau, *The Lin Piao Affair*; and Myers, Domes, and Yeh, *Chinese Politics*.

For collections of documents concerning the trials, see *A Great Trial in Chinese History*; Lishi shenpan bianjizu, *Lishi de shenpan*; Zhonggong yanjiu zazhishe, *Zhonggong shenpan "Lin-Jiang jituan" an*; and Zuigao renmin fayuan yanjiusuo, *Zhonghua renmin gongheguo zuigao renmin fayuan tebei fating shenpan Lin Biao, Jiang Qing fangeming jituan zhufan jishi*.

29. According to the official Chinese explanation, "571" is a pun or homophone for the Chinese characters for "armed uprising."

30. For a translation of some of these documents, see Kau, *The Lin Piao Affair*.

31. ZZB [7].

32. Lin's generals included Huang Yongsheng, the former chief of staff of the People's Liberation Army (PLA); Wu Faxian, the former commander-in-chief of the air force; Li Zuopeng, the former political commissar of the navy, and Qiu Huizuo, the former director of the Logistics Department of the PLA.

For information about the government's change of position, see the speech made by Wu Faxian's lawyer during the 1981–82 trial. *Renmin ribao*, December 19, 1980. See Chapter 7 for a more detailed discussion of this.

33. According to a CCP document (ZZB [6]), the Central Investigation Group for Special Cases was set up to handle Lin's case. The members included Zhou Enlai, Kang Sheng, Jiang Qing, Zhang Chunqiao, Yao Wenyuan, Ji Dengkui, Li Desheng, Wang Dongxing, Wu De, and Wu Zhong. Ji Dengkui and Wang Dongxing were in charge of the routine work of this group.

34. In his discussion of "situational groups," Lee identified four different groups during the Cultural Revolution: the purged, the survivors, the de facto beneficiaries, and the defenders. Each group's attitude toward the Cultural Revolution was based on its own experiences. See Lee, *From Revolutionary Cadres to Party Technocrats*, pp. 85–95.

35. For excerpts from the "Outline of Project 571," see Wang Nianyi, *Dadongluan*, pp. 417–21. For English translations of the excerpts, see Myers, Domes, and Yeh, *Chinese Politics*, vol. 2, pp. 147–53; and Kau, *The Lin Piao Affair*, pp. 81–90.

36. Shao Yihai, *Lin Biao wangchao heimu*, pp. 99–107; Wu De, "Lushan huiyi he Lin Biao shijian," pp. 143–44.

37. Li Zhisui, *The Private Life of Chairman Mao*, p. 540.

38. Interview with the author, Boston, Sept. 21, 1993.

39. During one of my recent lectures in China, a well-known scholar told me that he had always wondered why the "Outline" reflects the ideas of Deng Xiaoping instead of Lin Biao. He noted that everything said in the "Outline" has been realized by Deng Xiaoping since the 1980s. "How do you explain this?" he asked.

40. Kau, *The Lin Piao Affair*, p. 85.

41. Li's statement is fundamentally ambiguous. It is now known that Liguo did not go back to Beidaihe until the evening of September 12. Also, the statement that Liguo had "left it with Shou Zhang and the director at Beidaihe" does not prove that Lin Biao and Ye Qun knew about the plan. For Li Weixin's confession, see ZZB [16], pp. 40–46; and for an English version of Li Weixin's confession, see Kau, *The Lin Piao Affair*, pp. 90–95.

42. Earlier, several other high officials, such as Gao Gang and Peng Dehuai, were charged with "having illicit relations with a foreign country," but none of the charges was ever proved. Similarly, other high officials were charged with plotting coups, but all of them were later vindicated.

43. For the different theories of Lin Biao's demise, see Uhalley and Jin Qiu, "The Lin Biao Incident."

44. MacFarquhar and Fairbank, The *Cambridge History of China*, vol. 15, pt. 2, "Succession to Mao," pp. 305–36 and 407–26; Kau, *The Lin Piao Affair*, introduction; Wu Tien-wei, *Lin Biao and the Gang of Four*, pp. 15–21; Domes, *China After the Cultural Revolution*, pp. 77–103; Teiwes, *Leadership, Legitimacy, and Conflict in China*, pp. 113–18; and Thornton, *China, the Struggle for Power, 1917–1972*, pp. 336–41.

45. Teiwes and Sun, *The Tragedy of Lin Biao.*
46. Liu Suinian and Wu Qungan, *China's Socialist Economy*, p. 599.

CHAPTER 2. *Mao Zedong and Theories of the Cultural Revolution*

1. Wang Nianyi, *Dadongluan*, p. 434.
2. For more details on this argument, see Thurston, "The Politics of Survival," p. 100.
3. Gong Yuzhi, "Guanyu jixu geming de jige wenti."
4. Wang Li, *Xianchang lishi*, p. 86.
5. Tan Zongji, "Wuchan jieji zhuanzheng xia jixu geming lilun de laiyuan yu fazhan," p. 57; and Ye Yonglie, *Chen Boda*, pp. 418–19.
6. Ye Yonglie, *Chen Boda*, p. 419.
7. Xu Quanxing, *Mao Zedong wannian de lilun yu shijian*, pp. 361–62.
8. Wang Li, *Xianchang lishi*, p. 84.
9. Dittmer, *China's Continuous Revolution*, pp. 3–4.
10. When the word "legitimacy" is used in a discussion of Chinese politics, meaning "in accordance with established rules, or the acceptance of power," the concept can be discussed at three different levels: legitimacy of (1) party members, (2) people in general, and (3) other regimes. In this study, I discuss Mao's legitimacy only in relation to his party comrades and the Chinese people.
11. See Frederick Teiwes's detailed discussion of the legitimacy of Mao's power in Teiwes, *Leadership, Legitimacy, and Conflict in China.*
12. In 1949 the CCP consisted mostly of poorly educated youth. In his study of Chinese revolutionary cadres, Lee observes that in Helongjiang province 95 percent of the 18,903 party members came from the most disadvantaged social groups. Lee, *From Revolutionary Cadres to Party Technocrats*, p. 45.
13. Cong Jin, *Quzhe fazhan de suiyue*, pp. 305–6; and Xu Quanxing, *Mao Zedong wannian de lilun yu shijian*, p. 404.
14. Cong Jin, *Quzhe fazhan de suiyue*, p. 117.
15. "Hangzhou juiyi jianghua" ("Speech in Hangzhou"), in *Mao Zedong sixiang wansui*, M1400 12c, p. 203.
16. Editorial, *Hongqi* 4 (1968): 3.
17. Xiao Yanzhong insists that Mao always looked at the world condescendingly, as if he were one of its saviors. Consciously or unconsciously, he saw his personal will as the source and center of the nation's strength. Consequently, "belief in the people" was merely a substitute for "belief in oneself." See Xiao Yanzhong, *Wannian Mao Zedong*, p. 71. Mao's former personal physician, Dr. Li Zhisui, also provides witness to Mao's view of himself as an "emperor." For more discussion, see Li Zhisui, *The Private Life of Chairman Mao.*
18. Jing Hong and Wu Hua, comps., *Mao Zedong shenping shilu*, pp. 657–59.
19. Li Yinqiao, *Mao Zedong shiweizhang zaji*, pp. 94, 126–27.
20. B. J. Schwartz, "Thoughts on the Late Mao," in MacFarquhar, Cheek, and Wu, *The Secret Speeches of Chairman Mao*, p. 27.

21. See Lee, *From Revolutionary Cadres to Party Technocrats*, pp. 1–9.

22. According to Li Rui, Mao had expected that it would take 50 years to complete the transformation. Li Rui, *Lushan huiyi shilu*, p. 1.

23. One jin equals half a kilogram. For production figures, see Liu Suinian and Wu Qungan, *China's Socialist Economy*, p. 88.

24. Ibid., p. 595.

25. Ding Shu, *Ren huo*, p. 8.

26. Xu Quanxing, *Mao Zedong wannian de lilun yu shijian*, p. 135.

27. One mu equals approximately one-sixth of an acre. The newspaper account appeared in Ding Shu, *Ren huo*, pp. 61–67.

28. Xu Quanxing, *Mao Zedong wannian de lilun yu shijian*, pp. 137–38.

29. Cong Jin, *Quzhe fazhan de suiyue*, p. 155; emphasis added.

30. Ding Shu, *Ren huo*, p. 26.

31. Liu Suinian and Wu Qungan, *China's Socialist Economy*, p. 239; and Cong Jin, *Quzhe fazhan de suiyue*, p. 160.

32. Liu Suinian and Wu Qungan, *China's Socialist Economy*, pp. 239–40.

33. Wen Tiejun, "Guojia ziben zai fenpei yu minjian ziben zai jilei," p. 7.

34. For more details about the famine, see Ding Shu, *Ren huo*, pp. 173–203.

35. For analyses of the origins of the Great Leap Forward from other perspectives, see Bachman, *Bureaucracy, Economy, and Leadership in China*; and MacFarquhar, *The Origins of the Cultural Revolution 2*.

36. Shi Zhongquan, "Jianxin de kaituo" ("A Difficult Start"), in Xiao Yanzhong, *Wannian Mao Zedong*, p. 133.

37. Xiao Yanzhong, *Wannian Mao Zedong*, p. 66.

38. "Mao's speech at Beidaihe Conference, August 21," in MacFarquhar, Cheek, and Wu, *The Secret Speeches of Chairman Mao*, p. 417. For a version in Chinese, see Yan Yongsong and Wang Junwei, *Zuoqing ershi nian*, p. 141. The "supply system" he refers to was a system of payment in kind practiced during the revolutionary wars and in the early days of the PRC. Working personnel and their dependents were provided with the necessities of life instead of a salary.

39. Cong Jin, *Quzhe fazhan de suiyue*, pp. 158–62.

40. Zheng Qian and Han Gang, *Wannian suiyue*, p. 415.

41. Shi Zhongquan, "Jianxin de kaituo," in Xiao Yanzhong, *Wannian Mao Zedong*, p. 135.

42. Mao Zedong, "Jianding di xiangxin qunzhong de daduoshu," ("Firmly Believe in the Majority of the People"), in *Mao Zedong zhuzuo xuandu*, vol. 5, p. 484.

43. Tan Zongji, "Wuchan jieji zhuanzheng xia jixu geming lilun de laiyuan yu fazhan," p. 53.

44. Liu Suinian and Wu Qungan, *China's Socialist Economy*, pp. 244–46.

45. Cong Jin, *Quzhe fazhan de suiyue*, p. 165.

46. Li Rui, *Lushan huiyi shilu*, pp. 7–8.

47. For a copy of Mao's "May 7 Directive" and more discussion, see Wang Nianyi, *Dadongluan*, pp. 2–6.

48. Shi Zhongquan, "Jianxin de kaituo," in Xiao Yanzhong, *Wannian Mao Zedong*, p. 130.

49. Li Yinqiao, *Mao Zedong shiweizhang zaji*, pp. 121–22.

50. The purge of Gao Gang, chairman of the State Planning Commission, and Rao Shushi, director of the Central Organization Department, in 1955 and other purges before 1949 happened for the same reasons but under different circumstances.

51. Liu Suinian and Wu Qungan, *China's Socialist Economy*, p. 257.

52. Zhou Xiaozhou was a former secretary to Mao and later became party secretary for Hunan province. He was purged along with Peng Dehuai at Lushan in 1959.

53. It is a tradition in the CCP to ask a member who has made mistakes in his work, or is perceived to have done so, to make a self-criticism. The assumption is that once someone has made a self-criticism, admitting wrongdoing, he can be forgiven.

54. Cong Jin, *Quzhe fazhan de suiyue*, pp. 198–200.

55. The complete letter in Chinese can be found in Yan Yongsong and Wang Junwei, *Zuoqing ershi nian*, pp. 173–78. An English translation can be found in Peng Dehuai, *Memoirs of a Chinese Marshal*, pp. 510–20.

56. Cong Jin, *Quzhe fazhan de suiyue*, p. 206.

57. Li Rui, *Lushan huiyi shilu*, p. 74. Wang Renzhong was the governor of Hubei province at the time.

58. The chairman was known to have serious bouts of insomnia and was in a very bad mood whenever he could not sleep.

59. Li Rui, *Lushan huiyi shilu*, p. 128.

60. Both Luo Longji and Chen Mingshu were well-known "rightists" at the time.

61. For Mao's speech, see Li Rui, *Lushan huiyi shilu*, pp. 128–40. It is worth noting that this speech of Mao's is similar to several of his later speeches during the Cultural Revolution, such as those that criticized his colleagues' opposition to the Cultural Revolution during what is known as the "February Adversary Current" and Lin Biao and Chen Boda after the Lushan Conference of 1970.

62. Li Rui recorded Mao's instructions and other people's speeches in his notebooks. He was purged with Peng Dehuai and was in "exile" outside Beijing until 1979. The notebooks were taken from him during the Cultural Revolution, but he managed to get them back after returning to Beijing. These notebooks became precious sources for research on the Lushan Conference. For more about the notebooks, see Li Rui, *Lushan huiyi shilu*, pp. 10–11, 161.

63. Ibid., p. 158.

64. Tian Jiaying, Li Rui, and Zhou Xiaozhou had all worked as Mao's secretaries. They maintained good personal relationships among themselves.

65. For these records, see Li Rui, *Lushan huiyi shilu*, pp. 177–209. A more detailed discussion of the reasons for Peng's purge can be found in the next chapter, which discusses a pattern of purges in the CCP.

66. Cong Jin, *Quzhe fazhan de suiyue*, p. 219.

67. Center for Chinese Research Materials, *Xuexi wenxuan*, M1400 3, pp. 110–12.

68. See, for example, Cong Jin, *Quzhe fazhan de suiyue*, p. 403–4.

69. "Big-character posters" were used extensively in the Cultural Revolution as a means of expressing personal opinions. Individuals wrote messages in large print on poster-sized pieces of paper and posted them in public places. People usually used the posters to criticize leaders or others they disagreed with.

70. Cong Jin, *Quzhe fazhan de suiyue*, 713.

71. Ding Shu, *Ren huo*, p. 216.

72. Cong Jin, *Quzhe fazhan de suiyue*, pp. 429–31.

73. Zhu Jiaming, "Mao Zedong wannian dui jingji de zhuzhang yu xuanze" ("Mao Zedong's Basic Ideas and Choices in the Economy in His Later Years"), in Xiao Yanzhong, *Wannian Mao Zedong*, p. 91; and Wen Tiejun, "Guojia ziben zai fenpei yu minjian ziben zai jilei," p. 8.

74. Cong Jin, *Quzhe fazhan de suiyue*, p. 508.

75. Ibid., p. 510.

76. Ibid., p. 518.

77. Ibid., p. 526. The campaign of "five antis" was to eliminate "five evils," corruption, speculation, extravagance and waste, decentralization, and bureaucracy. The "four cleans" were political, economic, organizational, and ideological loyalty. Later, at the national working conference held by the Politburo in December 1964, the two movements were renamed the Socialist Education Movement.

78. Ibid., p. 526.

79. For Mao's and Liu's differences on the Socialist Education Movement, see Dittmer, *Liu Shao-ch'i and the Chinese Cultural Revolution*, pp. 228–29.

80. In answering a question from Edgar Snow in December 1970, Mao admitted that he gave serious thought to the problem of Liu in January 1965 when he was outlining the "23 items," a short title for the document entitled "On Questions of the Socialist Education Movement in the Countryside at Present," which was endorsed by the Working Conference of the Politburo in January 1964. "Mao Zhuxi huijian meiguo youhao renshi Snow de tianhua jiyao, 1970 nian 12 yue 18 ri" ("A Record of Chairman Mao's Talks to Friendly American Snow, Dec. 18, 1970"), CCP document, June 17, 1971, p. 13.

81. Cong Jin, *Quzhe fazhan de suiyue*, p. 533.

82. Ibid., p. 530.

83. Ibid., p. 604.

84. For the population decrease during the Great Leap Forward, see Bachman, *Bureaucracy, Economy, and Leadership in China*, pp. 4–5.

85. For details about this movement, see Cong Jin, *Quzhe fazhan de suiyue*, pp. 227–32.

86. During Mao's retreat from Yanan in 1945, he was hotly pursued by Liu Kan's seven brigades. Later, Mao referred to this experience whenever he en-

countered problems, because it was one of the most dangerous of his life. Chen Jin, *Mao Zedong de wenhua xingge*, p. 243.

87. Quan Yanchi, *Zouxia shentan de Mao Zedong*, pp. 26–30.

CHAPTER 3. *Chinese Gerontocracy and the Cultural Revolution*

1. Some exceptions are Lifton, *Revolutionary Immortality*; Pye, *Mao Tse-tung*; and Dittmer, "Mao Zedong and the Dilemma of Revolutionary Gerontocracy."

2. Shanas et al., *Old People in Three Industrial Societies*, pp. 18–19.

3. McIntyre, conclusion, in *Aging and Political Leadership*, p. 283.

4. Lifton, *Revolutionary Immortality*, p. 7. Stuart Schram also believes that the Cultural Revolution was Mao's attempt to erect a monument to himself in China for centuries to come. Schram, *Mao Tse-tung*, p. 345.

5. Integrity, as it is used by Erikson, refers to the ability to accept the facts of one's life and to face death without fear. B. M. Newman and P. R. Newman, "Later Adulthood," in Hendricks and Hendricks, *Dimensions of Aging*, p. 131.

6. Ibid., pp. 129–33.

7. Pye, *Mao Tse-tung*, p. 314.

8. Vertzberger, *The World in Their Minds*, pp. 190–91.

9. Ibid., p. 183.

10. Ibid., pp. 184–85.

11. For further discussion of this, see McIntyre, *Aging and Political Leadership*, pp. 290–98.

12. Roderick MacFarquhar suggested such a possibility. MacFarquhar and Fairbank, *The Cambridge History of China*, vol. 15, pt. 2, pp. 107–15.

13. Dittmer suggests such a hypothesis when he discusses the purge of a rather large proportion of China's leaders as the immediate result of Mao's mass mobilization efforts. Dittmer, "Mao Zedong and the Dilemma of Revolutionary Gerontocracy," pp. 163–70.

14. Ibid., p. 162.

15. Lifton, *Revolutionary Immortality*, p. 19.

16. Dittmer, "Mao Zedong and the Dilemma of Revolutionary Gerontocracy," pp. 151–59.

17. "Directives of July 3 (July 3, 1965)," in *Mao Zedong sixiang wansui*, M1400 12c, p. 185.

18. Chen, *Mao and the Chinese Revolution*, p. 53.

19. *Mao Zedong sixiang wansui*, p. 211.

20. Ibid., p. 153.

21. Snow, *The Long Revolution*, p. 169. Edgar Snow was among the first Americans to have contacts with Chinese communists. He visited Mao and his colleagues at Yanan as early as 1937 and remained Mao's friend until Mao died in 1976.

22. *Mao Zedong sixiang wansui*, M1400 12c, pp. 150–51.

23. Ibid., p. 127.

24. Cheng Qian, "Wenge mantan," pp. 9–10.

25. MacFarquhar and Fairbank, *The Cambridge History of China*, vol. 15, pt. 2, p. 143.

26. Wang Nianyi, *Dadongluan*, pp. 77–79.

27. On June 1, 1966, the Central Broadcast Station televised the content of one big-character poster to the nation from Peking University. The poster criticized the Party Committee of the university. This event is considered to be the beginning of the Cultural Revolution. For Mao's speech, see *Mao Zedong sixiang wansui*, M1400 12c, p. 148.

28. For more on Mao's criticism of Liu and Deng on the matter of work teams, see the discussion in the next chapter.

29. Dittmer, "Mao Zedong and the Dilemma of Revolutionary Gerontocracy," p. 164.

30. Xu Quanxing, *Mao Zedong wannian de lilun yu shijian*, p. 390.

31. On the paranoid suspicion of leaders, see Vertzberger, *The World in Their Minds*, p. 176.

32. The letter was also printed and distributed later, at the first Lushan Conference, with Mao's critical comments. Li Rui, *Lushan huiyi shilu*, pp. 47–53; Bo Yibo, *Ruogan zhongda juece yu shijian de huigu*, pp. 861–62.

33. For an excerpt from Liu's speech, see Xu Quanxing, *Mao Zedong wannian de lilun yu shijian*, p. 237.

34. Li Rui, *Lushan huiyi shilu*, p. 95.

35. In 1940 the general headquarters of the Eighth Route Army under the CCP launched large-scale offensives against the Japanese troops who invaded China proper in 1937. This was known as the Hundred Regiments Campaign. As the major organizer of this campaign, Peng Dehuai was criticized later at a meeting at Yanan for failing to get permission from CCP central headquarters to launch the campaign. For more on the campaign, see Hu Sheng, ed., *A Concise History of the Communist Party of China*, pp. 249–52. For more on the meeting at Yanan, see Bo Yibo, *Lingxiu, yuanshuai, zhanyou*, pp. 105–8. For Peng's defense of his actions, see Peng Dehuai, *Memoirs*, pp. 434–47.

36. Bo Yibo, *Huigu*, p. 880; Xu Quanxing, *Mao Zedong wannian de lilun yu shijian*, p. 233.

37. Li Yinqiao, pp. 137–38.

38. Xu Quanxing, *Mao Zedong wannian de lilun yu shijian*, p. 233.

39. Li Rui, *Lushan huiyi shilu*, p. 139.

40. Shao Yang, *Beijing: Zhongguo de gaogang zidimen*, pp. 8–9.

41. Li Yinqiao, *Mao Zedong shiweizhang zaji*, p. 139.

42. Xu Quanxing, *Mao Zedong wannian de lilun yu shijian*, p. 236.

43. Hollingworth, *Mao and the Men Against Him*, pp. 98–99.

44. Xu Quanxing, *Mao Zedong wannian de lilun yu shijian*, p. 36; emphasis added.

45. Li Rui, *Lushan huiyi shilu*, pp. 141–42.

46. Peng Dehuai, p. 505.

47. Cong Jin, *Quzhe fazhan de suiyue*, p. 304.

48. Xu Quanxing, *Mao Zedong wannian de lilun yu shijian*, p. 237.

49. Li Rui, *Lushan huiyi shilu*, p. 142.

50. Xu Quanxing, *Mao Zedong wannian de lilun yu shijian*, p. 383.

51. For instance, see Mao's personal letter to Jiang Qing in Kau, *The Lin Piao Affair*, p. 62.

52. Li Rui, *Mao Zedong de zaonian yu wannian*, pp. 313–15.

53. Snow, *The Long Revolution*, pp. 70–71.

54. Wu Xiaomei and Liu Peng, *Mao Zedong zouchu hongqiang*, p. 164.

55. Hai Rui was a minister of the Ming dynasty who was known to be outspoken about the emperor's mistakes. By mentioning Hai Rui, Mao actually encouraged others to criticize him.

56. Jia Sinan, *Mao Zedong renji jiaowang shilu*, p. 166.

57. Pye, *Mao Tse-tung*, pp. 36–37.

58. Gao Zhi and Zhang Ni'er, *Jiyao mishu de sinian*, pp. 155–56.

59. Xiao Feng and Ming Jun, *Mao Zedong zhimi*, p. 94. Sir Bernard Law Montgomery was the British officer who during World War II commanded the British troops and the Allied advance through Normandy. When he visited China in 1961, Mao received him.

60. Chen, *Mao's Papers*, p. 75.

61. Dittmer, "Mao Zedong and the Dilemma of Revolutionary Gerontocracy," p. 158.

62. Dittmer, *Liu Shao-ch'i and the Chinese Cultural Revolution*, pp. 50–51.

63. At a previous meeting, Liu had interrupted Mao's speech to disagree with him. Xiao Xinli, *Xunshi dajiang nanbei de Mao Zedong*, p. 359.

64. Li Zhisui, Mao's physician, discussed only minor illnesses Mao suffered between 1957 and 1971, such as colds, pneumonia, and skin infections. For more information, see Li Zhisui, *The Private Life of Chairman Mao*.

65. Xiao Feng and Ming Jun, *Mao Zedong zhimi*, p. 56.

66. Snow, *The Long Revolution*, pp. 195–96.

67. Ibid., p. 57.

68. Eduard Bernstein was a German Social Democratic leader. He was considered a revisionist because he rejected the arguments of Karl Marx and Friedrich Engels for the violent overthrow of capitalism. Karl J. Kautsky was a German Marxist theorist and one of the early leaders of the German Social Democratic Party. He rejected the Russian Revolution of October 1917. In one of his books, V. I. Lenin, the leader of the revolution, accused him of being a traitor to the communist revolution. N. S. Khrushchev was the Soviet communist leader after Stalin. He and Mao accused each other of Marxist revisionism because they could not agree on several major issues concerning Marxist theory and world politics. Zheng Qian and Han Gang, *Wannian suiyue*, p. 440.

69. Cong Jin, *Quzhe fazhan de suiyue*, p. 602. In Chinese, "to scold the mother" means "to scold others using vulgar language."

70. Ibid., p. 605.

71. Xi Xuan, "Guanyu wenhua dageming de qiyin de tantao," p. 56.

72. Wang Nianyi, "'Wenhua dageming' de youlai," p. 61.

73. Xi Xuan, "Guanyu wenhua dageming de qiyin de tantao," p. 57.
74. Ibid.
75. Xu Quanxing, *Mao Zedong wannian de lilun yu shijian*, p. 367.
76. Kau, *The Lin Piao Affair*, p. 328.
77. Xu Quanxing, *Mao Zedong wannian de lilun yu shijian*, pp. 367–68.
78. In July 1966 a big-character poster appeared on the campus of Peking University claiming that the Beijing municipal government had had a plan in February of that year to station troops from the Beijing garrison at Peking University and People's University. The poster also claimed that this was part of a conspiracy of the mayor, Peng Zhen, and the vice-mayor, Liu Ren. Later, Kang Sheng of the Central Cultural Revolution Small Group levied similar charges against Peng and Liu, as well as against Marshal He Long, who was supposedly a patron of Peng and Liu, using the poster as evidence. The charges were dropped later, however. For more about the "February Mutiny," see Jin Chunming, Huang Yuchong, and Zhang Huimin, *"Wenge" shiqi guishiguiyu*, pp. 8–9; and Xiao Di, Zhi Wu, and Tian Yi, *"Wenge" zhi mi*, pp. 22–26.
79. Dittmer makes a similar argument in his analysis of the case of Liu Shaoqi in terms of the "politics of mass criticism." For further discussion, see Dittmer, *Liu Shao-ch'i and the Chinese Cultural Revolution*, pp. 109–18.
"Mass criticism" means "criticism by the masses." Before the Cultural Revolution, the criticism of party leaders was conducted only within the party. During the Cultural Revolution, Mao asked the masses—the general public—to criticize Liu, Deng, and others. The party publicized the leaders' "mistakes" or "crimes" and asked the people to hold meetings and create big-character posters to criticize them.
80. Although it sounds self-serving, Mao did show sympathy to Liu and others in 1970 when he told Snow that one of the two things that made him most unhappy during the Cultural Revolution was the maltreatment of "captives"—party leaders and others removed from power. Snow, *The Long Revolution*, p. 174.
81. Wang Li, *Xianchang lishi*, p. 84.
82. Li Junru, *Mao Zedong yu dangdai zhongguo*, p. 216.
83. "Mass organizations" during the Cultural Revolution were organizations of the people; they had no affiliation with the government or with previously established (permanent) organizations. Many were temporary and arbitrary in nature. Red Guard organizations were one type of mass organization. There were thousands of others organized by workers, peasants, and other Chinese citizens.
84. Qi Benyu, "Aiguo zhuyi hai shi maiguo zhuyi—ping fandong yinpian *Qinggong mishi*" ("Patriotic or Disloyal to the Country—Criticism of a Counter-revolutionary Movie, *Secret History of a Qing Palace*"), *Hongqi* 5 (March 1967): 9–23.
85. Dittmer, *Liu Shao-ch'i and the Chinese Cultural Revolution*, p. 33.
86. Lu Dingyi was minister of propaganda of the Party Central Committee; Tan Zheng was director of the General Political Department of the PLA; Peng

Zhen was mayor of Beijing; Luo Ruiqing was chief of staff of the PLA; He Long was a marshal of the PLA and the director of the State Commission of Sports; Wan Li was vice-premier; Li Jingquan was the governor of Sichuan province; Liu Ren was vice-mayor of Beijing; and Chen Zaidao was commander of the Wuhan Military Region. Li Yang, *Tejian yishi*, pp. 11–15.

87. Wang Li, *Xianchang lishi*, pp. 63, 96.

88. Ibid., pp. 94–95.

89. Ye Yonglie, *Chen Boda*, p. 458.

90. Wang Nianyi, *Dadongluan*, pp. 311–15.

91. For further discussion of succession problems in China, see Dittmer, "Mao Zedong and the Dilemma of Revolutionary Gerontocracy," pp. 157–58.

92. Nearly all scholars in China take it for granted that Mao had the right to choose his own successor. So far, I have not encountered a single Chinese author who questions Mao's right to do so.

93. Mao characterized each major power struggle as a "line struggle"—a struggle for the party line, the direction the party policy should take. For example, the fall of Liu Shaoqi was the result of the "ninth line struggle" and that of Lin Biao the result of the tenth. Before 1980, the official party history also characterized these power struggles as conflicts over party policy.

94. Dittmer, "Mao Zedong and the Dilemma of Revolutionary Gerontocracy," p. 166.

CHAPTER 4. *Lin Biao and the Cultural Revolution*

1. Li Tianmin, "The Mao-Lin Relationship" (Jan. 1973), p. 81; and Leys, "The Death of Lin Biao," in *The Burning Forest*, p. 142.

2. Robinson, "Lin Piao as an Elite Type," in Scalapino, *Elites in the People's Republic of China*, p. 158.

3. The Jinggang Mountain period refers to the early years of the CCP and the early operations of an armed forces under Mao and his comrades. Mao and others set up their first bases in the area of the Jinggang Mountains in Jiangxi province in 1927, where they operated until they were driven out by the Nationalist forces in 1934.

4. Li Tianmin, *Lin Biao pingzhuan*, p. 12.

5. Huang Chenxia, *Zhonggong junren zhi*, p. 209.

6. Thomas Robinson, Donald Klein, and Anne Clark believe that Lin became commander of the Fourth Red Army in the summer of 1930. See Robinson, *Biography of Lin Piao*, pt. 1, p. 17; and Klein and Clark, *Biographic Dictionary of Chinese Communism: 1921–1965*, vol. 1, p. 560.

7. Li Tianmin, *Zhonggong shouyao shiliao huibian*, p. 5; and Huang Chenxia, *Zhonggong junren zhi*, p. 220.

8. Robinson, *Biography of Lin Piao*, p. 19.

9. Ibid., pp. 22–23.

10. Gong Chu, "Canjia zhonggong wuzhuang douzheng jishi," *Ming Pao Monthly*, March 1972, p. 99.

11. Li Tianmin, *Lin Biao pingzhuan*, p. 11; Gong Chu, "Canjia zhonggong wuzhuang douzheng jishi," *Ming Pao Monthly*, March 1972, p. 99; April 1972, p. 100; and May 1972, p. 99.

12. Huang Chenxia, *Zhonggong junren zhi*, p. 209.

13. A commander with "warlord habits" acted on his own, without consulting the party. Zhu had been a warlord before joining the party. Gong Chu, "Canjia zhonggong wuzhuang douzheng jishi," *Ming Pao Monthly*, May 1972, pp. 99–100; and Li Tianmin, *Lin Biao pingzhuan*, p. 28.

14. Liu Yuen-sun, *The Current and the Past of Lin Piao*, p. 38.

15. Li Tianmin, *Lin Biao pingzhuan*, p. 12.

16. After the Lin Biao incident in 1971, however, Lin was condemned for opposing the resolution in 1929. Li Tianmin, *Lin Biao pingzhuan*, p. 14.

17. Robinson, *Biography of Lin Piao*, p. 16.

18. For a detailed analysis of the letter and the Mao-Lin relationship, see Li Tianmin, "The Mao-Lin Relationship" (Oct. 1973), pp. 78–85.

19. Robinson, *Biography of Lin Piao*, p. 15.

20. Smedley, *The Great Road*, p. 310.

21. Robinson, *Biography of Lin Piao*, p. 24.

22. Snow, *Red Star over China*, p. 194. Both Edgar Snow and Agnes Smedley provide vivid descriptions of this battle. See also Smedley, *The Great Road*.

23. In June 1935, when Mao and Zhang joined forces, the CCP held a Politburo meeting at Lianghekou. During the meeting, Mao's Central Army argued with Zhang's Fourth Army Corps over a series of questions, including the legitimacy of the Party Central Committee, which had been altered during the Zunyi meeting, the administrative system of the Chinese Soviets, and the route the Red Army should take later. Zhang opposed Mao's idea of going to northern Shaanxi province, suggesting that the Red Army go first to Sichuan province and then to Xinjiang. The two forces reached a temporary compromise.

In August 1935, the CCP held two meetings near a small town called Maoergai in Gansu province in an attempt to smooth over disputes between Mao and Zhang Guotao. These meetings came to be known as the Maoergai meetings. Historians disagree about the time and place of the meetings, but all concur that the meetings failed to achieve their main purpose, so immediately afterward, Mao and Zhang openly split with each other.

24. Li Tianmin, *Lin Biao pingzhuan*, pp. 32–33.

25. Robinson, *Biography of Lin Piao*, p. 27; and Hu Sheng, *A Concise History of the Communist Party of China*, pp. 186–87.

26. Salisbury, *The Long March*, chap. 24; and Li Tianmin, *Lin Biao pingzhuan*, pp. 38–42.

27. Snow, *Red Star over China*, p. 115.

28. Qin Bangxian was the secretary and nominal leader of the CCP at that time.

29. Wu Xiuquan was a Long March veteran and held important government positions after 1949. His memoirs are entitled *Wo de shengya: 1908–1949*

(*My Career: 1908–1949*) (Beijing: Renmin chubanshe, 1986). Otto Braun (also known as Li De), a German, was the representative of the Third Comintern to the CCP at that time.

30. Salisbury, *The Long March*, pp. 125–26.

31. Zhou Enlai was criticized as being responsible for the loss of the fifth encirclement battle at the Zunyi meeting and was removed from his position on the Military Committee. Hu Chi-hsi cites an article by Lin Biao in the Chinese Communist journal *Geming yu zhanzheng* (*Revolution and War*) in July 1934. It contains what Hu regards as a thinly veiled attack on Braun's strategy and implies support for Mao. Braun makes a rather condescending reference to Lin's article in his memoirs. Hu Chi-hsi, "Mao, Lin and the Fifth Encirclement Campaign," *China Quarterly* 82 (April–June 1980): 250–80.

32. Li Tianmin, *Lin Biao pingzhuan*, p. 38; and Robinson, *Biography of Lin Piao*, p. 25.

33. Salisbury gives several examples of Lin's dissatisfaction with Mao during the Long March. He notes, however, that some of these claims were probably exaggerated by Red Army survivors who fell victim to the Cultural Revolution. See Salisbury, *The Long March*, pp. 189–91.

34. Robinson, *Biography of Lin Piao*, pp. 31–32; Li Tianmin, *Lin Biao pingzhuan*, p. 42.

35. Robinson, *Biography of Lin Piao*, p. 49.

36. For details about this campaign, see Liu, "The Battle of P'inghsingkuan"; and Li Tianyou, "First Encounter at P'inghsingkuan Pass," pp. 1–23.

37. It is not certain just how and when Lin Biao was wounded. Smedley says that it was in early 1938, but Huang Chenxia believes that it was in September 1938. Both Robinson and Li say it was in March 1938. Smedley, *The Great Road*, p. 368; Huang Chenxia, *Zhonggong junren zhi*, p. 211; Robinson, *Biography of Lin Piao*, p. 39; and Li Tianmin, *Lin Biao pingzhuan*, p. 48.

38. Li Tianmin, *Lin Biao pingzhuan*, pp. 48–49.

39. Robinson, *Biography of Lin Piao*, pp. 40–41.

40. In 1940, *Communist International* (no. 8, New York) published the article "For the Third Anniversary of the Chinese National Liberation War" by a person named "Ling Pao," which had been published in Moscow in Russian sometime earlier. It is far from clear that Lin actually wrote this article, although he may have signed his name to it. For more on the authorship of this article, see Li Tianmin, *Lin Biao pingzhuan*, pp. 49–50; and Robinson, *Biography of Lin Piao*, p. 202.

41. Li Tianmin, *Lin Biao pingzhuan*, p. 50.

42. The Internationalists were 28 or so young people who had studied in the Soviet Union in the late 1920s and early 1930s. After returning to China, they formed a faction led by Wang Ming and dominated the party. With few exceptions, they were all removed from authoritative positions in the party by the end of the Rectification Movement of 1945.

43. I would like to thank Professor Niu Dayong of the History Department of Peking University for referring me to another source concerning the Mao-

Lin relationship at Yanan. According to the memoir of Shi Zhe, who worked as an interpreter for CCP leaders after the 1930s, Shi was surprised by Mao's warm welcome upon Lin Biao's return to Yanan. Shi Zhe contrasted Mao's attitude toward Lin with Mao's attitude toward Zhou Enlai and other CCP leaders: Mao remained in bed sleeping when Zhou and others returned from the Soviet Union, but he received Lin in person and held Lin's hand on their way to Mao's office. Shi Zhe, *Zai lishi juren shenbian*, pp. 231–33.

44. Li Tianmin, *Lin Biao pingzhuan*, p. 51.

45. Wang Ming, *Zhonggong ban shiji yu pantu Mao Zedong*, p. 171.

46. Whitson, *The Chinese High Command*, p. 309.

47. The creation of the Fourth Field Army began in November 1948 and was completed in March 1949. The Field Army, based on the Northeast People's Army, included approximately 75 divisions, 24 corps, and 9 armies. It became Lin's power base in his later political career. During the Cultural Revolution, many former leading officers of the Fourth Field Army were promoted to key positions in the PLA, including Lin's four primary assistants, Huang Yongsheng, Wu Faxian, Li Zuopeng, and Qiu Huizuo. A good history of the Fourth Field Army appears in Whitson, *The Chinese High Command*.

48. A collection of materials about Lin Biao published in Hong Kong maintains that he was the commander-in-chief of the Chinese Volunteers in Korea. See also Kau, *The Lin Piao Affair*, p. xx. Martin Ebon quotes an American historian who claimed that it was Lin Biao who attacked the U.S. I and IX Corps. Ebon, *Lin Piao*, p. 32. Most scholars, however, believe that Lin Biao was not in Korea during the war. See, for example, Li Tianmin, *Lin Biao pingzhuan*, p. 76; and Robinson, *Biography of Lin Piao*, pp. 6–14. A recently published memoir by Hong Xuezhi, the former vice-commander-in-chief of the Volunteers confirms that Lin was not involved in the war. Hong Xuezhi, *Kang mei yuan chao zhanzheng huiyi*, p. 19. For the latest account of Lin's opposition to Mao's decision to enter the Korean War and his refusal to head the troops there, see Goncharov, Lewis, and Xue Litai, *Uncertain Partners*, pp. 167, 176.

49. Hong Xuezhi, *Kang mei yuan chao zhanzheng huiyi*, p. 17; and Li Tianmin, *Lin Biao pingzhuan*, p. 78.

50. Li Yinqiao, "Zouxiang shentian de Mao Zedong" ("Mao on His Way to Becoming a God"), quoted in Xu Quanxing, *Mao Zedong wannian de lilun yu shijian*, p. 407.

51. Cong Jin, *Quzhe fazhan de suiyue*, pp. 305–6.

52. Wu Faxian, Manuscript, hel5004, pp. 7–8.

53. Xu Quanxing, *Mao Zedong wannian de lilun yu shijian*, pp. 411–12.

54. "Ye Jianying tongzhi 10 yue 5 ri zai Beijing gongren tiyuguan jundui yuanxiao wuchan jieji wenhua dageming dongyuan dahui shang de jianghua" ("Comrade Ye Jianying's October 5 Speech at the Meeting of Army Schools for the Mobilization of the Great Proletarian Cultural Revolution at Beijing Workers' Stadium"), in *Zai wuchan jieji wenhua dageming zhong zhongyang fuze tongzhi jianghua chaolu* (*A Collection of the Speeches by the Central Lead-*

ers During the Great Proletarian Cultural Revolution) (Stanford, Calif.: Hoover Institution, 1967), pp. 18–21.

55. Wang Nianyi, "Zhengque zongjie 'wenhua dageming' de lishi jiaoxun," p. 157.

56. Jia Sinan, *Mao Zedong renji jiaowang shilu*, pp. 269–70. Huang was purged with Peng Dehuai in 1959. He was rehabilitated after Mao's death.

57. Chinese scholars have debated when and why Mao wrote the letter. Some even question its authenticity. Recent evidence suggests that Mao wrote it while visiting his hometown of Shaoshan in the summer of 1966. See Jin Chunming, "Yipian qite de ziwo jiepou"; Hu Xiongwei, "Ziwo jiepou de qite haishi ziwo xinxin de xianyi"; and Xu Quanxing, "Mao Zedong wannian zai jiebanren wenti shang de chouchu."

58. Kau, *The Lin Piao Affair*, p. 120.

59. Jin Chunming, "Yipian qite de ziwo jiepou," p. 54; and Xu Quanxing, "Mao Zedong wannian zai jiebanren wenti shang de chouchu," pp. 85–86.

60. Kau, *The Lin Piao Affair*, p. 119.

61. Mao and Jiang Qing held a birthday dinner to which they invited the members of the Central Cultural Revolution Small Group, including Chen Boda, Zhang Chunqiao, Wang Li, Guan Feng, Qi Benyu, and Yao Wenyuan.

62. Wang Li, *Xianchang lishi*, pp. 100–110.

63. According to Chinese folklore, Zhong Kui had the power to chase away ghosts and evil spirits.

64. The Chinese expression is "Wangpo mai gua, zimai zikua." Chinese often use this phrase to mock those who brag about something that is not true.

65. *Jiefangjun bao*, Jan. 16, 1961. For a translation of this resolution, see Cheng, *The Politics of the Chinese Red Army*, pp. 66–94.

66. Cheng, *The Politics of the Chinese Red Army*, pp. 67–68.

67. Chiang I-shan, "Military Affairs," p. 186.

68. Gittings, *The Role of the Chinese Army*, p. 247.

69. Jordan, "Political Orientation of the PLA," p. 8.

70. *Guangming ribao*, Nov. 17, 1961.

71. Meisner, *Mao's China*, p. 297.

72. Center for Chinese Research Materials, *Xuexi ziliao*, vol. 3, p. 72.

73. *Renmin ribao*, "Quanguo bixue xuexi remin jiefangjun" ("The Whole Country Must Learn from the PLA"), Feb. 1, 1964.

74. Gittings, *The Role of the Chinese Army*, p. 257.

75. Lei Feng was a soldier known for his "high political consciousness" in following the party unconditionally. He became a model for others after he died in an accident in 1964. In using Lei Feng as a good example, the General Political Department often used the metaphor of a nail to describe his unconditional devotion to the party. Being "a nail of the party" meant that no matter what the party asked him to do, he did his share devotedly without conditions, just as a nail does when it is hammered into something.

76. Powell, "Commissars in the Economy," pp. 136–38; and Gittings, *The Role of the Chinese Army*, pp. 257–58.

77. Jordan, "Political Orientation of the PLA," p. 9.

78. According to a Chinese party historian, Zhou Enlai suggested to Mao after he had seen the letter at Wuhan that he go to Dalian to talk to Lin Biao, and Mao agreed. Xu Quanxing, "Mao Zedong wannian zai jiebanren wenti shang de chouchu," p. 86.

79. "Lin Biao tongzhi 1967 nian 8 yue 9 ri tong Zeng Siyu he Liu Feng tongzhi de tanhua," p. 221.

80. Hong Haiyan, *Wuxian fengguang zai xianfeng*, p. 66.

81. Xiao Sike, *Chaoji shenpan*, vol. 1, p. 77.

82. Xu Quanxing, *Mao Zedong wannian de lilun yu shijian*, p. 408.

83. Zhang Yunsheng, *Maojiawan jishi*, p. 373; and Zhang Yunsheng, "True Account," p. 18.

84. Wang Nianyi, *Dadongluan*, pp. 481–83.

85. Guan Weixun, *Wo suo zhidao de Ye Qun*, p. 215.

86. ZZB [1], pp. 9–10. It was considered a virtue in Chinese tradition to make the modest gesture of refusing an appointment even if one wanted it very much.

87. Wu Faxian, Manuscript, he15004, p. 1.

88. A more dramatic version of this meeting between Mao and Lin says that Lin begged Mao on his knees not to appoint him. Interview with a party historian, Beijing, August 15, 1994.

89. In a discussion of the Lin Biao incident, one party historian told me that he had seen Mao's criticism of Lin in written material kept in the central archives.

90. Guan Weixun, *Wo suo zhidao de Ye Qun*, p. 215.

91. Zhang Yunsheng, *Maojiawan jishi*, pp. 230–36, 226.

92. Zhang Yunsheng, "True Account," pp. 12–13.

93. Quan Yanchi, *Tao Zhu zai "wenhua dageming" zhong*, p. 215.

94. "Lin Biao jianghua huibian" (Collection of Lin Biao's Speeches) (n.p.: East Asian Collection at the Hoover Institution, Stanford University, n.d.), p. 167.

95. Conference documents, June 6, 1972.

96. There are more profound social and political reasons behind the formation and development of the Red Guard movement than can be described here. For detailed discussion of the movement, see Lee, *The Politics of the Cultural Revolution*; Rosen, *Red Guard Factionalism and the Cultural Revolution in Guangzhou*; Hinton, *Hundred Day War*; Lin Jing, *The Red Guards' Path to Violence*; Bennett and Montaperto, *Red Guard*; Chan, *Children of Mao*; and Gao Yuan, *Born Red*.

97. Gao Shu and Xin Bing, *Juren Mao Zedong*, pp. 1461–63.

98. "East Wind" comes from a famous statement of Mao's: "The East Wind prevails over the West Wind." He meant that the peoples of the East would triumph over the peoples of the West.

99. Yan Jiaqi and Gao Gao, *Turbulent Decade*, pp. 89–98.

100. Chen Donglin and Du Pu, *Zhonghua renmin gongheguo shilu*, p. 153.

101. Wang Nianyi, *Dadongluan*, p. 73.

102. Chen Donglin and Du Pu, *Zhonghua renmin gongheguo shilu*, pp. 159–60.

103. Lee, *Politics of the Cultural Revolution*, pp. 68–69.

104. For more discussion of this couplet, see Chan, *Children of Mao*, pp. 132–38; and Lee, *Politics of the Cultural Revolution*, pp. 68–77.

105. At the beginning of the Cultural Revolution, "black gang" was a term used to refer to those who either had "bad" class origins or were considered to have some kind of political problem. For detailed discussion of the humiliation of the professors at the hands of the Red Guards, see Jin Xianlin, *Niupeng zayi*; and Zhou Yiliang, *Bijing shi shusheng*.

106. For more information, see Yan Jiaqi and Gao Gao, *Wenhua dageming shinian shi*, chap. 4, pp. 89–125; Wang Nianyi, *Dadongluan*, pp. 64–92; and Xiao Di, Zhi Wu, and Tian Yi, *"Wenge" zhi mi*, pp. 71–88.

107. For the details of this meeting, see MacFarquhar and Fairbank, *The Cambridge History of China*, pp. 150–51; and Wang Nianyi, *Dadongluan*, pp. 100–117.

108. Wang Nianyi, *Dadongluan*, pp. 113–14.

109. Dittmer, *Liu Shao-ch'i and the Chinese Cultural Revolution*, pp. 119–47; Lee, *Politics of the Cultural Revolution*, pp. 26–63; and Wang Nianyi, *Dadongluan*, pp. 33–49.

110. For the Mao-Liu conflict during the Socialist Education Movement, see Lieberthal, "The Great Leap Forward and the Split in the Yan'an Leadership, 1958–65," in MacFarquhar, *The Politics of China: 1949–1989*, pp. 137–39; Dittmer, *Liu Shao-ch'i and the Chinese Cultural Revolution*, pp. 241–43; and Cong Jin, *Quzhe fazhan de suiyue*, pp. 529–43.

111. During the Cultural Revolution, cadres who could not be trusted to continue their work but had not committed serious enough "mistakes" to be ousted would be asked to "step aside" pending a final decision on their political future.

112. Wang Li, *Xianchang lishi*, pp. 66–67.

113. Zhang Yunsheng, *Maojiawan jishi*, p. 108.

114. Ibid, p. 84; and Zhang Yunsheng, "True Account," p. 25.

115. Li Ke and Hao Shengzhang, *Wenhau dageming zhong de zhongguo renmin jiefangjun*, p. 225.

116. Zhang Yunsheng, *Maojiawan jishi*, 42–43; and Zhang Yunsheng, "True Account," pp. 21–33; and Wu Faxian, Manuscript, hel5004, pp. 11–12.

117. All documents regarding the Cultural Revolution required final approval from the Central Cultural Revolution Small Group.

118. Wang Nianyi, *Dadongluan*, p. 96.

119. Ibid., pp. 97–98. For the document itself, see Guofang daxue, *Wenhua dageming yanjiu ziliao*, vol. 1, pp. 132–33.

120. Zhang Yunsheng, *Maojiawan jishi*, p. 56; Wang Nianyi, *Dadongluan*, p. 119; and Wu Faxian, Manuscript, hel5004, p. 13.

121. Wu Faxian, Manuscript, hel5004, pp. 12–15. Only Mao, Lin, Zhou, Jiang Qing, and members of a few Cultural Revolution groups belonged to proletarian headquarters; Liu Shaoqi had authority over the "bourgeois headquarters."

122. Zhang Yunsheng, *Maojiawan jishi*, pp. 68–75.

123. Lin was known for trusting and caring for his subordinates, especially those who had followed him through the war years. See Quan Yanchi, *Tao Zhu zai "wenhua dageming" zhong*, pp. 124–25.

124. Wang Nianyi, *Dadongluan*, p. 151; and Chen Donglin and Du Pu, *Zhonghua renmin gongheguo shilu*, pp. 164, 206.

125. Zhang Yunsheng, "True Account," p. 24.

126. Zhang Yunsheng, *Maojiawan jishi*, pp. 40–42.

127. Ibid., p. 63.

128. Wang Li, *Xianchang lishi*, pp. 53–54.

129. Tie Zhuwei, *Shuang zhong se yu nong*, pp. 109–11; and Wang Nianyi, *Dadongluan*, p. 119.

130. Li Ke and Hao Shengzhang, *Wenhau dageming zhong de zhongguo renmin jiefangjun*, pp. 30–36.

131. Wu Faxian, Manuscript, hel5004, p. 16.

132. See Wang Nianyi, *Dadongluan*, pp. 150–51; Xu Xiangqian, *Lishi de huigu*, pp. 821–23; and Wu Faxian, Manuscript, hel5004, p. 17.

133. Zhang Yunsheng, *Maojiawan jishi*, pp. 65–68.

134. Wu Faxian, Manuscript, hel5005, pp. 11–12.

135. Zhang Yunsheng, *Maojiawan jishi*, pp. 163–64; and Wu Faxian, Manuscript, hel5005, pp. 12–14.

136. Xue Yesheng, *Ye Jianying de guanhui yisheng*, p. 333.

137. Xu Xiangqian, *Lishi de huigu*, vol. 3, p. 829; Wu Faxian, Manuscript, hel5005, p. 11; Zhang Yunsheng, *Maojiawan jishi*, pp. 76–78, and "True Account," pp. 24–26.

138. For the document, see Xu Xiangqian, *Lishi de huigu*, vol. 3, pp. 829–30; and Guofang daxue, *Wenhua dageming ziliao huibian*, vol. 1, p. 262.

139. Zong Huaiwen, *Years of Trial, Turmoil, and Triumph*, p. 140; MacFarquhar and Fairbank, *The Cambridge History of China*, vol. 15, pt. 1, p. 177; and Jin Chunming, *"Wenhua dageming" lunxi*, pp. 114–38.

140. Wang Nianyi, *Dadongluan*, p. 101.

141. Xiao Jinguang, *Xiao Jinguang huiyilu*, p. 271.

142. Wang Nianyi, *Dadongluan*, p. 172, n. 1.

143. Quan Yanchi, *Tao Zhu zai "wenhua dageming" zhong*, p. 124.

144. Ibid., pp. 207–11; and Ye Yonglie, *Chen Boda*, pp. 342–43.

145. Dong Baocun, *Tan Zhenlin waizhuan*, p. 105.

146. Lin Qing, *Zhou Enlai de zhaixiang shengya*, p. 116.

147. Wang Li, *Xianchang lishi*, p. 102.

148. Quan Yanchi, *Tao Zhu zai "wenhua dageming" zhong*, pp. 232–33.

149. Ye Yonglie, *Chen Boda*, 348; and Cheng Qian, "Wenge mantan," p. 43.

150. For details of the meeting, see Wang Nianyi, *Dadongluan*, p. 150; Ye Yonglie, *Chen Boda*, p. 348, and Wang Li, *Xianchang lishi*, pp. 29–32.

151. Wang Li, *Xianchang lishi*, p. 148; and Ye Yonglie, *Chen Boda*, pp. 365–68.

152. Cheng Qian found this draft, dated August 12, in the central archives. Item no. 6 advised the provinces not to encourage students to come to Beijing. Those who had already arrived were to go back to the provinces immediately.

Item no. 7 asked the schools to advise their students to stay at school. Cheng Qian, "Wenge mantan," pp. 7–8.

153. Ibid., pp. 8–9.

154. Wang Li, *Xianchang lishi*, p. 148.

155. Ibid., p. 147.

156. Ibid., p. 34; and Ye Yonglie, *Chen Boda*, p. 378.

157. Tan Zhenlin zhuan bianji weiyuanhui, *Tan Zhenlin zhuan*, p. 356.

158. Wang Li, *Xianchang lishi*, pp. 29–37.

159. According to the minutes of the meeting that day, Chen Yi complained because he had received criticism during the movement. That was why Mao later suspected that Chen wanted to "reverse the case." Xiao Sike, *Chaoji shenpan*, vol. 1, pp. 330–32. Chen's biographers, however, believed that when Chen mentioned the Yanan Rectification Movement he was criticizing Kang Sheng, who was in charge of the purge of a large number of cadres at Yanan. Tie Zhuwei, *Shuang zhong se yu nong*, p. 182; and Chen Yi zhuan bianji zu, *Chen Yi zhuan*, p. 609.

160. Zong Huaiwen, *Years of Trial, Turmoil, and Triumph*, pp. 140–41.

161. Wu Faxian, Manuscript, hel5005 p. 15.

162. MacFarquhar and Fairbank, *The Cambridge History of China*, p. 178; and Zhang Yunsheng, *Maojiawan jishi*, p. 93. For Tan's letter of February 17, see Dong Baocun, *Tan Zhenlin waizhuan*, pp. 125–26; and Ye Yonglie, *Chen Boda*, pp. 376–78.

163. Wang Li, *Xianchang lishi*, p. 31.

164. MacFarquhar and Fairbank, *The Cambridge History of China*, vol. 15, pt. 1, pp. 177–78.

165. A resolution of the Central Secretariat dated March 20, 1943, granted Mao veto power over the party decision. Hei Yannan, *Shinian dongluan*, p. 172.

166. Wang Nianyi, *Dadongluan*, p. 216.

167. Ibid., p. 216; and Li Ke and Hao Shengzhang, *Wenhau dageming zhong de zhongguo renmin jiefangjun*, p. 212.

168. Li Ke and Hao Shengzhang, *Wenhau dageming zhong de zhongguo renmin jiefangjun*, p. 213; and Wang Li, *Xianchang lishi*, p. 35.

169. Wang Nianyi, *Dadongluan*, p. 216, n. 3.

170. Jiang had asked Zhou several times before to join the CCRSG meetings, but Zhou had always refused. Wu Faxian, Manuscript, hel5006, pp. 4–5.

171. Jin Chunming, *"Wenhua dageming" lunxi*, p. 131.

172. Hei Yannan, *Shinian dongluan*, pp. 174–78.

173. For details, see Wu Faxian, Manuscript, hel5007, pp. 12–14; and Li Ke and Hao Shengzhang, *Wenhau dageming zhong de zhongguo renmin jiefangjun*, p. 48.

CHAPTER 5. *The Conflict Between Power Groups*

1. *A Great Trial in Chinese History*, pp. 149–50.

2. Terrill, *Madame Mao: The White-Boned Demon*, p. 305.

3. Lin Biao and his followers were charged with conducting an abortive coup attempt during the Second Plenum of the Ninth Party Central Committee in August 1970.

4. Wu Faxian, Manuscript, hel5006, pp. 12–14; and Zhang Yunsheng, *Maojiawan jishi*, pp. 112–23.

5. Wang Nianyi, *Dadongluan*, pp. 286–87.

6. Snow, *The Long Revolution*, p. 174.

7. Wang Nianyi, *Dadongluan*, pp. 286–87.

8. Wu Faxian, Manuscript, hel5006, pp. 2–3.

9. Wang Nianyi, *Dadongluan*, p. 380.

10. Guofang daxue, *Wenhua dageming yanjiu ziliao*, vol. 2, p. 28.

11. Wu Faxian, Manuscript, hel5006, pp. 20–22.

12. Ibid., p. 22.

13. For several years, only these eight operas were allowed on stage. Interestingly, the opera troupes that originally performed the model operas later became part of Jiang Qing's power base.

14. Wu Faxian, Manuscript, hel5006, pp. 22–23; and Zhang Yunsheng, *Maojiawan jishi*, pp. 133–35.

15. For more accounts of this event, see Xiao Sike, *Chaoji shenpan*, vol. 1, p. 334.

16. For other accounts of this event, see Zhang Yunsheng, *Maojiawan jishi*, pp. 138–40.

17. Ji Xichen, "'Yang-Yu-Fu' shijian neiqing," pp. 136–37. It is not clear why Ye Qun was interested in the affairs. It seems that she must have had a motive other than protecting her son's friends. For one such interpretation, see Zhang Yunsheng, *Maojiawan jishi*, pp. 138–41.

18. Wu Faxian, Manuscript, hel5006, p. 25; and Zhang Yunsheng, *Maojiawan jishi*, pp. 141–45.

19. "Lin Biao zai jundui ganbu dahui shang de jianghua," p. 87. Also see Xiao Sike, *Chaoji shenpan*, vol. 1, p. 337; Li Ke and Hao Shengzhang, *Wenhau dageming zhong de zhongguo renmin jiefangjun*, p. 56; and Ji Xichen, "Shijian neiqing," pp. 137–38.

20. Dong Baocun, "Yang Yu Fu mengnanji" ("Yang, Yu, and Fu Were in Trouble"), in Guofang daxue, *Wenhua dageming yanjiu ziliao*, vol. 2, pp. 67–70.

21. "Lin Biao Jianghua, 1968 nian 3 yue 24 ri," (Lin Biao's Speech, March 24, 1968"), in Guofang daxue, *Wenhua dageming yanjiu ziliao*, vol. 2, p. 87; and Wang Nianyi, *Dadongluan*, p. 291. Xie Fuzhi was then the first political commissar of the Beijing Military Region. Han Xianchu was commander of the Fuzhou Military Region.

22. Wang Nianyi, *Dadongluan*, p. 289.

23. Zhang Yunsheng, *Maojiawan jishi*, pp. 151–54; and Wang Nianyi, *Dadongluan*, pp. 285–93.

24. Terrill, *Madame Mao*, p. 200.

25. Ibid., p. 299.

26. Wu Faxian, Manuscript, he15007, pp. 1–2; Wang Nianyi, *Dadongluan*, pp. 385–86; and Zhang Yunsheng, *Maojiawan jishi*, pp. 202–4.

27. Wang Nianyi, *Dadongluan*, p. 386.

28. Ibid., pp. 386–87; and Zhang Yunsheng, *Maojiawan jishi*, pp. 206–9.

29. Ye Yonglie, *Chen Boda*, p. 448.

30. Zhang Yunsheng, *Maojiawan jishi*, pp. 179–80.

31. Ibid., pp. 209–15.

32. Cheng Qian, "Wenge mantan," pp. 66–71.

33. Wu Faxian, Manuscript, he15007, p. 9; Wang Dongxing, *Wang Dongxing huiyi*, pp. 15–17; and Ye Yonglie, *Chen Boda*, pp. 456–59.

34. Ye Yonglie, *Chen Boda*, pp. 462–63.

35. Ibid., pp. 460–61.

36. Ibid.; and Wu Faxian, Manuscript, he15007, p. 6.

37. Zhang Yunsheng, *Maojiawan jishi*, pp. 214–15; and Wang Dongxing, *Wang Dongxing huiyi*, p. 17.

38. The account of Wang Dongxing's relationship with Lin Biao here is based on the written materials of Lin Doudou (Lin Liheng) and Zhang Qinglin. In his recently published memoir, Wang Dongxing reveals little to support their account. Wang's stand is understandable, since the Chinese government still adheres to Mao's version of the Lin Biao incident for political reasons.

39. Lin Liheng and Zhang Qinglin, "Shangsu cailiao," pt. 2, p. 93.

40. Wu Faxian, Manuscript, he15007, p. 3.

41. Li Zhisui, *The Private Life of Chairman Mao*, p. 511. For another account of Wang Dongxing's relationship with Lin, see Wu Faxian, Manuscript, he15007, p. 519.

42. Lin Liheng and Zhang Qinglin, "Shangsu cailiao," pt. 2, pp. 94–95.

43. Li Zhisui, *The Private Life of Chairman Mao*, pp. 510, 358.

44. Wu Faxian, Manuscript, he15007, pp. 1–12.

45. Ibid., pp. 7–8.

46. Ibid., pp. 10–13.

47. Wu Faxian, Manuscript, he17001 p. 1. See also Wang Dongxing, *Wang Dongxing huiyi*, pp. 19–20. Wang's account, however, is different from Wu's on several points. For instance, Wang believes that he brought Mao's instructions to the Politburo on March 8, not May 8. And Wang does not mention the subsequent meeting with Ye Qun and Lin's generals.

48. Wu Faxian, Manuscript, he17001, p. 2.

49. Wang Dongxing, *Wang Dongxing huiyi*, p. 21.

50. See Ye Yonglie, *Zhang Chunqiao zhuan*, pp. 251–52; and Shao Yihai, *Lin Biao wangchao heimu*, pp. 62–64.

51. Interview with the one of Lin Biao's former secretaries, Beijing, Aug. 21, 1994.

52. Wu Faxian, Manuscript, he17001, p. 4; Wang Dongxing, *Wang Dongxing huiyi*, pp. 25–28; and Yu Nan, "Jiujie erzhong quanhui shang de yichang fengbo," p. 84.

53. Wang Dongxing, *Wang Dongxing huiyi*, p. 36.

54. Shao Yihai, *Lin Biao wangchao heimu*, pp. 77–79; and Yu Nan, "Jiujie erzhong quanhui shang de yichang fengbo," p. 84.

55. For Lin's speech at the opening session of the Second Plenum, see ZZB [16].

56. Wang Dongxing, *Wang Dongxing huiyi*, pp. 37–39.

57. Ye Yonglie, *Zhang Chunqiao zhuan*, pp. 253–54; and Wang Dongxing, *Wang Dongxing huiyi*, pp. 41–44.

58. Tie Zhuwei, *Shuang zhong se yu nong*, pp. 255–56.

59. Ibid., p. 257.

60. Wang Nianyi, *Dadongluan*, p. 401.

61. Wang Dongxing, *Wang Dongxing huiyi*, p. 45.

62. Ibid., pp. 45–46.

63. Wang Nianyi, *Dadongluan*, p. 402; Wang Dongxing, *Wang Dongxing huiyi*, pp. 45–46; and Yu Nan, "Lin Biao jituan xingwang chutan," p. 89.

64. Wang Dongxing, *Wang Dongxing huiyi*, p. 99.

65. Ibid., pp. 48–49.

66. Ibid., p. 51.

67. "The Summary of Chairman Mao's Talks to Responsible Local Comrades During His Tour of Inspection," in Kau, *The Lin Piao Affair*, pp. 59–60.

68. Wu admits that he distorted the facts under heavy pressure from the Special Case Group. He made marks next to several untrue statements in the original text of his "confessions" in case he should forget later. In his manuscript, he makes several corrections of false testimony he was forced to give. Ye's alleged statement was one of them. Wu Faxian, Manuscript, hel7001, pp. 6–7.

69. Wang Dongxing, *Wang Dongxing huiyi*, p. 26.

70. Ibid., p. 44; emphasis added.

71. Wu De, "Lushan huiyi he Lin Biao shijian," pp. 132–33; and Wang Dongxing, *Wang Dongxing huiyi*, p. 48.

72. See also Zhang Yunsheng, *Maojiawan jishi*, pp. 330–33.

73. Interview with the author, Beijing, Aug. 21, 1994.

74. Lin Liheng and Zhang Qinglin, "Shangsu cailiao," pt. 3, p. 17.

75. Zhang Yunsheng, *Maojiawan jishi*, pp. 329–30.

76. Wang Nianyi, *Dadongluan*, pp. 392–94.

77. Zhang Youyu, "Guanyu huifu guojia zhuxi ji qita"; and Wang Nianyi, *Dadongluan*, pp. 392–93.

78. Yu Nan, "Jiujie erzhong quanhui shang de yichang fengbo," p. 86.

79. "Summary of Chairman Mao's Talks to Responsible Local Comrades (Mid-Aug. to Sept. 12, 1971)," in Kau, *The Lin Piao Affair*, p. 60.

80. Wu Faxian, Manuscript, hel7013, p. 6.

81. Wang Dongxing, *Wang Dongxing huiyi*, pp. 48–49.

82. Ibid., pp. 66–77.

83. Wang Nianyi, *Dadongluan*, p. 368.

84. Wu Faxian, Manuscript, hel7021, pp. 2–3.

85. Wang Dongxing, *Wang Dongxing huiyi*, p. 67.

86. Wang Nianyi, *Dadongluan*, p. 412.

87. Wang Dongxing, *Wang Dongxing huiyi*, pp. 72–74. At the beginning of the Cultural Revolution, Lin Biao was the first to use "the Four Greats" to refer to Mao. Later it became a ritual that whenever Mao's name appeared in the media the Four Greats would be mentioned as well.

88. Ibid., pp. 74–75.

89. Ibid., pp. 75–76.

90. Mao used the expression "boarding the pirate ship" (*shang zeichuan*) to mean joining the side of his political opponents. Later, the party frequently employed it to refer to those who "made political mistakes."

91. Wu Faxian, Manuscript, hel7021, pp. 4–5.

92. For Mao's talk with Xiong Xianghui, see *Mao Zedong de shengqian sihou*, pp. 140–45; and Xiong Lei, "9.13 qian hou de Mao Zedong," pp. 79–83.

93. Kau, *The Lin Piao Affair*, pp. 59–66. The comment about a "super genius" was a reference to Lin Liguo, Lin Biao's son. Mao had learned that Liguo's colleagues in the air force referred to him as a "super genius." For details, see the discussion in Chapter 7. Also see Myers, Domes, and Yeh, *Chinese Politics*, p. 60.

94. Wu Faxian, Manuscript, hel8003, p. 11.

CHAPTER 6. *Families in Chinese Politics*

1. I define the Lin Biao incident in two ways. In the narrow sense, the incident was what happened to Lin Biao and his family on the night of September 12–13, 1971. In a broader sense, the incident was the result of the events that developed between the Second Plenum of the Ninth Party Central Committee in August 1970, when the rupture between Mao and Lin began, and September 1, 1971.

2. Mencius, *The Works of Mencius*, bk. 2, pt. 2, p. 171, quoted in Lang, *Chinese Family and Society*, p. 9.

3. Baker, *Chinese Family and Kinship*, p. 122.

4. Lang, *Chinese Family and Society*, pp. 9–10.

5. Ibid., p. 18; and Baker, *Chinese Family and Kinship*, p. 118.

6. Baker, *Chinese Family and Kinship*, pp. 113–21.

7. Chu Tung-tsu, *Han Social Structure*, p. 26; and Baker, *Chinese Family and Kinship*, pp. 113–14.

8. Lang, *Chinese Family and Society*, p. 22.

9. Baker, *Chinese Family and Kinship*, p. 27.

10. Pelzel, "Japanese Kinship: A Comparison," in Freedman, *Family and Kinship in Chinese Society*, p. 238.

11. Brook and Frolic, p. 3.

12. For more details on this, see Pye, *Mao Tse-tung*, pp. 111–42.

13. Yanan was a town in the central part of Shaanxi province. Communists under Mao established their headquarters there in 1936 and remained until they were driven out by the Nationalist troops in early 1947.

14. Terrill, *Madame Mao*, p. 150.

15. For a detailed account of the affair, see Terrill, *Madame Mao*, pp. 142–48; and Wang Xingjuan, *Li Min, He Zizhen yu Mao Zedong*, pp. 29–36.

16. Wang Xingjuan, *Li Min, He Zizhen yu Mao Zedong*, pp. 127–28.

17. Ibid., p. 188.

18. Salisbury, *The New Emperors*, pp. 278–79.

19. For more information, see Quan Yanchi, *Tao Zhu zai "wenhua dageming" zhong*, pp. 31–32 and 138–39; Wang Xingjuan, *Li Min, He Zizhen yu Mao Zedong*, pp. 188–89; and Jin Feng, *Deng Yingchao zhuan*, vol. 1, pp. 105–22.

20. Wang Xingjuan, *Li Min, He Zizhen yu Mao Zedong*, pp. 34–35.

21. Ibid., p. 8.

22. In China, the private lives of high officials, including their family life and health, are considered top secret and are carefully kept from the public.

23. Wang Xingjuan, *Li Min, He Zizhen yu Mao Zedong*, pp. 216–17.

24. Ibid., pp. 164–65.

25. Uhalley, *A History of the Chinese Communist Party*, p. 191.

26. Quan Yanchi, *Tao Zhu zai "wenhua dageming" zhong*, pp. 143–44, 146–49.

27. Li Zhisui, *The Private Life of Chairman Mao*, pp. 227–29, 256–57, and 259–60.

28. Terrill, *Madame Mao*, p. 154.

29. On Jiang's hypochondria, see Li Zhisui, *The Private Life of Chairman Mao*, p. 224. He Zizhen also suffered from the fear of being poisoned. See Wang Xingjuan, p. 204.

30. Li Zhisui, *The Private Life of Chairman Mao*, p. 143.

31. Ibid., pp. 259, 45.

32. Ibid., pp. 258, 154–55.

33. For more on this, see Guo Jinrong, *Mao Zedong de wannian shenghuo*, pp. 117–21; and Li Zhisui, *The Private Life of Chairman Mao*, pp. 570–71.

34. According to Dr. Li, Ye was probably born in 1920, but another source describes Ye as in her forties in 1970. Li Zhisui, *The Private Life of Chairman Mao*, p. 662; and Jiao Ye, *Ye Qun zhi mi*, p. 220.

35. Jiao Ye, *Ye Qun zhi mi*, pp. 236, 362–63; and Zhang Yunsheng, *Maojiawan jishi*, p. 429.

36. Li Zhisui, *The Private Life of Chairman Mao*, p. 315.

37. Guan Weixun, *Wo suo zhidao de Ye Qun*, pp. 206–7.

38. Ibid., pp. 213–14.

39. Quan Yanchi, *Shenghuo zhong de lingxiumen*, pp. 186–87.

40. Li Zhisui, *The Private Life of Chairman Mao*, pp. 453–54.

41. Guan Weixun, *Wo suo zhidao de Ye Qun*, p. 214.

42. Ibid., p. 225; and my interviews with Lin's family members and staff, Beijing, August 1994.

43. Salisbury, *The New Emperors*, pp. 284–85.

44. For more details on this, see Zhang Yunsheng, *Maojiawan jishi*, pp. 78–83, 164–67, and 250–52; Guan Weixun, *Wo suo zhidao de Ye Qun*, pp. 91–94, 219–20; and Jiao Ye, *Ye Qun zhi mi*, pp. 369–79. This account is also based on my interviews with Lin's family members and former secretaries.

45. Guan Weixun, *Wo suo zhidao de Ye Qun*, p. 171; and Zhang Yunsheng, *Maojiawan jishi*, p. 408.

46. Guan Weixun, *Wo suo zhidao de Ye Qun*, pp. 217–27.

47. Terrill, *Madame Mao*, prologue.

48. Li Zhisui, *The Private Life of Chairman Mao*, pp. 480–81.

49. The two women were Zhang Yufeng and Meng Jingyun. Mao trusted only these two women to take care of him. Mao met Zhang Yufeng when she worked on the train designated for Mao's personal use. In the 1970s she was transferred to Zhongnanhai and then became Mao's "secretary" until Mao died in 1976. She may have a couple of children with Mao. Meng was a former member of the air force performing arts troupe and was transferred to Zhongnanhai in 1974 to help Zhang take care of Mao. For more details on this, see Guo Jinrong, *Mao Zedong de wannian shenghuo*; and Wang Xingjuan, *Li Min, He Zizhen yu Mao Zedong*, pp. 271–73.

50. Wang Xingjuan, *Li Min, He Zizhen yu Mao Zedong*, p. 117.

51. Lin Liheng and Zhang Qinglin, "Shangsu cailiao," pt. 2, pp. 33–37.

52. Ibid., p. 37.

53. Ibid., p. 13.

54. Zhang Yunsheng, *Maojiawan jishi*, p. 224.

55. Ibid., pp. 78–80.

56. The prologue is written in a question-and-answer format.

57. Once Doudou attempted suicide after Ye had humiliated her. This is discussed later in the text. Zhang Yunsheng, *Maojiawan jishi*, pp. 428–29; and Guan Weixun, "Heiwu li de Lin Doudou de sanci zisha," pp. 167–70.

58. For one that does, see Guo Xin and He Pin, *Zhonggong taizitang*.

59. Lin Liheng and Zhang Qinglin, "Shangsu cailiao," pt. 2, pp. 2–3.

60. Guan Weixun, "Heiwu li de Lin Doudou de sanci zisha," p. 170.

61. Lin Liheng and Zhang Qinglin, "Shangsu cailiao," pt. 2, p. 3.

62. Guan Weixun, "Heiwu li de Lin Doudou de sanci zisha," pp. 167–70.

63. Ibid., p. 175.

64. Ibid., pp. 170–73. It is said that after Ye Qun found out that Yan Weibing had written letters, she retaliated against her during the Cultural Revolution by helping to arrange for Lu Dingyi's fall. For details of this episode, see Zhang Yunsheng, *Maojiawan jishi*, pp. 47–52.

65. Tao Siliang, "Gongheguo de gongzhumen," p. 349.

66. Cao Weidong, *Hong bingli*, pp. 136–37.

67. Guan Weixun, "Heiwu li de Lin Doudou de sanci zisha," p. 169; and Cao Weidong, *Hong bingli*, p. 136.

68. Interview with the author, Beijing, Sept. 16, 1994.

69. It was general practice among Chinese high officials to change their children's surname. Both of Mao's daughters use the family name Li. Mao occasionally used the false name "Li Desheng," and Jiang Qing had the alternative name "Li Jing." See Zhang Xiaolin, *Lingxiu yizu*, pp. 24–26.

70. Zhang Ning, *Chen jie*, p. 325.

71. The party requires a nominee to have two recommendations from party

members before he can join the party. Liguo's other recommendation came from Zhou Yuchi, who later helped Liguo conspire against Mao.

72. For a literary account of the activities of the "small fleet," see Shao Yi-hai, *"Lianhe jiandui" de fumie*, pp. 32–61.

73. Wu Faxian, Manuscript, hel5007, pp. 20–22; and Zhang Yunsheng, *Mao-jiawan jishi*, pp. 324–28.

74. For a detailed account of Lin Liguo's independent activity, see Zhang Yunsheng, *Maojiawan jishi*, pp. 325–26.

75. Wu Faxian, Manuscript, hel7021, p. 19.

76. Ibid., hel5007, pp. 21–23.

77. Ibid., hel7013, pp. 6–7.

78. Both He and Lu were alleged members of Liguo's "small fleet." Ibid., hel7021, pp. 18–19.

79. Interview with the author, Beijing, August 1979.

80. The "pen" refers to Jiang Qing's group. Zhang Chunqiao and Yang Wenyuan were known for their debatable skill in composing theories. The "gun" refers to the military.

81. Wang Nianyi, *Dadongluan*, pp. 417–21. For another translation of the "Outline," see Kau, *The Lin Piao Affair*, pp. 81–90.

CHAPTER 7. *The Lin Biao Incident*

1. For details of Mao's inspection tours, see Wang Dongxing, *Wang Dong-xing huiyi*, pp. 87–176.

2. Zhang Ning, *Chen jie*, pp. 190–92. Li Wenpu had been one of Lin's body-guards since the 1940s and was one of the key witnesses to the Lin Biao incident.

3. Ye Qun held the position of director of Lin Biao's General Office. For some reason, her children never referred to her as their mother. Instead, they always called her "the director."

4. In Lin's house, everybody used "Shou Zhang," meaning "commander," to refer to Lin Biao.

5. Both Liu and Peng died at the hands of the Special Case Group after they were out of power.

6. Zhang Ning, *Chen jie*, pp. 193–94. For consistency, I have changed the name of Lin Liheng to Doudou.

7. Ibid., p. 281; and interview with one of Lin's family members, Beijing, Aug. 10, 1994.

8. Interview with the author, Beijing, Aug. 21, 1994. Also see Zhang Ning, *Chen jie*, pp. 213–14.

9. Lin Liheng and Zhang Qinglin, "Shangsu cailiao," pt. 1, pp. 56–57.

10. Zhang Ning, *Chen jie*, pp. 251–52.

11. Ibid., pp. 213–14, 196–97, and 222.

12. Ibid., p. 280.

13. Interview with Zhang Ning, New Jersey, Aug. 25, 1993. For the details

of Zhang Ning's conversation with Ye Qun, see Zhang Ning, *Chen jie*, pp. 223–33.

14. Wu Faxian, Manuscripts, he17021, pp. 16–17.

15. Interview with the author, Beijing, Aug. 8, 1994.

16. Zhou Yuchi was a secretary in the General Office of the Party Committee of the air force. He was one of the key figures in Liguo's plot. He committed suicide after failing to escape from Beijing by helicopter on September 13.

17. Jiang Tengjiao was deputy chief of staff of the air force central headquarters and the political commissar of the air force in the Nanjing Military Region. Li Weixin was on the staff of the Political Department of the Fourth Air Force Army. He was on the helicopter with Zhou and later surrendered to the local militia when the helicopter was forced down.

18. ZZB [20].

19. See "Jiang Tengjiao's Confession (9/24/71)," in ZZB [20], p. 66; and his testimony during the trial. Zuigao renmin fayuan yanjiusuo, *Zhonghua renmin gongheguo zuigao renmin fayuan tebie fating shenpan Lin Biao, Jiang Qing fangeming jituan zhufan jishi*, p. 124.

20. "Cheng Hongzhen's Confession, 9/16/71," in ZZB [20].

21. "Jiang Tengjiao's Confession, 9/28/71," in ZZB [20].

22. Bonavia, *Verdict in Peking*, pp. 163–65.

23. Mao's speeches to the provincial leaders are discussed in detail later.

24. Zuigao renmin fayuan yanjiusuo, *Zhonghua renmin gongheguo zuigao renmin fayuan tebie fating shenpan Lin Biao, Jiang Qing fangeming jituan zhufan jishi*, 126–30.

25. "Wang's Confession (9/28/71)," in ZZB [20]. Yu Xinye was another secretary in the General Office of the Party Committee of the air force. He committed suicide along with Zhou Yuchi after their helicopter was forced down on September 13, 1971.

26. Interview with the author, Beijing, Aug. 5, 1994.

27. Mao left Shanghai around 1 P.M. on September 11. See Wang Dongxin, *Wang Dongxing huiyi*, pp. 166–69.

28. "Jiang Tengjiao's Confession, 9/28/71" in ZZB [20].

29. Liu Shiying was deputy director of the General Office of the Party Committee of the air force. He Dequan was director of the Department of Intelligence of the air force. Zhu Tiezheng was another secretary in the General Office with Zhou Yuchi, Yu Xinye, Liu Peifeng, and Liu Shiying. Zheng Xinghe was deputy director of military training of the air force.

30. Zuigao renmin fayuan yanjiusuo, *Zhonghua renmin gongheguo zuigao renmin fayuan tebie fating shenpan Lin Biao, Jiang Qing fangeming jituan zhufan jishi*, pp. 139–42; Shao Yihai, "*Lianhe jiandui*" *de fumie*, pp. 230–32.

31. Zuigao renmin fayuan yanjiusuo, *Zhonghua renmin gongheguo zuigao renmin fayuan tebie fating shenpan Lin Biao, Jiang Qing fangeming jituan zhufan jishi*, p. 148.

32. Interview with the author, Aug. 16, 1994.

33. Zhang Yunsheng, *Maojiawan jishi*, pp. 173–75.

34. Interview with the author, Beijing, Aug. 21, 1994.

35. Zhang Ning, *Chen jie*, p. 254.

36. The following account concerning Doudou's activities is based on Lin Liheng and Zhang Qinglin, "Shangsu cailiao," pt. 1.

37. Of the two, Doudou trusted Liu more, because Liu did not get along with Liguo. Li Wenpu was much closer to Liguo than to Doudou. This explains why the two had different interpretations of what Doudou told them.

38. Lin Liheng and Zhang Qinglin, "Shangsu cailiao," pt. 1, pp. 61–66.

39. According to Zhang Yaoci, who was commander of Unit 8341, it was 9:50 P.M. when Doudou went to the office to report on Ye Qun and Liguo. It was he who first received the report from Beidaihe. He then reported the matter to Wang Dongxing and Zhou Enlai. Zhang Yaoci, *Huiyi Mao Zedong*, pp. 108, 109.

40. Shao Yihai, *"Lianhe jiandui" de fumie*, p. 271.

41. There is great confusion among the accounts available about where Ye told people to go. Some accounts of the incident mention Guangzhou, but most mention Dalian. Since there is no way to know for sure, I must go along with whatever the source materials say. It is possible that Lin himself insisted on going to Dalian.

42. Shao Yihai, *"Lianhe jiandui" de fumie*, pp. 271–72.

43. Interview with the author, Beijing, Aug. 10, 1994.

44. "Reminiscence of Little Zhang," in Shao Yihai, *"Lianhe jiandui" de fumie*, p. 275.

45. "Reminiscence of Little Zhang," in ibid., p. 275.

46. "Reminiscence of Little Chen," in ibid., p. 277.

47. "Reminiscence of Lin Liheng [Lin Doudou]," in ibid., p. 272.

48. "Reminiscence of Liu Jichun," in ibid., p. 274.

49. Ibid., p. 272.

50. "Reminiscence of Li Wenpu," in ibid., pp. 273–80.

51. By this time, General Wu had already arrived at Xijiao airport to check with Hu about the Trident 256 upon Zhou Enlai's orders. We will discuss this later.

52. This is one of the key points on which Doudou and Li Wenpu cannot agree. Doudou does not believe Lin asked this question. There is circumstantial evidence to support her belief. Even available accounts by eyewitnesses, which were probably tailored to match the official version, provide no evidence that Lin wanted to go anywhere other than Dalian up to the point when he got into the car. It is to be hoped that Li will speak out someday to clear up these doubts. Also see Zhang Ning, *Chen jie*, pp. 249–50, 269–70.

53. Interview with the author, Beijing, Aug. 10, 1994. Also see Zhang Ning, *Chen jie*, p. 270. The Chinese government, however, claimed later that it was Lin Liguo who shot Li Wenpu. For more information on this, see ZZB [3]; Zhang Yaoci, *Huiyi Mao Zedong*, p. 110.

54. "Reminiscence of Liu Jichun," and "Reminiscence of Jiang Zuoshou," both in Shao Yihai, *"Lianhe jiandui" de fumie*, pp. 274, 281.

55. "Reminiscence of Yu Zhongtang," in ibid., pp. 282–83.

56. ZZB [4].

57. Wu Faxian was commander-in-chief of the air force, deputy chief of staff of the PLA, and a Politburo member at the time. The following account is based on his memoirs. Wu Faxian, Manuscript, he17022.

58. Hu Ping was the deputy chief of staff of the air force and the former division commander of the 34th Air Force Division. He was hospitalized at the time of the incident. His medical problem was not acute, however, so he could leave the hospital temporarily.

59. For more information, see Yu Nan, "Guanyu Lin Biao shijian ruogan lishi wenti de kaocha," p. 187.

60. Li Zuopeng was the political commissar of the navy, the deputy chief of staff of the PLA, and a Politburo member. I would like to thank Dongdong, the son of Huang Yongsheng, for allowing me to read the manuscript of General Li Zuopeng. The following account is based on that manuscript as well as secondary sources.

61. Bonavia, *Verdict in Peking*, pp. 166–70.

62. "The Record of the Phone Calls of the Control Tower of the Shanhaiguan Airport on September 12," in ZZB [20].

63. Xiao Sike, *Chaoji shenpan*, vol. 1, pp. 250–51.

64. Ibid., p. 339.

65. Ibid., pp. 138–39; vol. 2, pp. 647–48.

66. Ibid., vol. 2, p. 648.

67. Ibid., vol. 1, p. 139.

68. Interview with the son of Huang Yongsheng, Beijing, June 22, 1994.

69. Lin Qing, *Zhou Enlai de zhaixiang shengya*, p. 207.

70. Xie Shouzhen, Quan Yonglin, and Ye Deben, *Xinwen renwu jinxi*, p. 65.

71. Chen Runjiang, "Xingman shifang de Qiu Huizuo," p. 425.

72. *People's Daily*, December 19, 1980, p. 4.

73. Wang Dongxing, *Wang Dongxing huiyi*, p. 203; and Ke Yan, *Mao Zedong de licheng*, p. 368.

74. Lin Qing, *Zhou Enlai de zaixiang shengya*, pp. 202–3. There is a discrepancy between Lin Qing's assumption about the content of Doudou's report and Doudou's own account. Doudou insists that she never told Zhou that Lin intended to "escape from the country."

75. Zhang Ning, *Chen jie*, pp. 276–77.

76. There are some questions about the details of Wang's report of Zhou's talk with Ye Qun. Ye probably would never have used the terms "my son" and "his father" to refer to Lin Liguo and Lin Biao.

77. A war wound had damaged Lin Biao's central nervous system. Whenever he was nervous and perspired, he became seriously ill. Ye often used this as an excuse to prevent other people from seeing him in order to manipulate the communications between Lin and others.

78. Wang Dongxing, *Wang Dongxing huiyi*, pp. 205–6; and Ke Yan, *Mao Zedong de licheng*, pp. 368–69.

79. Yu Nan, "Zhou Zongli chuzhi '9.13' Lin Biao pantao shijian de yixie qingkuang"; and Lin Qing, *Zhou Enlai de zhaixiang shengya*, p. 205.

80. Interview with a member of Lin's family, Beijing, Aug. 10, 1994.

81. Ibid. However, according to the materials recently available, Mao told Hua Guofeng before Hua left for Beijing on August 31 that he could tell Zhou about Mao's talks in Hunan. Gong Guzhong, Tang Zhennan, and Xia Yuansheng, *Mao Zedong hui Hunan jishi*, p. 76.

82. ZZB [2], p. 4.

83. Zhang Ning, *Chen jie*, pp. 276–77.

84. Wang Zhenghua, *Lin Biao wangchao xingshuai shilu*, pp. 263–64.

85. Li Zhisui, *The Private Life of Chairman Mao*, pp. 536–37.

86. Yu Nan, "Zhou Zongli chuzhi '9.13' Lin Biao pantao shijian de yixie qingkuang," p. 59; and Lin Qing, *Zhou Enlai de zhaixiang shengya*, p. 205.

87. Wang Dongxing, *Wang Dongxing huiyi*, pp. 208–9; Zhang Yaoci, *Huiyi Mao Zedong*, p. 112; and Ke Yan, *Mao Zedong de licheng*, pp. 370–71.

88. The sources for the list are Wang Dongxing, *Wang Dongxing huiyi*, pp. 56–82; and Gong Guzhong, Tang Zhennan, and Xia Yuansheng, *Mao Zedong hui Hunan jishi*, pp. 137–97.

89. Wang Dongxing, *Wang Dongxing huiyi*, pp. 88–97.

90. Ibid., pp. 99–100.

91. Ibid., p. 126.

92. Wang Dongxing, "Mao zhuxi zai fensui Lin Biao fangeming zhengbian yinmo de rizi li," p. 57.

93. Dishuidong was one of Mao's secret villas in his hometown. Mao often went to Dishuidong when he wanted absolute privacy. He spent several days there before deciding to purge Liu Shaoqi and before starting the Cultural Revolution in 1966.

94. According to Bu, the CCP document that contains Mao's speeches from his inspection tour was largely based on their draft of Mao's speech in Hunan. See ZZB [18].

95. Gong Guzhong, Tang Zhennan, and Xia Yuansheng, *Mao Zedong hui Hunan jishi*, pp. 290–98.

96. Ibid., p. 298.

97. Ibid., pp. 316–17.

98. Li Desheng, "Cong Lushan huiyi dao '9.13' shijian de ruogan huiyi," p. 9.

99. This was a pun on Wu De's name. In Chinese, "Wu" means "not have" and "De" means "virtue." By "You Wu De have De," Mao means Wu De has virtue, although his name literally means "does not have virtue."

100. Wu De, "Lushan huiyi he Lin Biao shijian," pp. 136–38.

101. Zhang Ning, *Chen jie*, p. 276.

102. Interviews with the author, Beijing, July 30 and Aug. 1, 1994.

103. Xiao Sike, *Zhiqingzhe shuo*, vol. 3, pp. 334–35.

104. Yu Nan, "Guanyu Lin Biao shijian ruogan lishi wenti de kaocha," in Xiong Huayuan and An Jianshe, *Lin Biao fangeming jituan fumie jishi*, p. 191.

105. Interview with Zhang Ning, New Jersey, March 27, 1991.
106. Zhang Ning, *Chen jie*, pp. 249–50, 304–27.
107. Ibid., p. 280.
108. Xiao Sike, *Zhiqingzhe shuo*, pp. 328–29.
109. Chapter 8 discusses these points in more detail.

CHAPTER 8. *Conclusion: The Tragedy of Lin Biao*

1. See Bass, *Leadership, Psychology, and Organizational Behavior*, p. 18.
2. In his study of rebel leadership, James Downton suggests that personal authority is an especially important aspect of leader-follower relations among rebels. For a detailed discussion of this idea, see Downton, *Rebel Leadership*, pp. 72–74.
3. For a detailed analysis of the difference between small group and collective movements, see Smelser, *Theory of Collective Behavior*, pp. 6–7; see also Downton, *Rebel Leadership*, pp. 101–3.
4. For an account of Mao's collapse, see the comments of a senior photographer who worked in Zhongnanhai for more than 30 years. Du Xiuxian, "Lin Biao dui Mao Zedong de 'buci erbie'" ("Lin Biao's 'Leave Without a Word' from Mao Zedong"), in Xiong Huayuan and An Jianshe, *Lin Biao fangeming jituan fumie jishi*, pp. 57–58; also see Zhang Yaoci, *Huiyi Mao Zedong*, pp. 118, 129–36.
5. Ye Yonglie, *Lishi xuanzele Mao Zedong*, p. 460.
6. Ibid., p. 462.
7. Kau, *The Lin Piao Affair*, p. 120. According to Chinese folklore, Zhong Kui had the power to chase away ghosts and evil spirits.
8. Interview with one of Lin's secretaries, Beijing, Aug. 21, 1994.
9. Li Zhisui, *The Private Life of Chairman Mao*, pp. 508–12.
10. Cheng Qian, "Wenge mantan," p. 162.
11. Wang Li, *Xianchang lishi*, p. 96.
12. Wu Faxian, Manuscript, he15007, p. 11.
13. Quan Yanchi, *Hongqiang neiwai*, p. 276.
14. Li Zhisui, *The Private Life of Chairman Mao*, p. 497.
15. Downton, *Rebel Leadership*, p. 73.
16. Ibid., pp. 75–76.
17. The Institute of Party History et al., "'Wuhao shijian' de qianqian houhou" ("On the 'Wuhao Event'"), in An Jianshe, *Zhou Enlai de zuihou suiyue*, pp. 66–67.
18. For the details of this argument, see Dittmer, *Liu Shao-ch'i and the Chinese Cultural Revolution*, pp. 109–18.
19. Zhang Xiaolin, *Lingxiu yizu*, pp. 152–53.
20. Diandian, *Feifan de niandai*, pp. 252–53.

■ Bibliography

Ahn, Byung-joon. "Ideology, Policy, and Power in Chinese Politics and the Evolution of the Cultural Revolution, 1959–1965." Ph.D. diss., Columbia University, 1972.

———. *Chinese Politics and the Cultural Revolution: Dynamics of Policy Processes.* Seattle: University of Washington Press, 1976.

An Jianshe, comp. *Zhou Enlai de zuihou suiyue, 1966–1976 (Zhou Enlai's Last Years).* Beijing: Zhongyang wenxian chubanshe, 1995.

An, Tai Sung. *Mao Tse-tung's Cultural Revolution.* New York: Pegasus, 1972.

Bachman, David. *Bureaucracy, Economy, and Leadership in China: The Institutional Origins of the Great Leap Forward.* Cambridge: Cambridge University Press, 1991.

Baker, Hugh D. R. *Chinese Family and Kinship.* New York: Columbia University Press, 1979.

Barnett, A. Doak, ed. *Cadres, Bureaucracy, and Political Power in Communist China.* New York: Columbia University Press, 1967.

———, ed. *Chinese Communist Politics in Action.* Seattle: University of Washington Press, 1969.

Barnouin, Barbara, and Yu Changgen. *Ten Years of Turbulence: The Chinese Cultural Revolution.* London: Kegan Paul International, 1993.

Bass, Bernard. *Leadership, Psychology, and Organizational Behavior.* New York: Harper and Row, 1960.

Bennett, Gordon A., and Ronald N. Montaperto. *Red Guard: The Political Biography of Da Hsiao-ai.* New York: Doubleday, 1971.

Bernstein, Richard. "New Doubts Cast on Fate of Mao's Early Heir Apparent." *Honolulu Star-Bulletin,* April 27, 1990.

Bonavia, David. *Verdict in Peking: The Trial of the Gang of Four.* New York: Putnam, 1984.

Bo Yibo. *Lingxiu, yuanshuai, zhanyou (Leaders, Marshals, and Comrades).* Beijing: Zhonggong zhongyang dangxiao chubanshe, 1992.

———. *Ruogan zhongda juece yu shijian de huigu (Reminiscences About Several*

Important Policies and Events). Beijing: Zhonggong zhongyang dangxiao chubanshe, 1993.

Bridgham, Philip. "The Fall of Lin Piao." *China Quarterly* 55 (July–Sept. 1973): 427–49.

Brook, Timothy, and B. Michael Frolic, eds. *Civil Society in China*. Armonk, N.Y.: M. E. Sharpe, 1977.

Brugger, Bill. *China: The Impact of the Cultural Revolution*. Canberra: Australian National University Press, 1978.

Bullard, Monte. *China's Political-Military Evolution*. Boulder, Colo.: Westview, 1985.

Burchett, Wilfred. "Lin Piao's Plot—The Full Story." *Far Eastern Economic Review*, Aug. 20, 1973, 22–24.

Cao Weidong. *Hong bingli* (*Red Medical Records*). Taiyuan: Shanxi renmin chubanshe, 1993.

Center for Chinese Research Materials. *Xuexi ziliao* (*Study Materials*). 9 vols. Oakton, Va., 1989.

Center of Chinese Studies. *Lin Biao zhuanji* (*Collected Materials on Lin Biao*). Hong Kong: Zi lian Press, 1970.

Chan, Anita. *Children of Mao: Personality Development and Political Activism in the Red Guard Generation*. Seattle: University of Washington Press, 1985.

Chang, C. P. "The Death of Lin Paio." *Issues and Studies* 8 (Sept. 1972): 8–9.

Chang, Parris H. "Regional Military Power: The Aftermath of the Cultural Revolution." *Asian Survey* 12 (Dec. 1972): 999–1013.

———. *Power and Policy in China*. 2d enlarged ed. University Park: Pennsylvania State University Press, 1978.

Charles, David A. "The Dismissal of Marshal P'eng Teh-huai." *China Quarterly* 8 (Oct.–Dec. 1961): 63–76.

Chen Donglin and Du Pu. *Zhonghua renmin gongheguo shilu* (*True Records of the People's Republic of China*). 11 vols. Changchun: Jilin renmin chubanshe, 1994.

Chen, Jerome. *Mao and the Chinese Revolution*. Oxford University Press, 1965.

———, ed. *Mao's Papers*. London: Oxford University Press, 1970.

Chen Jin. *Mao Zedong de wenhua xingge* (*The Cultural Character of Mao Zedong*). Beijing: Zhongguo qingnian chubanshe, 1991.

———. *Mao Zedong zhi hun* (*The Soul of Mao Zedong*). Changchun: Jilin renmin chubanshe, 1993.

Chen Lisheng. *Zhongguo "wenhua geming" he zhengzhi douzheng* (*The Chinese "Cultural Revolution" and Political Struggles*). Taipei: Li Ming Cultural Press, 1974.

Chen Runjiang. "Xingman shifang de Qiu Huizuo" ("Qiu Huizuo After His Release"). In *"Wenhua dageming" fengyun renwu fangtan lu* (*Interviews with the Celebrities of the "Cultural Revolution"*), comp. Si Ren. Beijing: Zhongyang minzu xueyuan chubanshe, 1993.

Chen Yi zhuan bianji zu. *Chen Yi zhuan* (*A Biography of Chen Yi*). Beijing: Dangdai zhongguo chubanshe, 1991.

Cheng Chu-yuan. "Power Struggle in Red China." *Asian Survey* 9 (Sept. 1966): 469–84.

Cheng, J. Chester, ed. *The Politics of the Chinese Red Army: A Translation of the Bulletin of Activities of the People's Liberation Army.* Stanford, Calif.: Hoover Institution, 1966.

Cheng Qian. "Wenge mantan" ("Sketches of the Cultural Revolution"). Manuscript.

Chiang I-shan. "Military Affairs." In *Communist China, 1961.* Vol. 2. Hong Kong: Union Research Institute, 1962.

———. "Military Affairs." In *Communist China, 1963.* Vol. 2. Hong Kong: Union Research Institute, 1965.

———. "Military Affairs." In *Communist China, 1964.* Vol. 2. Hong Kong: Union Research Institute, 1965.

———. "Communist China's Military Affairs in 1965." In *Communist China, 1965.* Vol. 1. Hong Kong: Union Research Institute, 1967.

———, ed. *Source Book on Military Affairs in Communist China.* Hong Kong: You lian Institute, 1965.

Chien Tieh. "A Study of a Document Concerning the Lin Piao Incident." *Issues and Studies* 8 (June 1972): 38–56; (July 1972): 87–95; (Aug. 1972): 51–60; and (Sept. 1972): 41–46.

Chien Yu-shen. *China's Fading Revolution: Army Dissent and Military Divisions, 1967–1968.* Hong Kong: Center for Contemporary Chinese Studies, 1969.

Chu Tung-Tsu. *Han Social Structure.* Ed. Jack L. Dull. Seattle: University of Washington Press, 1972.

Chuan Tsun. "The Lin Piao Incident and Its Effect on Mao's Rule." *Issues and Studies* 8 (Feb. 1972): 21–28.

Cong Jin. *Quzhe fazhan de suiyue (Years of Zigzag Developments).* Zhengzhou: Henan renmin chubanshe, 1989.

"The Conspiracy and Death of Lin Biao by Yao Ming-le." *New Republic,* June 12, 1983, 31.

Dangdai zhongguo yanjiu suo. *Zhonggong zhongyang zhengzhi douzheng shiliaoji (Materials on the Political Struggles in the Central Committee of the Chinese Communist Party).* Vol. 1. Hong Kong: Contemporary China Research Institute, 1972.

Daubier, Jean. *A History of the Chinese Cultural Revolution.* Trans. Richard Seaver. New York: Vintage, 1974.

Delfs, Robert. "Marshal's Mystery." *Far Eastern Economic Review,* May 10, 1990, 14–15.

Diandian. *Feifan de niandai (The Extraordinary Years).* Shanghai: Shanghai wenyi chubanshe, 1992.

Ding Shu. *Ren huo (Manmade Disasters).* Hong Kong: The Nineties Monthly / Going Fine, 1993.

Dittmer, Lowell. *Liu Shao-ch'i and the Chinese Cultural Revolution: The Politics of Mass Criticism.* Berkeley: University of California Press, 1974.

————. *China's Continuous Revolution: The Post-Liberation Epoch, 1949–1989*. Berkeley: University of California Press, 1987.

————. "Mao Zedong and the Dilemma of Revolutionary Gerontocracy." In *Aging and Political Leadership*, ed. Angus McIntyre, 151–180. Albany: State University of New York Press, 1988.

————. "Chinese Informal Politics." *China Journal* 34 (July 1995): 1–34.

Dittmer, Lowell, and Samuel S. Kim, eds. *China's Quest for National Identity*. Ithaca, N.Y.: Cornell University Press, 1993.

Domes, Jurgen. "The Cultural Revolution and the Army." *Asian Survey* 8 (May 1968): 349–63.

————. *China After the Cultural Revolution: Politics Between Two Party Congresses*. Berkeley: University of California Press, 1975.

Dong Baocun. *Tan Zhenlin waizhuan (An Unofficial Biography of Tan Zhenlin)*. Beijing: Zuojia chubanshe, 1992.

Downton, James V., Jr. *Rebel Leadership: Commitment and Charisma in the Revolutionary Process*. New York: Collier-Macmillan, 1973.

Ebon, Martin. *Lin Piao: The Life and Writings of China's New Ruler*. New York: Stein and Day, 1970.

Edinger, Lewis J. *Kurt Schumacher: A Study in Personality and Political Behavior*. Stanford, Calif.: Stanford University Press, 1965.

Eisebstadtn, S. N., and L. Roniger. *Patrons, Clients, and Friends*. Cambridge: Cambridge University Press, 1984.

Fan, K., ed. *Mao Tse-tung and Lin Piao: Post-Revolutionary Writing*. New York: Doubleday, 1972.

Fessler, Loren. "The Long March of Lin Piao." *New York Times Magazine*, Sept. 10, 1967, 61–65.

Fleron, Frederic J., Jr., ed. *Communist Studies and the Social Sciences*. Chicago: Rand McNally, 1969.

Freedman, Maurice, ed. *Family and Kinship in Chinese Society*. Stanford, Calif.: Stanford University Press, 1970.

Fu Hao. "Addenda on the Handling of the Lin Biao Affair." *Wen wei po*, Feb. 14, 1988, 3. In *Foreign Broadcast Information Service-China* (*FBIS-CHI*), Feb. 16, 1988, 23–24.

————. "'9.13' shijian buyi" ("Addenda on the Handling of the 'September 13 Incident'"). *Xinhua wenzhai* (*New China Digest*) (February 1990): 150–51.

Gao Shu and Xin Bing. *Juren Mao Zedong (Mao Zedong, a Giant)*. Beijing: Renmin chubanshe, 1993.

Gao Yuan. *Born Red: A Chronicle of the Cultural Revolution*. Stanford, Calif.: Stanford University Press, 1987.

Gao Zhi and Zhang Ni'er. *Jiyao mishu de sinian (The Memories of a Secretary)*. Beijing: Zhonggong zhongyang dangxiao chubanshe, 1993.

Gelman, Harry. "Mao and the Permanent Purge." *Problems of Communism* 15 (Nov.–Dec. 1966): 2–14.

Ginneken, Jaap van. *The Rise and Fall of Lin Piao.* Trans. Danielle Adkinson. New York: Avon, 1972.

Gittings, John. "The 'Learn from the Army' Campaign." *China Quarterly* 18 (April–June 1964): 153–59.

———. *The Role of the Chinese Army.* London: Oxford University Press, 1967.

Goldstein, Avery. *From Bandwagon to Balance-of-Power Politics.* Stanford, Calif.: Stanford University Press, 1991.

Goncharov, Sergei N., John W. Lewis, and Xue Litai. *Uncertain Partners: Stalin, Mao, and the Korean War.* Stanford, Calif.: Stanford University Press, 1993.

Gong Chu. "Canjia zhonggong wuzhuang douzheng jishi" ("Joining in the Armed Struggle of the Chinese Communist Party"). *Ming Pao Monthly* (November 1971): 94–99; (December 1971): 96–101; (January 1971): 98–105; (February 1972): 100–104; (March 1972): 99–104; (April 1972): 96–100; and (May 1972): 99–103.

Gong Guzhong, Tang Zhennan, and Xia Yuansheng, comps. *Mao Zedong hui Hunan jishi, 1953–1975 (True Records of Mao Zedong's Returns to Hunan, 1953–1975).* Changsha: Hunan chubanshe, 1993.

Gong Yuzhi. "Guanyu jixu geming de jige wenti" ("Several Questions on Continuing the Revolution"). In vol. 1 of *"Wenhua dageming" ziliao yanjiu (Materials for Research on the "Cultural Revolution"),* 611–17. Beijing: Guofang daxue dangshi jiaoyanshi, 1988.

"The Great Lin Biao Mystery." *The Economist,* Sept. 13, 1986, 43.

A Great Trial in Chinese History. Beijing: New World Press, 1981.

Guan Weixun. "Heiwu li de Lin Doudou de sanci zisha" ("Lin Doudou's Three Suicide Attempts in the Dark Room"). *Bai xin (Common People),* Feb. 1, 1993, 40–43.

———. *Wo suo zhidao de Ye Qun (The Ye Qun I Knew).* Beijing: Zhongguo wenxue chubanshe, 1993.

Gudoshnikov, L. M., R. M. Neronov, and B. P. Barakhta. *China: Cultural Revolution and After.* New Delhi: Sterling, 1978.

Guo Jinrong. *Mao Zedong de wannian shenghuo (Mao Zedong's Later Life).* Beijing: Jiaoyu kexue chubanshe, 1993.

Guo Xin and He Pin. *Zhonggong taizitang (The Princes' Party of the Chinese Communist Party).* 2d ed. Hong Kong: Mirror Books, 1995.

Guofang daxue. *Wenhua dageming yanjiu ziliao (Research Materials on the Cultural Revolution).* 3 vols. Beijing: Guofang daxue dangshi jiaoyanshi, 1988.

Harding, Harry. *The Purge of Lo Jui-ching: The Politics of Chinese Strategic Planning.* Santa Monica, Calif.: Rand, 1971.

———. *Organizing China: The Problem of Bureaucracy, 1949–1976.* Stanford, Calif.: Stanford University Press, 1981.

Hei Yannan. *Shinian dongluan (Ten Years of Turmoil).* Xi'an: Guoji wenhua chuban gongsi, 1988.

Hendricks, Jon, and C. Davis Hendricks. *Dimensions of Aging*. Cambridge, Mass.: Winthrop, 1979.

Hiniker, Paul J. "The Cultural Revolution Revisited: Dissonance Reduction or Power Maximization." *China Quarterly* 94 (June 1983): 282–302.

Hinton, William. *Hundred Day War: The Cultural Revolution at Tsinghua University*. New York: Monthly Review Press, 1972.

Hoffmann, Erik P. "Methodological Problems of Kremlinology." In *Communist Studies and the Social Sciences: Essays in Methodology and Empirical Theory*, ed. Frederick Fleron, Jr., 129–49. Chicago: Rand McNally, 1969.

Hollingworth, Clare. *Mao and the Men Against Him*. London: Jonathan Cape, 1985.

Hong Haiyan. *Wuxian fengguang zai xianfeng: Jiang Qing tongzhi guanyu wenyi geming de jianghua* (*Excellent Scenery Can Be Found on Perilous Peaks: The Speeches of Comrade Jiang Qing on the Art Revolution*). Tianjin: Nankai daxue, 1968.

Hong Xuezhi. *Kang mei yuan chao zhanzheng huiyi* (*Recollections of the War to Resist U.S. Aggression and Aid Korea*). Beijing: Jiefangjun wenyi chubanshe, 1990.

Houn, Franklin W. *Chinese Political Traditions*. Washington, D.C.: Public Affairs Press, 1965.

Hu Chi-hsi. "Mao, Lin, and the Fifth Encirclement Campaign." *China Quarterly* 82 (April–June 1980): 250–80.

Hu Sheng. "Mao Zedong yisheng suo zuo de liangjian dashi" ("The Two Life Achievements of Mao Zedong"). *Renmin ribao* (*People's Daily*), Dec. 17, 1993.

———, ed. *A Concise History of the Communist Party of China*. Beijing: Foreign Language Press, 1994.

Hu Xiongwei. "Ziwo jiepou de qite haishi ziwo xinxin de xianyi" ("Peculiarity of Self-analysis or Demonstration of Self-confidence"). *Dangxiao luntan* (*Forum of Party Schools*) 8 (Aug. 5, 1989): 45–49.

Hua Fang. "Lin Biao's Abortive Counter-Revolutionary Coup d'État." *Beijing Review*, Dec. 22, 1980, 19–28.

Huang Chenxia, ed. *Zhonggong junren zhi* (*Mao's Generals*). Hong Kong: Research Institute of Contemporary History, 1968.

Huntington, Samuel P., and Clement H. Moore, eds. *Authoritarian Politics in Modern Society: The Dynamics of Established One-Party Systems*. New York: Basic Books, 1970.

———. *Political Order in Changing Societies*. New Haven, Conn.: Yale University Press, 1981.

Janowitz, Morris. *The Military in the Political Development of New Nations*. Chicago: Phoenix Books, 1964.

Ji Xianlin. *Niupeng zayi* (*Talks from the Cowshed*). Beijing: Zhonggong zhongyang dangxiao chubanshe, 1998.

Ji Xichen. "'Yang-Yu-Fu' shijian neiqing" ("The Inside Story of the 'Yang-Yu-Fu Incident'"). In *Zhongnanhai renshi chenfu* (*Ups and Downs at Zhongnanhai*). Hong Kong: Xianggang wenhui chuban youxian gongsi, 1991.

Jia Sinan, ed. *Mao Zedong renji jiaowang shilu* (*True Accounts of Mao's Relationships with People*). Nanjing: Jiangsu wenyi chubanshe, 1989.

Jiang Yishan, ed. *Zhonggong junshi wenjian huibian* (*A Source Book on Military Affairs in Communist China*). Hong Kong: You lian Institute, 1965.

Jiao Ye. *Ye Qun zhi mi* (*The Mystery of Ye Qun*). Beijing: Zhongguo wenlian chubanshe, 1993.

Jin Chunming. *"Wenhua dageming" lunxi* (*Analyses of the "Cultural Revolution"*). Shanghai: Shanghai renmin chubanshe, 1985.

———. "Yipian qite de ziwo jiepou" ("A Peculiar Self-analysis"). *Dangxiao luntan* (*Forum of Party Schools*) 5 (May 1989): 54–58.

Jin Chunming, Huang Yuchong, and Zhang Huimin, comps. *"Wenge" shiqi guishiguiyu* (*Strange Events and Talk During the "Cultural Revolution"*). Beijing: Quishi chubanshe, 1989.

Jin Daying. "'9.13 shijian' jishi" ("The Record of the 'September 13 Incident'"). *Shidai de baogao* (*Contemporary Report*) 4 (1988): 124–59.

Jin Feng. *Deng Yingchao zhuan* (*A Biography of Deng Yingchao*). 2 vols. Beijing: Renmin chubanshe, 1993.

Jin Qiu, "The Fall of Lin Biao: A Reappraisal." Master's thesis, University of Hawaii, 1991.

Jing Hong and Wu Hua, comps. *Mao Zedong shengping shilu* (*The Actual Life of Mao Zedong*). Changchun: Jilin renmin chubanshe, 1992.

Joffe, Ellis. "The Chinese Army in the Cultural Revolution: The Politics of Intervention." *Current Scene* 8, no. 18 (Dec. 7, 1970): 1–25.

———. *Between Two Plenums: China's Intraleadership Conflict, 1959–1962*. Ann Arbor: Center for Chinese Studies, University of Michigan, 1975.

———. *The Chinese Army After Mao*. Cambridge, Mass.: Harvard University Press, 1988.

Johnson, Chalmers. "Lin Piao's Army and Its Role in Chinese Society." *Current Scene* 4 (July 1, 1966): 1–9; and 5 (July 15, 1966): 1–11.

———. *Change in Communist Systems*. Stanford, Calif.: Stanford University Press, 1970.

———. *Ideology and Politics in Contemporary China*. Seattle: University of Washington Press, 1973.

Jordan, James D. "Political Orientation of the PLA." *Current Scene* 11 (June 1, 1973): 1–15.

Joseph, William A. *The Critique of Ultra-Leftism in China, 1958–1981*. Stanford, Calif.: Stanford University Press, 1984.

Kane, Penny. *Famine in China, 1959–1961*. New York: St. Martin's, 1988.

Kau, Michael Y. M. "The Case Against Lin Piao." *Chinese Law and Government* (Fall–Winter 1972–73): 3–30.

———, ed. *The Lin Piao Affair: Power Politics and Military Coup*. New York: International Arts and Sciences Press, 1975.

Kau, Michael Y. M., and Pierre M. Perrolle. "The Politics of Lin Piao's Abortive Military Coup." *Asian Survey* 14 (June 1974): 558–77.

Keesing's Research Report. *The Cultural Revolution in China: Its Origins and Course.* New York: Scribner's, 1967.

Ke Yan, comp. *Mao Zedong de licheng (Mao's Road).* Beijing: Jiefangjun wenyi chubanshe, 1996.

Klein, Donald, and Anne Clark. *Biographic Dictionary of Chinese Communism: 1921–1965.* 2 vols. Cambridge, Mass.: Harvard University Press, 1971.

K'ung Te-liang. "The Impact of the Lin Piao Incident on the Chinese Communist Party and Government." *Issues and Studies* 8 (June 1972): 23–29.

Lampton, David. *Path to Power: Elite Mobility in Contemporary China.* Ann Arbor: Center for Chinese Studies, University of Michigan, 1986.

Lang, Olga. *Chinese Family and Society.* New Haven, Conn.: Yale University Press, 1946.

Lasswell, Harold D. *Power and Personality.* New York: Viking, 1962.

Lee, Hong Yung. *The Politics of the Cultural Revolution.* Berkeley: University of California Press, 1978.

———. *From Revolutionary Cadres to Party Technocrats in Socialist China.* Berkeley: University of California Press, 1991.

Lewis, John W., ed. *Party Leadership and Revolutionary Power in China.* Cambridge: Cambridge University Press, 1970.

Leys, Simon. "The Death of Lin Biao." In *The Burning Forest: Essays on Chinese Culture and Politics,* 141–51. New York: New Republic Books, 1985.

Li Desheng. "Cong Lushan huiyi dao '9.13' shijian de ruogan huiyi" ("Reminiscences of events between the Lushan Conference and the 'September 13 Incident'"). *Yanhuang chunqiu (Autumn and Spring in China)* (November 1993): 4–10.

Li Junru. *Mao Zedong yu dangdai zhongguo (Mao Zedong and Contemporary China).* Fuzhou: Fujian renmin chubanshe, 1991.

Li Ke and Hao Shengzhang. *Wenhua dageming zhong de zhongguo renmin jiefangjun (The People's Liberation Army in the Cultural Revolution).* Beijing: Zhongyang wenxian chubanshe, 1988.

Li Li. "Zhang Ning da pu shenshi yu guanchang neimu" ("Zhang Ning Exposes Her Life and the Inside Story"). *Jing bao (The Mirror)* 2 (1989): 45–51.

Li Rui. *Mao Zedong de zaonian yu wannian (Mao Zedong in His Early and Late Years).* Guiyang: Guizhou renmin chubanshe, 1992.

———. *Lushan huiyi shilu (A True Record of the Lushan Conference)* 2d ed. Zhengzhou: Henan renmin chubanshe, 1995.

Li Tianmin. "Lin Piao's Situation." *Issues and Studies* 8 (Nov. 1971): 66–74.

———. "The Mao-Lin Relationship as Viewed from the Article 'A Single Spark Can Start a Prairie Fire.'" *Issues and Studies* 9 (Jan. 1973): 78–85.

———. "The Mao-Lin Relationship as Viewed from the Article 'A Single Spark Can Start a Prairie Fire.'" *Issues and Studies* 10 (Oct. 1973): 78–85.

———. *Lin Biao pingzhuan (A Biography of Lin Biao).* Hong Kong: Mingbao Monthly, 1978.

———, ed. *Zhonggong shouyao shiliao huibian (Collected Materials of the Chinese Communist Party).* Taipei: Zhonggong yanjiu zazhishe, 1969.

Li Tianyou. "First Encounter at P'inghsingkuan Pass." In *Saga of Resistance to Japanese Invasion*, 1–23. Beijing: Foreign Languages Press, 1959.

Li Yang. *Tejian yishi* (*Sketches of a Special Prison*). Beijing: Renmin zhongguo chubanshe, 1992.

Li Yinqiao. *Mao Zedong shiweizhang zaji* (*Anecdotes from Mao's Chief Bodyguard*). Hong Kong: Cultural and Education Press, 1989.

Li Zhisui. *The Private Life of Chairman Mao*. Ed. Anne Thurston. Trans. Tai Hongchao. New York: Random House, 1994.

Liang Heng. "Room at the Top." Trans. Judith Shapiro. *New York Review of Books*, July 21, 1983, 35–36.

Lifton, Robert Jay. *Revolutionary Immortality: Mao Tse-tung and the Chinese Cultural Revolution*. New York: Random House, 1968.

"Lin Biao tongzhi 1967 nian 8 yue 9 ri tong Zeng Siyu he Liu Feng tongzhi de tanhua" ("Comrade Lin Biao's Speech to Comrades Zeng Siyu and Liu Feng, August 9, 1967"). In *Lin Biao jianghua* (*Lin Biao's Speeches*). N.p.: Library of the John Fairbank Center at Harvard University, n.d.

"Lin Biao zai jundui ganbu dahui shang de jianghua" ("Lin Biao's Speech at the Meeting of Military Cadres, March 24, 1968"). In *"Wenhua dageming" yanjiu ziliao* (*Research Materials on the "Cultural Revolution*), ed. Guofang daxue, vol. 2, 87–94. Beijing: Guofang daxue dangshi jiaoyanshi, 1988.

Lin Jing. *The Red Guards' Path to Violence: Political, Educational, and Psychological Factors*. New York: Praeger, 1991.

Lin Liheng and Zhang Qinglin. "Shangsu cailiao" ("Written Materials"). 3 parts.

"Lin Piao and the Cultural Revolution." *Current Scene* 8, no. 14 (Aug. 1, 1970): 1–13.

Lin Qing. *Zhou Enlai de zaixiang shengya* (*Zhou Enlai as Minister*). N.p.: Changcheng wenhua chubanshe, 1991.

Lin Qingshan. *Lin Biao zhuan* (*A Biography of Lin Biao*). 2 vols. Beijing: Zhishi chubanshe, 1988.

Lishi shenpan bianjizu, ed. *Lishi de shenpan* (*A Trial of History*). Beijing: Qunzhong chubanshe, 1981.

Liu Guokai. *A Brief Analysis of the Cultural Revolution*. Armonk, N.Y.: M. E. Sharpe, 1987.

Liu Huinian, Zhao Qi, Xu Xinhua, Zhou Cilin, and Yang Jinzhou. "Lin Biao fangeming zhenbian pochan ji" ("The Failure of Lin Biao's Counter-revolutionary Coup"). *People's Daily*, Nov. 24, 1980.

Liu, Sidney. "The Battle of P'inghsingkuan: A Significant Event in Lin Piao's Career." *China Mainland Review* 3 (Dec. 1956): 161–73.

Liu Suinian and Wu Qungan, eds. *China's Socialist Economy: An Outline History (1949–1984)*. Beijing: Beijing Review Press, 1986.

Liu Yuen-sun. *The Current and the Past of Lin Piao*. Trans. Robert Liang. Santa Monica, Calif.: Rand, 1967.

Lotta, Raymond, ed. *And Mao Makes 5: Mao Tse-tung's Last Great Battle*. Chicago: Banner Press, 1978.

MacFarquhar, Roderick. *The Origins of the Cultural Revolution 1: Contradictions Among the People, 1956–1967*. New York: Columbia University Press, 1974.
———. *The Origins of the Cultural Revolution 2: The Great Leap Forward, 1958–1960*. New York: Columbia University Press, 1983.
———. *The Origins of the Cultural Revolution 3: The Coming of the Cataclysm, 1961–1966*. New York: Columbia University Press, 1997.
———, ed. *The Politics of China: 1949–1989*. New York: Cambridge University Press, 1993.
MacFarquhar, Roderick, Timothy Cheek, and Eugene Wu, eds. *The Secret Speeches of Chairman Mao*. Cambridge, Mass: Council on East Asian Studies/Harvard University, 1989.
MacFarquhar, Roderick, and John K. Fairbank, eds. *The Cambridge History of China*. Vol. 15, *The People's Republic*. Part 2, *Revolution Within the Chinese Revolution, 1966–1982*. Cambridge: Cambridge University Press, 1991.
McIntyre, Angus, ed. *Aging and Political Leadership*. Albany: State University of New York Press, 1988.
Mao Zedong. *Mao Zedong zhuzuo xuandu (Selected Works of Mao)*. Vol. 5. Beijing: Renmin chubanshe, 1977.
Mao Zedong de shengqian sihou (Mao Zedong: Before and After His Death). Hong Kong: Wen wei Publishing Company, 1993.
Mao Zedong sixiang wansui (Long Live Mao Zedong Thought). M1400 12c. Oakton, Va.: Center for Chinese Research Materials, 1989.
Meisner, Maurice. *Mao's China: A History of the People's Republic*. New York: Free Press, 1977.
Mencius. *The Works of Mencius*. Trans. James Legge. London: Oxford University Press, 1895.
Moody, Peter R., Jr. *The Politics of the Eighth Central Committee of the Communist Party of China*. Hamden, Conn.: Shoe String Press, 1973.
Morgan, D. H. J. *The Family, Politics and Social Theory*. London: Routledge, 1985.
Mosca, Gaetano. *The Ruling Class*. New York: McGraw Hill, 1965.
Murphy, Charles J. V. "Who Killed Lin Biao?" *National Review*, June 8, 1973, 625–34.
Myers, James T., Jurgen Domes, and Milton D. Yeh, eds. *Chinese Politics: Documents and Analysis*. Vol. 2. Columbia: University of South Carolina Press, 1989.
Nathan, Andrew J. "A Factionalism Model for CCP Politics." *China Quarterly* 53 (Jan./Mar. 1973): 34–66.
Nelson, Harvey W. "Military Forces in the Cultural Revolution." *China Quarterly* 51 (July–Sept. 1972): 444–74.
New Culture Supply Company, ed. *Lin Biao shijian yu Mao-gong nei-hong (The Lin Biao Incident and the Inner Struggle of Mao's Communists)*. Hong Kong: Southeast Press, 1972.
Nicholas, Ralph W. "Faction: A Comparative Analysis." In *Friends, Followers, and Factions: A Reader in Political Clientelism*, ed. Steffen W. Schmidt, Laura

Guasti, Carl Landé, and James C. Scott, 55–74. Berkeley: University of California Press, 1977.

Oksenberg, Michel. "Occupational Groups in Chinese Society and the Cultural Revolution." In *The Cultural Revolution: 1967 in Review.* Ann Arbor: Michigan Papers in Chinese Studies, no. 2, 1968.

———. "Source and Methodological Problems in the Study of Contemporary China." In *Chinese Communist Politics in Action*, ed. A. Doak Barnett, 577–606. Seattle: University of Washington Press, 1969.

———. "Exit Patterns for Chinese Politics and Its Implication." *China Quarterly* 67 (Sept. 1976): 501–18.

O'Sullivan, Noel, ed. *Revolutionary Theory and Political Reality.* New York: St. Martin's, 1983.

Parish, William L., Jr. "Factions in Chinese Military Politics." *China Quarterly* 56 (Oct.–Dec. 1973): 667–99.

Peng Dehuai. *Memoirs of a Chinese Marshal: The Autobiographical Notes of Peng Dehuai (1898–1974).* Trans. by Zheng Longpu. Ed. Sara Grimes. Beijing: Foreign Languages Press, 1984.

———. "Wo weishenme yao xiexin gei Mao zhuxi" ("Why I Wanted to Write to Chairman Mao"). *Xinhua Wenzhai* (*New China Digest*), November 1990, 140–42.

Peng Dehuai zishu (*A Biography of Peng Dehuai*). Beijing: Renmin chubanshe, 1981.

Perlmutter, Amos, and Valerie Plave Bennett. *The Political Influence of the Military.* London: Yale University Press, 1980.

Perry, Elizabeth J., and Li Xun. *Proletarian Power: Shanghai in the Cultural Revolution.* Boulder, Colo.: Westview, 1997.

Powell, Ralph L. "Commissars in the Economy: 'Learn from the PLA' Movement in China." *Asian Survey* 5 (March 1965): 126–38.

———. "The Increasing Power of Lin Piao and the Party-Soldiers, 1959–1966." *China Quarterly* 34 (April–June 1968): 38–65.

Pye, Lucian W. *Mao Tse-tung: The Man in the Leader.* New York: Basic Books, 1968.

———. *The Dynamics of Factions and Consensus in Chinese Politics.* Santa Monica, Calif.: Rand, 1981.

———. "Reassessing the Cultural Revolution." *China Quarterly* 108 (Dec. 1986): 597–612.

———. *The Mandarin and the Cadre: China's Political Cultures.* Ann Arbor: Center for Chinese Studies, University of Michigan, 1988.

———. *The Spirit of Chinese Politics: A Psychocultural Study of the Authority Crisis in Political Development.* New ed. Cambridge, Mass.: Harvard University Press, 1992.

Qin Zhihua. *Xinzhi yu zhengzhi: lun zhongguo dezhi zhuyi chuantong* (*Rule by Heart and Politics: On the Chinese Tradition of Ruling by Ethics*). Nanning: Guangxi renmin chubanshe, 1993.

Quan Yanchi. *Zouxia shentan de Mao Zedong* (*Mao Zedong, Man, Not God*). Beijing: Zhongwai wenhua chuban gongsi, 1989.

———. *Hongqiang neiwai* (*Inside and Outside the Red Walls*). Beijing: Kunlun chubanshe, 1989.

———. *Tao Zhu zai "wenhua dageming" zhong* (*Tao Zhu in the "Cultural Revolution"*). Beijing: Zhonggong zhongyang dangxiao chubanshe, 1991.

———. *Shenghuo zhong de lingxiumen* (*Leaders in Their Lives*). Kunming: Yunnan renmin chubanshe, 1993.

Ra'anan, Uri. "Peking's Foreign Policy Debate, 1965–1966." In *China in Crisis*. Vol. 2, *China's Policies in Asia and America's Alternatives*, ed. Tang Tsou, 23–72. Chicago: University of Chicago Press, 1968.

Resolution on CCP History (1949–81). Beijing: Foreign Languages Press, 1981.

Rigby, Thomas H., and Ferenc Feher. *Political Legitimation in Communist States*. London: Macmillan, 1982.

Riskin, Carl. *China's Political Economy: The Quest for Development Since 1949*. Oxford: Oxford University Press, 1987.

Robinson, Thomas W. *A Politico-Military Biography of Lin Piao*. Pt. 1, 1907–1949. Santa Monica, Calif.: Rand, 1971.

———. "Lin Pao as an Elite Type." In *Elites in the People's Republic of China*, ed. Robert Scalapino, 149–95. Seattle: University of Washington Press, 1972.

———, ed. *The Cultural Revolution in China*. Berkeley: University of California Press, 1971.

Rosen, Stanley. *Red Guard Factionalism and the Cultural Revolution in Guangzhou (Canton)*. Boulder, Colo.: Westview, 1982.

Russett, Bruce M. *International Regions and the International System: A Study in Political Ecology*. Chicago: Rand McNally, 1967.

Salisbury, Harrison E. *The Long March: The Untold Story*. New York: Harper and Row, 1985.

———. *The New Emperors: China in the Era of Mao and Deng*. New York: Avon, 1992.

Scalapino, Robert A., ed. *Elites in the People's Republic of China*. Seattle: University of Washington Press, 1972.

Schram, Stuart. *Mao Tse-tung*. London: Penguin, 1967.

Schurmann, Franz. "The Attack of the Cultural Revolution on Ideology and Organization." In *China in Crisis*. Vol. 1, *China's Heritage and the Communist Political System*, ed. Ping-ti Ho and Tang Tsou, 525–78. Chicago: University of Chicago Press, 1968.

———. *Ideology and Organization in Communist China*. 2d ed. Berkeley: University of California Press, 1968.

———. *People's China: Social Experimentation, Politics, Entry onto the World Scene, 1966 through 1972*. New York: Random House, 1974.

Scott, James C. "Patron-Client Politics and Political Change in Southeast Asia." In *Friends, Followers, and Factions: A Reader in Political Clientelism*, ed. Steffen W. Schmidt, Laura Guasti, Carl H. Landé, and James C. Scott, 123–46. Berkeley: University of California Press, 1977.

Shanas, Ethel, Peter Townsend, Dorothy Wedderburn, Henning Friis, Poul Milhoj, and Jan Stehouwer. *Old People in Three Industrial Societies*. New York: Atherton, 1968.

Shao Yang, comp. *Beijing: Zhongguo de gaogang zidimen* (*Beijing: Children of High Officials in China*). Beijing: Shidai wenyi chubanshe, 1993.

Shao Yihai. *"Lianhe jiandui" de fumie* (*Destruction of a "Joint Fleet"*). Beijing: Chunqiu chubanshe, 1988.

————. "Lin Biao chutao zhenxiang" ("The Truth About Lin Biao's Escape"). *Zhui qiu* (*Pursuit*) 6 (1988): 78–105.

————. *Lin Biao wangchao heimu* (*Inside the Dark Dynasty of Lin Biao*). Chengdu: Sichuan wenyi chubanshe, 1988.

Shapiro, Judith. "Wild History." *New Republic*, June 13, 1983, 31–33.

Shi Zhe. *Zai lishi juren shenbian* (*On the Side of Historical Giants*). Beijing: Zhongyang wenxian chubanshe, 1991.

Singer, J. David. *Human Behavior and International Politics: Contributions from the Social-Psychological Sciences*. Chicago: Rand McNally, 1967.

Smedley, Agnes. *The Great Road: The Life and Times of Chu Teh*. New York: Monthly Review Press, 1956.

Smelser, Neil. *Theory of Collective Behavior*. New York: Free Press, 1963.

Snow, Edgar. *Red Star over China*. New York: Grove, 1968.

————. *The Long Revolution*. New York: Vintage, 1973.

Solomon, Richard. *Mao's Revolution and the Chinese Political Culture*. Berkeley: University of California Press, 1971.

Starr, John B. *Ideology and Culture: An Introduction to the Dialectic of Contemporary Chinese Politics*. New York: Harper and Row, 1973.

————. *Continuing the Revolution: The Political Thought of Mao*. Princeton, N.J.: Princeton University Press, 1979.

Tan Zhenlin zhuan bianji weiyuanhui. *Tan Zhenlin zhuan* (*A Biography of Tan Zhenlin*). Hangzhou: Zhejiang renmin chubanshe, 1992.

Tan Zongji. "Wuchan jieji zhuanzheng xia jixu geming lilun de laiyuan yu fazhan" ("The Source and Development of the Theory of Continuing the Revolution Under the Dictatorship of the Proletariat"). *Dangshi yanjiu* (*Study of the Party History*) 2 (1987): 57–63.

Tan Zongji and Zheng Qian, eds. *Shinian hou de pingshuo* (*Comments After Ten Years*). Beijing: Zhonggong dangshi ziliao chubanshe, 1987.

Tao Siliang. "Gongheguo de gongzhumen: Li Na, Lin Doudou, Nie Li he Tao Siliang" ("Princesses of the People's Republic: Li Na, Lin Doudou, Nie Li, and Tao Siliang"). In *Lingxiu yizu: gongheguo xinshengdai jishi* (*Descendants of the Leaders: True Accounts of the New Generation of the People's Republic*), comp. Zhang Xiaolin, 339–65. Beijing: Tuanjie chubanshe, 1993.

Teiwes, Frederick C. *Leadership, Legitimacy, and Conflict in China: From a Charismatic Mao to the Politics of Succession*. Armonk, N.Y.: M. E. Sharpe, 1984.

————. *Politics at Mao's Court: Gao Gang and Party Factionalism in the Early 1950s*. Armonk, N.Y.: M. E. Sharpe, 1990.

————. *Politics and Purges in China*. 2d ed. New York: M. E. Sharpe, 1993.

Teiwes, Frederick C., and Warren Sun. *The Tragedy of Lin Biao: Riding the Tiger During the Cultural Revolution, 1966–1971*. Honolulu: University of Hawaii Press, 1996.

Terrill, Ross. *Mao: A Biography*. New York: Harper and Row, 1980.

———. *Madame Mao: The White-Boned Demon*. New York: Simon and Schuster, 1992.

Thomsen, Robert. "Mongolian Officials Refute Lin Biao Plane Crash." *South China Morning Post*, April 19, 1990, 11.

Thornton, Richard C. *China, the Struggle for Power, 1917–1972*. Bloomington: Indiana University Press, 1973.

Thurston, Anne F. "The Politics of Survival: Li Zhisui and the Inner Court." *China Journal* 35 (January 1996): 97–105.

Tie Zhuwei. *Shuang zhong se yu nong: Chen Yi zai wenhua da geming zhong* (*The Heavier the Frost, the Brighter the Color: Chen Yi in the Cultural Revolution*). Beijing: Jiefangjun chubanshe, 1986.

Townsend, James R. *Political Participation in Communist China*. Berkeley: University of California Press, 1969.

Tsou, Tang. "The Cultural Revolution and the Chinese Political System." *China Quarterly* 38 (April–June 1969): 63–79.

———. "Prolegomenon to the Studying of Informal Groups in CCP Politics." *China Quarterly* 65 (March 1976): 98–114.

———. *The Cultural Revolution and Post-Mao Reforms: A Historical Perspective*. Chicago: University of Chicago Press, 1986.

Uhalley, Stephen, Jr. "A Compelling but Unlikely Account of Lin Biao's Death." *Asian Wall Street Journal*, June 13, 1983.

———. *A History of the Chinese Communist Party*. Stanford, Calif.: Hoover Institution Press, 1988.

Uhalley, Stephen, Jr., and Jin Qiu. "The Lin Biao Incident: More Than Twenty Years Later." *Pacific Affairs* 66 (Fall 1993): 386–98.

Unger, Jonathan, ed. *Using the Past to Serve the Present: Historiography and Politics in Contemporary China*. Armonk, N.Y.: M. E. Sharpe, 1993.

Union Research Institute. *The Case of P'eng Teh-huai*. Hong Kong: Union Press, 1968.

United States, Defense Intelligence Agency. *The Chinese Armed Forces Today: The U.S. Defense Intelligence Agency Handbook of China's Army, Navy, and Air Force*. Englewood Cliffs, N.J.: Prentice-Hall, 1979.

United States, Department of State, Bureau of Intelligence and Research. *Directory of Chinese Communist Officials: Biographic Reference Aid*. Washington, D.C.: U.S. Government Printing Office, 1963.

United States, Office of Coordinator of Information, Research and Analysis Branch, Far Eastern Section. *Chinese Politico-Military Factions*. Washington, D.C.: Coordinator of Information, Far Eastern Section, 1942.

Vertzberger, Yaacov. *The World in Their Minds: Information Processing, Cognition, and Perception in Foreign Policy Decisionmaking*. Stanford, Calif.: Stanford University Press, 1990.

Vlasov, Victor. "The Last Days of Lin Biao." *Far Eastern Affairs* 6 (1990): 150–59.

Vogel, Ezra F. *Canton Under Communism: Programs and Politics in a Provincial Capital, 1949–1968.* Cambridge, Mass.: Harvard University Press, 1969.

Wakeman, Frederic E., Jr. *History and Will: The Origins of Maoism.* Berkeley: University of California Press, 1973.

Wang Dongxing. "Mao zhuxi zai fensui Lin Biao fangeming zhengbian yinmo de rizi li" ("Chairman Mao in the Days of Crushing Lin Biao's Counter-revolutionary Conspiracy of Coup d'État"). *Zhonggong dangshi ziliao (Materials on the History of Chinese Communist Party)* 49 (1994): 56–82.

———. *Wang Dongxing huiyi: Mao Zedong yu Lin Biao fangeming jituan de douzheng (Wang Dongxing's Memoir: The Struggle Between Mao Zedong and Lin Biao's Counter-revolutionary Clique).* Beijing: Dangdai zhongguo chubanshe, 1997.

Wang Li. *Xianchang lishi (Witness to History).* Hong Kong: Oxford University Press, 1993.

Wang Ming. *Zhonggong ban shiji yu pantu Mao Zedong (Fifty Years of the Chinese Communist Party and the Traitor Mao Zedong).* Hong Kong: Wanhai yuyan chubanshe, 1989.

Wang Nianyi. "Zhengque zongjie 'wenhua dageming' de lishi jiaoxun" ("To Correctly Summarize the Lessons from the 'Cultural Revolution'"). Paper presented at the National Forum on the History of the Chinese Communist Party, Beijing, Aug. 1987.

———. *Dadongluan de niandai (Years of Turmoil).* Zhengzhou: Henan renmin chubanshe, 1988.

———. "'Wenhua dageming' de youlai" ("Origins of the 'Cultural Revolution'"). *Zheng ming (Challenge)* 1 (January 15, 1989): 55–63.

Wang Shaoguang. *Failure of Charisma: The Cultural Revolution in Wuhan* (New York: Oxford University Press, 1995).

Wang Xingjuan. *Li Min, He Zizhen yu Mao Zedong (Li Min, He Zizhen, and Mao Zedong).* Beijing: Zhongguo wenlian chuban gongsi, 1993.

Wang Zhenghua. *Lin Biao wangchao xingshuai shilu (A True Account of the Rise and Fall of Lin Biao's Dynasty).* Hong Kong: Tai Ping Shan Publishing and Cultural Company, 1995.

Weber, Max. *Methodology of the Social Sciences.* Trans. and ed. Edward A. Shils and Henry A. Finch. Glencoe, Ill.: Free Press, 1949.

———. *The Theory of Social and Economic Organization.* Ed. Talcott Parsons. New York: Free Press, 1964.

Wen Feng. *Zouxia shentan de Lin Biao (Lin Biao: Man, Not God).* Beijing: Zhongguo huaqiao chubanshe, 1993.

Wen Tiejun. "Guojia ziben zai fenpei yu minjian ziben zai jilei" ("The Redistribution of National Assets and the Reaccumulation of Public Capital"). *Gaige yu shiyan (Reform and Experiment)* 2 (February 10, 1993): 1–21.

White, Gordon. *The Politics of Class and Class Origin: The Case of the Cultural Revolution.* Canberra: Australian National University, 1976.

White, Lynn. *Policies of Chaos.* Princeton, N.J.: Princeton University Press, 1990.

Whitson, William W. "The Field Army in Chinese Communist Military Politics." *China Quarterly* 37 (Jan.–March 1969): 1–30.

———. *The Chinese High Command: A History of Communist Military Politics, 1927–71*. New York: Praeger, 1973.

———. *Chinese Military and Political Leaders and the Distribution of Power in China, 1956–1971*. Santa Monica, Calif.: Rand, 1973.

———, ed. *PLA Unit History*. Washington, D.C.: Office of the Chief of Military History, 1967.

———, ed. *The Military and Political Power in China in the 1970s*. New York: Praeger, 1973.

Willey, Fay. "Was Lin Biao Murdered?" *Newsweek*, May 16, 1983, 55.

Wilson, Dick. *The People's Emperor*. New York: Doubleday, 1980.

———. "To Unseat the Chairman." *Times Literary Supplement*, June 24, 1983, 654–56.

———, ed. *Mao Tse-tung in the Scales of History*. Cambridge: Cambridge University Press, 1977.

Witke, Roxane. *Comrade Chiang Ch'ing*. Boston: Little, Brown, 1977.

Womack, Brantly. *Contemporary Chinese Politics in Historical Perspective*. Cambridge: Cambridge University Press, 1991.

Wright, Arthur F., and Denis Twichett, eds. *Confucian Personalities*. Stanford, Calif.: Stanford University Press, 1962.

Wu De. "Lushan huiyi he Lin Biao shijian" ("The Lushan Conference and the Lin Biao Incident"). In *Zhou Enlai de zuihou suiyue, 1966–1976* (*Zhou Enlai's Last Years, 1966–1976*), comp. An Jianshe, 127–53. Beijing: Zhongyang wenxian chubanshe, 1996.

Wu Faxian. Manuscript.

Wu Tien-wei. *Lin Biao and the Gang of Four: Contra-Confucianism in Historical and Intellectual Perspective*. Carbondale: Southern Illinois University Press, 1983.

Wu Xiaomei and Liu Peng. *Mao Zedong zouchu hongqiang* (*Mao Zedong Came out of the Red Walls [of Zhongnanhai]*). Beijing: Zhonggong zhongyang dangxiao chubanshe, 1993.

Wu Xiuquan. *Wo de shengya: 1908–1949* (*My Career: 1908–1949*). Beijing: Renmin chubanshe, 1986.

Xi Xuan. "Guanyu wenhua dageming de qiyin de tantao" ("On the Origins of the Cultural Revolution"). *Zhonggong dangshi yanjiu* (*Study of the History of the CCP*) 5 (September 25, 1988): 51–60.

Xiao Di, Zhi Wu, and Tian Yi, comps. "*Wenge*" *zhi mi* (*Mysteries of the "Cultural Revolution"*). Beijing: Zhao hua chubanshe, 1993.

Xiao Feng and Ming Jun, comps. *Mao Zedong zhi mi* (*The Mystery of Mao Zedong*). Beijing: Zhongguo renmin daxue chubanshe, 1992.

Xiao Jinguang. *Xiao Jinguang huiyilu* (*Xiao Jinguang's Memoirs*). Beijing: Jiefangjun chubanshe, 1988.

Xiao Sike. *Chaoji shenpan* (*The Super Trials*). 2 vols. Jinan: Jinan chubanshe, 1992.

————. *Zhiqingzhe shuo* (*Stories of Eyewitnesses*). Vol. 3. Beijing: Zhongguo qingnian chubanshe, 1997.

Xiao Xiao. "Lin Biao nu'er dadan pilu fuqin chuzou xiangqing" ("Lin Biao's Daughter Boldly Exposes the Details of Her Father's Flight"). *Jing bao* (*The Mirror*) 6 (June 1988): 16–23.

Xiao Xinli, comp. *Xunshi dajiang nanbei de Mao Zedong* (*The Mao Zedong Who Traveled the Country*). Beijing: Zhongguo shehui kexueyuan, 1993.

Xiao Yanzhong, ed. *Wannian Mao Zedong* (*Mao Zedong in His Later Years*). Beijing: Chunqiu chubanshe, 1989.

Xie Shouzhen, Quan Yonglin, and Ye Deben, comps. *Xinwen renwu jinxi* (*Accounts About the Celebrities Today*). Yanji: Yanbian daxue chubanshe, 1991.

Xiong Huayuan and An Jianshe, comps. *Lin Biao fangeming jituan fumie jishi* (*A True Account of the Destruction of the Lin Biao Counter-revolutionary Clique*). Beijing: Zhonggong zhongyang wenxian chubanshe, 1995.

Xiong Lei. "9.13 qianhou de Mao Zedong." In *Lin Biao fangeming jituan fumie jishi* (*A True Account of the Destruction of the Lin Biao Counter-revolutionary Clique*), comp. Xiong Huayuan and An Jianshe, 77–89. Beijing: Zhonggong Zhongyang wenxian chubanshe, 1995.

Xu Quanxing. "Mao Zedong wannian zai jiebanren wenti shang de chouchu" ("Mao Zedong's Hesitation on the Question of a Successor in His Later Years"). *Mao Zedong sixiang yanjiu* (*Study of Mao Zedong Thought*) 3 (1990): 85–90.

————. *Mao Zedong wannian de lilun yu shijian, 1956–1976* (*Theories and Practices of Mao Zedong in His Later Years, 1956–1976*). Beijing: Zhongguo da baike quanshu chubanshe, 1993.

Xu Wenyi. "Inside Story of the Lin Biao Plane Crash Affair and the Whole Process of Diplomatic Negotiations," *Wen Wei Po*, Jan. 12 and 13, 1988, 2 (for each installment); in *FBIS-CHI*, Jan. 14, 1988, 13–16; *Wen Wei Po*, Jan. 14, 1988, 2; in *FBIS-CHI*, Jan. 14, 1988, 11–13; *Wen Wei Po*, Jan. 23, 1988, 3; Jan. 24, 1988, 2; and Jan. 25, 1988, 2; in *FBIS-CHI*, Jan. 26, 1988, 19–23; *Wen Wei Po*, Jan. 26, 1988, 3; in *FBIS-CHI*, Jan. 27, 1988, 25–26.

————. "A Special Mission History Entrusted to Me." Part 1, *Beijing Review*, May 23–29, 1988, 26–30, and Part 2, May 30–June 5, 1988, 23–27.

Xu Xiangqian. *Lishi de huigu* (*Reminiscences on History*). 3 vols. Beijing: Jiefangjun chubanshe, 1987.

Xue Yesheng. *Ye Jianying de guanghui yisheng* (*The Glorious Life of Ye Jianying*). Beijing: Jiefangjun chubanshe, 1987.

Yahuda, Michael. "Kremlinology and the Chinese Strategic Debate, 1965–1966." *China Quarterly* 49 (Jan.–March 1972): 32–75.

Yan Jiaqi and Gao Gao. *Wenhua dageming shinian shi* (*Ten-Year History of the Cultural Revolution*). 2d ed. Taiwan: Yuanliu chuban shiyie gufen youxian gongsi, 1990.

————. *Turbulent Decade: A History of the Cultural Revolution*. Trans. and ed. D. W. Y. Kwok. Honolulu: University of Hawaii Press, 1996.

Yan Yongsong and Wang Junwei, comps. *Zuoqing ershi nian, 1957–1976* (*Twenty Years of Leftism, 1957–1976*). Henan: Nongcun duwu chubanshe, 1993.

Yang Kelin, ed. *Wenge bowuguan* (*Cultural Revolution Museum*). Pt. 2. Hong Kong: Dongfeng chuban youxian gongsi, 1995.

Yao Ming-le. *The Conspiracy and Death of Mao's Heir*. New York: Knopf, 1983.

Yao Xinwu and Yin Hua. *Zhongguo changyong renkou shujuji* (*Basic Data on China's Population*). Beijing: Zhongguo renkou chubanshe, 1994.

"Ye Jianying tongzhi 10 yue 5 ri zai Beijing gongren tiyuguan jundui yuanxiao wuchan jieji wenhua dageming dongyuan dahui shang de jianghua" ("Comrade Ye Jianying's October 5 Speech at the Meeting of Army Schools for the Mobilization of the Great Proletarian Cultural Revolution at Beijing Workers' Stadium"). In *Zai wuchan jieji wenhua dageming zhong zhongyang fuze tongzhi jianghua chaolu* (*A Collection of the Speeches by the Central Leaders During the Great Proletarian Cultural Revolution*). N.p. Hoover Institution Library, 1967.

Ye Yonglie. *Yao Pengzi yu Yao Wenyuan* (*Yao Pengzi and Yao Wenyuan*). Hong Kong: South China Press, 1989.

———. *Chen Boda*. Hong Kong: Wenhua jiaoyu chuban youxian gongsi, 1990.

———. *Lishi xuanzele Mao Zedong* (*History Chose Mao Zedong*). Shanghai: Shanghai renmin chubanshe, 1992.

———. *Zhang Chunqiao zhuan* (*A Biography of Zhang Chunqiao*). Beijing: Zuojia chubanshe, 1993.

Yu Nan. "Lin Biao jituan xingwang chutan" ("Initial Research on the Rise and Fall of the Lin Biao Clique"). In *Shinian hou de pingshuo* (*Comments After Ten Years*), ed. Tan Zongji and Zheng Qian, 57–110. Beijing: Zhonggong dangshi ziliao chubanshe, 1987.

———. "Zhou Zongli chuzhi '9.13' Lin Biao pantao shijian de yixie qingkuang" ("How Premier Zhou Handled the 'September 13' Incident of Lin Biao's Escape"). *Dangshi yanjiu* (*Study of the Party History*) 9 (June 28, 1991): 59.

———. "Jiujie erzhong quanhui shang de yichang fengbo" ("Problems at the Second Plenum of the Ninth Central Committee"). *Dang de wenxian* (*Party Literature*) 3 (March 1993): 83–86.

———. "Guanyu Lin Biao shijian ruogan lishi wenti de kaocha" ("A Study on Several Historical Issues Related to the Lin Biao Incident"). In *Lin Biao fangeming jituan fumie jishi* (*A True Record of the Destruction of the Lin Biao Counter-revolutionary Clique*), ed. Xiong Huayuan and An Jianshe, 167–93. Beijing: Zhongyang wenxian chubanshe, 1995.

Yuan Yue. *Lin Biao shijian yuanshi wenjian huibian* (*A Collection of the Original Documents Concerning the Lin Biao Incident*). Taipei: Institute of the Problems of Mainland China, n.d.

Zagoria, Donald. "The Strategic Debate in Peking." In *China in Crisis*." Vol. 2, *China's Policies in Asia and America's Alternatives*, ed. Tang Tsou, 237–68. Chicago: University of Chicago Press, 1968.

Zhang Ning. "Niuqu de hong" ("The Distorted Rainbow"). *Dongfang jishi* (*Eastern Affairs*) 3 (March 1988): 45–68.

———. *Chen jie* (*Predestinated Fate*). Hong Kong: Mingbao chubanshe, 1997.

Zhang Xiaolin, comp., *Lingxiu yizu: gongheguo xinshengdai jishi* (*Descendants of the Leaders: True Accounts of the New Generation of the People's Republic*). Beijing: Tuanjie chubanshe, 1993.

Zhang Yaoci. *Huiyi Mao Zedong* (*In Memory of Mao Zedong*). Beijing: Zhonggong zhongyang dangxiao chubanshe, 1996.

Zhang Youyu. "Guanyu huifu guojia zhuxi ji qita" ("On Restoration of the Position of State Chairman and Other Questions"). *Beijing wanbao* (*Beijing Evening News*), April 28, 1982.

Zhang Yunsheng. *Maojiawan jishi: Lin Biao mishu huiyilu* (*True Account of Maojiawan: Reminiscences of Lin Biao's Secretary*). Beijing: Chunqiu chubanshe, 1988.

———. "The True Account of Maojiawan: Reminiscences of Lin Biao's Secretary." Trans. Nancy Liu. Ed. Lawrence R. Sullivan. *Chinese Law and Government* 26 (March–April 1993): 1–85.

Zhang Zhenlong. *Xuehong xuebai* (*White Snow, Red Blood*). Beijing: Jiefangjun chubanshe, 1989.

Zhao Cong. *Wenge yundong licheng shulun* (*The History of the Cultural Revolution*). 4 vols. Hong Kong: Friendship Association Press, 1971–79.

Zheng Qian and Han Gang. *Wannian suiyue: 1959 nian hou de Mao Zedong* (*Mao Zedong's Late Years After 1959*). Beijing: Zhongguo qingnian chubanshe, 1993.

Zhonggong yanjiu zazhishe, ed. *Zhonggong shenpan "Lin-Jiang jituan" an* (*The Trial of Lin-Jiang Clique by the Chinese Communist Party*). 2 vols. Taipei: Zhonggong yanjiu zazhishe, 1981.

Zhou Songnai. "'9.13' hou de Lin Doudou" ("Lin Doudou after September 13"). *Xinhua wenzhai* (*New China Digest*), May 1988, 147–49.

Zhou Yiliang. *Bijing shi shusheng* (*An Intellectual After All*). Beijing: Beijing shiyue wenyi chubanshe, 1998.

Zong Huaiwen, comp. *Years of Trial, Turmoil, and Triumph: China from 1949 to 1988*. Beijing: Foreign Languages Press, 1989.

Zuigao renmin fayuan yanjiusuo, ed. *Zhonghua renmin gongheguo zuigao renmin fayuan tebie fating shenpan Lin Biao, Jiang Qing fangeming jituan zhufan jishi* (*The True Account of the Trials of Chief Defendants of the Lin Biao and Jiang Qing Counter-revolutionary Cliques by the Special Court of the Supreme Court of the People's Republic of China*). Beijing: Falu chubanshe, 1982.

ZZB (Zhonggong zhongyang bangongting), CCP Documents on the Lin Biao incident

[1] "Lin Biao zai 1966 nian 8 yue 13 ri zhongyang gongzuo huiyi shang de jianghua" ("Lin Biao's Speech at the Central Working Conference, August 13, 1966"). A document prepared for a conference, Beijing, July 1, 1972, 9–10.

[2] "Zhonggong zhongyang tongzhi" ("Circular of the CCP Central Committee"). Zhongfa no. 57 (1971), Sept. 18, 1971.

[3]   "Zhonggong zhongyang guanyu kuoda chuanda (1971) 57 hao wenjian de tongzhi" ("Circular of the CCP Central Committee on Issuing Document no. 57 (1971) on an Enlarged Scale"). Zhongfa no. 60 (1971), Sept. 28, 1971.

[4]   "Zhonggong zhongyang tongzhi" (Circular of the CCP Central Committee). Zhongfa no. 61 (1971), Sept. 29, 1971.

[5]   "Zhonggong zhongyang tongzhi" ("Circular of the CCP Central Committee"). Zhongfa no. 62 (1971), Oct. 3, 1971.

[6]   "Zhonggong zhongyang tongzhi" ("Circular of the CCP Central Committee"). Zhongfa no. 64 (1971), Oct. 3, 1971.

[7]   "Zhonggong zhongyang tongzhi" ("Circular of the CCP Central Committee"). Zhongfa no. 65 (1971), Oct. 6, 1971.

[8]   "Zhonggong zhongyang tongzhi" ("Circular of the CCP Central Committee"). Zhongfa no. 67 (1971), Oct. 24, 1971.

[9]   "Zhonggong zhongyang tongzhi" ("Circular of the CCP Central Committee"). Zhongfa no. 69 (1971), Oct. 29, 1971.

[10]   "Zhonggong zhongyang tongzhi" ("Circular of the CCP Central Committee"). Appendix, "Fangeming zhenbian gangling, '571 gongcheng jiyao' he yingyin jian" ("The Outline of the Counter-revolutionary Coup d'État, 'The Outline of Project 571' and a Photocopy"). Zhongfa no. 74 (1971), Nov. 14, 1971.

[11]   "Guanyu xiang guiguo huaqiao chuanda 'zhonggong zhongyang tongzhi' wenti de buchong tongzhi ("Circular on How to Pass on the 'Circular of the CCP Central Committee' to the Returned Overseas Chinese"). Zhongfa no. 75 (1971), Nov. 30, 1971.

[12]   "Guanyu jiaqiang baomi gongzuo de tongzhi" ("Circular on How to Heighten Awareness of the Necessity of Maintaining Secrecy"). Zhongfa no. 76 (1971), Nov. 30, 1971.

[13]   "Zhonggong zhongyang tongzhi" ("Circular of the CCP Central Committee"). "Fensui Lin Chen fandang jituan zhengbian de douzheng (cailiao zhiyi)" ("Struggles to Smash the Counter-revolutionary Coup d'État of the Lin and Chen Anti-Party Clique [Part 1]"). Zhongfa no. 77 (1971), Dec. 7, 1971.

[14]   "Zhonggong zhongyang tongzhi" ("Circular of the CCP Central Committee"). Zhongfa no. 83 (1971), Dec. 29, 1971.

[15]   "Zhonggong zhongyang tongzhi" ("Circular of the CCP Central Committee"). Zhongfa no. 3 (1972), Jan. 13, 1971.

[16]   "Zhonggong zhongyang tongzhi" ("Circular of the CCP Central Committee"). "Fensui Lin Chen fandang jituan fangeming zhengbian de douzheng (cailiao zhi'er)" ("Struggles to Smash the Counter-revolutionary Coup d'État of the Lin and Chen Anti-Party Clique [Part 2]"). Zhongfa no. 4 (1972), Jan. 10, 1972.

[17]   "Zhonggong zhongyang tongzhi" ("Circular of the CCP Central Committee"). "Lin Biao zai jiujie erzhong quanhui kaimuhui shang de jiang-

hua" ("Lin Biao's Speech at the Opening Session of the Second Plenum of the Ninth Central Committee"). Zhongfa no. 5 (1972), Jan. 13, 1972.

[18] "Zhonggong zhongyang tongzhi" ("Circular of the CCP Central Committee"). "Mao zhuxi zai waidi xunshi qijian tong yantu gedi fuze tongzhi de tanhua." ("Chairman Mao's Talks to Responsible Local Comrades During His Tours of Inspection"). Zhongfa no. 12 (1972), Mar. 18, 1972.

[19] "Zhonggong zhongyang chongshen baomi tongzhi" ("Circular of the CCP Central Committee on Reemphasizing [the Necessity of] Maintaining Secrecy"). Zhongfa no. 13 (1972), Mar. 23, 1972.

[20] "Zhonggong zhongyang tongzhi" ("Circular of the CCP Central Committee"). "Fensui Lin Chen fandang jituan fangeming zhengbian de douzheng (cailiao zhisan)" ("Struggles to Smash the Counter-revolutionary Coup d'État of the Lin and Chen Anti-Party Clique [Part 3]"). Zhongfa no. 24 (1972), July 3, 1972.

■ Index of Persons

In this and the following index an "f" after a number indicates a separate reference on the next page, and an "ff" indicates separate references on the next two pages. A continuous discussion over two or more pages is indicated by a span of page numbers, e.g., "57–59." *Passim* is used for a cluster of references in close but not consecutive sequence. Annotations are provided for only those persons involved the Lin Biao incident or the Cultural Revolution. Unless otherwise indicated, all titles and offices pertain to the period during the Cultural Revolution.

Bai Chongshan (commander, Fifth Air Force Army), 191
Baker, Hugh, 138–39
Bandaranaike, Sirimavo, 7
Bo Gu (a.k.a. Qin Bangxian; secretary and nominal leader of CCP during time of Long March), 65f
Bo Yibo (vice-premier; chairman, State Economic Commission), 24
Braun, Otto, 66, 224–25nn29, 31
Brezhnev, Leonid, 56
Bu Zhanya (political commissar, Hunan Military Region), 190, 191–92

Cao Cao, 129
Cao Diqiu (mayor, Shanghai; ousted January 1967), 99
Chen Boda (chief, CCRSG), 8, 60, 86, 100f, 109, 112, 116, 120ff, 124, 127, 130, 193, 204; and Cultural Revolution, 17, 83, 87f, 90, 92–93, 104–5, 117–18; and PLA, 95, 114; criticism of, 102–3, 132–33, 134
Chen Liyun (political commissar, Fifth Air Force Army), 191

Chen Mingshu (well-known "rightist" in late 1950s), 32
Chen Pixian (party secretary, Shanghai; ousted January 1967), 103
Chen Suiqi (wife of Wu Faxian), 181
Chen Yi (PLA marshal; PRC's first foreign minister; member, Central Military Committee), 30, 53, 71f, 74, 93, 103ff, 125, 141, 212n16, 231n159
Chen Yun (vice-premier in charge of economic policy), 35f, 60, 71
Chen Zaidao (commander, Wuhan Military Region), 59, 222–23n86
Cheng Hongzhen (secretary, General Office of the Party Committee, air force), 168–69
Cheng Qian, 206
Cheng Shiqing (commander, Jiangxi Military Region), 128, 190
Chiang Kai-shek, *see* Jiang Jieshi
Confucius, 78, 138

Deng Tuo (party secretary, Bejing; committed suicide May 18, 1966), 203

Index of Topics

Library of Congress Cataloging-in-Publication Data
Jin, Qiu
    The culture of power : the Lin Biao incident in the
Cultural Revolution / Jin Qiu.
        p.   cm.
    Includes bibliographical references and index.
    ISBN 0-8047-3529-8 (alk. paper)
    1.   China—History—Cultural Revolution,
1966–1976.   2. Lin, Piao, 1908–1971.   3. China—
Politics and government—1949–1976.   I. Title.
II. Title: Lin Biao incident in the Cultural Revolution.
DS778.7.J56   1999
951.05'6—dc21   98-54159
                                                            Rev

   ∞   This book is printed on acid-free, recycled paper.
Original printing 1999
Last figure below indicates year of this printing:
08   07   06   05   04   03   02   01   00   99

Designed by Eleanor Mennick
Typeset by James P. Brommer in 9.5/12 Palatino
and Nueva display